D1432951

Marriage and Family
in the Biblical World

E D I T E D   B Y

Ken M. Campbell

InterVarsity Press
Downers Grove, Illinois

InterVarsity Press
P.O. Box 1400, Downers Grove, IL 60515-1426
World Wide Web: www.ivpress.com
E-mail: mail@ivpress.com

©2003 by Ken M. Campbell

All rights reserved. No part of this book may be reproduced in any form without written permission from InterVarsity Press.

InterVarsity Press® is the book-publishing division of InterVarsity Christian Fellowship/USA®, a student movement active on campus at hundreds of universities, colleges and schools of nursing in the United States of America, and a member movement of the International Fellowship of Evangelical Students. For information about local and regional activities, write Public Relations Dept., InterVarsity Christian Fellowship/USA, 6400 Schroeder Rd., P.O. Box 7895, Madison, WI 53707-7895, or visit the IVCF website at <www.ivcf.org>.

Scripture quotations, unless otherwise noted, are from the New Revised Standard Version of the Bible, *copyright 1989 by the Division of Christian Education of the National Council of the Churches of Christ in the USA. Used by permission. All rights reserved.*

Cover design: Cindy Kiple

Cover image: Erich Lessing/Art Resource, NY

ISBN 0-8308-2737-4

Printed in the United States of America ∞

Library of Congress Cataloging-in-Publication Data

Marriage and family in the biblical world / edited by Ken M.
Campbell.
      p. cm.
Includes bibliographical references and index.
   ISBN 0-8308-2737-4 (pbk.: alk. paper)
   1. Marriage—Biblical teaching. 2. Family—Biblical teaching. I.
Campbell, Ken M., 1940-
   BS680.M35.M34 2003
   220.8'3068—dc21

                                                                              2003010911

P	17	16	15	14	13	12	11	10	9	8	7	6	5	4	3	2	1
Y	15	14	13	12	11	10	09	08	07	06	05	04	03				

Contents

Abbreviations of Serials, Series and Reference Works

AB	Anchor Bible
ABD	D. N. Freedman. *Anchor Bible Dictionary.* 6 vols. New York: Doubleday, 1992.
ABRL	Anchor Bible Reference Library
AbrN	*Abr-Nahrain*
AfOB	Archiv für Orientforschung: Beiheft
AGJU	Arbeiten zur Geschichte des antiken Judentums und des Urchristentums
AJAH	*American Journal of Ancient History*
ANEP	J. B. Pritchard. *The Ancient Near East in Pictures Relating to the Old Testament.* Princeton, N.J.: Princeton University Press, 1954.
ANET	J. Pritchard, ed. *Ancient Near Eastern Texts Relating to the Old Testament,* 3rd ed. Princeton, N.J.: Princeton University Press, 1969.
AOAT	Alter Orient und Altes Testament
ARM	Archives royales de Mari
ArOr	*Archiv Orientální*
ASNU	Acta seminarii neotestamentici upsaliensis
AuOr	*Aula Orientalis*
AUSS	*Andrews University Seminary Studies*
BA	*Biblical Archaeologist*
BASOR	*Bulletin of the American Schools of Oriental Research*
BBR	*Bulletin for Biblical Research*
BDAG	W. Bauer, F. W. Danker, W. F. Arndt and F. W. Gingrich. *Greek-English Lexicon of the New Testament and Other Early Christian Literature.* 3rd ed. Chicago: University of Chicago Press, 1999.
BE	Babylonian Expedition of the University of Pennsylvania, Series A: Cuneiform Texts
BGU	*Aegyptische Urkunden aus den Königlichen [Staatlichen] Museen zu Berlin. Griechische Urkunden.* 15 vols. Berlin, 1895-1983.
BIDR	*Bulletino internazionale di diritto romano*
BJS	Brown Judaic Studies
BLS	Bible and Literature Series
BM	Tablets in the collections of the British Museum
BN	*Biblische Notizen*

BT	*The Bible Translator*
BZ	Biblische Zeitschrift
BZAW	Beihefte zur Zeitschrift für die alttestamentliche Wissenschaft
CAD	*The Assyrian Dictionary of the Oriental Institute of the University of Chicago.* Chicago: University of Chicago Press, 1956-.
CANE	J. Sasson, ed. *Civilizatons of the Ancient Near East.* 4 vols. New York: Scribner, 1995.
CBC	Cambridge Bible Commentary
CBET	Contributions to Biblical Exegesis and Theology
CBQ	*Catholic Biblical Quarterly*
CCTC	Cambridge Classical Texts and Commentaries
Chm	*Churchman*
CIJ	*Corpus inscriptionum Judaicarum*
CJ	*Classical Journal*
CP	*Classical Philology*
CQ	Classical Quarterly
CRINT	Compendia rerum iudaicarum ad novum testamentum
CSHJ	Chicago Studies in the History of Judaism
CSSH	*Comparative Studies in Society and History*
CT	Cuneiform Texts from Babylonian Tablets in the British Museum
DCH	David J. A. Clines, ed. *Dictionary of Classical Hebrew.* Sheffield: Sheffield Academic Press, 1993-.
DJD	Discoveries in the Judaean Desert
DJG	Joel B. Green, Scot McKnight and I. Howard Marshall, eds. *Dictionary of Jesus and the Gospels.* Downers Grove, Ill.: InterVarsity Press, 1992.
DLNTD	Ralph P. Martin and Peter H. Davids, eds. *Dictionary of the Later New Testament and Its Developments.* Downers Grove, Ill.: InterVarsity Press, 1997.
DNTB	Craig A. Evans and Stanley E. Porter, eds. *Dictionary of New Testament Background.* Downers Grove, Ill.: InterVarsity Press, 2000.
DPL	Gerald F. Hawthorne, Ralph P. Martin and Daniel G. Reid, eds. *Dictionary of Paul and His Letters.* Downers Grove, Ill.: InterVarsity Press, 1993.
EBC	Expositor's Bible Commentary
EMC	*Echos du monde classique/Classical Views*
EncJud	*Encyclopaedia Judaica.* 16 vols. Jerusalem: Keter, 1972.
ErIsr	*Eretz-Israel*
ETS	Evangelical Theological Society

EuroJTh	*European Journal of Theology*
EvQ	*Evangelical Quarterly*
ExpTim	*Expository Times*
GBE	Grove Booklets on Ethics
GR	*Greece and Rome*
GTJ	*Grace Theological Journal*
HALOT	L. Kohler, W. Baumgartner and J. J. Stamm, *The Hebrew and Aramaic Lexicon of the Old Testament.* Translated and edited under the supervision of M. E. J. Richardson. 4 vols. Leiden: E. J. Brill, 1994-1999.
HG	J. Kohler et al. *Hammurabi's Gesetz.* 5 vols. Leipzig: Pfeiffer, 1904-1911.
HJPAJC	Emil Schürer, *The History of the Jewish People in the Age of Jesus Christ (175 B.C.-A.D. 135).* Edited by Geza Vermes, et al. Revised English edition. 3 vols. Edinburgh: T & T Clark, 1973-1987.
HS	*Hebrew Studies*
HTR	*Harvard Theological Review*
HUCA	*Hebrew Union College Annual*
IEJ	*Israel Exploration Journal*
ISBE	G. Bromiley, ed. *International Standard Bible Encyclopedia.* 4 vols. Grand Rapids, Mich.: Eerdmans, 1979-1988.
ISBL	Indiana Studies in Biblical Literature
JAC	*Jahrbuch für Antike und Christentum*
JAOS	*Journal of the American Oriental Society*
JBL	*Journal of Biblical Literature*
JBS	Jerusalem Biblical Studies
JCS	*Journal of Cuneiform Studies*
JDS	Judean Desert Studies
JECS	*Journal of Early Christian Studies*
JEOL	*Jaarbericht van het Vooraziatisch-Egyptisch Gezelschap (Genootschap) Ex oriente lux*
JEN	Joint Expedition with the Iraq Museum at Nuzi
JESHO	*Journal of the Economic and Social History of the Orient*
JETS	*Journal of the Evangelical Theological Society*
JJP	*Journal of Juristic Papyrology*
JJS	*Journal of Jewish Studies*
JNES	*Journal of Near Eastern Studies*
JNSL	*Journal of Northwest Semitic Languages*
JÖAI	*Jahreshefte des Österreichischen archäologischen Instituts*

JQR	*Jewish Quarterly Review*
JRE	*Journal of Religious Ethics*
JRelS	*Journal of Religion Studies*
JRS	*Journal of Roman Studies*
JSOT	*Journal for the Study of the Old Testament*
JSOTSup	Journal for the Study of the Old Testament: Supplement Series
JSPSup	Journal for the Study of the Pseudepigrapha: Supplement Series
KAR	E. Ebeling, ed. *Keilschrifttexte aus Assur religiösen Inhalts.* Leipzig: J. C. Hinrichs, 1919-1923.
LCL	Loeb Classical Library
LSJ	H. G. Liddell, R. Scott and H. S. Jones. *A Greek-English Lexicon.* 9th ed. with rev. supplement. Oxford: Clarendon Press, 1996.
NAC	The New American Commentary
NewDocs	G. H. R. Horsley and S. Llewelyn. *New Documents Illustrating Early Christianity.* North Ryder, N.S.W.: Macquarie University, 1981-.
NICNT	New International Commentary on the New Testament
NICOT	New International Commentary on the Old Testament
NIDOTTE	W. A. VanGermeren, ed. *New International Dictionary of Old Testament Theology and Exegesis.* 5 vols. Grand Rapids: Zondervan, 1997.
NIGTC	New International Greek Testament Commentary
NovT	*Novum Testamentum*
NPNF	*Nicene and Post-Nicene Fathers,* Series 2
NSBT	New Studies in Biblical Theology
OBO	Orbis biblicus et orientalis
OBT	Overtures to Biblical Theology
OCD	S. Hornblower and A. Spawforth, eds. *Oxford Classical Dictionary,* 3rd ed. Oxford: Oxford University Press, 1996.
OCuT	Oxford Editions of Cuneiform Texts
OTL	Old Testament Library
OTP	J. H. Charlesworth, ed. *Old Testament Pseudepigrapha.* 2 vols. New York: Doubleday, 1983, 1985.
PapCol	Papyrologica Coloniensia
PBS	Publications of the Babylonian Section, University Museum, University of Pennsylvania
PBSR	*Papers of the British School at Rome*
PG	Patrologia graeca [= Patrologiae cursus completus: Series graeca]. Edited by J.-P. Migne. 162 vols. Paris: Mignen, 1857-1886.

PNTC	Pillar New Testament Commentary
RA	*Revue d'assyriologie et d'archéologie orientale*
RB	*Revue biblique*
SAOC	Studies in Ancient Oriental Civilizations
SBH	Georg A. Reisner, *Sumerisch-babylonische Hymnen nach Thontafeln griechischer Zeit.* Berlin: Spemann, 1896.
SBJT	*The Southern Baptist Journal of Theology*
SBLDS	Society of Biblical Literature Dissertation Series
SBLMS	Society of Biblical Literature Monograph Series
SBLSBS	Society of Biblical Literature Sources for Biblical Study
SCE	*Studies in Christian Ethics*
SE	*Studia Evangelica I, II, III* (=TU 73 [1959], 87 [1964], 88 [1964], etc.)
SFSHJ	South Florida Studies in the History of Judaism
SJ	Studia Judaica
SNTSMS	Society for New Testament Studies Monograph Series
SR	*Studies in Religion*
STDJ	Studies on the Texts of the Desert of Judah
SVTP	Studia in Veteris Testamenti pseudepigraphica
TAPA	*Transactions of the American Philological Association*
TDNT	G. Kittel and G. Friedrich, eds. *Theological Dictionary of the New Testament.* Trans. G. W. Bromiley. 10 vols. Grand Rapids, Mich.: Eerdmans, 1964-1976.
Them	*Themelios*
TIM	Texts in the Iraq Museum
TJ	*Trinity Journal*
TLOT	E. Jenni et al., ed. *Theological Lexicon of the Old Testament.* Trans. M. E. Biddle. 3 vols. Peabody, Mass.: Hendrickson, 1997.
TS	*Theological Studies*
TSAJ	Texte und Studien zum antiken Judentum
TU	Texte und Untersuchungen
TynBul	*Tyndale Bulletin*
UF	*Ugarit-Forschungen*
UrET	Ur Excavations, Texts
VAS	Vorderasiatische Schriftdenkmäler
VC	Vigiliae Christianae
VTSup	Vetus Testamentum Supplements
WO	*Die Welt des Orients*
WTJ	*Westminster Theological Journal*
WUNT	Wissenschaftliche Untersuchungen zum Neuen Testament

YCS   Yale Classical Studies
YOS   Yale Oriental Series, Babylonian Texts
ZA   *Zeitschrift für Assyriologie*
ZAH   *Zeitschrift für Althebräistik*
ZBK   Zürcher Bibelkommentare
ZNW   *Zeitschrift für die neutestamentliche Wissenschaft und die*
           Kunde der älteren Kirche
ZPE   *Zeitschrift für Papyrologie und Epigraphik*

Abbreviations of Ancient Works

Ag. Ap.	Josephus, *Against Apion*
'Abot	*'Abot*
Abraham	Philo, *On the Life of Abraham*
Add Esth	Additions to Esther
Alleg. Interp.	Philo, *Allegorical Interpretation*
Ant.	Josephus, *Jewish Antiquities*
b.	Babylonian Tractates
2 Bar.	*2 Baruch (Syriac Apocalypse)*
B. Bat.	*Baba Batra*
Ber.	*Berakot*
CD	Cairo Genizah copy of the *Damascus Document*
CE	Code of Eshnunna
CH	Code of Hammurabi
Contempl. Life	Philo, *On the Contemplative Life*
Embassy	Philo, *On the Embassy to Gaius*
Flight	Philo, *On Flight and Finding*
Giṭ.	*Giṭṭin*
Heir	Philo, *Who Is the Heir?*
Ḥev	Naḥal Ḥever
Ḥev/Se	Naḥal Ḥever/Seiyal
HL	Hittite Laws
Hypothetica	Philo, *Hypothetica*
Jdt	Judith
Jos. Asen.	*Joseph and Aseneth*
Jub.	*Jubilees*
J.W.	Josephus, *Jewish War*
Ker.	*Kerithot*
Ketub.	*Ketubbot*
L.A.B.	*Liber antiquitatum biblicarum* (Pseudo-Philo)
Life	Josephus, *The Life*
LL	Laws of Lipit-Ishtar
LU	Laws of Ur-Nammu
LXX	Septuagint
1-2-3-4 Macc	1-2-3-4 Maccabees
m.	Mishnah
MAL	Middle Assyrian Laws
Menaḥ.	*Menaḥot*

Mur	Wadi Murabbaʿat
Nat.	Pliny the Elder, *Naturalis historia*
Ned.	*Nedarim*
Nid.	*Niddah*
Pesaḥ.	*Pesaḥim*
Posterity	Philo, *On the Posterity of Cain*
Praep. ev.	Eusebius, *Praeparatio evangelica*
Ps.-Phoc.	Pseudo-Phocylides
Pss. Sol.	*Psalms of Solomon*
P. Yadin	Papyrus Yadin
Qidd.	*Qiddušin*
Q	Qumran
Sacrifices	Philo, *On the Sacrifices of Cain and Abel*
Sanh.	*Sanhedrin*
Sib. Or.	*Sibylline Oracles*
Sir	Sirach/Ecclesiasticus
Sobriety	Philo, *On Sobriety*
Spec. Laws	Philo, *On the Special Laws*
Tob	Tobit
t.	Tosefta
Taʿan.	*Taʿanit*
T. Jac.	*Testament of Jacob*
T. Job	*Testament of Job*
T. Jos.	*Testament of Joseph, Testament of the Twelve Patriarchs*
T. Jud.	*Testament of Judah, Testament of the Twelve Patriarchs*
T. Levi	*Testament of Levi, Testament of the Twelve Patriarchs*
Tg. Ps.-J.	*Targum Pseudo-Jonathan*
Unchangeable	Philo, *That God Is Unchangeable*
Virtues	Philo, *On the Virtues*
Wis	Wisdom of Solomon
Yebam.	*Yebamot*

Preface

The essays presented in this volume represent a comparative and theological survey of six cultural settings in which the human family existed in biblical times. No one today needs to be reminded of how controversial the subject of family became in the Western world, particularly in the United States, in the last decades of the twentieth century. Scholars of all viewpoints were drawn into this debate and unfortunately tended frequently either to mine the ancient texts for their own (Western, modern) views or to make generalized statements based on imperfect knowledge of the large variety of sources that the ancient world has bequeathed to us.

In this volume, six specialists offer a summary of and commentary on the source evidence from the ancient world on the topic of marriage and family. These cultures provided the platform upon which modern ideas and practices have developed: the ancient Near East, Old Testament Israel, Greece, Rome, Second Temple Judaism, and the New Testament. The reader is invited to appreciate the similarities and the differences, across time and culture, of the beliefs and customs of families in the ancient world.

One of the fallacies of modern biblical scholarship inherited from the old history-of-religions school, is the assumption that the practices (and even beliefs) of the biblical cultures reflected in the Scriptures are derivative from the societies and religions that surrounded them. The historical reality is of course that influence seldom travels one way. All the societies discussed in this book interacted from time to time with one another, sometimes in positive ways and sometimes negatively. Ideas and practices in this area as in others were considered and either emulated or rejected, sometimes casually and other times vigorously. Careful scholarship requires us to compare and contrast both synchronically and diachronically in order to understand why societies behaved the way they did within the context of their own *Weltanschauung*.

My thanks go to each of the scholars who have undertaken this difficult task in the midst of heavy schedules and teaching responsibilities. My hope is that more informed discussion will take place in future when scholars and students examine the nature and history of the family, particularly in relation to biblical teaching.

Ken M. Campbell

I
—

Marriage and Family
in the Ancient Near East

VICTOR H. MATTHEWS

An examination of the laws and customs that deal with marriage and family in the ancient Near East is necessarily incomplete. Scholars are limited in their conclusions by the fragmentary nature of the available evidence from that distant time. Therefore, much of what will be said below will be subject to change as new discoveries come to light. The following view, however incomplete, of life in ancient Mesopotamia is based on law codes, personal correspondence, business records, the annals of kings, religious documents, and archaeological data. This examination of marriage customs and family life will deal with the patriarchal nature of ancient society, the arrangement of marriage alliances, the importance of children, social problems such as divorce and adultery, and finally the protections afforded to widows.

PATRIARCHY

While there are some who would suggest that matriarchal social structures existed or even dominated in the ancient Near East,[1] the weight of evidence indicates that male dominance was the rule and that patriarchal lineage and inheritance systems were the norm in both Egypt and Mesopotamia. One of the clearest indications of this situation is found in the mandate for a woman to worship the personal or household god of her male protector. Thus, initially, a woman would worship the god of her father, and then, once her marriage contract had been arranged and she had officially joined the new household of her husband, she would transfer her worship to the god of her husband.[2] This practice is also echoed in the story of Rebekah's betrothal to

---

[1] Johann Jakob Bachofen, *Mutterrecht und Urreligion: Eine Auswahl* (Stuttgart: A. Kröner, 1954).

[2] See Karel van der Toorn's discussion in "Torn Between Vice and Virtue: Stereotypes of the Widow in Israel and Mesopotamia," in *Female Stereotypes in Religious Traditions,* ed. Ria Kloppenborg and Wouter J. Hanegraaff (Leiden: Brill, 1995), pp. 1-2. For reference to a salu-

Isaac and her quick decision to leave her father's household once the marriage contract was concluded (Gen 24:50-60).

The head of household or paterfamilias, whether the father (the eldest male) or the eldest son, had complete charge of the household's property, represented the household in court, and was responsible for maintaining its prosperity and credibility within the community.[3] He determined which children would inherit the household's property, and in this (at least with respect to texts from Nuzi, Alalakh and Ugarit) he was not bound by the tradition of primogeniture.[4] As a result, his dignity had to be upheld, even if it required him to exercise summary judgment over members of his family. No father could tolerate the public humiliation associated with a disrespectful or criminal son: "If a child should strike his father, they shall cut off his hand" (CH §195).[5] Similarly, if charges of adultery were made against his wife, it was her responsibility "for the sake of her husband's honor" to submit to the River Ordeal (CH §132). In this way no shame was attached to the household (identified with the male), and its/his standing within the community was maintained.[6]

This ancient household generally consisted of the extended family—including not only the wife/wives and children of the father but also perhaps his unmarried sisters, his widowed mother, and minor children of his deceased father.[7] While wives were entrusted with the management of the domestic aspects of the household, they ordinarily did not own property, could not testify in court, and were required to uphold the honor of the household through their chaste behavior and social correctness.

There were also categories of women in ancient Near Eastern society who were free of the male-dominated household (barmaids, prostitutes,

---

tation, blessing a woman in the name of her husband's god, see Stephanie Dalley, C. B. F. Walker and J. D. Hawkins, *The Old Babylonian Tablets from Tell Al Rimah* (London: British School of Archaeology in Iraq, 1976), no. 116:4-5.

[3]Karel van der Toorn, *Family Religion in Babylonia, Syria and Israel* (Leiden: Brill, 1996), p. 21. See also Ignace J. Gelb, "Household and Family in Early Mesopotamia," in *State and Temple Economy in the Ancient Near East,* ed. Edward Lipinski (Leuven: Peeters, 1979), 1:1-97.

[4]Shalom M. Paul, "Adoption Formulae: A Study of Cuneiform and Biblical Legal Clauses," *Maarav* 2 (1979-1980): 178, n. 8.

[5]Martha T. Roth, *Law Collections from Mesopotamia and Asia Minor* (Atlanta: Scholars Press, 1995), p. 120. There is no evidence that such a harsh punishment was ever actually carried out. However, it does indicate how seriously respect for parental authority was taken in the ancient world.

[6]See discussion in Victor H. Matthews, "Honor and Shame in Gender-Related Legal Situations in the Hebrew Bible," in *Gender and Law in the Hebrew Bible and the Ancient Near East,* ed. Victor H. Matthews et al., JSOTSup 262 (Sheffield: Sheffield Academic Press, 1998), pp. 106-7.

[7]K. R. Nemet-Nejat, *Daily Life in Ancient Mesopotamia* (Westport, Conn.: Greenwood, 1998), p. 127.

some widows), but their liminal status removed them from ordinary social discourse. While they figured into legal texts,[8] these unattached females operated outside the household and did not have either the restrictions or the guarantees associated with submitting to husbands or fathers.

CLAN AND KINSHIP

It is generally assumed that the culture of ancient Mesopotamia was a traditional society and as such clan based and kin oriented. However, textual evidence on kinship ties, clan or ethnic identity, and loyalties to peoples rather than to a king or city-state is not always consistent. In general it can be said that members of family groups and clans would be expected to come to one another's aid (financial and otherwise), but it is not clear how far this obligation actually went. To be sure, since many extended families lived in close proximity to one another within the cities, one would expect them to work together to maintain businesses and work fields that were owned jointly by the related households.[9]

Several terms appear in Akkadian texts for the family, including *kimtu,* which may refer to "family houses," and appears to include husband, wife and children as well as the wife's brothers. There is some textual evidence that indicates that a *kimtu* included members in more than one city or village.[10] *Nišūtu* is a generic term for "people" and is used in much the same way as *kimtu; illatu* can be used both for clan or kin-group as well as a group of confederates or associates.[11]

The Mari texts from eighteenth-century B.C. northern Mesopotamia also use social designations to refer to family groups and their property. Thus government officials employed *nawûm* as a collective term for tribal pastoralists as well as their animals and even the area in which they pitched their camp.[12]

---

[8]For instance, in CH §§108 and 109 there are legal restraints on the activities of women working as innkeepers or barmaids, but no mention is made about their husbands or fathers. In MAL A.42, a prostitute is prevented from wearing a veil because that garment is reserved for "respectable" wives, daughters and concubines—all women who have submitted to the male-dominated social system.

[9]See Igor M. Diakonoff, "On the Structure of Babylonian Society," in *Beiträge zur sozialen Struktur des alten Vorderasien,* ed. Horst Klengel (Berlin: Academie, 1971), pp. 15-31.

[10]Van der Toorn, *Family Religion,* p. 22 n. 65.

[11]Daniel C. Snell, *Life in the Ancient Near East 3100-332 B.C.E.* (New Haven, Conn.: Yale University Press, 1997), p. 52.

[12]Michael B. Rowton, "Urban Autonomy in the Nomadic Environment," *JNES* 32 (1973): 253, notes a different usage in other Old Babylonian texts for this term. There, rather than referring to a specific social group, *nawûm* is used as the designation for the "countryside between the cities, including settlements, villages and livestock."

A more obvious term for a social unit is *hibrum,* which is defined as a group of families who share a common migratory pattern.[13] It can be translated as "clans" but is generally tied to the name of the chief member of the group or perhaps an eponymous ancestor.[14] A third term applied in the texts is *um-matum,* which seems to refer to a tribal unit. It most often appears as the designation for a fighting unit and thus may reflect the common practice in ancient military conscription to levy troops from tribal or kinship groups.[15]

Some of this diversity in terminology probably results from the influx of new ethnic groups throughout Mesopotamian history. The Akkadians, the Amorites, the Hurrians, the Kassites, the Assyrians and the Chaldeans supplanted the Sumerian culture, which continued to influence all subsequent civilizations in the Tigris-Euphrates Valley. Each new people adopted the use of cuneiform writing, a temple-palace hierarchy of power and a pantheon of gods centered on fertility concerns. New peoples assimilated quickly and thus may not have chosen in their legal and civil documents to emphasize ethnic differences.

In fact, the continuous settling of portions of the seminomadic tribal groups sloughing off into the village culture may have been prompted by the desire of the newly settled people to mask or submerge their former life in favor of that of their neighbors. In this way, they could more easily do business without the cultural frictions associated with strictly maintained ethnic customs and tribal identity. Evidence that this was not always totally successful can be found in the Old Babylonian Mari documents, which refer to several tribal groups occupying portions of the northern Syrian steppe region. For instance, ARM 3/16:5-6 refers to the "villages of the Yaminites" near the urban center of Terqa. At least for government purposes, these tribesmen retained their tribal name, if not their former pastoral lifestyle.

CORPORATE IDENTITY

K. van der Toorn asserts that the concept of corporate identity in ancient Mesopotamia is to be found in the repeated use of the phrase "flesh and blood."[16] The close quarters in which the people had to live in their small

---

[13]See Abraham Malamat, "Mari and the Bible," *JAOS* 82 (1962): 143-46.

[14]Victor H. Matthews, *Pastoral Nomadism in the Mari Kingdom (ca. 1830-1760 B.C.)* (Cambridge, Mass.: ASOR, 1978), pp. 65-66. For Mari texts containing this term, see Georges Dossin, "*Adaššum* et Kirhum dans des textes de Mari," *RA* 66 (1972): 118; A.2801:14-19; and ARM 8/11.

[15]A. Malamat, "Ummatum in Old Babylonian Texts and Its Ugaritic and Biblical Counterparts," *UF* 11 (1979): 528.

[16]Van der Toorn, *Family Religion,* p. 20.

cities,[17] surrounded by the noise of children playing, domestic arguments brewing and merchants hawking their wares, prevented the family from isolating itself from the culture. However, these conditions also encouraged the family, the *bīt abim,* to more rigidly identify with its own members so that there was a clear differentiation between "brothers" and "strangers."[18]

In the light of this social attitude, the legal principle of *lex talionis* also could be seen as an expression of corporate identity. A man was responsible in equal measure for his actions, both civil and criminal. In addition, the punishment for injurious actions could affect him or members of his family as the principle of reciprocity was brought into play. For example, if a building contractor used shoddy materials or poor workmanship, which contributed to the collapse of a house and the death of the owner, then that builder was to be executed (CH §229). If the son of the owner was killed in the collapse, then the builder must surrender his own son to be executed (CH §230). This principle even extended to the property of the builder. If a slave was killed in the collapse, then the builder must supply a slave of equal value as compensation for the loss (CH §231).

There does seem to be some attempt in the Mesopotamian legal corpus to limit the degree of liability a parent or spouse might have for the actions of a daughter or a wife. Thus in MAL A.2 it states that no claim may be made against the husband, son or daughter of a woman (either a wife or daughter) who "speaks disgracefully or blasphemously." As in Ezekiel 18:1-20, this woman alone must bear the responsibility for her offense.

CLASS

Textual evidence for differentiation into class is not readily available prior to the Akkadian period in Mesopotamia.[19] With the establishment of monarchies and temple bureaucracies, however, evidence of distinctions of privi-

---

[17]J. N. Postgate, *Early Mesopotamia. Society and Economy at the Dawn of History* (London: Routledge, 1992), p. 20, estimates that these small urban centers seldom exceeded four thousand inhabitants.

[18]Van der Toorn, *Family Religion,* pp. 18-20. For additional material on the Mesopotamian family, see Elizabeth C. Stone, *Nippur Neighborhoods,* SAOC 44 (Chicago: Oriental Institute, 1987), and Claus Wilcke, "Familiengründung im alten Babylonien," in *Geschlechtreife und Legitimation zur Zeugung,* ed. E. W. Müller (Freiburg: Alber, 1985), pp. 213-317.

[19]The social structure in Egypt consisted of a similar pattern below the level of the royal family. Texts reveal mention of royal officials (a large and diverse body ranging from advisers to the king to local magistrates), priests (again a diverse and hierarchical group), warriors and commoners. Slaves also figure into Egyptian society but are not a factor in the arrangement of marriage contracts or household ownership of property except with regard to their assignment as property. See Snell, *Life in the Ancient Near East,* pp. 108-9.

lege and power become more evident. The nobility and priesthood in some ways stood outside the ordinary class system since their status transcended the normal legal and social patterns of the majority of the population. It would have been unheard of for a member of the royal family to marry beneath himself or herself since that would have been a waste of economic and political clout. Similarly, the restrictions placed on the priestly community ensured that temple property remained untouched by marriage agreements and inheritance allocations.

Still, Hammurabi's Code makes it clear that there were class differences recognized within the general population that were necessarily addressed in the legal statutes. The *awîlum* class designated those persons with full citizenship rights who were not legally attached or dependent upon temple or palace. Within the legal code, their independent status is tied to higher fines and punishments if injury is inflicted upon them.[20] A much larger group was known as the *muškēnū,* who were commoners tied to either the royal authority or the temple complex.[21] They owed labor or military service to their patron and worked assigned plots of land, giving back a portion of the harvest in rent or tithe.[22] Finally, at the bottom of the social scale were slaves, in many cases prisoners of war or persons who had fallen into debt slavery (CH §117) and had been assigned to the service of the king, the temple or private households.[23] While they had no rights over their persons, the law protected them from unjustifiable abuse[24] and their worth was certainly recognized in the fines imposed on persons who injured or killed them (CH §§199, 213, 219).

MARRIAGE

The natural order of life in ancient Mesopotamia assigned particular roles to each person—whether king, priest, soldier, farmer or slave, male or female. Once a person had managed to survive childhood, the expectation was that he or she would become a contributing member of the household and the community. M. Stol notes that the Sumerian Hymn to Gula includes the following stages of a woman's life: "I am daughter, I am bride, I am spouse, I

---

[20]Ibid., p. 60.

[21]Samuel Greengus, "Legal and Social Institutions of Ancient Mesopotamia," in *Civilizations of the Ancient Near East,* ed. Jack M. Sasson (New York: Charles Scribner's Sons, 1995), 2:476-77.

[22]Snell, *Life in the Ancient Near East,* p. 54.

[23]Hans Jochen Boecker, *Law and the Administration of Justice in the Old Testament and Ancient East,* trans. Jeremy Moiser (Minneapolis: Augsburg, 1980), p. 77.

[24]Note that CH §282 does allow the owner to cut off the ear of a slave who defiantly asserts "You are not my master." See also in LU §25 the insolent slave woman who compares herself to her mistress and subsequently has her mouth scoured with salt.

am housekeeper."[25] A similar list could be created for the man: "I am son, I am bridegroom, I am husband, I am head of household." Thus all members had tasks to perform in managing their lives and the lives of those who depended upon them. In the section below, the role of the parents in caring for their children and preparing them for their future lives will be discussed.

Betrothal. Within the patriarchal household, typically the father or the eldest brother negotiated the arrangement of marriage with the bride's parents or "guardians."[26] Of course, if the groom's father had died and the groom was an adult, then he could negotiate on his own behalf.[27] The negotiator had to consider social parity, economic advantage and expansion of the kinship network. Social parity was always a minimum goal. No family wanted to marry "down" socially, at least when arranging the contract for the first wife.[28] Thus the participants must at least be of the same social class and have approximately the same economic standing. In this way marriages served not only to produce children and a new generation to inherit property, but they also established social ties, economic connections and a network of association that was designed to benefit both parties.

Although a full picture has not yet emerged from the ancient texts, it seems likely that there was a formal set of rites and procedures that accompanied the arrangement of a marriage alliance. This would have been necessary since no evidence of a formal, written contract of marriage has surfaced thus far.[29] What textual evidence we do have deals with legal protections for both parties as well as economic details associated with the feeding of marriage parties, sometimes during an extended period prior to the transfer of the young woman to her husband's household.[30]

There does not appear to be a legal term for betrothal in the Old Babylonian materials, perhaps because once a contractual agreement had been made, the young woman was transformed immediately from a daughter to a *kallatum*, "daughter-in-law."[31] As Westbrook notes,[32] the appearance of

---

[25]Marten Stol, "Private Life in Ancient Mesopotamia," in *CANE*, 2:486-87.

[26]Samuel Greengus, "Old Babylonian Marriage Ceremonies and Rites," *JCS* 20 (1966): 59.

[27]Both BE 6/1.101 and CT 8.2a make no mention of a father-in-law, indicating that the negotiations were transacted by the groom himself.

[28]See Raymond Westbrook, *Old Babylonian Marriage Law, AfOB* 23 (Horn: Berger, 1988), p. 66, for instances in which a slave marries a free man.

[29]Samuel Greengus, "The Old Babylonian Marriage Contract," *JAOS* 89 (1969): 512.

[30]Meir Malul, "*SILLÂM PATÂRUM* 'To Unfasten the Pin' *copula carnalis* and the Formation of Marriage in Ancient Mesopotamia," *Ex Oriente Lux* 32 (1991-1992): 71.

[31]Fritz R. Kraus, *Vom mesopotamischen Menschen der altbabylonischen Zeit und seiner Welt* (Amsterdam: North-Holland, 1973), pp. 51-52.

[32]Westbrook, *Old Babylonian Marriage Law*, p. 17.

the term *kallatum* in CH §156 in a context clearly prior to the consummation of the marriage is indicative of a betrothal period, even if no formal
term is used for it.

To begin the process, preliminary contacts were made between the
families. It was first necessary for the groom's representative to make a
formal request, asking (*šalum*) the prospective bride's father/guardian for
consent to the betrothal. The Laws of Eshnunna (CE §27) provide a clear
statement of the necessity for obtaining parental consent. Under this statute, no marriage may be recognized unless the groom has asked "her father and mother" and has settled "a *kirrum* and contract with her father
and mother."[33] Although the word *kirrum* actually refers to an earthen-
ware vessel used to contain beer,[34] it was also applied to the public ceremony in which the announcement of agreement was made. This was
the occasion when a ceremonial libation was shared between the families. Eventually the meaning of *kirrum* was expanded to include the marriage feast.[35]

The contractual arrangement consisted of several parts in addition to the
mutual agreement for the couple to wed. These included the giving of a
bride-price, the *terhatum,* and prenuptial agreements regarding potential divorce by either party. There might also be stipulations on the need for polygamous marriage (usually due to illness or infertility), obligations
regarding debts or other obligations during the betrothal period, and, depending on the social status of the bride, the exact inheritance rights of their
children. Each of these points will be dealt with below.

Once consent was given, it was to the advantage of the bridegroom's
family immediately to take the next step and deliver the bride-price (*terhatum*) to the bride's household. This insured, based on the good faith of her
parents,[36] his right to the marriage and also protected her from sexual advance or abuse during the betrothal period.[37] This gift was apparently presented on a table or tray and included clothing, jewelry and consumables:
food, drink and oil.[38] Acceptance of the gift or payment, symbolized by the

---

[33]Reuven Yaron, *The Laws of Eshnunna* (Jerusalem: Magnes Press, 1969), pp. 32-33. See also
Greengus, "Old Babylonian Marriage Ceremonies," p. 62.

[34]*CAD* 8:408-10. See Fritz Rudolf Kraus, "Briefschreibübungen im altbabylonischen Schulunter-
richt," *JEOL* 16 (1964): 24.

[35]Greengus, "Old Babylonian Marriage Ceremonies," p. 57.

[36]However, the penalty in CH §160 for withdrawing of parental consent to marry after receipt
of the *terhatum* indicates that "good faith" was not always present in these transactions.

[37]Westbrook, *Old Babylonian Marriage Law,* p. 36.

[38]Greengus, "Old Babylonian Marriage Ceremonies," pp. 58-60.

drinking of beer by both parties,[39] was tantamount to marriage under the law, whether the physical consummation was to occur within days or was to be delayed for months or even years.[40] The disparity in age between bride and groom (age twelve to fourteen versus age twenty-five to thirty, respectively) may have governed how soon the bride was actually taken from her father's house.[41]

While several ancient laws mention the condition of the prospective bride in terms of occupation (prostitute or priestess)[42] and previous marriage status (widow or divorcee),[43] Mesopotamian documents, at least prior to the Neo-Babylonian era,[44] did not categorically indicate that the young woman was a virgin prior to the arrangement of her betrothal in marriage.[45] This is a curious omission considering the importance placed on virginity prior to marriage in biblical law, as in Deuteronomy 22:13-21. In most traditional societies, the honor of the household was bound up in its guarantee that the bride was a virgin at the time of marriage and thus brought a "clean slate" to her husband's bed.[46] This insured that his property would only be transmitted to his offspring and reciprocally maintained the honor and political status of the bride's household.[47]

---

[39]Ibid., pp. 62-66. See also Benno Landsberger, "Neue Lesungen und Deutungen im Gesetzbuch von Ešnunna," in *Symbolae Iuridicae et Historicae Martino David Dedicatae,* ed. J. A. Ankum et al. (Leiden: Brill, 1968), 2:76-82.

[40]Westbrook, *Old Babylonian Marriage Law,* p. 32 n. 31, points out that in YOS 8.51 there is "a contractual promise to give a bride in marriage (in the far future!)."

[41]See Martha T. Roth, "Age at Marriage and the Household," *Comparative Studies in Society and History* 29 (1987): 715-47.

[42]Lipit-Ishtar Code #30 forbids a man to arrange a marriage with a prostitute after divorcing his wife. CH §§137, 144-47 deal with the marriage rights of a *naditu* priestess.

[43]Ur-Nammu #11 makes it clear that a widow must obtain a formal marriage contract to insure her legal rights if her second husband chooses to divorce her.

[44]Benno Landsberger, "Jungfräulichkeit: Ein Beitrag zum Thema 'Beilager und Eheschliessung'," in *Symbolae Iuridicae et Historicae Martino David Dedicatae,* ed. J. A. Ankum et al. (Leiden: Brill, 1968), 2:43.

[45]Malul, "To Unfasten the Pin," p. 73. Westbrook, *Old Babylonian Marriage Law,* p. 59, cites CT 48.53 as evidence that a "*terhatum* is paid for a woman who already has a child." For a full examination of the issue of virginity prior to marriage in Israelite law, see Clemens Locher, *Die Ehre einer Frau in Israel: Exegetische und rechtvergleichende Studien zu Deuteronomium 22,13-21,* OBO 70 (Frieburg: Universitätsverlag; Göttingen: Vandenhoeck & Ruprecht, 1986).

[46]Nancy Tapper, "Direct Exchange and Brideprice: Alternative Forms in a Complex Marriage System," *Man* 16 (1981): 391. See also Maureen J. Giovannini, "Female Chastity Codes in the Circum-Mediterranean: Comparative Perspectives," in *Honor and Shame and the Unity of the Mediterranean,* ed. David D. Gilmore (Washington, D.C.: American Anthropological Association, 1987), pp. 61-74.

[47]Victor H. Matthews and Don C. Benjamin, *Social World of Ancient Israel, 1250-587 B.C.E.* (Peabody, Mass.: Hendrickson, 1993), p. 178.

In any case, the acceptance of the bride-price by the bride's household was then the basis of her transfer from their legal control to that of her husband's household. The term used for this transfer was *ahāzum,* "to take in marriage."[48] Again, this does not necessarily imply immediate physical transport from her father's house or sexual intercourse.[49] However, it did bind the parties to a set of legal constraints that restricted all sexual rights from that moment on to the household of the bridegroom. Any infringement of these rights by other men, including the groom's father after the marriage was consummated (CH §155),[50] constituted an act of adultery (CE §28) or rape (CH §130). There were also guarantees regarding the *terhatum,* requiring that it be forfeited if the bridegroom chose to withdraw from the marriage agreement prior to the actual wedding (CH §159). In addition, the father of the bride was required to refund twice the amount of the bride-price if he gave his daughter to another man after once accepting the *terhatum* (CH §§160-61).

To this point in the transaction, what had taken place was a transfer of legal responsibility. The parents of the bride had given their consent to what amounted to an adoption of their daughter by her prospective bridegroom and his household. They had agreed to a *riksātim,* "a contract concerning their daughter,"[51] after receipt of a bride-price. There is no indication that the bride was in any way involved in the negotiations, nor that she was required to make a formal declaration consenting to the marriage. However, this is not to say that she was to be considered chattel, or that the marriage agreement was treated in the same light as the sale of land or other property.[52]

To complete this transaction of a first marriage for a newly pubescent female, rituals involving a status change were performed to mark and celebrate the physical transformation of the bride from a child to an adult. These

---

[48]See Westbrook, *Old Babylonian Marriage Law,* pp. 10-11 nn. 8-10, for textual citations of its usage.

[49]Ibid., pp. 11-16.

[50]Note the exception in CH §156. In this case, presumably after the bride has been transported to the groom's house (unlike in CH §130), his own father has intercourse with her before the groom has consummated his marriage. The result is a large fine (thirty shekels of silver), the return of her dowry and the legal right to marry "a husband of her choice." Westbrook, *Old Babylonian Marriage Law,* p. 37, suggests that this is not a case of adultery (as indicated by the lighter penalty) because the transfer of the bride was made to his household, not just to the groom. If the groom has not yet had intercourse with her, then there can be no claim of adultery.

[51]Westbrook, *Old Babylonian Marriage Law,* p. 31.

[52]Contra Paul Koschaker, "Eheschließung und Kauf nach altem Recht, mit besonderer Berücksichtigung der älteren Keilschriftrechte," *ArOr* 18.3 (1950): 210-96. For a full analysis of Koschaker's theory of *Kaufehe,* see Westbrook, *Old Babylonian Marriage Law,* pp. 53-58.

ceremonies began with the giving of gifts by the groom's family. They were brought on a tray by an official known as the *susapinnu*.[53] This appointed official was exclusively associated with the bride and apparently functioned as the guarantor of her chastity during the betrothal period.[54] He also functioned as a guardian on the wedding night, with sword in hand, to protect the couple from demons, who might kidnap the bride or otherwise disrupt the consummation of the marriage.[55]

On the day of the groom's entrance into his father-in-law's house, the bride bathed and was anointed with oil, an initial ritual of transformation marking her incorporation into her husband's household.[56] One example of this is found in a Sumerian ritual marriage text[57] that describes the preparation of the marriage bed/couch[58] and the bathing and anointing of the goddess Inanna. The groom's marriage party, made up of his *ibrim* (friends) and possibly his parents, was fed and housed by the bride's family. Economic registers of the costs for feeding the marriage party included expenditures for grain, oil, beer and sheep.[59]

Further evidence of these preparations made by the bride is found in a lament over the death of Enlil, *SBH,* 69. In this fragmentary document, the bride is adorned in a wedding garment, and an encircling headband is placed on her head.[60] This finery, which also included a veil in Ur III and Middle Assyrian texts,[61] may have simply been a means of honoring her bridegroom or displaying the wealth of her father's household. However,

---

[53]Greengus, "Old Babylonian Marriage Ceremonies," p. 61, 70.

[54]Meir Malul, "*SUSAPINNU:* The Mesopotamian Paranymph and His Role," *JESHO* 32 (1989): 270-75. It is unlikely (contra W. G. Lambert, *Babylonian Wisdom Literature* [Oxford: Clarendon Press, 1960], pp. 339-40) that the paranymph's role included the ritual deflowering of the bride, according to the supposed legal principle of *ius primae noctis.* More likely he served as a witness of the consummation of the marriage and possibly as the official in charge of determining if the bride was a virgin at the time of first intercourse. See Malul's opinion on this in "*SUSAPINNU,*" pp. 262, 264.

[55]For texts dealing with concern over demons, see Jacob J. Finkelstein, "*ana bīt emim šasû,*" *RA* 61 (1967): 132; Sylvie Lackenbacher, "Note sur l'*ardat-lili,*" *RA* 65 (1971): 119-54.

[56]Greengus, "Old Babylonian Marriage Ceremonies," pp. 65-66. See MAL A.42-43 for anointing in the Middle Assyrian period.

[57]"SRT 1: A hymn to Iddin-Dagan" is dealt with by Adam Falkenstein in *Sumerische und Akkadische Hymnen und Gebete* (Zurich: Artemis, 1953) no. 18, pp. 90-99.

[58]Compare Prov 7:16-17.

[59]Greengus, "Old Babylonian Marriage Ceremonies," pp. 55-58. Nemet-Nejat, *Daily Life,* p. 135, notes that these wedding parties could last from several days to weeks for wealthy families. Such ostentatious and extravagant expenditure of resources must have served as a method of garnering respect and honor.

[60]See Malul's translation in "*SUSAPINNU,*" p. 248.

[61]Greengus, "Old Babylonian Marriage Ceremonies," p. 72 nn. 118-19. See esp. MAL A.40-41.

the garments also differed distinctly from the daily toilette and set the stage for the eventual consummation of the marriage. Wearing the veil also functioned as a symbol of her honorably married state and her membership in her husband's household.[62]

The final step in completing the marriage ritual was the physical consummation. The legal phrase is *ana bīt emim šasûm,* "to claim at the house of the father-in-law," and it occurs in the context of the entrance of the bridegroom into the bridal chamber.[63] As noted above, the groom brought witnesses, his "friends," who would have accompanied him to the house of his father-in-law. It may also be surmised that the *susapinnu* actually entered the bridal chamber with the couple to witness their sexual joining.[64] At that point, a ritual described in an Old Babylonian legal text (TIM 4.48) and a magical text[65] marked the moment when the bride submitted fully to her husband. The phrase used in the text is to "unfasten the pin of her virginity." This most likely refers to the unpinning of an undergarment (*sillûm*) arrayed around the waist prior to sexual intercourse.[66]

Having physically joined in marriage, the legal status of both parties was also transformed or at least further clarified. Since the moment when her betrothal had been solemnized by her father/guardian and the groom's representative, the bride had been referred to as an *aššatu,* "wife." However, her rights to compensation in the event of divorce,[67] her rights to property as a widow,[68] and for that matter her rights to marry the man with whom she had originally been contracted[69] were not officially set until intercourse had taken place. By consummating the marriage, both parties fulfilled the oral arrangements and legal technicalities that had been set by their representatives, thus changing their legal status and their social standing within the community.[70] In addition, the wife now lived under her husband's name and benefited from his protection and social standing.[71] The implications of this

---

[62]Van der Toorn, *Family Religion,* p. 47.

[63]See Finkelstein, "*ana bīt emim,*" pp. 127-36; F. R. Kraus, "Altbabylonische Heiratsprobleme," *RA* 68 (1974): 111-20.

[64]Malul, "To Unfasten the Pin," p. 73 n. 39.

[65]Lackenbacher, "Note sur l'*ardat-lilî,*" p. 136, lines 9-24.

[66]Malul, "To Unfasten the Pin," p. 70.

[67]Ibid., p. 75 n. 56.

[68]Martha T. Roth, "The Neo-Babylonian Widow," *JCS* 43-45 (1991): 1-26.

[69]Nemet-Nejat, *Daily Life,* pp. 134-35, emphasizes that the bride married into her husband's household. Thus, if he died prior to the consummation of the marriage, or changed his mind about the match (CH §159), she was still obligated to marry one of his brothers.

[70]Westbrook, *Old Babylonian Marriage Law,* pp. 58-59.

[71]Van der Toorn, *Family Religion,* p. 47.

transformation were now defined in terms of inheritance law and the statutes regarding divorce and remarriage that will be discussed below.

Dowry. Unlike the marriage agreement, which was presented orally by the parties involved, the terms of the dowry[72] were enumerated on a tablet, spelling out in exact detail what the young woman was bringing with her to her new household. The technical term *nudunnûm* was most commonly used in "documents of [legal] practice" during both the Old Babylonian and Neo-Babylonian periods, but *šeriktum* appears in the law codes (CH §§171-79 and MAL A.27, 29). Westbrook, following the suggestion of Wilcke,[73] persuasively argues that the legal distinction between these terms is based on the total property that constituted the dowry. Thus the *nudunnûm* equaled both the property given to her by her own family as well as gifts given to her by her husband. The impersonal law codes, not concerned with specific individuals and never attaching their names to the text, used *šeriktum,* which only referred to that portion of the dowry that derived exclusively from the bride's family.[74]

It is quite likely that the total value of this property would have intentionally matched the value of the bride-price presented by the groom's family.[75] It should also be noted that the bride's family would have released the dowry only after the marriage had been consummated.[76] The following formulaic text (*CT,* 48, 50), from the reign of Ammi-ditana in the Old Babylonian period, provides an excellent example of a dowry register:

> Sabītum the daughter of Ibbatum—Ibbatum her father has given her as a wife into the house of Ilšu-ibni her father-in-law for his son Warad-Kubi.
>
> Two beds, two chairs, one table, two chests, one grindstone, one grindstone for ZÍD.GU-flour, one 10-litre container, one empty *šikkatum*-jar.
>
> All of this is what Ibbatum gave to his daughter Sabītum, and arranged for her to enter into the house of her father-in-law Ilšu-ibni. Ibbatum has received ten shekels of silver as her "brideprice"; he has kissed (?) (it?), and he has tied it into the fringe of his daughter Sabītum('s dress). It will be given back to Warad-Kubi. Should Sabītum say to her husband Warad-Kubi: "You are no

---

[72]Westbrook, *Old Babylonian Marriage Law,* p. 24 n. 119, lists citations for *nudunnûm.*

[73]Claus Wilcke, "Zwei spät-altbabylonischen Kaufverträge aus Kiš, Zikir *šumim,*" in *Festschriften für F. R. Kraus,* ed. G. van Driel et al. (Leiden: Brill, 1982), pp. 440-41.

[74]Westbrook, *Old Babylonian Marriage Law,* pp. 25-27.

[75]Nemet-Nejat, *Daily Life,* p. 133.

[76]Westbrook, *Old Babylonian Marriage Law,* p. 46. He further argues on p. 90 that the property that composed the dowry might well have been set aside for some time, was identifiable and was therefore subject to legal dispute in cases where the marriage agreement was violated, as in CH §142.

longer my husband," they shall tie her up and throw her into water. And should Warad-Kubi say to his wife **Sabitum**: "You are no longer my wife," he shall pay her 1/3 of a mina of silver as separation money. Emuq-Adad is her "father"; he is responsible for what she says (or: for her legal affairs).[77]

These rather modest items are perhaps more typical of the average dowry than ones that included slaves (*CT,* 48 55), land and a house (BM 92550), and gold jewelry (*HG,* 3:9). They all, however, are a clear reflection of the bride's interests and relative status.

While it was generally the father who provided the dowry for his daughter, there were circumstances, perhaps the absence or death of the father, in which the mother or brothers were the signatories.[78] Like the bride-price paid by the groom's family, the dowry served as an economic incentive to establish the marriage bond. However, the precision with which the dowry texts are written suggests that they were intended to protect the bride's property should her husband die or the marriage end in divorce. For example, S. Dalley notes that even something as minuscule as a half-full container of oil had to be returned in exact measure to the woman if her dowry was to be returned to her.[79]

The dowry remained the property of the wife once she had given birth to children. This in turn became her legacy to them, and her father's household and her brothers must not lay any claim against it (CH §162). In fact, if the wife died after giving birth to children and her husband remarried, her children still retained their full right to her dowry and no other children by their father were allowed to take a share (CH §167). And, reflecting how complicated marriage patterns could become, if a widow with children remarried and had children by her second husband, then all her children shared in the distribution of her dowry (CH §173). Apparently, the only claim that a husband could make on the dowry occurred when his wife died without birthing children and for some reason the *terhatum* was not returned by her family. He could then deduct the amount of the bride-price from her dowry (CH §163).

Polygamy. While most Mesopotamian marriages seem to have been monogamous, there are a number of legal and civil texts that mention a man with more than one wife—in many cases involving marriage with a priest-

---

[77]This translation is taken from Stephanie Dalley, "Old Babylonian Dowries," *Iraq* 42 (1980): 57-58.

[78]Westbrook, *Old Babylonian Marriage Law,* p. 89, cites several of these texts, including CT 8.2a and YOS 2.25.

[79]Dalley, "Old Babylonian Dowries," p. 54.

ess.[80] Certainly, whenever more than one spouse was involved, whether concurrently or in succession due to divorce or death, this would have complicated inheritance awards and other legal matters.[81] In the cuneiform texts, the reasons for the addition of a second wife seem to center primarily on the problems associated with infertility or illness on the part of the first wife.

Marriage to a *nadītu*-priestess, who was not allowed to have children herself, required a form of surrogacy in which the *nadītum* provided her husband with a slave-woman to impregnate (CH §144). If this slave gave birth to children, then they were the legal offspring of the *nadītum*, but it was necessary for the husband to legitimize them as his heirs. Westbrook suggests that the restriction in CH §145 prohibiting the husband from marrying a second wife, a *šugītum*, if the *nadītum*'s slave had given birth to children was a form of legal pressuring designed to encourage him to legitimize the slave's children.[82]

When a man's first wife was diagnosed with an incapacitating disease that made it impossible for her to continue to have sexual relations with her husband,[83] then he was free to contract a second marriage (CH §148). However, this did not end or diminish his responsibility to support and honor his first wife for the rest of her life. She did have the option in this case to return to reclaim her dowry and return to her father's house (CH §149) if she did not choose to remain in the house with a second wife.

The only other legal basis for adding a second wife is found in CH §141. This case involves a disaffected wife, who not only wishes to leave her husband's household but maliciously "appropriates goods, squanders her household possessions, or disparages her husband" and is convicted of these acts.[84] Under these circumstances, the husband was within his rights to divorce her without a financial settlement. However, if he chose not to divorce her, perhaps as a means of shaming her before the entire commu-

---

[80]See the list of texts containing polygamy contracts in Westbrook, *Old Babylonian Marriage Law*, pp. 103-8. For additional studies on *nadītu* marriage arrangements, see Claus Wilcke, "CT 45, 119: Ein Fall legaler Bigamie mit *nadītu* und *šugītum*," *ZA* 74 (1984): 170-80; Klaus R. Veenhof, "Three Old Babylonian Marriage Contracts Involving *nadītu* and *šugītum*," in *Reflets des deux fleuves: Volume de mélanges offerts à André Finet*, ed. Marc Lebeau and Philippe Talon (Louvain: Peeters, 1989), pp. 181-89.

[81]Note that slave-concubines were not to be considered wives in this context. Their children were not allowed to inherit their father's property unless he specifically legitimized them and named them his heirs (CH §§170-171).

[82]Westbrook, *Old Babylonian Marriage Law*, p. 107.

[83]Marten Stol, *Epilepsy in Babylonia* (Groningen: STYX, 1993), p. 143, suggests that *la'bu* disease may be a contagious skin disease.

[84]Roth, *Law Collections*, p. 108.

nity, then he might marry a second wife and relegate the first wife to the position of a household slave.[85]

CHILDREN

Mesopotamian culture was based upon a cyclical understanding of the universe. As a result, each successive generation was expected to maintain continuity with the past, upholding traditions and performing rituals designed to protect the household and effectively manage its resources. Thus, the object of marriage, beyond the economic considerations of the families who had arranged it, was to produce children who would inherit the parents' property, care for them as they aged, and continue to make the offerings necessary to the ancestor cult.

There is a clear association in the ancient texts between honoring one's father and the ability to become a father. In a first millennium omen text (*KAR,* 300), the prosperity and the virility of the head of the household is also tied to continuous and pious observance of religious ritual:

> [If a man] does not honour his father:
>> [his virility] will soon be taken [away].
> [If] in [a man's] fireplace fire reignites regularly:
>> the blessing of the god is constant to him in his house.[86]

The parallel here reflects the duty of a son to his living father as well as previous generations of the fathers, all of whom represent the identity and honor of the household. As long as the family continues to perpetuate itself, the household is immortal and the cult of the ancestors can be maintained.[87]

The desire for economic and social continuity required a male heir, but the relatively high infant mortality rate as well as the uncertainty of any child living to adulthood made it necessary for couples to produce several children.[88] This also provided additional hands to work the fields or labor in a

---

[85]Westbrook, *Old Babylonian Marriage Law,* p. 108, suggests that the phrase *ki-ma gemé,* "like a slave," simply means to reverse seniority in the household, placing the first wife as the inferior of the second. However, it seems more likely that she, like the adopted son who repudiates his father and is disinherited or even sold as a slave (see the section below on adoption), loses her rights as a free woman.

[86]Van der Toorn, *Family Religion,* pp. 129-30.

[87]Note also the plea in the Ugaritic epic of Aqhat in which the hero's father prays for a son "who sets up the stelae of his ancestral spirits" (*ANET,* p. 150).

[88]One might wonder at the low average family size (1.43 children/household) found in Harran census lists and cited by Snell, *Life in the Ancient Near East,* p. 81. However, this may simply reflect how few children lived to an age of accountability.

shop or home industry (weaving, carving, etc). Too many children, especially daughters, could be a financial disaster for even the wealthy family since each would expect to receive equal treatment with regard to betrothal expenses as well as a dowry.[89] This may explain the fairly frequent mention of exposing infants, literally "casting [them] to the dog's mouth."[90] The adoption of these abandoned children by childless couples or craftsmen seeking apprentices (CH §188) will be discussed below.

Some daughters were dedicated to the goddess as *nadu*-priestesses. These "fallow" females lived a cloistered life that in most circumstances required them to remain childless.[91] An initial expense, dowering them to the temple would have been required, but this arrangement usually lessened the drain on the family's property or land.[92]

Despite the problems and concerns that a household full of children might present, in all circumstances, infertility or impotence would have been considered a catastrophe for the family. This was of course a more serious problem for childless couples, but a wife might even feel threatened if she was not able to continue to conceive or provide her husband with children. This could be grounds for divorce (CH §138). If her problem was associated with a debilitating disease, her husband might choose to marry a second wife, but CH §148 indicates that she could not be divorced for this reason, and he must continue to support her as before for the rest of her life.

Anxiety over the problems of female infertility could explain the appearance of magic texts prescribing remedies for this condition: "Total: 21 stones to help a barren woman become pregnant; you string them on a linen thread and put them around her neck."[93] Since this is not simply a female problem, a remedy for male impotence appears in a Middle Hittite text. The patient is encouraged to achieve arousal through the use of incantations, the ingestion

---

[89]See Greengus, "Old Babylonian Marriage Ceremonies," p. 58, for expenses incurred in hosting the marriage party of the groom.

[90]See Meir Malul, "Adoption of Foundlings in the Bible and Mesopotamian Documents: A Study of Some Legal Metaphors in Ezekiel 16.1-7," *JSOT* 46 (1990): 104-6.

[91]See Rivkah Harris, "The Organization and Administration of the Cloister in Ancient Babylonia," *JESHO* 6 (1963): 121-57; Elizabeth Stone, "The Social Role of the *Naditu* Women in Old Babylonian Nippur," *JESHO* 25 (1982): 50-70. Note the use of a slave woman as a surrogate mother by a *naditu* in CH §146.

[92]Snell, *Life in the Ancient Near East,* p. 53. See also Rivkah Harris, "Biographical Notes on the *Naditu* Women of Sippar," *JCS* 16 (1962): 1-12. Note the clause in CH §180 that states a *naditu* may benefit from a portion of the parental estate in her lifetime but that it "belongs only to her brothers."

[93]Text quoted from Robert D. Biggs, "Medicine, Surgery, and Public Health in Ancient Mesopotamia," *CANE,* 3:1917.

of ritual meals and sleeping before a table filled with offerings to a goddess.[94]

Adoption. There were two basic types of adoptive practices in ancient Mesopotamia. The first was simply a means of redressing problems in the makeup of the family structure. This addressed the need to care for children without families (orphans, bastards and foundlings), the need to provide for childless couples and the need to provide an individual person or a couple with an heir to transferable property.[95] The second type of adoption practice was a hybrid of the first. It provided for a legal fiction in which a person who was not a member of a family was adopted into that family in order to transfer land or other inheritable property for a payment of silver. This is the case in a group of adoption texts from mid-second-millennium Nuzi[96] in which a single person is attested as being "adopted" by over two hundred people.[97] For the purposes of this study, only the first type will be dealt with in depth.

Since the ancient world did not have government programs that attempted to provide for the needs of the aged and the infirm, it fell upon the extended family to take up these duties. One of the chief purposes, therefore, of having children, aside from insuring that there would be an orderly inheritance pattern, was to create caregivers for their aging parents. Failure either to conceive children or to raise them to adulthood because of disease, famine or war would have forced the head of the household either to obtain another wife or concubine or to impregnate a slave.[98]

One means of obtaining an adopted child was reclaiming one that had been abandoned by its parents. Financial exigency or some other calamity might drive a parent or parents either to expose a child or relinquish their rights to a child. For instance in PBS 8/2.107, a couple made the following legal arrangements:

> Yasirum and Ama-Suen have taken as their son a suckling baby called Ili-awili the son of Ayartum, from Ayartum his mother and Eriштum her husband. As

---

[94]Harry A. Hoffner, Jr., "Paskuwatti's Ritual Against Sexual Impotence (CTH 406)," *AuOr* 5 (1987): 271-87. A portion of the text is provided by Gabriella Frantz-Szabó, "Hittite Witchcraft, Magic, and Divination," *CANE*, 3:2014.

[95]Jack Goody, "Adoption in Cross-Cultural Perspective," *CSSH* 2 (1969): 55-78.

[96]E. M. Cassin, *L'Adoption à Nuzi* (Paris: Adrien-Maissoneuve, 1938).

[97]Maynard Maidman, "A Socio-Economic Analysis of a Nuzi Family Archive" (Ph.D. diss., University of Pennsylvania, 1976).

[98]Nemet-Nejat, *Daily Life*, pp. 126-27, notes that on the average only 50 percent of children survived to adulthood.

payment for his upbringing Yasirum and Ama-Suen have given [ ] shekels of silver and 2 mina of wool to Ayartum and Eristum. Yasirum and Ama-Suen [will take] Ili-awili from Ayartum and Eristum.[99]

Interestingly, the rescuing of the foundling has come into ancient Near Eastern literature as the basis for the rise of great leaders such as Moses (Ex 2:1-10) and Sargon of Akkad.[100] In some cases, the adopted foundling even retained a personal name reflecting his origins, such as *Šapī-kalbi*, "He-of-the-dog's-mouth," or *Sūqā'a*, "He-of-the-street."[101]

Legal rights to an abandoned child were relinquished when its parents chose not to legitimize it by cleansing the child of amniotic fluid and blood.[102] Such a nameless waif was "cast into the dog's mouth," and the person who chose to adopt the infant reversed the fatal process by "picking him up from the dog's mouth."[103] As CH §185 clearly states, the adoptive parents could take the child into their household without any fear of a later claim on that child: "If a man has taken in adoption an infant while still (bathed in) his amniotic fluid and raised him up, that adopted child shall not be (re)claimed!"[104]

An older couple, who had remained childless or whose children had all preceded them in death, might have to resort to adopting a slave from their household or an adult to be their son in order to care for their needs. There are a number of legal formulae employed in the cuneiform sources for adoption. These texts, duly witnessed, dated and sealed, provide a record of a solemn ritual in which both parties would have declared publicly their new relationship. The father may say *māru^{meš}-ú-a*, "you are my sons" (HL 170.45), or the son may declare orally and in writing to his adoptive father

---

[99]Translation taken from Elizabeth C. Stone and David I. Owen, *Adoption in Old Babylonian Nippur and the Archive of Mannum-mešu-lissur* (Winona Lake, Ind.: Eisenbrauns, 1991), pp. 48-49.

[100]*ANET*, p. 119. For comparisons between the Sargon and Moses stories, see Samuel E. Loewenstamm, "Die Geburtsgeschichte Moses," in *Studies in Jewish Religious and Intellectual History Presented to Alexander Altmann on the Occasion of His Seventieth Birthday*, ed. Siegfried Stein and Raphael Loewe (Tuscaloosa: University of Alabama Press, 1979), pp. 195-213.

[101]Malul, "Adoption of Foundlings," pp. 105, 121 n. 67. See also Johann Jakob Stamm, *Die Akkadische Namengebung* (Leipzig: Hinrichs, 1939), pp. 251, 320-25.

[102]Claus Wilcke, "Noch einmal: *šilip rēmim* in die Adoption *ina mēšu*: Neue und alte einschlägige Texte," *ZA* 71 (1981): 94. See also Reuven Yaron's discussion of the legal implications of the phrase "in its amniotic fluid" in "Varia on Adoption," *JJP* 15 (1965): 171-83.

[103]A Neo-Babylonian text containing this adoption formula is found in J. N. Strassmaier, *Inschriften von Nabuchodnosor König von Babylon, 604-561 v. Chr.* (Leipzig: Pfeiffer, 1889), no. 439.

[104]Translation taken from Malul, "Adoption of Foundlings," p. 106.

ana abušu īppuš, "He adopted him as his father" (Alalakh 16:3).[105]

The most common type of adoption was one in which a man adopted one or more sons. In exchange for a portion of the inheritable property, certain responsibilities were placed on the adopted son(s) within the contract. In most cases this meant that the son(s) provided a set amount of food for his new parents (PBS 8/2.153), and in some cases he even paid off a debt owed by his adoptive father (BE 6/2.28). The most important concern of the parents was addressed by the adoption, turning over to the son(s) the responsibility of managing the financial affairs of the parental estate and seeing to it that the parents received their monthly ration of food and other necessities of life.[106] This, of course, also required a transfer of property, but debts or concern over caregiving may have outweighed this consideration.[107]

This solution, however, obviously had its hazards and uncertainties. This is why many of the adoption texts include severe penalties for noncompliance with the terms or for repudiation of the agreement, including fines or disinheritance. To address the most severe case, the Sumerian Laws (#4) contain an instance in which the adopted son makes a public statement, for whatever reason, denying his responsibilities: "You are not my father" . . . "You are not my mother." In this instance, the parents were within their rights to cancel the adoption contract and sell the oathbreaker as a common slave.[108] Similarly, an adopted son who seriously violated his adoption agreement might be turned into the street after being forced to leave his garment hanging on the doorpost.[109] Perhaps more common was the payment of a fine of 1/3 mina of silver by the son, a penalty mentioned in TIM 4.13 and PBS 8/2.153.[110]

Naturally, both parties were expected to abide by the agreement. Thus stipulations are contained in the contract should either party repudiate the arrangement by either saying "you are not my son" or "you are not my fa-

---

[105]Paul, "Adoption Formulae," pp. 179-81. See also Martin David, *Dei Adoption im altbabylonischen Recht* (Leipzig: Weicher, 1927), pp. 47-48, 79-80, 90-91, for additional legal formulae.

[106]Stone and Owen, *Adoption in Old Babylonian Nippur,* pp. 3-5. See also Mark Van De Mieroop's review of Stone and Owen's volume in *JCS* 43-45 (1991-1993): 128.

[107]Stone and Owen, *Adoption in Old Babylonian Nippur,* pp. 9-10, cite OCuT 8.20 [no. 23] and OCuT 8.17/18 [no. 24 and 53] as evidence of a couple whose debts have forced them to adopt a temple official as their son and heir despite the existence of natural children.

[108]BE 6/2.4 contains a similar penalty for a woman who states to her adoptive mother, "you are not my mother." She may then be "given away for silver."

[109]Jean Noveayrol et al., *Ugaritica 5: Nouveaux Textes Accadiens, Hourrites et Ugaritiques des Archives et Bibliotheques Privées D'ugarit* (Paris: Geuthner, 1968), 83:8-10.

[110]See Stone and Owen, *Adoption in Old Babylonian Nippur,* pp. 38-42, for translations of these adoption texts.

ther." TIM 4.14 prescribes the same penalty for either party who chooses to set aside the agreement. Both parties are required to relinquish legal claims to "all houses, fields, and orchards and pay 1/3 mina of silver" should they fail in their sworn obligations.[111]

Abortion. While various forms of birth control were used in both Mesopotamia and Egypt (including castration, sexual abstinence and celibacy, chemical anti-spermicides, and *coitus interruptus*),[112] the desire to have children was very strong in the ancient world. The large number of infant deaths because of disease, birth defects, and accidents[113] and the need to both replenish or increase the labor force as well as provide heirs to facilitate the orderly transmission of property made it imperative to have large families.

Still there were instances when a pregnancy was unexpected, unwanted or illegal. For example, some priestesses were restricted from having children as part of their vows.[114] Should one of these *entu*-priestesses become pregnant, she might try to hide the fact until the birth and then expose the child, as appears to be the case in the birth narrative of Sargon of Agade.[115] However, there is evidence from both cuneiform texts[116] and Egyptian sources[117] that chemical remedies were concocted to end a pregnancy before term. There is no mention of surgical methods of abortion, but since surgical procedures were used for other types of cases, this cannot be ruled out.[118]

The only law in the Mesopotamian corpus that deals explicitly with self-induced abortion by the mother is MAL A.53. It states that if it is proven and she is convicted of aborting her fetus "by her own actions," then she is to be impaled on a stick, and her body is to remain unburied. Even if she dies

---

[111]Ibid., p. 41.

[112]See Andrew E. Hill, "Abortion in the Ancient Near East," in *Abortion: A Christian Understanding and Response,* ed. James K. Hoffmeier (Grand Rapids, Mich.: Baker Book House, 1987), pp. 31-36, for a full discussion of these contraceptive methods.

[113]See the inclusion in several law codes (Lipit-Ishtar, Sumerian, Hammurabi, Middle Assyrian) of liability clauses covering the loss of a fetus if someone strikes (either intentionally or unintentionally) a pregnant woman and causes her to have a miscarriage. See LL d-f; Sumerian Laws Exercise Tablet 1'-2'; CH §§209, 211-14; MAL A.21, 50-52.

[114]Michael Astour, "Tamar the Hierodule," *JBL* 85 (1966): 188.

[115]*ANET,* p. 119: "My mother, the high priestess, conceived me, in secret she bore me. She set me in a basket of rushes, with bitumen she sealed my lid. She cast me into the river which rose not over me."

[116]*CAD,* 11/1:79, in the article on *nadû,* cites CT 14.36 79-7-8, 22 r.5, which describes an herb used to induce miscarriage and to expel afterbirth.

[117]Cyril P. Bryan, *Ancient Egyptian Medicine: The Papyrus Ebers* (Chicago: Ares, 1974 [1930]), p. 83, cites a chemical recipe to induce abortion: "Dates, Onions, and the Fruit-of-the-Acanthus, were crushed in a vessel with Honey, sprinkled on a cloth, and applied to the Vulva."

[118]Hill, "Abortion in the Ancient Near East," p. 37.

as a result of her attempted abortion, her corpse is to be publicly displayed on a stick and left unburied. The severity of this punishment is a clear indication of the value attached to the child, and her action may well have been considered a form of theft from her husband, or an indication of another crime such as adultery (compare the trial by ordeal of the woman accused of adultery in Num 5:12-31).

An unrelated set of laws in Hammurabi's Code may also shed some light on this issue. In CH §34, a slave woman has secretly given her child to another man's daughter to raise, and in CH §35 a slave woman who belongs to the palace has secretly given her child to a *muskenum* to raise. In both cases the rights of the slave owner are upheld even if years have passed and the owner recognizes the now-grown child on the street. CH §36, unfortunately fragmentary, takes this a step further, adding a fine equal to the value of the child as punishment for the person who accepted the child from the slave woman. In this way it is made clear that children belong to husbands, fathers and slave owners, not to their mothers. Thus if the mother chooses to try to end her pregnancy or pass a child off to another person, she has violated the terms of her marriage or condition as a slave.

WIDOWS

Since death was a common companion for the ancients, it is not surprising to find very explicit legal statutes guaranteeing the rights of widows and their children.[119] In fact, economic and administrative documents indicate that there were a fairly large number of elderly females, presumably widows, in the general population.[120] With their husbands deceased and therefore not present to protect them, the widow could easily have become the subject of economic or even physical abuse.[121] If she had not been provided for in her husband's will, or if she was either childless or neglected by her children, the widow could end up in a form of ancient poorhouse grinding grain into flour alongside female slaves.[122] She might also become a ward of

---

[119]See the comparison made with biblical widows in F. Charles Fensham, "Widow, Orphan, and the Poor in Ancient Near Eastern Legal and Wisdom Literature," *JNES* 21 (1962): 129-39.

[120]Martha T. Roth, "The Neo-Babylonian Widow," *JCS* 43-45 (1991-1993): 1 n. 2, provides a long list of texts and sources depicting population trends, illustrating the importance of consulting household lists as primary data. On p. 5 she shows evidence for a large number of widows who represented their daughters in arranging a marriage (eleven of forty-five cases).

[121]See in J. N. Postgate, *Taxation and Conscription in the Assyrian Empire* (Rome: Pontifical Biblical Institute, 1974), pp. 363-67, taxation rolls from the Assyrian period that listed widows.

[122]Wolfgang Heimpel, "The Nanshe Hymn," *JCS* 33 (1981): 82. See also van der Toorn, "Torn Between Vice and Virtue," p. 3.

the temple complex, along with elderly slave women, working at menial tasks or weaving garments.[123]

Simply holding the legal status of widow, however, did not mean that the woman was necessarily destitute.[124] The term that most often appears in the text for a widow is *almattu,* but it apparently holds additional social meaning beyond marital status.[125] Household records of the Middle Assyrian period demonstrate that the legal term *almattu* was used only for widows who were economically and legally independent. These women could serve as heads of households (VAS 21.6), even if they had adult children. However, a widow who was subject to either a court authority or even another woman could not be labeled an *almattu.* Despite this evidence, the use of *almattu* is not always consistent from one period to the next. For instance, in the Neo-Babylonian period *almattu* is applied to impoverished women, who have no financial support from their families.[126]

Remarriage would have been one remedy for the problems associated with becoming a widow while still of childbearing age. However, the financial arrangements of the first marriage, especially the dowry might make this either impossible or difficult. For example, a "testament" from Nuzi (JEN 4.444:19-23) penalizes the widow for remarrying because her first husband's family did not want to lose the financial benefits of her dowry.[127] Similarly, Roth cites a Borsippa text that indicates a tendency to encourage endogamy. In this way, if a spouse died it would be expected that the widow would marry another member of his family and thus keep the financial package associated with their marriage intact.[128]

Where the law codes do deal with providing a financial settlement for the widow, they take into account a variety of factors. The settlement might depend on whether the widow brought a dowry into the marriage, whether she had children and whether her husband's will included a separate widow's settlement (see Neo-Babylonian Laws 12, 13). Roth emphasizes that

[123]Maurice Birot, "Un recensement de femmes au royaume de Mari," *Syria* 35 (1958): 9-26. See also Ignace J. Gelb, "The Arua Institution," *RA* 66 (1972): 1-32. For similar remedies for widows in the Neo-Babylonian period, see Martha T. Roth, "Women in Transition and the *bit mar banî,*" *RA* 82 (1988): 131-38.

[124]See the discussion in David I. Owen, "Widow's Rights in UR III Sumer," *ZA* 70 (1980): 174.

[125]Karel van der Toorn, *From Her Cradle to Her Grave: The Role of Religion in the Life of the Israelite and the Babylonian Woman* (Sheffield: JSOT Press, 1994), p. 134.

[126]Roth, "Neo-Babylonian Widow," p. 3.

[127]Raymond Westbrook, "Adultery in Ancient Near Eastern Law," *RB* 97 (1990): 560 n. 66.

[128]Roth, "Neo-Babylonian Widow," p. 4. HL 193 may be the extreme case of forced endogamy, although it is probably also a form of levirate obligation (see Deut 25:5-10).

the financial aspects of these laws clearly provided an incentive for younger widows to remarry.[129] The laws also would have provided the financial security necessary for an older widow to remain independent of another marriage, giving her a place to live and freedom from having to make an arrangement with the temple.

Both Hammurabi's Code and the Middle Assyrian Laws contain statutes suggesting that widows had the right to contract their own marriage agreements. In CH §177, the widow may remarry "without the consent of the judges," although safeguards are also included in the law to prevent any misuse of her deceased husband's estate. MAL 45 shows that widows could have a missing husband declared legally dead after a two-year waiting period and then could marry "the husband of her own choice." In the latter case, it was to the advantage of the state to give her this option since it also freed up a parcel of land that could be distributed to another farmer.

If the widow did not have a financial settlement that could serve as an inducement to obtain a marriage on a par with her first husband, she might simply seek the protection of a man outside of wedlock or as a prostitute.[130] This could be a dangerous choice, however, since no marriage contract had been signed. Thus in LU §11 a man may divorce a widow who has been living with him without having to pay a settlement fee. A slightly more humane solution is provided in MAL 34, which states that the widow can obtain status as a common-law wife after a two-year period of cohabitation.

There is simply too much variation in the cuneiform record to make many generalizations about the fate of widows. Many of the younger women probably remarried, while a large percentage of the older women went to live with their adult sons or in a house that was part of her dowry. Some received financial settlements from their deceased husbands' estates, and some were left destitute and wards of the temple. The complexity of the legal and social factors make this a particularly difficult aspect of ancient family life to adequately define and describe.

DIVORCE

Not every marriage lasted a lifetime in the ancient world. The law provided a variety of grounds for a divorce, but the texts do not always make it clear

---

[129]Roth, "Neo-Babylonian Widow," p. 6. See MAL A.35 which states the new husband's right to claim all property brought by the widow into his house, providing the widow an incentive to remarry.

[130]Van der Toorn, "Torn Between Vice and Virtue," p. 12. See Roth's discussion in "Neo-Babylonian Widow," p. 22.

whether the husband needed any more justification to divorce his wife than that he chose to do so for his own private purposes or possibly economic gain. Clearly, it also was easier for the husband to divorce his wife than for the wife to leave a marriage. The decision to divorce, like that to marry, carried with it economic and social implications and therefore would not have been made frivolously. Marriage agreements in fact contained penalty clauses in the case of divorce without grounds.[131]

Divorce rituals and legal forms reversed those associated with betrothal and marriage. Just as the husband had formalized his legal and social ties to his wife by stating in her presence "You are my wife," he breaks those ties by pronouncing their divorce (*ezēbša iqtabi* in CH §141), saying, "You are not my wife." It also may be assumed that witnesses would have been present since a marriage party had originally accompanied the groom.[132]

The symbolism attached to marriage preparations as described above is negated by parallel symbolism at the time of divorce. For instance, at the time of marriage, the bride is clothed and veiled to represent her new status and her transfer of membership into her husband's household. At the dissolution of that bond, the husband cuts the hem of his wife's garment *(sissiktam batāqum),* thereby sundering their association and making it possible for them to establish new marriage links.[133] This reversal is not necessarily designed to shame the wife, although in several texts it apparently is symbolic of the forfeiture of the wife's dowry as the price of her freedom.[134] More drastic measures, literally stripping the woman naked and driving her from the house,[135] were employed if the woman had repudiated her husband or had violated other social norms, such as giving family property to an outsider.[136]

The complicating factor in divorce cases is whether the marriage has

---

[131]Westbrook, *Old Babylonian Marriage Law,* p. 78, asserts that these penalties could only be imposed when a husband divorced his wife without legal grounds. See his n. 67 for the list of texts involved.

[132]Ibid., p. 70, cites VAS 8.9-10, in which witnesses testify to having seen a husband cut off the hem of his wife's garment as part of a divorce proceeding.

[133]Jacob J. Finkelstein, "Cutting the *sissiktu* in Divorce Proceedings," *WO* 8 (1976): 236-40. See also Klaas R. Veenhof, "The Dissolution of an Old Babylonian Marriage According to CT 45, 86," *RA* 70 (1976): 153-64, esp. 159.

[134]See Westbrook, *Old Babylonian Marriage Law,* pp. 70-71, for the treatment of several texts involving this ritual in both inchoate as well as consummated marriages.

[135]Meir Malul, *Studies in Mesopotamian Legal Symbolism* (Kevelaer: Butzon & Bercker; Neukirchen-Vluyn: Neukirchener Verlag, 1988), pp. 122-38. Note the parallels with Hos 2:2-3.

[136]See van der Toorn, *Family Religion,* pp. 46-47, for discussion of this ritual severing a woman's ties to a household for violation of the marriage agreement.

produced children. If the wife has borne children, or in the case of a *nadītum* who provided her husband with children through a surrogate, then the penalties imposed on the husband if he wishes to divorce her are greater (see CH §137). Presumably, this was a means of protecting the economic rights of both the wife and the children so that they were not left destitute. CE §59 follows this same pattern, expelling the husband from his house and leaving his children in his wife's custody. YOS 14.344 expands this law to include adopted children. In this case, the husband forfeits ownership of his house and custody of the children, thereby insuring their right to inherit the property even if he remarries and has additional children.[137]

The set of laws composing CH §§138-140 addresses the situation of divorce in a childless marriage. It is possible that the husband has chosen to set aside his wife because of her infertility,[138] but it is equally possible that he simply wishes to dissolve this relationship and establish another one. This might be compared to CH §159, in which the groom, after giving his father-in-law the bride-price, changes his mind, formally declares "I will not marry your daughter," and forfeits his marriage payment. However, there is a further complication once the marriage has been consummated.[139] Then the blameless wife is the injured party and thus is entitled to the restoration of her dowry as well as a divorce settlement equal in value to the *terhatum,* bride-price (CH §138).[140]

There is some dispute over whether wives actually had the right to divorce their husbands in ancient Mesopotamia.[141] However, the presence of a penalty clause for the reciprocal statement in marriage contracts in which either the husband or the wife may repudiate their spouse argues for this

---

[137]See Westbrook, *Old Babylonian Marriage Law,* pp. 78-79, 85, for discussion of these texts as well as other divorce settlements involving children.

[138]Koschaker, "Eheschließung und Kauf nach altem Recht," p. 190.

[139]Westbrook, *Old Babylonian Marriage Law,* pp. 71-72, draws on the parallel situation in CH §156, in which a betrothed woman's father-in-law has sexual relations with her prior to marriage. Her consummation includes the restoration of her dowry as well as a hefty fine of thirty shekels of silver. Like the divorced wife in CH §138, the deflowered bride in CH §156 may now arrange a new marriage of her choice.

[140]Note the variations in CH §§139 and 140, which allow for marriages arranged with the payment of a *terhatum* and for the assumed poverty of a *muškēnum*. LU §§9 and 10 provide varying marriage settlements depending on whether this was the wife's first marriage or whether she had previously been a widow.

[141]For the arguments against, see Godfrey R. Driver and John C. Miles, *The Babylonian Laws* (Oxford: Oxford University Press, 1955), pp. 291-92; Paul Koschaker, "In der Tat dürfte in VAS 8.4-5 der Schreiber sich versehen und im Ausdruck vergiffen haben," *ZA* 35 (1945): 208, argues that such a right would be "unthinkable" in a patriarchal society.

right.[142] It should also be noted that a woman who has been abandoned by her husband may enter the household of another man, and her first husband may not reclaim her (CH §136). The one law in Hammurabi's Code that seems explicitly to address the right of the wife to divorce her husband, CH §142, is also a disputed statute. On the surface, it provides her with the necessary grounds to end her marriage: a "wayward" husband, who disparages her publicly. Once the facts of the case have been investigated and determined in her favor, she is then, according to the law, allowed to return to her father's house with her dowry and without penalty to herself.[143]

Where this argument breaks down, however, is in the lack of a marriage settlement. As noted above, marriage contracts contained a penalty clause, and even the corollary to this law, CH §143, prescribes that the wife who has not been able to prove her case against her husband shall be executed by drowning. Why is it that her husband is not required to pay a divorce settlement if he is found to be at fault? And, is this another case of a childless marriage since no children are mentioned within the body of the law? Westbrook's argument that this is a case of an inchoate marriage, one that has not yet been consummated, seems to answer these questions.[144] If the couple is still betrothed, but not yet married, then the resolution of the dispute between them that dissolves the marriage agreement would be a parallel with CH §159, in which the prospective groom changes his mind about the union. He does have to forfeit the bride-price, but there is no other penalty. In CH §142, the betrothed bride leaves with only her dowry—in other words with what she had brought to the table as her portion of the marriage pact.

ADULTERY

Somewhat clearer are those divorce cases in which there are definite grounds for the dissolution of the marriage. Chief among these is adultery. In its violation of the marriage agreement, adultery also violated a taboo of society and angered the gods. It could be the object of the Babylonian "Counsels of Wisdom,"[145] which decries the actions of those persons who

---

[142]See the argument for this in Westbrook, *Old Babylonian Marriage Law*, p. 80. For a further study on one of these texts, VAS 8.4-5, see Koschaker, "In der Tat dürfte," pp. 208-11.

[143]Samuel Greengus, "A Textbook Case of Adultery in Ancient Mesopotamia," *HUCA* 40-41 (1970): 38, notes these as the only circumstances under which the woman may leave her husband with either a physical or economic penalty.

[144]Westbrook, *Old Babylonian Marriage Law*, pp. 14-15, 82-83.

[145]Lambert, *Babylonian Wisdom Literature*, p. 106; *CAD*, "*ikkibu*," 2b, 7:57.

stoop "to create trust and then to abandon, to [promise] and not to give" as "an abomination to Marduk."[146] As a result, a woman who is accused of adultery either by her husband or another person, even if she has not been caught in the act, has no option but to submit to a trial by ordeal in order to reestablish her husband's honor (CH §§131-32).[147]

Each of the major law codes of the ancient Near East contains statutes regarding adultery:[148]

LU §7: If the wife of a young man, on her own initiative, approaches a man and initiates sexual relations with him, they shall kill that woman; that male shall be released.

CE §28: If he concludes the contract and the nuptial feast for her father and mother and he marries her, she is indeed a wife; the day she is seized in the lap of another man, she shall die, she will not live.

CH §129: If a man's wife should be seized lying with another male, they shall bind them and throw them into the water; if the wife's master allows his wife to live, then the king shall allow his subject to live.

MAL A.13: If the wife of a man should go out of her own house, and go to another man where he resides, and should he fornicate with her knowing that she is the wife of a man, they shall kill the man and the wife.

In each of these instances, it can be seen that the crime of adultery is a violation of the husband's right to exclusive sexual access to his wife. However, there are escape clauses in CH §129 and MAL A.14 that set aside the punishment for the man who has been caught in adultery. In the first instance, if the husband chooses not to punish his wife, then the king may pardon the man. The Assyrian law places the entire blame on the woman, suggesting that she has either seduced her lover or disguised her identity as a married woman. In that instance, the duped male cannot be held lia-

---

[146]See William W. Hallo, "Biblical Abominations and Sumerian Taboos," *JQR* 76 (1985): 21-40, for the implications of violating the taboos and angering the gods.

[147]See discussion of this case as it compares to Num 5:11-31 in Matthews, "Honor and Shame in Gender-Related Legal Situations in the Hebrew Bible," pp. 102-8.

[148]Each of the translations below comes from Roth, *Law Collections*. Egyptian sources do not contain laws on adultery. However, literary sources, such as "The Tale of Two Brothers" (Miriam Lichtheim, *Ancient Egyptian Literature* [Berkeley: University of California Press, 1976], 2:203-11) and "King Cheops and the Magicians" (William K. Simpson, *The Literature of Ancient Egypt* [New Haven, Conn.: Yale University Press, 1973], pp. 16-19), indicate that charges of adultery or the act itself is both a major disrupter of family harmony and a crime that Pharaoh and the gods will vindicate.

ble for her fraudulent activity. There is thus no crime if the husband chooses not to punish his wife, or if the court determines the honest intentions of the "entrapped" lover.[149]

There are cases mentioned in the law codes in which an aggrieved husband discovers his wife and her lover in their sexual embrace. The Hittite law (HL 197) absolves the husband of all legal liability if, in his passionate rage, he kills the adulterers. While court procedures are described in MAL A.15 after a man has caught his wife committing adultery, the range of punishments he can inflict on them (death, disfigurement, castration) again indicates a waiving of normal legal restraint.[150] When the cuckolded husband cannot take revenge for the wrong done him, as in CH §153, where his wife has him murdered in order to continue her affair with her lover, then the state may step in and have her executed by impalement.

The wife's violation of her marriage vows, of course, were grounds for divorce. A text from Nippur, first published by Jan van Dijk,[151] contains the trial of a woman named Ištar-ummi, whose husband, Irra-malik, brings several charges, including adultery, against her before the city assembly. According to his testimony, she had previously established a pattern of criminal and disrespectful behavior. She had been burglarizing his granary storeroom by boring a hole in the adjoining wall,[152] and she had secretly tapped into one of his jars of sesame oil, covering up her theft with a cloth.[153] Now she has been caught in the arms of another man. Based on these charges, he is granted a divorce and a variety of punishments are inflicted upon his unfaithful wife.

Since she is to have an arrow drilled through her nostrils and her pudenda shaved, some speculation has arisen that her husband might have re-

---

[149]See Westbrook's discussion in "Adultery in Ancient Near Eastern Law," pp. 549-51. The issue of "entrapment" is further explained on pp. 554-55.

[150]Ibid., pp. 552-53. See also Yaron, *Laws of Eshnunna,* pp. 284-85.

[151]Jan van Dijk, "Neusumerische Gerichtsurkunden in Bagdad," *ZA* 55 (1963): 70-77. He had originally interpreted this case as one in which a wife discovers her husband engaging in a homosexual act. However, I agree with Greengus, "Textbook Case of Adultery," p. 37, that it is the husband who discovers his wife in an act of adultery.

[152]Compare MAL A.3, which describes a wife who steals from both a deceased or ill husband as well as a healthy husband. In the former case she is to be executed, while in the latter her punishment is left to the discretion of her husband.

[153]Greengus, "Textbook Case of Adultery," pp. 35-36. He also compares (p. 38) this case to CH §141, in which a woman is charged with being a wasteful and thieving mistress over her husband's household. Although this is not a case of adultery, it is grounds for divorce. See on these charges against a "loose woman," Jacob J. Finkelstein, "Sex Offenses in Sumerian Laws," *JAOS* 86 (1966): 362-63.

duced her to the status of a slave.[154] However, both Roth[155] and Westbrook[156] disagree with this position, the former suggesting that she is shaved, "making her a prostitute," and the latter seeing it as a means of inflicting public humiliation since she is also to be escorted about the city in her mutilated condition. In any case, it is the civil authority that carries out sentence on the woman, not her husband.[157]

Having been driven from her husband's home, mutilated and stripped of her dowry and her self-esteem, the unfaithful wife would have found it practically impossible to obtain another husband. Remarriage would have been an honorable option for the divorced woman only if it could be proven that she was blameless. Only CH §142 provides an instance in which a woman regains her freedom and reclaims her dowry in the face of a wayward and verbally abusive husband. However, this was most likely an inchoate marriage,[158] in which case it would have been an annulment rather than a divorce. Still, if this betrothed woman were proven to be "wayward," a squanderer and one who "disparages her husband," then she would be subject to capital punishment just like a wife who commits adultery (CH §143).

HOMOSEXUALITY

While homosexuality does not figure very largely in ancient Near Eastern legal tradition, it did exist in the cultures of Mesopotamia and was variously tolerated, despised and legislated against. Perhaps the most common role for male homosexuals was as members of the cultic community.[159] Several terms are used for these individuals: *assinnu, kulu'u, sinnišanu* (generally translated "effeminate man") and *pilpilû*. Some of these priests apparently were cross-dressers and skilled dancers since they performed within the rituals of the fertility cult of Ishtar.

---

[154]Greengus, "A Textbook Case of Adultery," pp. 34, 41.

[155]Martha T. Roth, "The Slave and the Scoundrel: CBS 10467, A Sumerian Morality Tale?" *JAOS* 103 (1983): 282.

[156]Westbrook, "Adultery in Ancient Near Eastern Law," pp. 559-60. He points out in p. 559 n. 63 that persons have their heads shaved when they are cast into slavery.

[157]Ibid., p. 563. He further cites UrET 5.203 and the Egyptian text "Cheops and the Magicians," in which the king orders the execution of the unfaithful wife.

[158]Westbrook, *Old Babylonian Marriage Law,* p. 81.

[159]Marten Stol, "Private Life in Ancient Mesopotamia," in *Civilizations of the Ancient Near East,* ed. Jack M. Sasson (New York: Charles Scribner's Sons, 1995), 1:494. Harry A. Hoffner, "Incest, Sodomy and Bestiality in the Ancient Near East," in *Orient and Occident,* ed. Harry A. Hoffner, AOAT 22 (Neukirchen-Vluyn: Neukirchener Verlag, 1973), p. 82, is more cautious, simply stating that "there is no agreement among scholars" on whether these cult figures were actually homosexuals.

The only explicit legal pronouncement outlawing sodomy is found in MAL A.19-20. The first of these laws involves a false accusation of engaging in sodomy. These unsubstantiated charges are punished by a form of corporal punishment (fifty blows with a rod); the accuser's hair is shaved off, marking him as a slave of the king for a month; and a heavy fine of 3600 shekels of lead is imposed. It is interesting to note that this is the same punishment prescribed for a man who falsely accuses another man's wife of adultery (MAL A.18) and thus indicates the level of concern attached to both adultery and sodomy in Assyrian society.[160]

In MAL A.20, the charge of sodomy is proven, and the penalty is based on the desire for reciprocity as well as prevention of any possible repetition of the act.[161] The culprit is sentenced to be sodomized, presumably by several individuals, and he is then castrated and left to live the rest of his life as a eunuch.[162] Stol[163] suggests that homosexuals were despised because they opted to engage in sexual activities that "did not serve the purpose of having children" and thus were not productive citizens of the community.

The Hittite Laws also briefly address sodomy, but in the context of incest and bestiality. Thus in HL 189 the law juxtaposes an illegal *(hurkel)* coupling between a man and his mother with a coupling between a man and his son. Both are judged to be inappropriate and incestuous. However, there does not appear to be a concern raised here over same-sex intercourse. What makes this *hurkel* is the fact that the man has sexual relations with his own son.[164]

CONCLUSIONS

Over two thousand years of history and several different geographical regions within Mesopotamia and northern Syria have been tapped for information in this examination of ancient family life and custom. While the area

---

[160]Jacob J. Finkelstein, "Sex Offenses in Sumerian Law," *JCS* 86 (1966): 367, notes that unsubstantiated accusations "serve to exemplify the 'lawgiver's' zealous concern for strict justice," and the principle of reciprocity (also found in Deut 19:19-21) provides both a means of prevention of frivolous charges and an indicator of those crimes considered particularly harmful to society. On this legal concern, see Tikva Frymer-Kensky, "Tit for Tat: The Principle of Equal Retribution in Near Eastern and Biblical Law," *BA* 43 (1980): 230-34.

[161]Roth, *Law Collections,* p. 192 n. 15, indicates that the translation of "sodomy" for the Akkadian *nâku* is based on context since this word is generally translated "fornication."

[162]This stands in contrast to the use of the death penalty to punish those who engage in homosexual acts in Lev 29:13. Tikva Frymer-Kensky, *ABD,* 5:1145, argues that this is one instance in which the Holiness Code is clearly not basing its prohibitions on ancient Near Eastern law. Instead she links it to "a desire to keep the categories of 'male' and 'female' intact."

[163]Stol, "Private Life," p. 494.

[164]Hoffner, "Incest, Sodomy and Bestiality," p. 83.

is uniformly patriarchal in its orientation, local variations, the cupidity of individual families, and the variant usage of technical, legal terms make it virtually impossible to describe a universal set of marriage laws and customs. The simple comparison of law codes demonstrates how legal trends evolved. Although the codes contain many of the same legal issues, they vary from the relatively sketchy statutes in the laws of Ur-Nammu to the convoluted and repetitious legal clauses of the Middle Assyrian Laws.

Under these circumstances it may be enough to say that the households of ancient Mesopotamia took the various stages of life very seriously. They carefully evaluated the social and economic advantages and disadvantages of every marriage agreement. They ritualized the betrothal process and created symbolic acts to mark each stage of the nuptial display as the couple moved from feasting to the marriage chamber.

Provisions were made for as many eventualities as possible. Inheritance patterns were carefully established to insure that property was held within the extended family. In the case of childlessness, adoption, surrogacy and divorce were all recognized as options. Criminal statutes were also put in place to deter adultery, murder and the theft of property. Penalties were prescribed for those who would not follow custom, and guarantees were made to protect widows and orphans from deception, fraud and homelessness.

In sum, the culture of ancient Mesopotamia was complex, resilient and innovative. Its people cared about many of the same things we do today. They wanted financial security for themselves and their children, and they took great pleasure in the religious and civil festivals that marked their lives. Although their choice of a spouse was more limited than ours, it is possible to relate to their reasoning and their faith in proper manners and behavior.

2

Marriage and Family
in Ancient Israel

DANIEL I. BLOCK

The task of recapturing ancient Israelite perspectives on family life is difficult, being complicated by several factors. First, we must ask what we mean by *Israelite*. Some modern authors insist that historically the name was restricted to the northern kingdom, whose capital city from the ninth to the seventh centuries B.C. was Samaria, and that the application of the name to the kingdoms of Israel and Judah was a late ideologically driven development.[1] However, according to the consistent witness of the biblical writings themselves, the term *Israel* could be applied variously: (a) to the putative eponymous ancestor of the nation of Israel, otherwise known as Jacob; (b) to the nation consisting of twelve tribes whose genealogical origins are traced back to the sons of Jacob; (c) to the northern kingdom of Israel, dominated by the tribe of Ephraim, which seceded from the Davidic Kingdom after the death of Solomon in the tenth century B.C.; (d) to the community of Judean exiles in Babylon after the fall of Jerusalem in 586 B.C.; and (e) to the new commonwealth of restored exiles concentrated in Jerusalem and the surrounding Judean countryside after 538 B.C.[2] Since the narratives and laws recorded in the Old Testament derive from a time span exceeding a millennium and from periods of vastly different socioeconomic realities, it would be foolish to suppose that family and marriage customs were uniform throughout this period or even throughout the nation at any given time.

---

[1]Thus Karel van der Toorn, *Family Religion in Babylonia, Syria, and Israel: Continuity and Change in the Forms of Religious Life,* Studies in the History and Culture of the Ancient Near East (Leiden: Brill, 1996), pp. 182-83. But one may respond with equal force that this modern interpretation is also ideologically driven, reflecting a minimalist disposition toward the value of the biblical texts for reconstructing ancient realities.

[2]Strictly speaking, Abraham, Isaac and even Jacob, prior to his return to Bethel from exile in Harran (Gen 32:9-12), were not Israelites, though the biblical stories about them obviously reflect Israelite perspectives.

Second, we recognize the inadequacy of the sources available for reconstructing a coherent and complete picture of ancient Israelite family and marriage practices. Our sources are essentially two: archaeological and biblical. With respect to the former, the Israelites have left us only a limited amount of textual material reflecting domestic realities, the most important type of documentation being provided by personal stone seals and clay seal impressions. For the rest we are dependent upon material cultural remains on the basis of which we may try to recover a picture of ancient family life.[3] With respect to the Old Testament record, we recognize the wide variety of literary genres that yield information on ancient family life: laws, narratives, polemical prophetic texts, songs, didactic wisdom compositions, etc.[4] Not only do many of these texts derive from a much later time than the events they describe, but they also provide inconsistent pictures. The frankness of the accounts of people's behavior often flies in the face of ideals promulgated elsewhere. Accordingly, when we try to reconstruct a picture of family life in ancient Israel we must always ask ourselves whether the texts we are reading present a normative picture, or whether the authors have consciously described a deviation from the norm.[5] Historical realities should not be confused with domestic ideals.

Third, modern Western notions of "family" should not be imposed upon ancient evidence. Much of the pro-family rhetoric of American evangelicals, for example, tends to be driven by the desire to maintain the nuclear family, that is, a family unit consisting of husband and wife and biological and/or adopted children. But domestic paradigms adhered to in many cultures in the Second and Third Worlds bear a much closer resemblance to the biblical picture than patterns currently operative in Western countries. Accordingly, if Western readers are not able to shed their biases when they examine ancient records, they must at least be aware of their biases and try to interpret the data in the light of the values that prevailed at the time the documents were produced.

These difficulties not withstanding, we now turn our attention to recon-

---

[3]For a recent attempt, see Lawrence E. Stager, "The Archaeology of the Family in Ancient Israel," *BASOR* 260 (1985): 1-35. For an extremely helpful study of a broad range of subjects relating to life in ancient Israel, based on biblical and archeological sources, see Philip J. King and Lawrence E. Stager, *Life in Biblical Israel* (Louisville, Ky.: Westminster John Knox, 2001).

[4]Unless otherwise indicated, the translations of biblical texts in this chapter are the author's own.

[5]Many feminist scholars treat a composition like the book of Judges, for example, as if it represents normative biblical patriarchy. But my point is that little is normative or normal in the book. The pictures of family life painted in the book of Judges provide disturbing domestic evidence of the Canaanization of Israelite values and culture. For a commentary on the book reflecting this perspective, see Daniel I. Block, *Judges, Ruth,* NAC, vol. 6 (Nashville: Broadman & Holman, 1999).

structing ancient Israelite perspectives on marriage and family life. After considering general questions concerning the basic structure of the family, this discussion will investigate in turn the status and roles of husbands and fathers, wives and mothers, children, and the elderly within the extended family unit. Comments on specific topics like polygamy, adultery, abortion and adoption will be integrated into these discussions as deemed appropriate. Whereas contemporary discussions of family roles in the Bible tend to focus on the power of the male head and the subject status of the rest of the members, this study will emphasize the responsibilities each member bears in the effective functioning of the family unit.

THE ANCIENT ISRAELITE VOCABULARY OF FAMILY

It is impossible to understand the Israelite family without recognizing the broader sociological context within which families functioned. Critical scholarship generally questions the reliability of Israel's traditions, but the biblical texts from Genesis to Malachi assume that common descent from an eponymous ancestor provides the basis for Israel's ethnic unity and that the Israelites perceived themselves as one large extended kinship group.[6] The hierarchy of the nation's genealogical social structure may be represented diagrammatically as in figure 1.

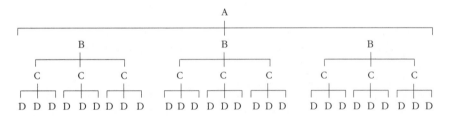

Figure 1. The social structure of ancient Israel

In figure 1, **A** represents *ʿam,* "people"; **B** represents *šēbeṭ maṭṭeh,* "tribe"; **C** represents *mišpāḥâ,* "clan"; and **D** represents *bêt ʾāb,* "house of a father." Each of these expressions deserves further comment.

The biblical writers' perception of Israel's ethnic cohesion is reflected in the ubiquitous references to the nation or portions thereof as *ʿam,* "people,"

---

[6]The extension of this sense of ethnic cohesion to the population of the entire world, presented as one large kinship group descended from Noah, in the so-called Table of Nations in Gen 10, is without parallel in the ancient Near East. On the text, see Daniel I. Block, "Table of Nations," *ISBE,* 4:707-13.

from a root signifying "paternal uncle," which often (though not always) implies internal blood relationship.[7] The frequent use of compound collective phrases like *běnê yiśrā'ēl,* "sons of Israel," and *bêt yiśrā'ēl,* "house/household of Israel," reinforces this impression of the nation's ethnic cohesion.[8] The nation of Israel was subdivided into twelve tribes, designated variously as *šēbeṭ* or *maṭṭeh,* and identified by the names of their eponymous ancestors, the twelve sons of Jacob/Israel.[9] As the book of Judges indicates, in times of crisis caused by external threats to the nation, tribal identity was important, and military levies tended to be based on tribal structures.

Despite the Israelites' clear sense of tribal identification, the everyday life of individual Israelites was determined more by the next two levels of the hierarchy, the clan and the local household. Because anthropologists and sociologists tend to define a clan as an exogamous kinship group (marriage within the clan is forbidden), to render *mišpāḥôt* as "clan" is misleading. Nevertheless, in the absence of a better expression *clan* will probably continue to be used by biblical scholars to designate the subgroup smaller than the tribe but larger and more complex than the family.[10] Inasmuch as the land of Canaan was divided among the Israelites according to their *mišpāḥôt,*[11] which then often gave their names to the territories held, the term also functioned as a technical term for hereditary land tenure.[12] Typically the territory

---

[7]See discussion in Daniel I. Block, "The Foundations of National Identity: A Study in Ancient Near Eastern Perceptions" (Ph.D. diss., University of Liverpool, 1983), pp. 1-83.

[8]For discussion of the former, see Daniel I. Block, "'Israel'—'Sons of Israel': A Study in Hebrew Eponymic Usage," *SR* 13 (1984): 301-26; for discussion of the latter, see idem, "Israel's House: Reflections on the Use of *byt yśr'l* in the Old Testament in the Light of Its Ancient Near Eastern Environment," *JETS* 29 (1985): 257-75. This sense of ethnic cohesion is expressed even more explicitly in variations of the phrase *zera' yiśrā'ēl,* "seed of Israel."

[9]Inasmuch as Joseph's descendants were divided into two tribes, Ephraim and Manasseh, the number of tribes should be adjusted upward to thirteen. But the geographical twelve-tribe system was maintained by withholding a contiguous territory from the tribe of Levi, to whom was ascribed a special spiritual role within the nation.

[10]For more detailed discussion of the sociological significance of *mišpāḥâ,* see Norman K. Gottwald, *The Tribes of Yahweh: A Sociology of the Religion of Liberated Israel, 1250-1050 B.C.E.* (Maryknoll, N.Y.: Orbis, 1979), pp. 257-84, 301-5; Christopher J. H. Wright, *God's People in God's Land: Family, Land, and Property in the Old Testament* (Grand Rapids, Mich.: Eerdmans, 1990), pp. 48-53; Francis I. Andersen, "Israelite Kinship Terminology and Social Structure," *BT* 20 (1969): 29-39; C. H. J. de Geus, *The Tribes of Israel: An Investigation into Some of the Presuppositions of Martin Noth's Amphictyony Hypothesis* (Assen: Van Gorcum, 1976), pp. 133-37.

[11]Josh 13:15, 23, 24, 28, 29, 31; 15:1, 12, 20; 16:5, 8; 17:2; 18:11, 20, 21, 28; 19:1, 10, 16, 17, 23, 24, 31, 32, 39, 40, 48.

[12]Similarly William Johnstone, "Old Testament Technical Expressions in Property Holding: Contributions from Ugarit," *Ugaritica* 6 (1969): 313.

of a clan incorporated the villages and towns where the members of the *mišpāḥâ* lived, along with the agricultural land between. Although individual families possessed the right to the produce of their assigned parcels of land, ownership of the land rested with the clan.[13] As the records of Israel's military forces in Numbers 1 and 26 indicate,[14] tribal forces were called up or organized according to their clans.

Socially and religiously the *mišpāḥâ* played an extremely important role in the daily life of the Israelites. Within the territory of the clan each household farmed its smaller piece of patrimonial land *(nāḥălâ)*; the *mišpāḥâ*, however, was ultimately responsible for maintaining the integrity of the patrimonial holdings, among other ways through the institution of the *gō'ēl*, the "kinsman redeemer."[15] Although intermarriage among clans (exogamy) did occur, for the most part Israelite marriages occurred within the clan (endogamy). This endogamous arrangement was undoubtedly driven in some measure by economics (money exchanged in marriages and land inherited by orphaned women who had no brothers would remain within the clan),[16] but social considerations were also important. The practice facilitated the identification of appropriate wives for the men while ensuring that married women would not live too far from their family of origin. In addition to protecting the integrity of patrimonial holdings and inhibiting the introduction of foreign elements into the clan community, the *mišpāḥâ* bore responsibility for the administration of justice within the community:[17] enforcing blood vengeance in the case of capital crimes (2 Sam 14:7) and ensuring in the year of Jubilee that land would return to its rightful owner and that those who had sold themselves into slavery because of poverty would be released (Lev 25:10, 41). The clan was also engaged in religious affairs: guarding the community against Molech cult rituals (Lev 20:5), arranging for the Passover celebrations (Ex 12:21), participating in community sacrifices (1 Sam 20:6, 29), mourning the deaths of their mem-

---

[13]For a discussion of undivided inheritance, see Raymond Westbrook, *Property and the Family in Biblical Law,* JSOTSup 113 (Sheffield: JSOT Press, 1991), pp. 118-41; Wright, *God's People in God's Land,* pp. 66-70.

[14]These lists are commonly referred to as censuses, but the repeated references to war, the fact that only those men twenty years and older were counted, the frequent use of the verb *pāqad,* "to muster," and the references to the numbered persons as *ṣābā',* "military host," demonstrate that the primary purpose of the documents is not to record the population of the nation but to register tribal and clan contributions to the military forces.

[15]Cf. Jer 32:6-15; Ruth 4:1-10. On other obligations of the *gō'ēl* see further below.

[16]See Num 27:1-11; 36:1-12. So also van der Toorn, *Family Religion,* p. 201.

[17]With the heads of the households functioning as the elders *(zĕqēnîm)* of the clan.

bers (Zech 12:10-14), and in later times celebrating the Festival of Purim (Esther 9:28).

The fourth level of Israel's kinship structure was the *bêt 'āb*, "family," literally, "father's house."[18] Unlike modern Western notions of nuclear families consisting of husband, wife, and biological or adopted children (not to mention alternative definitions of family that include households composed of same-sex domestic partners), ancient Israelite *mišpāḥôt* consisted of numerous smaller units, "fathers' houses," that in reality were large extended families. These families were made up of a single living male ancestor, his wife/ wives, the man's sons and their wives, grandsons and their wives, and conceivably even great grandchildren; any unmarried male or female descendants (married female descendants were excluded, having left the household to live with the families of their husbands) and unrelated dependents; male and female hired servants and slaves, along with their families; resident laborers; and on occasion resident Levites (Judg 17:7-13). Assuming monogamous marriages, an average life span of forty or fifty years,[19] and average fertility rates, a *bêt 'āb* could have consisted of several nuclear (two-generation) families and totaled twenty to twenty-five persons, though a smaller count of fifteen was probably more common.[20]

Joshua 7:16-26 provides the most impressive illustration of this family structure. The process whereby Achan was exposed as the cause of Israel's defeat at Ai was complex, involving a serial examination of the Israelites as a whole (*'am*), the tribes (*šěbāṭîm*), the clans (*mišpāḥôt*), the households (*bāttîm*), and the nuclear families. By a process of isolation Joshua identified Achan, the son of Carmi, of the house (*bayit*) of Zabdi, of the clan (*mišpāḥâ*) of Zerah, of the tribe (*šēbeṭ*) of Judah, as the guilty person. Achan was a married man with children, but he was still considered a part of the house of his grandfather Zerah. Similarly Judges 6—8 presents Gideon as the father of several sons (Judg 8:20) and a man with at least ten servants of his own

---

[18]Cf. the discussion by King and Stager, *Life in Biblical Israel*, pp. 39-40.

[19]The figures of seventy or eighty years given in Psalm 90:10 are highly optimistic and ideal. According to 1 and 2 Chronicles, the average ages of kings of Judah when they died was forty-four. Given the special privileges and health services available to royalty, the life span of ordinary citizens will have been shorter. So also H. W. Wolff, *Anthropology of the Old Testament*, trans. M. Kohl (Philadelphia: Fortress, 1974), pp. 119-20.

[20]This is the sociological picture envisaged in the second covenantal principle of the Decalogue: Yahweh visits the sins of the fathers on the children, on the third and fourth generations (Ex 20:5; Deut 5:9). This statement is commonly interpreted vertically, that is from one generation to another even after the decease of the previous. However, it is preferable to interpret it horizontally, in which case "to the third and fourth generations" incorporates all those persons that constitute a *bêt 'āb* at a given moment.

(Judg 6:27), though he still lived under the protection and authority of his father Joash (Judg 6:11, 28-32; 7:14).[21] On the basis of these texts we may represent a typical household diagrammatically as in figure 2.

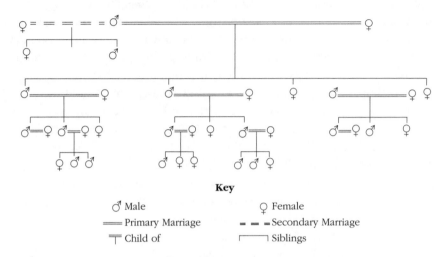

Key

♂ Male   ♀ Female

══ Primary Marriage   = = = Secondary Marriage

┬ Child of   ┌──┐ Siblings

Figure 2. The *bêt 'āb* in Israel: The kinship structure of a typical household

A combination of the biblical and archaeological evidence yields a reasonable picture of the physical circumstances in which these households might have lived.[22] In the Iron Age nuclear family units tended to live in houses between fifty and one hundred square meters in area, depending on the status and wealth of the residents, and the space available for construction. Amihai Mazar describes a typical house as follows:

> The most advanced form was the so-called four room house. This was a rectangular building with average dimensions of 10 x 12 m. The entrance usually led directly into a rectangular courtyard flanked by various spaces on three of its sides. One of the spaces along the courtyard was usually a pillared roof area. There were many variations to this plan: pillars were sometimes found on both sides of the courtyard; in other cases no pillars at all were used.[23]

---

[21]A similar picture of the *bêt 'āb* is reflected in the regulations concerning sexual conduct in Lev 18. For detailed redactional and sociological analysis of this passage, see Friedrich Fechter, *Die Familie in der Nachexilszeit: Untersuchungen zur Bedeutung der Verwandtschaft in Ausgewählten Texten des Alten Testaments,* BZAW 264 (Berlin: deGruyter, 1998), pp. 115-227.

[22]See the discussion by Wright in *God's People in God's Land,* pp. 53-58.

[23]Amihai Mazar, *Archaeology of the Land of the Bible 10,000-586 B.C.E.* (New York: Doubleday, 1990), p. 486. For a more detailed discussion, see Stager, "Archaeology of the Family," pp. 11-18; King and Stager, *Life in Biblical Israel,* pp. 28-35.

The compounds that represented the home of the *bêt ʾāb* were as significant as the dwellings of the so-called nuclear families, for this was the focus
of village life. Judges 17—18 provides a literary picture of one such *bêt ʾāb*.
This household consisted of its head, Micah the Ephraimite, his mother, an
unspecified number of sons, a wandering Levite whom he had engaged as
priest (Judg 17:7-13), a significant number of men whom he could muster in
defense of the household (Judg 18:22), and, we may assume, wives and
daughters of many of these men. The compound itself consisted minimally
of the principal residence occupied by Micah, presumably shared with his
widowed mother,[24] the cult shrine, a residence for the Levitical priest, and
houses for the men referred to in Judges 18:22,[25] all of which were apparently enclosed by a wall since access to the compound could be gained only
through a gate (cf. Judg 18:16-17). This literary portrayal of Micah's compound accords with the picture of numerous Iron Age sites that archaeolo-
gists have reconstructed. These settlements were composed of clusters of
dwellings consisting of several individual houses, which may have been free
standing or may have shared one or two common walls. Access to the
houses from a central open courtyard was gained through separate door-
ways. Some settlements comprised several compounds separated by paths,
streets, or stone walls.[26]

THE STATUS AND ROLES OF HUSBANDS AND FATHERS IN ANCIENT ISRAEL

The status of husband and father. The Hebrew designation of an extended family unit as a *bêt ʾāb,* "father's house," reflects not only the andro-
centricity of Israelite society in general but the patricentricity of families in
particular. Like most ancient Near Eastern cultures, Israelite families were
patrilineal (official lines of descent were traced through the father's line),[27]
patrilocal (married women joined the households of their husbands), and
patriarchal (the father governed the household).[28] Although scholars gener-

---

[24]The absence of any reference to his father and the initiative taken by his mother in Judg 17:1-
4 suggest that Micah's father had died and that Micah had now assumed the role of head of
the household, though he was still obligated to honor and care for his mother.

[25]The description of the men's residences as *babāttîm ʾăšer ʿim bêt mîkâ,* may be translated either
"in the houses that were near Micah's house" or "in the houses comprising [*sic*] the household
of Micah." Thus Stager, "Archaeology of the Family," p. 22.

[26]For more detailed description, see ibid., pp. 18-23.

[27]See the genealogies in Genesis 5, 10, 36, and so on.

[28]For discussion, see Raphael Patai, *Family, Love and the Bible* (London: Macgibbon & Kee,
1960), pp. 17-18.

ally use the term *patriarchy* to identify the Israelite social structure, I prefer to speak of *patricentrism* for several reasons.

First, the term *patriarchy,* literally, "the rule of the father," places inordinate emphasis on the power a father exercised over his household.[29] In recent years feminist interpreters have performed a valuable service in pointing out the dark side of patriarchy reflected in many biblical narratives.[30] However, such approaches tend to interpret obviously abusive male behavior as natural and normal expressions of patriarchy, despite the fact that in many instances the author cites such conduct deliberately to demonstrate the degeneracy of the times.[31] By definition, heads of households exercised authority over their families, but when Israelites lived by Canaanized standards, normative patriarchy rapidly degenerated to cancerous, corrupt, irresponsible, self-centered and exploitative exercise of power. But this was a far cry from the normative ideal of patriarchy. Because many associate this term *a priori* with this kind of abuse, the expression is best avoided.[32]

Second, *patricentrism* reflects the normative biblical disposition toward the role of the head of a household in Israel more accurately than does the word *patriarchy*. It is clear that if the *bêt ʾāb* was the nucleus of the *mišpāḥâ,* then the *ʾāb* was the nucleus of the *bêt ʾāb*. And just as in a physical sense the house inhabited by the head of the extended family represented the nucleus of the compound, so the head of the family functioned as its center. Like the spokes of a wheel, family life radiated outward from him (see figure 3). In fact, as Johannes Pedersen noted long ago, "wherever a man goes he

---

[29]See, for example, Patai's discussion of "The Powers of the Patriarch," ibid., pp. 114-24.

[30]These interpreters are correct in characterizing as abusive Abraham's passing off his wife Sarah as his sister to save his own skin (Gen 12:10-20); Lot's offer of his two daughters to the thugs of Sodom (Gen 19:8); Jephthah's sacrifice of his daughter (Judg 11:34-40); the Israelite men's authorization of the remnant of Benjamite warriors to ambush and seize their daughters as they are engaged in celebrative religious dance (Judg 21:19-24); David's adultery with Bathsheba and his murder of her husband (2 Sam 11:1-27); and Amnon's rape of his half sister Tamar (2 Sam 13:1-19), to name just a few horrendous episodes recounted in Scripture. For keen analyses of some of these troubling texts see Phyllis Trible, *Texts of Terror: Literary Feminist Readings of Biblical Narratives,* OBT 13 (Philadelphia: Fortress, 1984).

[31]Nowhere is this more evident than in the book of Judges, the central thrust of which is to expose the Canaanization of Israelite society. Indeed, the horrendous abuse of women in the book represents but one of the symptoms of a culture gone wrong. For a discussion of the issue, see Daniel I. Block, "Unspeakable Crimes: The Abuse of Women in the Book of Judges," *SBJT* 2, no. 3 (1998): 46-55.

[32]Carol Meyers is correct in preferring to characterize Israelite society in general as androcentric rather than patriarchal ("The Family in Early Israel," in *Families in Ancient Israel,* ed. Leo G. Perdue et al. [Louisville: Westminster John Knox, 1997], pp. 34-35), but as the phrase *bêt ʾāb* suggests, families in particular were patricentric.

takes 'his house' with him."[33] Biblical genealogies trace descent through the male line;[34] a married couple resided within the household of the groom; in references to a man and his wife or a man and his children, the man is generally named first (Gen 7:7); children were born to the father (Gen 21:1-7); fathers negotiated family disputes (Gen 13:1-13; 31:1-55); God generally addressed heads of the household;[35] when families worshiped, the head of the household took the initiative;[36] and when men died without descendants their "name" died.[37] In short, the community was built around the father; in every respect it bore his stamp.

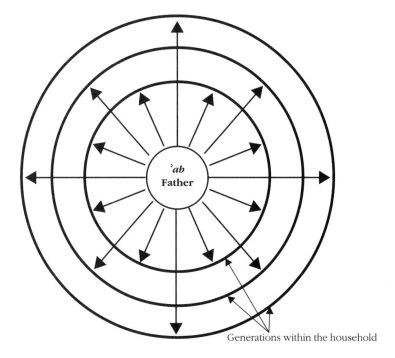

Generations within the household

Figure 3. The *bêt 'āb*: The patricentric family structure of ancient Israel

---

[33]Johannes Pedersen, *Israel: Its Life and Culture,* SFSHJ 1 (Atlanta: Scholars Press, 1991 [1926]), 1:51. See, for example, the deliverance of Noah and his house, which included his wife and his sons' wives (Gen 7:1, 13).

[34]The exceptional inclusion of four women in the genealogy of Jesus in Matt 1 is driven by the rhetorical aims of the evangelist.

[35]Gen 3:9; 12:1; 35:1. This normal pattern throws into even sharper relief the exceptional character of Judg 13:1-23, where the divine envoy prefers to address an otherwise unnamed woman concerning the birth of a child to her husband, Manoah, who is named.

[36]Gen 9:13-22; 12:7-8; 35:2-15; cf. Job 1:4-5.

[37]Deut 25:5-6; Ruth 4:5,10; 1 Sam 24:18-22.

Third, although the man did indeed function as the ruler of the household,[38] the Old Testament pays relatively little attention to the power of the husband and father.[39] The only reference to a man's status as ruler over his wife occurs in Genesis 3:16, but here it highlights the fundamentally negative effects of the Fall on marital relations: as a result of sin, responsible headship degenerates to an inappropriate exercise of power over *(māšal)* the woman.[40] Accordingly, we do a disservice to the biblical record if we are preoccupied with the power the *'āb* wielded. In healthy and functional households the male head was neither despot nor dictator. On the contrary, since the family members were perceived as extensions of the progenitor's own life, the head's own interests depended upon the well-being of the household. Rather than evoking images of "ruler" or "boss," the term *'āb* expressed confidence, trust and security.[41] This emphasis on the responsibilities associated with headship over the household (as opposed to

---

[38]Witness the references to a head of a household as its *ba'al*, "owner, master" (Ex 22:8 [Eng. 7]), and *'ǎdôn*, "lord, sovereign," of his wife/wives (Gen 18:12), children, slaves, livestock, movable property and land. For discussions of the former term, see J. Kühlewein, *TLOT*, 1:247-51; for the latter, see E. Jenni, *TLOT*, 1:23-29.

[39]The fifth command of the Decalogue addresses children's duty to honor parents, rather than parents' power to demand the respect of the child.

[40]Taken out of context, Ps 105:21 could be interpreted as highlighting the authority of a father over his household ("He [Yahweh] made him lord *['ǎdôn]* of his house *[bêtô]*, and ruler *[mōšēl]* of all his possessions *[qinyānô]*"), except that this statement refers to Joseph, whom the pharaoh put in administrative charge of his kingdom. Elsewhere, the verb *māšal*, "to rule," occurs in association with the government of a household only in Prov 17:2, which speaks of a wise servant ruling over a foolish son and sharing in the inheritance. But see also Is 3:12, which speaks of an upside-down world in which children oppress and women rule the people of Yahweh.

[41]This is evident in texts like Ps 68:5-6, which portrays the father figure as the protector of orphans, defender of widows, host for the homeless and savior of the prisoner; or Job 29:12-17, where, as one dressed in righteousness and justice, Job describes himself as a savior to the poor in distress, a helper for the orphan, a blessing to the perishing, a joy for the widow, eyes for the blind, feet for the lame, a father to the needy, defender of the stranger and rescuer of the victims of the wicked. Although the term *'āb*, "father," always connoted authority, it also suggested protection and security, even when *'āb* was used in a metaphorical sense. Cf. Judg 17:10; 18:19, according to which the unnamed Levitical priest was engaged as priest and "father," first by Micah, then by the Danites. He was not expected to govern either the household or the tribe, but he was expected to guarantee security, to serve as a kind of "rabbit's foot." When Naaman's servants addressed Elijah as *'āb*, they expressed both their respect and their dependence upon him (2 Kings 5:13). At the ascension of Elijah, Elisha's exclamation, "My father! My father!" reflected not so much his subjection to his mentor as the warmth of the relationship between the two men, comparable to Isaac's similar utterance to his literal father in Gen 22:7. The same applies when Yahweh is portrayed as divine Father of Israel (Deut 32:6; Is 63:16; 64:7; Jer 31:9; Mal 1:6), of the members of the community of faith (Mal 2:10), of orphans (Ps 68:6) and of the king of Israel (2 Sam 7:14; Ps 89:27)—or when an idol is addressed as the father of the devotee (Jer 2:27).

its privileges and power) is consistent with the overall tenor of the Old Testament, which views leadership in general to be a privilege granted to an individual in order to serve the interests of those who are led.[42] The pervasive nature of this perspective is illustrated by the Decalogue. Addressed to the head of the household, the second commandment strengthens the prohibition on idolatry by declaring that consequences of the father's actions extend to the third and fourth generation, that is, to the entire *bêt 'āb* (Ex 20:4-5; Deut 5:8-9). This concern is even clearer in the fourth commandment, which prohibits the head of a household from exploiting his people or animals by having them work while he rests (Ex 20:10; Deut 5:14-15).[43] Similarly, the eighth and tenth commands rein in the power of greedy heads of households by forbidding them to covet and seize neighbors' property (including that of family members; Ex 20:15, 17).

Having demonstrated the general biblical emphasis on paternal responsibility (rather than privilege), I would like to explore how headship was exercised in real life. The question may be answered in part by examining the role of the husband in the marriage itself. Ancient Israelites viewed marriage as a covenant relationship. Accordingly, Proverbs 2:17 speaks of matrimony as a "covenant of God" *(běrît 'elôhîm),*[44] and Malachi 2:14 refers to the bride as "the wife of his [the groom's] covenant" *('ēšet běrîtô).* But apart from the fact that weddings were civil rather than religious affairs, the Old Testament provides little information on the nature of Israelite weddings. From Ezekiel's parabolic description of Yahweh's marriage to Jerusalem/Israel (Ezek 16:8-13), we may infer a series of elements involved in an ancient wedding. (1) The groom covered his bride with his garment,[45] a symbolic act signifying "the establishment of a new relationship and the symbolic declaration of

---

[42]The so-called Mosaic Charter for Kingship (Deut 17:14-20) prohibited kings from ruling in their own interests but commanded them to lead the people in scrupulous observance of the Torah. See also the oracle on righteous rule by Lemuel's mother in Prov 31:2-9. But these idealistic statements contrast with Samuel's warning of the oppressive nature of kingship in 1 Sam 8:11-18 and the preaching of the prophets, which frequently denounced abuse of power by kings and other government officials (e.g., Ezek 34:1-19).

[43]The Deuteronomic version strengthens the humanitarian concern by adding "so your male servant and female servant may rest as well as you," and reminding the head of the household of the Israelites' own experience of exploitative labor in Egypt.

[44]This is the most likely interpretation of the phrase (thus also R. B. Y. Scott, *Proverbs. Ecclesiastes: Introduction, Translation, and Notes,* AB 18 (Garden City, N.Y.: Doubleday, 1965), pp. 42-43. Alternatively, the forgotten "covenant of God" could also be Yahweh's covenant with Israel made at Sinai.

[45]Ezek 16:8; cf. Ruth 3:9; Deut 23:1 (Eng. 22:30); 27:20; Mal 2:16.

the husband to provide for the sustenance of the future wife."[46] (2) The groom swore an oath *(nisba')* of fidelity to the bride. Presumably this would involve a physical gesture of raising the hand *(nāśā' yād)* to heaven, thereby invoking God as a witness and guarantor of the covenant.[47] (3) The groom entered into covenant *(bô' bĕrît 'et)* with his bride so that she became his. This part of the ceremony would involve a verbal formulaic declaration something like "I, PN, will be your husband, and you, PN, shall be my wife."[48] (4) The groom bathed his bride and anointed her with oil as a tender expression of love and devotion.[49] (5) Depending upon the economic resources of the groom, he would dress her up in the finest garments and jewelry he could afford.[50] (6) He prepared his finest meal for her, and they would feast together in his house. Based on several written marriage contracts recovered from the fifth-century B.C. Jewish colony at Elephantine and references in extrabiblical legal codes,[51] it seems likely that at some point in the ceremony written copies of the marriage covenant were prepared and deposited for safe keeping in a secure place.

As in most cultures, weddings provided occasions for great celebration. Song 3:11 and Isaiah 61:10 speak of the bridegroom wearing his diadem, and, from a later period, 1 Maccabees 9:39 observes the groom's friends accompanying the couple with musical instruments as they proceed to his house. The bride herself will have been veiled until the couple was alone in the bridal chamber (Song 4:1, 3; 6:7), but she also had her attendants, who sang love songs as the procession made its way to the groom's house (Ps

---

[46]Thus Paul A. Kruger, "The Hem of the Garment of Marriage: The Meaning of the Symbolic Gesture in Ruth 3:9 and Ezek 16:8," *JNSL* 12 (1984): 86. Cf. Block, *Judges, Ruth*, p. 691.

[47]The idiom occurs elsewhere in divine covenantal contexts promising the land of Canaan to Abraham (Ex 6:8; Num 14:30; Neh 9:15; Ezek 20:5, 6, 28, 42; 47:14; cf. Deut 32:40; Ezek 16:15, 22, 23 for additional contexts). The invocation of gods was a fundamental part of all ancient covenants, inviting them to impose devastating curses on those who would be unfaithful to their covenant promises.

[48]The following formula derives from a marriage contract from the Aramaic-speaking Jewish colony at Elephantine in Egypt: *hy 'ntty w'nh b'lh mn ywm' znh w'd 'lm,* "She is my wife, and I am her husband from this day and forever." For further discussion of the formula and bibliography, see Daniel I. Block, *The Book of Ezekiel 1-24,* NICOT (Grand Rapids, Mich.: Eerdmans, 1997), p. 483. These two elements (the oath and the declaration) are present also in Ezek 20:5, which refers to Yahweh's analogous covenant with Israel: "I raised my hand to the descendants of the house of Jacob. . . . I raised my hand to them saying: I am Yahweh your God" (my translation).

[49]The gesture finds an analogue in the Old Babylonian reference to "a day of bathing" as part of the marriage ritual. See Block, *Ezekiel 1-24,* p. 484, for discussion and bibliography.

[50]Ezek 16:10-13; cf. Ps 45:14-15; Is 61:10.

[51]CH §128, *ANET,* p. 171.

45:15; Jer 16:9). The Song of Songs probably preserves the kind of love songs that were sung at such occasions. The celebrations reached their climax in a great feast, which could last an entire week (Gen 29:27; Judg 14:12). Generally the marriage would be physically consummated the night of the wedding. Deuteronomy 22:13-21 suggests that the sheet stained with the virginal bleeding produced by the first coitus would be kept by the bride's parents to be produced in a legal hearing should the husband ever suspect her of not having been a virgin at the time of the wedding.

In ancient Israelite marriages a primary concern of a husband was the fathering of children, which added to the significance of the consummation of the marriage in sexual intercourse.[52] Although the Song of Songs celebrates love and lovemaking as an egalitarian affair, Hebrew expressions for marriage[53] and sexual intercourse reflect male initiative. The latter is described as a man "knowing" *(yāda‘)* a woman,[54] "entering" *(bô’ ‘el)* a woman,[55] "lying" *(sākab)* with a woman,[56] and giving a woman his penis *(nātan šěkobtô);*[57]

---

[52]On the importance of children, see further below.

[53]Typically a man "takes" *(lāqaḥ)* a woman in marriage. For references, see *DCH*, 4:573. The male initiative in marriage is also reflected in other idioms: (1) a man (or his *nepeš,* "person, soul") "clings to" *(dābaq bě)* his wife (Gen 2:24); (2) a man "loves" *(’āhēb)* a woman (Gen 24:67; 29:18, 20, 30, 32; Judg 16:4, 15; 1 Sam 1:5; 2 Sam 13:1, 4, 15; 2 Chron 11:21; Esther 2:17; and others; for additional references see *DCH* 1:138-39; Michal's love for David (1 Sam 18:20, 28) represents the singular exception, on which see Susan Ackerman, "The Personal Is Political: Covenantal and Affectionate Love *[’āhēb, ’ahābâ]* in the Hebrew Bible," *VT* 52 [2002]: 452-53); note also Leah's craving, not to love but to be loved (Gen 29:31-33); (3) a man "finds" *(māṣā’)* a woman (Prov 31:10); (4) a man "covers" a woman with his garment (Ruth 3:9; Ezek 16:8); (5) the man pledges himself *(nišba’ lě)* to a woman (Ezek 16:8). In Jer 31:22 Jeremiah envisages a radically new situation created by Yahweh in which a woman (Israel) will embrace *(těsôbēb)* a mighty man (Yahweh).

[54]Gen 4:1; 19:8; 38:26; Num 31:17; Judg 11:39; 19:25; 21:11; 1 Sam 1:19; 1 Kings 1:41.

[55]Gen 6:4; 16:2,4; 29:23; 29:21,30; 30:3, 4; 38:2, 8, 9, 16, 18; 39:14, 17; Deut 21:13; 22:13; Judg 15:1; 16:1; Ruth 4:13; 2 Sam 3:7; 12:24; 16:21, 22; 17:25; 20:3; 1 Chron 2:21; 7:23.

[56]Gen 26:10; 30:15, 16; 34:2, 7; 35:22; 39:12, 14; Lev 15:18, 24, 33; 18:22; 19:20; 20:11, 12, 13, 18, 20; Num 5:13, 19; Deut 22:25; 27:20, 21, 22, 23; 35:22; 1 Sam 2:22; 2 Sam 11:11; 13:14; Ezek 23:8. With the exception of Gen 30:15, 16 and 2 Sam 11:11, all of these involve illicit sexual relations: incest, adultery, homosexuality and bestiality. The only exceptions to male initiative occur in extraordinary contexts. According to Gen 19:32-35, Lot's daughters "lay with" their father because they thought there was no one left to "lie with" them—"according to universal custom" *(kěderek kol hā’areṣ).* In 2 Sam 13:11, in quoted speech, Absalom demanded that Tamar his sister "lie with" him, though in 1 Sam 13:14 the narrator identifies the true nature of this abusive act by saying he abused and lay with her.

[57]Lev 18:20, 23; 20:15; Num 5:20. The evidence is limited but refers to a woman receiving *(lāqah)* a penis. While assonantally related to *šākab,* "to lie [with]," *šěkōbet,* "penis," derives from a homonymous root meaning "to pour out." Compare the Hebrew reference to "semen," as *šikbat zera‘,* literally "discharge of seed" (Lev 15:16-18, 32; 19:20; 22:4; Num 5:13). For discussion of these expressions, see Jacob Milgrom, *Leviticus 1-16,* AB 3 (New York: Doubleday, 1991), p. 927.

in unwilling contexts a man "humiliates" *(ʿinnâ)* a woman.[58] But in family terms, the goal of such action was to build a family (cf. Ruth 4:11), which begins with conception and pregnancy.[59]

A husband and father's responsibilities increased as the household was established and the membership increased. Among his growing obligations, he had a number of responsibilities to the family as a whole. Whether the man was the head of the extended family *(rōʾš bêt ʾāb)* or the nuclear family within the *bêt ʾāb,* he was obligated to serve the family by (1) personally modeling strict personal fidelity to Yahweh;[60] (2) leading the family in the national festivals, thereby keeping alive the memory of Israel's salvation;[61] (3) instructing the family in the traditions of the Exodus and the Torah;[62] (4) managing the land in accordance with the regulations of the Torah to ensure the family's security with God;[63] (5) providing the basic needs of food, shelter, clothing, rest; (6) defending the household against outside threats;[64] (7) functioning as elder and representing the household in the gate, viz., the official assembly of the citizens;[65] (8) maintaining the well-being of the individuals in the household and the harmonious operation of the family unit; (9) implementing decisions made at the level of the *mišpāḥâ,* especially decisions involving the *gōʾēl*—blood vengeance, redemption of persons and property, and levirate marriage. In addition to these general duties, the fa-

---

[58]Gen 34:2; Judg 19:24; 20:5; 2 Sam 13:12,14, 22, 32; Lam 5:11. The verb used in this sense never involves a female subject and a male object.

[59]The natural progression is reflected in the following sequence of verbs: "A man knew *(yādaʿ)* his wife, and she conceived *(wattahar)* and gave birth *(wattēled)*." See Gen 4:1; 1 Sam 1:19-20. According to Josephus *(Ag. Ap.* 2.199), "the Law recognizes no sexual connections, except the natural union of man and wife, *and that only for the creation of children*" (emphasis added). Compare the divine blessing of humankind with the command to "be fruitful and multiply, and fill the earth" in Gen 1:28.

[60]Note: (1) the example of Noah, described as righteous, blameless and one who walked with God (Gen 6:9); (2) God's demand of Abraham that he walk before him and be blameless that his covenant might be established with him and his descendants after him (Gen 17:1-7) and the divine declaration of the fulfillment of this promise because of satisfaction with Abraham (Gen 26:5); (3) Joshua's challenge to his people to follow him as he leads his household in serving Yahweh (Josh 24:15); and (4) Hezekiah's following the example of David his father in doing what was right in the sight of Yahweh (2 Kings 18:3). Deut 6:4-9 charges fathers to commit themselves to loving Yahweh before demanding them to teach "these words" to their children. Functioning as "the wings of Yahweh," Boaz models these qualities even before he is married (Ruth 2:12).

[61]Passover (Ex 12:1-20); Festival of Weeks (Deut 16:9-12); Festival of Booths (Deut 16:13-17).

[62]Addressed to fathers, Deut 6:4-9 speaks of deep personal commitment. Cf. also Deut 6:20-25; 11:18-25.

[63]See the regulations concerning the Sabbatical Years and the year of Jubilee in Lev 25, obviously addressed to the heads of households.

[64]See the example of Micah in Judg 18:21-25.

[65]See Ruth 4:1-11.

ther had specific responsibilities to the other members of the household. These will be discussed in more detail below.

The husband's responsibilities toward his wife/wives. While monogamous marriage represents the biblical norm (Gen 2:21-24), and seems to have prevailed among the common folk, polygyny apparently was not uncommon.[66] In addition to the regular wife or wives,[67] a man might also have one or more secondary wives or concubines who would bear children for him. The most explicit statement prescribing a husband's behavior toward a wife occurs in Exodus 21:7-11. This text concerns a concubine, to be sure, but according to the rabbinic principle of *qal wa-homer* (what applies in a minor case will also apply in a major case), one may assume that husbands were to treat their wives with even greater dignity.[68] Because of uncertainties in the meanings of the three critical words in verse 10, there is some question concerning the obligations placed upon the man. However, on the analogy of extrabiblical formulas, *šě'ēr, kěsût* and *'ōnâ* are best understood as "food," "clothing" and "ointment/ oil," respectively.[69] These specific expressions capture the man's general responsibility to provide peace, permanence and security for his wives. All of these expressions are covered by the term *měnuhâ,* "rest," in Ruth 1:9. Beyond these obligations of husbands to meet the daily needs of their wives, they were also expected to provide their wives with proper burials.[70] A fuller discussion of the relationship of husband and wife will follow later, but the narrative of Genesis 1—2 suggests that in an ideal world men were obligated to treat their wives with dignity, as their ontological equals.[71]

---

[66]Jacob married sisters, Leah and Rachel (Gen 29:15-30); Esau had three wives, apparently of equal rank (Gen 26:34; 28:9; 36:1-5); and Elkanah had two wives, though, as in the case of Jacob, initially the favored one was barren (1 Sam 1:2). Polyandry (multiple husbands) is unheard of in the Old Testament.

[67]The Old Testament has no specific designation for wife, other than *'iššâ,* "woman."

[68]Raymond Westbrook ("The Female Slave," in *Gender and Law in the Hebrew Bible and the Ancient Near East,* ed. Victor H. Matthews et al., JSOTSup 262 [Sheffield: Sheffield Academic Press, 1998], p. 236) notes that "The duty of a husband to provide his wife with sustenance was so self-evident that it went virtually unmentioned in ancient Near Eastern sources."

[69]Tanakh interprets the last word, a *hapax legomenon,* traditionally as "conjugal rights." However, Shalom M. Paul has argued convincingly for the meaning "oil, ointment," in "Exod. 21:10: A Threefold Maintenance Clause," *JNES* 28 (1969): 48-51; idem, *Studies in the Book of the Covenant in the Light of Cuneiform and Biblical Law,* VTSup 18 (Leiden: Brill, 1970), pp. 56-61. So also Westbrook, "The Female Slave," p. 218. For a convenient brief discussion of these terms, see Nahum Sarna, *Exodus,* The JPS Torah Commentary (Philadelphia: Jewish Publication Society, 1991), p. 121.

[70]Gen 23:16; 35:19-20.

[71]If the man was created to function as vice-regent and king in God's world (see Manfred Hutter, "Adam als Gärtner und König," BZ 30 [1986]: 258-62), then the woman was created as queen. According to Ezek 16:1-14, this is how Yahweh treated Jerusalem, his wife.

As in any society, in ancient Israel the reality of human experience often made the ideal of peaceful and secure marital relations seem like a distant dream, and some marriages ended in divorce. It is impossible to determine how often this might have occurred, but the absence of a single divorce case in the Old Testament narratives and the limitation of legislation to a single text (Deut 24:1-4) are indicative of how far removed this ancient society was from the modern Western "culture of divorce." The Old Testament provides only the vaguest of hints at Israelite procedures for divorce. Based upon Hosea 2:4 (Eng. 1), some think it involved a verbal declaration, something like "She (PN) is not my wife, and I (PN) am not her husband," which represents a reversal of the formula recited at the time of marriage.[72] Conceivably the proceedings would also involve tearing up the original marriage contract and the drawing up of a formal severance document *(sēper kĕrîtut)*, as required by Deuteronomy 24:1. Because of the silence of the Old Testament on women suing for divorce, some conclude that they had no legal recourse to the dissolution of a marriage and that only the husband could initiate divorce proceedings. It is reasonable to suppose that in a patricentric and patrilocal culture it would have been extremely difficult for a woman to deal with the hostility her attempts at divorce might have provoked in her husband's clan. And given the fragility of single women's economic status, divorce would surely have been a last resort. Nevertheless, Judges 19:1-2 testifies to at least one instance in which a woman (identified as a *pilegeš*, "concubine") left her husband and returned to her father's house.

As noted above, Deuteronomy 24:1-4 contains the only explicit reference to divorce in the Old Testament legislation. This text is illuminating for several reasons.

First, it deals only with the case of divorce initiated by the husband.

Second, it demonstrates that divorce in Israel, rather than being a matter for the public courts, belonged to the realm of internal family law.[73]

Third, it identifies the motivation behind the divorce in only the vaguest of terms: the husband has found *ʿerwat dābār* in his wife. Literally the expression means "nakedness of a matter," but based on a comparison with the only other occurrence of this phrase (Deut 23:15 [Eng 14]), in reference to excrement and other body wastes, John Walton has plausibly proposed that this is a euphemistic expression for menstrual irregularity that would

---

[72]In the Elephantine papyri, "I hate [i.e., divorce] my wife" functioned as the divorce formula. Cf. Roland de Vaux, *Ancient Israel: Its Life and Institutions* (New York: McGraw-Hill, 1961), p. 35.

[73]So also Wright, *God's People in God's Land*, pp. 216-17.

keep her in a state of ritual uncleanness and prohibit her husband from having intercourse with her (Lev 15:14). The woman could certainly not be blamed for this condition, but her inability to conceive a child provided her husband with an excuse for divorce.[74]

Fourth, the passage does not seek to regulate divorce per se but the conduct of the husband after the divorce has occurred. Having humiliated his wife by forcing her to declare herself unclean,[75] he may not reclaim her if she remarries and then loses her husband through divorce or death.[76]

Fifth, the legislation seeks to protect the woman by requiring the husband to produce a severance document as legal proof for the dissolution of the marriage. Without this document the husband could demand to have her back at any time, and if she would remarry he could accuse her of adultery.[77]

Sixth, the text provides no moral or theological justification for divorce; it deals only with its legality.

Whether or not divorce was morally justifiable, this text demonstrates that it was tolerated in ancient Israel as a legal reality. In fact, Exodus 21:10-11 and Deuteronomy 21:10-14 recognize that for humanitarian reasons, releasing a slave-wife or captive woman whom an Israelite warrior has married is preferable to the man's refusing in either case to fulfill his marital duties. Elsewhere (presumably as the lesser of two evils) narrative texts report God's directing Abraham to send away his slave-wife Hagar (Gen 21:8-14) and Ezra's commanding the Jews of postexilic Jerusalem to put away their foreign wives.[78]

The prophets occasionally countenance the notion of God's divorcing Israel (e.g., Is 50:1; Hos 2:2; Jer 3:1-8),[79] but this use of the motif should be

---

[74]John Walton, "The Place of the *hutqaṭṭēl* Within the D-stem Group and Its Implications in Deuteronomy 24:4," *HS* 32 (1991): 14-15. Some suggest it refers to adulterous "indecent exposure" to another man (the New Testament logically interprets the phrase as *porneia* [Mt 5:31-32; 19:7-9]); or perhaps it serves as an intentionally vague expression, spreading the net as broadly as possible for any "shameful behavior" or even "any reason whatsoever." Thus John J. Collins, "Marriage, Divorce, and Family in Second Temple Judaism," in *Families in Ancient Israel*, ed. Leo G. Perdue et al. (Louisville: Westminster John Knox, 1997), p. 65.

[75]Walton ("Place of the *hutqaṭṭēl*" pp. 7-17) argues convincingly for this interpretation of *huttammāʾâ* in Mal 2:4. This is one of only four *hutqaṭṭēl* forms in the Old Testament (cf. Lev 13:55, 56; Is 34:6).

[76]The fact that she remarries demonstrates that her second husband is more charitable than the first, inasmuch as he is willing to marry her despite public awareness of her condition. Thus also Walton, "Place of the *hutqaṭṭēl*," p. 14.

[77]So also Wright, *God's People in God's Land*, p. 217.

[78]For a discussion of these texts see Joe Sprinkle, "Old Testament Perspectives on Divorce and Remarriage," *JETS* 40 (1997): 533-38.

[79]For a discussion of these texts see ibid., 541-43.

interpreted as a rhetorical device intended to wake the people up to their own infidelities. The fact is at Sinai God bound himself eternally to Israel in a covenant relationship. It might appear that he had divorced them when he abandoned Israel in 586 B.C. However, according to Leviticus 26:44-45 and Deuteronomy 4:29-31; 30:1-10, the judgment could not be the last word. Estranged husband and wife would be reconciled.

Although the Old Testament recognizes divorce as a legal reality, the basic biblical stance toward the issue is expressed by Malachi, who, speaking for Yahweh, declares, "I hate divorce" (Mal 2:16). Despite numerous attempts to reinterpret this ambiguous text,[80] within its present context the statement declares a fundamental divine aversion to divorce.[81] But what is it about divorce that is so objectionable? Practically, in the ancient context, unless a woman was taken in by her father or her brothers, divorce put her in an extremely vulnerable economic position. Like the widow or the orphan, she would be without male provision and protection, and in many instances would turn to prostitution simply to earn a living.

But Malachi 2:10-16 is not concerned with the economic consequences of divorce for the woman. Rather, it concentrates on the spiritual and covenantal implications of such an eventuality, which may be summarized as follows.

First, within the general flow of the book, the prevalence of divorce is perceived as evidence of a fundamental lack of reverence and fear toward Yahweh.[82]

Second, divorce is perceived as an act of treachery against one's companion, and a fundamental breach of covenant commitment to one's wife (v. 14).[83]

Third, reflecting the communal implications of marriage, divorce is

---

[80]The Masoretic text reads *kî śānēʾ šallaḥ,* "For he hates divorce," but who is the subject of "hate"? And does *šallaḥ* actually mean "divorce"? For discussions of the options see Ralph L. Smith, *Micah-Malachi,* WBC 32 (Waco, Tex.: Word, 1984), pp. 320-25; Collins, "Marriage, Divorce, and Family in Second Temple Judaism," pp. 123-27; and Sprinkle, "Old Testament Perspectives on Divorce and Remarriage," pp. 539-40.

[81]As Collins notes ("Marriage, Divorce, and Family in Second Temple Judaism," p. 125) both words—*śānēʾ* and *šallaḥ* are common in contexts dealing with divorce in not only the Old Testament but the Elephantine papyri.

[82]Along with boredom and malpractice in worship (Mal 1:6-14), personal and professional priestly corruption (Mal 2:1-9), intermarriage with pagans ("daughters of a foreign god," Mal 2:10-12), cynicism and contempt for Yahweh (Mal 2:17-3:4; 3:13-14), abusive and exploitative conduct toward the vulnerable in society (Mal 3:5-6), and stinginess in temple contributions (Mal 3:7-12).

[83]*Beged,* "treachery," functions as the *Leitwort* in Mal 2:10-16, occurring five times (Mal 2:10, 11, 14, 15, 16).

considered together with marriage to pagans to be an act of treachery against the community ("brothers") and a profanation of God's covenant with Israel (v. 10).

Fourth, intact marriages are prerequisite to producing "godly offspring" (*zera*ʿ *ʾĕlōhîm*, v. 15). People may perform the animal functions of procreation apart from marriage, but a stable home is indispensable for the continuation of a people of faith.

Fifth, a person's treachery against a human covenant partner absolves God of his covenantal obligations to that person (Mal 2:15-16). God rejects the offerings of those guilty of marital treachery, and no matter how frantically they plead for his attention, his obligation to the unfaithful is suspended.

Sixth, treachery is committed in the spirit (*rûaḥ*) before it is committed in action. God is not fooled by external acts of devotion when the spirit is fundamentally treacherous. Significantly, in keeping with the overall tenor of the Old Testament, this passage treats divorce not as a moral right enjoyed by males but as a moral offense committed by males.

Paternal responsibilities toward sons. When scouring the Old Testament for evidence concerning the relationship between fathers and sons, it is tempting to concentrate on the authority that fathers exerted over their sons[84] and to forget that the father's own interests were best

---

[84]With respect to Abraham's offering of his son Isaac in Gen 22, Patai comments (*Family, Love and the Bible,* p. 116), "The absolute power of the father over the life and the death of his children is taken so completely for granted in the earliest narrative portions of the Bible that never is there any thought given to the fears, the desperation, or other feelings a son (or a daughter) may have when he learns that he has to die because of a decision of his father." But this conclusion is one-sided and superficial on several counts. At best it argues from silence. Patai continues, "The question of Isaac's role in the story, of his feelings, of his—to use a modern phrase—individual problem never arises, is never for a moment considered." But how does he know? The account is not exhaustive. At worst, it overlooks patently contrary evidence within the narrative of a close relationship between father and son within the account, which is transparent in portraying the attitude of the father toward the son. (1) God himself expresses an awareness of the relationship in his opening charge: "Take your son, your only son Isaac, whom you love" (Gen 22:2). (2) Abraham guardedly informs his servants that he and the son will return from worship (Gen 22:5). (3) Abraham carries the dangerous objects up the mountain (fire and knife), while Isaac carries the benign wood (Gen 22:6). (4) Twice the narrator observes, "the two of them walked on together" (Gen 22:6, 8). (5) When Abraham answers his son's question, "Where is the lamb?" with "God himself will provide," he expresses both the anguish of his heart and his trust in Yahweh. A calloused and unfeeling Abraham would have responded, "You're it." In all these respects this account differs dramatically from the story of Jephthah's sacrifice of his daughter in Judg 11. But Patai's interpretation also misconstrues the narrator's purpose. The primary aim of biblical narratives is not to provide modern readers with cases for psychoanalysis but to develop theological themes. This event is explicitly cast as a test of Abraham's faith in God, who had promised to provide him with progeny through Isaac.

served when he secured the well-being of his children. Under healthy circumstances fathers took their responsibilities toward children very seriously. The following list represents a summary of paternal obligations/dispositions toward sons in particular. First, although many children were named by their mothers,[85] fathers often did so as well.[86] In naming a child, responsible parents not only gave expression to their faith but also expressed their aspirations for the child. Second, in Israel fathers were responsible for consecrating their first-born sons to Yahweh.[87] Third, fathers circumcised their sons on the eighth day.[88] Fourth, fathers took delight in their sons (*rāṣâ,* Prov 3:12), showed compassion on them (*riḥam,* Ps 103:13) and loved them (*'āhab,* Prov 13:24; Hos 11:1-4). Fifth, fathers assumed responsibility for their sons' spiritual development, modeling before them deep personal commitment to Yahweh and his Torah (Deut 6:5-6), diligently instructing them in the Torah and the traditions of salvation and covenant,[89] and generally "wearing their faith on their sleeves," that is, giving public witness to their spiritual commitment.[90] Sixth, fathers guarded their own ethical conduct so that their sons would not be implicated in their sin.[91] Seventh, fathers instructed their sons in the way of wisdom, specifically developing their character and skills for life and vocation and teaching them to follow in their fathers' steps (Prov 1—9). Eighth, fathers disciplined their sons when they erred,[92] and when the latter refused to be corrected, they presented their sons to the communal leaders for discipline.[93] Ninth, fathers managed household affairs judiciously, especially in issues of inheritance, thereby ensuring a smooth transition to the next generation. Tenth, fathers arranged for the marriage of their sons to suitable wives.[94] Eleventh, fathers pronounced blessings

---

[85]Gen 29:31; 30:6; 35:18; 38:28; Judg 13:24; 1 Sam 1:20; 4:20; Is 7:14.

[86]Gen 16:15; 17:19; Ex 2:22; 2 Sam 12:24; Hos 1:4.

[87]Ex 13:2, 12-15; 22:29; 34:1-20; Num 3:11-13; 8:16-18; 18:15.

[88]Gen 17:12; 21:4; Lev 12:3.

[89]Ex 12:24; 13:8; Deut 6:7, 20-25.

[90]Deut 6:8-9. For a discussion of the fathers' didactic and catechetical responsibilities, see Wright, *God's People in God's Land,* pp. 81-84.

[91]Ex 20:5; Deut 5:9.

[92]Deut 8:5; 2 Sam 7:14; Prov 13:24; 19:18; 22:15; 23:13-14.

[93]Deut 21:18-21. Since parents (both father and mother) were not permitted to execute a rebellious son but were required to present him before the elders for the final determination of his fate, the notion of some that fathers exercised virtually unlimited *patria potestas,* "paternal power," even over the life and death of their children, is to be severely reined in, if not outrightly rejected. So also Wright, *God's People in God's Land,* pp. 30-38.

[94]Gen 24; Judg 14. Though V. P. Hamilton correctly observes ("Marriage," *ABD,* 4:562) that the Old Testament nowhere mandates the arrangement of marriages for one's son or daughter.

upon their children prior to their decease.[95] A list like this exposes how skewed are perceptions that focus only on the power of the father over his son.

Paternal responsibilities toward daughters. Given the generally androcentric perspective of the Old Testament, it is not surprising that the biblical evidence concerning fathers' obligations toward their sons is more complete than the evidence of obligations toward their daughters. Nevertheless, it is possible to combine some loose threads to develop a preliminary understanding of the issue. Because daughters were expected to leave the *bêt ʾāb* when they married, their economic significance for the household differed from that of sons. But this does not mean that they were not treasured by their fathers. On the contrary, when Ezekiel speaks of children as the desire of parents' eyes *(maḥmad ʿênêhem)* and the delight of their beings *(maśśāʾ napšām)*, he refers to both "sons and daughters" (Ezek 24:25). And the narratives provide occasional touching scenes of sympathetic heads of households responding favorably to their daughters when they bring exceptional requests.[96]

In addition to the general care responsible fathers provided for their daughters,[97] the biblical record also shows specific obligations. First, a father protected his daughter from male predators so she would marry as a virgin, thereby bringing honor to his name and purity to her husband (cf. Ex 22:16-17; Deut 22:13-21). He would also stand up in court for his daughter against her husband if the latter accused her of not having been a virgin at the time of the marriage. Second, a father arranged for the marriage of his daughter by finding a suitable husband for her and negotiating the terms of the marriage.[98] Third, a father ensured a measure of security for his daughter by providing her with a dowry from the patrimonial estate.[99] Fourth, a father protected his daughter from her own rash vows,[100]

---

[95]Gen 27; 48—49.

[96]See, for example, Caleb's response to his daughter Achsah in Judg 1:13-14. Compare also Moses' sensitive paternal response to the orphaned daughters of Zelophehad in Num 27:1-10.

[97]That fathers were involved in the care of even female infants and growing children is reflected in Ezek 16:1-7, which portrays Yahweh as an adoptive father diapering and caring for a foundling until she reached puberty.

[98]See further below.

[99]According to Paula S. Hiebert ("'Whence Shall Help Come to Me?' The Biblical Widow," in *Gender and Difference in Ancient Israel*, ed. Peggy L. Day [Minneapolis: Fortress, 1989], p. 136), "the dowry was property owned by the woman, her share of the family inheritance." The dowry often included female servants. Cf. Gen 29:24, 29.

[100]Num 30:2-15.

not as a high-handed exercise of control over the girl, but out of obligation for the welfare of the entire household.[101] Fifth, a father provided security for his daughter if her marriage failed, either because of the death of her husband or the disintegration of her marriage.[102] It is doubtful that under normal circumstances such actions would have been taken merely in fulfillment of legal obligations. Natural paternal affection would demand that a father continue to be concerned about the welfare of his daughter even after she had left home.[103]

While these were noble ideals, illustrations of paternal abuse of daughters in the Old Testament are numerous. The book of Judges in particular recounts episodes in which fathers sacrifice their daughters in the interests of male guests,[104] their own male military honor[105] and sentimental loyalty to distant male relatives.[106] Although commentators often assume such behavior was acceptable in a patriarchal society, these should be interpreted as evidences of patricentrism run amok, in direct violation of normative values

---

[101] According to Num 30:13, fathers (and husbands in the case of a married women) could act in the interests of their dependents by annulling vows of self-mortification and self-affliction. Where fathers overrode vows of their daughters, Yahweh would forgive the daughters. The situation was different for a widow or divorcee, who, as an independent person, was obligated to keep her vows, unless of course they had been annulled by her husband while she was still in his house (Num 30:9-12).

[102] The evidence on this issue is meager, but Gen 38:11 reports Judah instructing his daughter-in-law Tamar to return to her father's house *(bêt 'āb)* after the death of his son, her husband, Er. However, since Judah set the terms of her return ("until my son Shelah grows up"), and since he had authority to sentence Tamar to burning for her alleged crime (Gen 38:24), it appears that even if she went home she remained under the authority of her deceased husband's father. Elsewhere, we read of Samson's father-in-law taking back his daughter and trying to protect her from Samson after Samson left her (Judg 14:20—15:2). Admittedly this event involves a Philistine father, but the case of the Levite and his concubine in Judg 19:1-2 suggests similar customs in Israel. Ruth 1:8 presents an exceptional case in which one widow (Naomi) releases her two widowed daughters-in-law to return to their mothers' houses *(bêt 'ēm)*. Like many other features, this detail reflects the general gynocentricity of the chapter. See further Block, *Judges/Ruth,* p. 633.

[103] The account of Laban's pursuit of Jacob and his daughters in Gen 31 illustrates the potential for conflict within Israelite families, especially when fathers' and husbands' interests in women clashed.

[104] Judg 19:22-24. In this account the narrator deliberately echoes the story of Lot in Sodom in Gen 19:7-8 to illustrate the depth of Israel's moral depravity in the premonarchic era. On the relationship between these two texts and the significance of the latter within the overall structure of Judges, see Daniel I. Block, "Echo Narrative Technique in Hebrew Literature: A Study in Judges 19," *WTJ* 52 (1990): 325-41; idem, *Judges/Ruth,* pp. 518-20, 532-38.

[105] Judg 11:29-40.

[106] Judg 21:19-24. For a discussion of the significance of this unethical conduct in the overall message of Judges, see Daniel I. Block, "Unspeakable Crimes: The Abuse of Women in the Book of the Judges," *SBJT* 2 (1998): 46-55.

that governed specific legislation outlawing such exploitation of daughters.[107]

Paternal responsibility in the marriage of children.[108] The role of the ancient Israelite father in the marriage of his sons and daughters was noted earlier in passing, but in order to understand the institution of marriage the manner in which marriages were effected deserves a closer look. Nowhere does the Old Testament mandate parentally arranged marriages, but it is clear from expressions like "giving your daughter to their sons or taking their daughters for your sons" (Deut 7:3) that this tended to be the practice. The fact that marriages were arranged by parents suggests that the institution itself involved much more than the mere union of one man with one woman; this was a momentous occasion uniting families.[109]

Ideally, Israelites preferred endogamous marriages within the clan or the tribe, though there were no official prohibitions on marrying an Israelite from another tribe. Leviticus 18:1-18 prohibits a man from marrying his siblings, uncles and aunts, or in-laws while his spouse is still alive, though marriages between first cousins appears to have been common and acceptable (Jacob with Rachel and Leah). Because of priests' sacred status within the nation, Leviticus 21:7 outlaws them from marrying prostitutes or divorcees. Ezekiel 44:22 extends this prohibition to include widows, unless they were widows of priests. For religious reasons marriage with Canaanites was absolutely forbidden for all from the nation's outset.[110] In the postexilic period, out of concern for a "holy seed" (Ezra 9:2), Ezra extended the prohibition to Philistines. In Malachi's mind, marriage of Israelites to pagans was equivalent to marrying daughters of foreign gods (Mal 2:11).

---

[107]See Lev 19:29, which prohibits fathers from degrading *(hillēl)* their daughters and filling the land with depravity *(zimmâ)* by engaging them in harlotry. On this text, see Erhard S. Gerstenberger, *Leviticus: A Commentary,* trans. Douglas W. Scott, OTL (Louisville: Westminster John Knox, 1996), pp. 277-78.

[108]By discussing arranged marriages here, in the context of paternal responsibilities in the Israelite household, I do not suggest that mothers of sons or daughters were not involved. Rebekah's grief over Esau's marriage to two Hittite women (Gen 26:34-35) and her determination that Jacob not make the same mistake (27:46), as well as the involvement of Samson's mother in his marriage to the Philistine woman of Timna (Judg 14:1-9), demonstrate that mothers also had high stakes in their children's marriages. In fact, Gen 21:21 describes Hagar, Ishmael's mother, arranging his marriage to an Egyptian like herself. Abraham's role in this marriage is unknown, though he may have acquiesced, knowing that this son would establish his own family far removed from the *bêt ʾāb* (cf. Gen 21:8-20). However, as texts like Gen 34 and Judg 14:20—15:6 indicate, fathers generally took the initiative.

[109]So also Hiebert, "'Whence Shall Help Come to Me?'" p. 129.

[110]Ex 34:10-17; Deut 7:1-5; Josh 23:12.

But within these broad parameters parents still needed to make specific decisions concerning suitable spouses for their own children. How such decisions were made must have varied greatly. Genesis 24 describes Abraham sending a trusted servant to his relatives in another country to find a wife for his son Isaac. According to Genesis 28—29 Isaac and Rebekah sent Jacob to Paddan-aram with orders to get his own wife from the house of Bethuel, his mother's brother. Sometimes fathers invited competition for their daughters, challenging potential suitors to earn the right with deeds of heroism.[111] Today feminist scholars appeal to the way these fathers treated their daughters as abusive examples of male chauvinism. But these accounts must be interpreted within the context of the ancient culture that placed a high value on marriage and bearing progeny; to have been given in marriage to the military hero would have been deemed a high honor for an Israelite girl.[112]

As a matter of custom parents expected their children to marry in the order of their births (Gen 29:26), but Israel had no laws prescribing this practice. When parents deemed their child to be approaching marriageable age,[113] the father of the groom would contact the parents of the potential spouse and negotiate the terms of the marriage, specifically the nature and size of the *mōhar,* "marriage present."[114] While some have interpreted the *mōhar* as a purchase price, it is preferable to see it as a deposit delivered to the parents of the bride to promote the stability of the marriage and to strengthen the links between the families of those being married.[115] Agreement by the parents of the bride would signal the engage-

---

[111]Caleb gave Achsah to Othniel as a reward for capturing Othniel (Judg 1:11-15); Saul offered David his daughter Merab as a reward for fighting Yahweh's battles for him, though David humbly declined and she was given to another man (1 Sam 18:17-18). Later, for sinister political reasons, Saul promised Michal (who already loved David) to David as a reward for killing one hundred Philistines, which he promptly proceeded to do (1 Sam 18:20-29).

[112]Though practice did not always match law, these examples recall a clause from the Law of Eshnunna (ca. 2000 B.C.) that declares "If a man takes a(nother) man's daughter without asking the permission of her father and her mother and concludes no formal marriage contract with her father and her mother, even though she may live in his house for a year, she is not a housewife" (*ANET,* p. 162).

[113]Daughters tended to marry at the onset of puberty, that is, about thirteen years of age, whereas boys would marry a couple of years later.

[114]So also Grace I. Emmerson, "Women in Ancient Israel," in *The World of Ancient Israel,* ed. R. E. Clements (Cambridge: Cambridge University Press, 1989), p. 382.

[115]Wright, *God's People in God's Land,* 194. According to Raymond Westbrook (*Old Babylonian Marriage Law,* AfOB 23 [Horn: Berger, 1988], p. 60), the *mōhar* represented a price that was paid for the transfer of authority from a girl's father to her husband.

ment of the bride and groom, who would then be married after a period of betrothal.

The Deuteronomic laws recognize the purpose of betrothal. From the bride's perspective, with engagement the commitment to marriage was deemed so firm that a betrothed woman who willingly engaged in sexual intercourse with a man other than her husband was to be treated as an adulteress and stoned to death (Deut 22:23-27). From the vantage of the groom, during the period of engagement he was exempted from military duty (Deut 20:7). Both regulations arise out of a concern for progeny. The former sought not only to secure the sanctity of sexual union between husband and wife but also to protect the patrilineal cohesion of the family— adultery could introduce an alien element. The aim of the latter was to protect the life of the groom until the marriage has been consummated. If he should be killed in battle, his line would die out. But the betrothal period also had an extremely practical function. It provided the bride opportunity quickly to hone her domestic and child-rearing skills under the tutelage of mother and grandmother and gave her family time to prepare the dowry that would go with her to her new home.[116] Meanwhile the groom, assisted by his father and brothers, would spend the engagement period building a house for the couple to occupy when they were married and securing the economic and social position of this new household within the extended family.

Paternal responsibilities toward servants/slaves. As noted earlier, in addition to the blood relatives, the Israelite family *(bêt 'āb)* included a variety of individuals who had by their own choice or through economic necessity come to be associated with the household. These included (1) resident aliens *(gērîm* and *tôšābîm)*, persons who apparently voluntarily left their home village or tribe in time of crisis (war, famine or epidemic) and sought employment and shelter in an Israelite community;[117] (2) hired hands *(śĕkîrîm)*, persons who no longer possessed their own land but who contracted themselves to a householder for daily wages;[118] and (3) slaves, both male *('ăbādîm)*

---

[116]The dowry could be in the form of slaves (Gen 24:59, 61; 29:24, 29), movable property and, in exceptional endogamous cases, land (Judg 1:11-12).

[117]By the grace of their Israelite hosts, many will have committed themselves to Israel's national deity and the nation's spiritual values, but their rights with respect to land, marriage, participation in the cult and judicial affairs were seriously curtailed. The distinctions between *gērîm* and *tôšābîm* are not clear. For definitions, see *HALOT,* pp. 201 and 1712, respectively. For discussion, see Daniel I. Block, "Sojourner; Alien; Stranger," *ISBE,* 4:561-64.

[118]*HALOT,* p. 1327.

and female *(ʾāmôt, šiphôt)*,[119] who occupied the lowest rung on the social ladder. As the property of full citizens, slaves could be bought and sold like cattle.

Because of the vulnerability of all of these classes of economic dependents within a household, laws against abuse by householders figure prominently in the Pentateuchal legislation. The fourth statement of the Decalogue, addressed to heads of households, sought to guarantee humane treatment for all members of the household, including children (male and female), servants (male and female), and resident aliens (and livestock!) by prescribing rest from work for all one day in seven.[120] This statement commands heads of households to give consideration to all in their employ, without discriminating between Israelite and non-Israelite members. Elsewhere the Mosaic legislation distinguishes between these two classes of slaves/servants. Exodus 21:1—23:33 and Deuteronomy 15:12-18 seek to ensure that the legal freedom of landless "Hebrew" slaves, whose security depended upon selling their services to Israelite landholders, would not be exploited indefinitely by any one landowner. In its concern to preserve/restore the property, independence and integrity of Israelite households, the law of Jubilee (Lev 25) required that any Israelite who had been enslaved was to be released in the Year of Jubilee. Because Israelite creditor and debtor stood before God as equals—that is, they were all Yahweh's purchased slaves—they were forbidden to enslave each other.[121]

Whereas the persons protected in the regulations cited above were primarily male slaves *(ʿăbādîm)*, Exodus 21:7-11 specifically seeks to regulate cases involving Israelite women/girls who were sold by their fathers as female slaves *(ʾāmôt)*, presumably because of debt. Many commentators assume that this sale envisions marriage to the master or to his son,[122] but the

---

[119]These terms are often used interchangeably, but the connotations of the latter were more negative. Whereas the former were eligible to marry, the latter were less clearly so. Ingrid Riesener (*Der Stamm* עבד *im Alten Testament,* BZAW 149 [Berlin: de Gruyter, 1979], p. 83) suggests that ʾāmâ tends to be used when a woman's feminine qualities are highlighted (weakness, need for protection, sexual attractiveness), while šiphâ tends to occur when her economic value (as possession, laborer) is involved. Gordon J. Wenham (*Genesis 16-50,* WBC 2 [Dallas: Word, 1994], p. 6) observes that šiphâ tends to be used in contexts involving dowries that a rich woman brought with her to a marriage and where the slave is answerable to her mistress, whereas ʾāmâ is used when the woman answers to a master. For summary discussions, see R. Schultz, "אָמָה," *NIDOTTE* 1:418-21; idem, "שִׁפְחָה," *NIDOTTE* 4:211-13.

[120]Ex 20:10; Deut 5:21.

[121]For a detailed discussion of these slave release laws, see Wright, *God's People in God's Land,* pp. 249-59.

[122]Thus Gregory Chirichigno, *Debt-Slavery in Israel and the Ancient Near East,* JSOTSup 141 (Sheffield: JSOT Press, 1993), pp. 24-55; cf. also Sarna, *Exodus,* p. 120.

absence of marriage or divorce terminology in the passage suggests the purpose of the sale was concubinage.[123] The regulation safeguards the woman's rights in two respects. First, the purchaser may not treat her as an ordinary slave. If she proves not to please him, and he does not fulfill his contractual obligation to treat her as his own concubine (qere᾽), or assign her to his son (kethib), he may not treat her as an ordinary slave woman. Because he has failed to grant her the protection available to concubines through motherhood, she retains the right to redemption by her father.[124] Second, the purchaser may not sell her to a foreigner, that is a non-Israelite,[125] and thereby render her irredeemable because foreigners would not recognize her rights under Israelite law. The law apparently assumes that she could be sold to another Israelite but that she would not thereby lose her redeemability.

Although slaves were viewed as the property of heads of households, the latter were not free to brutalize or abuse even non-Israelite members of the household. On the contrary, explicit prohibitions of the oppression/exploitation (hônā) of slaves appear repeatedly in the Mosaic legislation.[126] In two most remarkable texts, Leviticus 19:34 and Deuteronomy 10:19, Yahweh charges all Israelites to love (᾽āhēb) aliens (gērîm) who reside in their midst, that is, the foreign members of their households, like they do themselves and to treat these outsiders with the same respect they show their ethnic countrymen (᾽ezrah). Like Exodus 22:20 (Eng. 21), in both texts Israel's memory of her own experience as slaves in Egypt should have provided motivation for compassionate treatment of her slaves. But Deuteronomy 10:18 adds that the Israelites were to look to Yahweh himself as the paradigm for treating the economically and socially vulnerable persons in their communities.

The extent to which ancient Israelites actually adhered to these lofty ideals is difficult to ascertain. The pre-Israelite Abraham appears to have treated his slaves well. In Genesis 15:2-3 he offered to designate Eliezer the heir of his property, and in Genesis 24 he left the procurement of a wife for his sons in the hands of a servant (᾽ebed), the senior member of

---

[123]So also Westbrook, "The Female Slave," pp. 218-20. According to Deut 15:12, where concubinage is not involved, the status of Israelite males and females sold into debt-slavery is identical.

[124]The designation of this breach as a "treacherous act against her" (beged bāh), rather than against her father, confirms that the law was concerned to protect her rights.

[125]Ex 21:8. Interpreting ῾am nokrî in its usual sense, "a foreign people." On the term, see Daniel I. Block, "Sojourner," ISBE, 4:562.

[126]Ex 22:20 (Eng. 21), Lev 19:33 and Deut 23:16-17 (Eng. 15-16). Compare Jer 22:3, where the prophet Jeremiah calls upon the king, his courtiers and the citizens of Judah to stop their oppression and violence against the stranger, the orphan and the widow.

his household and administrator of all his possessions *(hammōšēl bĕkol ʾăšer lô)*. However, in a much later period, the prophets repeatedly condemned those with political and social power for abusing and exploiting the weak and vulnerable. But abuses in actual experience do not negate Israel's noble ideals; nor should they be interpreted as symptomatic of fundamental flaws in the structure of society. The prophets did not view themselves as social engineers, charged with reordering the structures of society. If householders oppressed those under their authority, the problem was viewed to be personal, not systemic. And the solution the prophets demanded was repentance from the sin of exploitation and the replacement of stony hearts with hearts of flesh that were sensitive not only to Yahweh, who had revealed to Israel his righteous statutes (Deut 4:8), but also to the plight of the weak among them.[127]

THE STATUS AND ROLES OF WIVES AND MOTHERS IN ANCIENT ISRAEL

The status of wife and mother. In Israel the female counterpart to the male head of the household was identified either as *ʾiššā,* "woman, wife" (from the husband's perspective), or *ʾēm,* "mother" (from a child's perspective). Scholars have long assumed that in a patriarchal society like Israel's wives were little more than chattel owned by men. Anthony Phillips's assertion is typical: "They [women] had no legal status, being the personal property first of their fathers, and then of their husbands."[128] But the argu-

---

[127]See especially Jer 7:1-11 and Ezek 18; 36:22-32.

[128]*Ancient Israel's Criminal Law: A New Approach to the Decalogue* (Oxford: Blackwood; New York: Schocken, 1970), p. 15. The same perspective is represented in the popular and influential works by Paul Jewett (*Man as Male and Female* [Grand Rapids, Mich.: Eerdmans, 1975], pp. 86-90), James B. Hurley (*Man and Woman in Biblical Perspective* [Grand Rapids, Mich.: Zondervan, 1981]), Stephen B. Clark (*Man and Woman in Christ* [Ann Arbor, Mich.: Servant, 1980]), and Gilbert Bilezikian (*Beyond Sex Roles: What the Bible Says About a Woman's Place in Church and Family,* 2nd ed. [Grand Rapids, Mich.: Baker, 1985]), all of which highlight what the authors deem to be contrasts between Old and New Testament perspectives. Although the motivations differ, this perspective pervades much of feminist scholarship, which gloats every time a woman in the Old Testament is deemed to subvert patriarchalism, which is considered oppressive by definition. See, for example, the works of Mieke Bal, *Lethal Love: Feminist Literary Readings of Biblical Love Stories,* ISBL (Bloomington, Ind.: University of Indiana Press, 1987); *Death and Dissymmetry: The Politics of Coherence in the Book of Judges,* CSHJ (Chicago: University of Chicago Press, 1988); *Murder and Difference: Gender, Genre and Scholarship on Sisera's Death,* trans. M. Gumpert, ISBL (Bloomington, Ind.: Indiana University Press, 1988); idem, ed., *Anti-Covenant: Counter Reading Women's Lives in the Hebrew Bible,* JSOTSup 81/BLS 22 (Sheffield: Almond, 1989). See also Danna Nolan Fewell and David M. Gunn, *Gender, Power, and Promise: The Subject of the Bible's First Story* (Nashville: Abingdon, 1993).

ments for this position are not nearly as convincing as they are generally made out to be.[129]

First, to argue that since one of the Hebrew words for "husband" is *ba'al*,[130] and in some contexts the word appears to mean "owner,"[131] the wife was the property of the husband is naive. On the one hand, the noun may be often interpreted as "a ruler, one in authority over," just as well as "one who owns," and on the other, the verb tends to mean "to rule, to exercise authority over," rather than "to own." Even in marital contexts it may be understood as "to assume authority over [a woman]" rather than "to own [a woman]." Furthermore, even though *ba'al*, "lord," is used for husband, neither of the obverse expressions *'āmâ*, "female servant," or *šipḥâ*, "female slave," is ever used of a married person. As an expression of self-deprecation before men, a woman may refer to herself as an *'āmâ*,[132] but when she marries she becomes the man's *'iššâ*, "wife," the female counterpart to *'iš*, which is used for "husband" much more frequently than *ba'al*.

Second, to conclude from the listing of the neighbor's wife along with other possessions in the tenth statement of the Decalogue[133] that she lacked legal rights and was deemed as mere property is equally ludicrous. As Wright has observed, the common denominator in the entries in the list is not that they are items of property but that all are elements of a person's household that male neighbors typically covet.[134]

Third, to argue that the practice of the husband paying the father of a bride

---

[129]For a discussion and critique of many of these arguments, see Wright, *God's People in God's Land*, pp. 291-316.

[130]The Hebrew word for "husband," *ba'al*, derives from a common Semitic root meaning "lord, master." The verb, *bā'al*, means "to be lord, to rule," and in a derived sense signifies "to marry, to take possession of a woman as a bride or wife" (*HALOT*, pp. 142-43), from which it is concluded that in an Israelite marriage the wife was viewed merely as the property of the husband. The verb occurs with *'iššâ*, "woman, wife," as object in Deut 21:13; 24:1; with *bĕtûlâ*, "virgin," in Is 62:5; with *bat*, "daughter," in Mal 2:11. A married woman is often referred to with the passive participle, *bĕtûlâ*, "to be ruled." See especially the phrase *bĕ'ulat-ba'al*, "one ruled by a husband," Gen 20:3; Deut 22:22. The expression *ba'al 'iššâ*, "owner of/authority over a wife," occurs in Ex 21:3, 22; Lev 21:4; Deut 22:22; 24:4; 2 Sam 11:26; Prov 12:4; 31:11, 23, 28; Hos 2:18.

[131]Of an ox, Ex 21:28-29; 22:10-14; donkey, Is 1:3; pit, Ex 21:34, 36; house, Ex 22:7; Judg 19:22-23; debt, Deut 15:2; land, Job 31:39; goods, Eccles 5:10; riches, Eccles 5:12.

[132]See Ruth 3:9; 1 Sam 25:24-25, 41.

[133]Ex 20:17 and Deut 5:21 list the neighbor's wife among objects that an Israelite (male) was prohibited from coveting: house, wife, male servant, female servant, ox, donkey and any other possession.

[134]Wright, *God's People in God's Land*, p. 197.

a "bride-price" suggests a purchase transaction[135] is to misinterpret the term *mōhar*. As we have already noted, this term is more appropriately rendered "marriage present."[136] Its purpose was to promote the stability of the marriage and to strengthen the links between the families of those being married.[137]

Fourth, the use of the verb *qānâ* to describe Boaz's acquisition of Ruth in Ruth 4:10 need not be interpreted in a mercantile sense of purchase, like one buys a pot or a piece of land. The verb is capable of a broad range of meanings; it can mean "to buy" in a specific sense or "to acquire" in a general sense, as well as "to bring under one's authority" or "to create." In the present context it means either "to acquire" in a general sense or to bring under Boaz's authority/protection.[138]

Fifth, the claim that prohibitions of adultery with a neighbor's wife[139] and the taboo on sexual relations with the wife of a male relative (Lev 18:1-18) represent safeguards against property offenses[140] is contradicted by the severity of the penalties assigned for the crimes: the death penalty for both man and woman, that is, the execution of the man who violated a neighbor's property rights and the destruction of the property. But nowhere else are property offenses answered with the death penalty. Adultery was a capital crime because it undermined the integrity of marriage, it violated the sanctity of sexual union, it defiled a human being as the image of God, and it threatened the stability of the community. Similarly, intercourse with the wife of a relative represented a crime against the person of the husband and a threat to the stability and sanctity of marriage.[141] But if such acts violated the hus-

---

[135]Thus Ephraim Neufeld, *Ancient Hebrew Marriage Laws, with Special References to General Semitic Laws and Customs* (London: Longman, Green, 1944), pp. 95-110. The word occurs three times: Gen 34:12; Ex 22:16; 1 Sam 18:25. For discussion, see de Vaux, *Ancient Israel,* pp. 26-27.

[136]So also Emmerson, "Women in Ancient Israel," p. 382.

[137]See n. 115 above.

[138]Cf. Ruth 2:12, according to which Boaz views himself as the wings of Yahweh under whom Ruth has sought refuge, which is hardly a metaphor of oppressive ownership. Gen 31:15 recounts the only instance of the obverse to the notion of acquisition of a wife, that is, the selling *(mākar)* of a woman to another man to be his wife. But this is an exception that proves the rule. The daughters of Laban complain about abuse suffered at the hands of their father. The rhetorical effectiveness of their use of this term depends upon the father's purported action being contrary to custom.

[139]Ex 20:14 = Deut 5:18; Lev 18:20; 20:10; Deut 22:22; cf. Jer 7:9; Ezek 18:6, 11, 15.

[140]Louis Wallis, *The Bible Is Human* (New York: AMS, 1972 [1942]), p. 272; Phillips, *Ancient Israel's Criminal Law,* p. 117. By this interpretation, the concern is not for the woman or the sexual integrity of the marriage but for the maintenance of male honor and the integrity of his estate.

[141]Cf. Lev 18:8; 20:11; Deut 22:30; 27:20.

band, they also violated his wife since, according to Genesis 2:24, the two were considered "one body."

Sixth, to interpret the law requiring payment to a husband for injury to his wife and the premature birth of his child in Exodus 21:21-25 as compensation for damage to his property[142] overlooks the fact that the primary issue in Exodus 21:21 is not injury to the pregnant woman but the loss of the fetus/child. According to Exodus 21:22, if the woman experiences further injury, this is to be answered not with a compensatory payment but with talionic retribution.[143]

Seventh, while it is possible for degenerate males to interpret their right as heads of households to nullify vows made by a wife (Num 30:2-15) as a means of maintaining control over their property, this provision may also be interpreted positively. As the head of a household the husband and father was accountable for the welfare of all who came under his roof. Paternal and husbandly responsibility extended to protecting daughters and wives from potentially injurious consequences of rash vows. Since divorcees and widows were deprived of this umbrella of protection, their vows were as binding as those of adult males.

In light of these considerations, to view women in ancient Israel as chattel of their husbands and fathers is to commit a fundamental fallacy: the failure to distinguish between authority and ownership, legal dependence and servitude, functional subordination and possession. The consistent and unequivocally patricentric worldview of biblical authors cannot be denied,[144] but this does not mean that those under the authority of males were deemed their property. On the contrary, in keeping with the radical biblical ideal of servant leadership as a whole,[145] husbands and fathers were to exercise authority with the well-being

---

[142]Phillips, *Ancient Israel's Criminal Law,* p. 90.

[143]Cf. Wright, *God's People in God's Land,* p. 211.

[144]Contra Phyllis Trible's attempt in an epochal paper in 1973 to redeem Gen 1—3 of its patriarchal and sexist stance and to elevate Eve to equal status with Adam ("Depatriarchalizing on Biblical Interpretation," *JAAR* 41 [1973]: 30-48). Compare the response of David J. A. Clines (*What Does Eve Do To Help? and Other Readerly Questions to the Old Testament,* JSOTSup 94 [Sheffield: JSOT Press, 1990], p. 45), who rightly concluded that Gen 1—3 is "indefensibly androcentric." While this comment may be applied to the entire Old Testament, his added note that these chapters cannot be redeemed from their "patriarchal and sexist stance" is not only too negative and deconstructionist; it also assumes the need to redeem the social structures of ancient Israel, a perspective that is narrowly modern and Eurocentric.

[145]Kings were to rule in the interests of their subjects (Deut 17:14-20), judges to adjudicate for the sake of their clients (Ex 18:13-27; cf. Deut 10:17-19), priests to serve God and worshipers (Num 6:24-27; Deut 10:8-9), and prophets to proclaim the oracles of God for the sake of their hearers (Deut 18:14-22; 2 Kings 17:13-23).

of their households in mind. Undoubtedly the experience of many women in ancient Israel was very different. Illustrative of Genesis 3:16, in the hands of self-centered males the responsible and compassionate exercise of authority often degenerated to oppressive "rule" *(māšal bĕ)*. But this should be viewed as perversion of biblical norms, not their rigorous application. The normative Israelite view of "headship" *(rō'š)* always placed the well-being of those under the leader's authority ahead of the leader's own well-being.

Although ancient Israelite society was unequivocally patricentric, evidences of the elevated status of the wife and mother of the household are ubiquitous. The Genesis account of human origins yields the following observations. First, the creation of *'ādām,* the image and likeness of God, as male and female affirms the ontological equality of man and woman, husband and wife, before God (Gen 1:27). If in God's creation the man reigns as his vice-regent, then the woman is queen. Second, the use of plural pronouns and plural verbs in Genesis 1:28 assigns the privilege and responsibility of governing the world to both men and women, and precludes the treatment of either as ontologically inferior. Third, according to Genesis 2:18, when Yahweh solves the deficiency of Adam's "aloneness," he does not create an *'ebed,* "servant," or an *'āmâ,* "maidservant," or a *šiphâ,* "female slave," but an *'ēzer kĕnegdô,* "a helper corresponding/as a complement to him."[146] The phrase represents an extraordinary expression of human community: man and woman, husband and wife, complementing each other in the divine enterprise of governing and filling the earth. Fourth, the fact that "woman" is created from the rib of "man," rather than his head or his feet (Gen 2:22), also expresses complementarity: she is his equal, at his side and near/dear to his heart.[147] Fifth, when the woman is presented to the man, in identifying her as *'iššâ,* "woman," which is assonantally linked with *'îš,* "man," the man recognizes her as the feminine counterpart to himself.[148] Sixth, Genesis 1:24-25 highlights the mutuality of the marital relationship—together married man and woman constitute one body *(bāśār)* and stand naked before one another with perfectly mutual confidence and trust.[149]

---

[146]On the meaning of the phrase, see Gordon J. Wenham, *Genesis 1-15,* WBC 1 (Waco, Tex.: Word, 1987), p. 68; Claus Westermann, *Genesis 1-11: A Commentary,* trans. J. J. Scullion (Minneapolis: Augsburg, 1984), p. 227.

[147]Cf. Wenham, *Genesis 1-15,* p. 69.

[148]"She shall be called 'woman' *['iššâ],* for she was taken out of man *['îš]*" (Gen 2:23 NIV) represents a popular rather than semantic etymology. See further V. P. Hamilton, "אִשָּׁה," *NIDOTTE,* 1:537-40.

[149]This text is exceptional in its emphasis on the man leaving his father and mother and clinging to his wife. Elsewhere Israelite marriage is consistently presented as patrilocal, with woman leaving her father and mother and the man "taking" *(lāqah)* her as his wife.

Although these literary features point to ontological equality between male and female and a complementarity of roles within the marital relationship, the narrative is not univocal in this respect. On the contrary, it contains clear signals of functional ordering. (1) God created man and woman consecutively, rather than simultaneously. (2) God created woman specifically to resolve a deficiency in the man's experience; he was alone and needed help to fulfill his role as vice-regent in paradise.[150] (3) God created woman from man, rather than man from woman (the natural birth order), or both from the same preexistent material. (4) God presented woman to man, not man to woman. (5) By quoting the man's response to the creation of woman, rather than vice versa or both together, the text presents an essentially androcentric interpretation of creation. (6) Man named woman, rather than woman named man. And her name is popularly derivative from his, not vice versa.

The significance of these features is often lost to modern readers, but to the ancient Hebrews none would have been deemed incidental nor accidental.[151] And herein lies the genius of this account and in the biblical portrayal of the ideal marital relationship. In their status and dignity before one another and before God, husband and wife are fundamentally and ontologically equal, and in their masculinity and femininity they fulfill complementary roles. However, the focus on the man in Genesis 2 anticipates what follows, namely the male headship of the family unit. In a perfect environment these tensions would have been more apparent than real. But as a consequence of human sin, in subsequent narratives the ideal is twisted and bent often beyond recognition as the *patricentric* ideals degenerate into self-centered and abusive *patriarchal* exercises of power.

But this does not mean that the ideals of equality and complementarity were forgotten. Although the functional subordination of the wife to her husband is a constant, throughout the Old Testament one recognizes clear affirmations of the dignity of the wife and obvious room for significant influence within the household. The following represents a short list of evidence that could be adduced. First, in courtship and lovemaking husbands

---

[150]For what the man needs help is not specified, but within the broader context this seems to involve generally serving as God's image, that is, as his deputy and representative, bringing the world into subjection, and specifically multiplying and filling the earth (cf. Gen 1:28), on the one hand, and serving (ʿābad) and guarding (šāmar) the garden of Eden on the other (Gen 2:15). The verbs in Gen 2:15 are employed later to describe the priests' ministry in the tabernacle, creating the impression of paradise as a sacred garden of God. Cf. Ezek 28:11-19.

[151]Paul's argumentation in 1 Cor 11:7-12 and 1 Tim 3:8-15 is based on some of these features.

and wives related to one another as equals.[152] Second, in more cases than not, wives/mothers named their children.[153] Third, as the fifth statement of the Decalogue indicates, ascribing honor to fathers *and mothers* is built into the very fabric of the covenant community of Israel.[154] Fourth, both father and *mother* were to be involved in defense of their daughter if her husband falsely accused her of not being a virgin when they married. Fifth, biblical wisdom places the instructions of a mother on a par with the teaching of one's father.[155] Sixth, the alphabetic portrait of wifely nobility in Proverbs 31:10-31 highlights her initiative, creativity and energy; she is obviously subordinate to her husband, but she is not subservient to him.[156] Seventh, in marriage relationships wives often exerted great influence over their husbands and sometimes even had their way against the wishes of the man.[157]

---

[152]The Song of Songs presents love not as a composite of assertive masculinity and passive femininity but as an egalitarian delight, with man and woman reaching out to each other in a mutuality and egalitarianism that reflects the ideal metaphysics of love, even if it does not match the realities of life. On this subject, see Richard M. Davidson, "Theology of Sexuality in the Song of Songs: Return to Eden," *AUSS* 27 (1989): 1-19.

[153]Of the forty-six recorded instances of naming children in the Old Testament, in twenty-eight the name is given by the mother. It is generally accepted that name giving in the Old Testament represented an expression of authority (cf. Gen 2:19-20).

[154]Ex 20:12; Deut 5:16. Lev 19:3 reverses the order of parents, citing the mother as the recipient of honor first. Biblical law calls for the death penalty for a rebellious son who curses or assaults his father or mother (Ex 21:15-17; Lev 20:9; Deut 27:16; cf. Ezek 22:7). According to Deut 21:18-21, if a rebellious son refuses to obey his father or mother, together the two parents shall turn the youth over to the judicial authorities.

[155]Prov 1:8; 6:20. Roger N. Whybray (*Wisdom in Proverbs* [Naperville, Ill.: Allenson, 1965], p. 42) observes that by placing father and mother "on exactly the same footing as teachers of their children," Hebrew wisdom adapts an Egyptian tradition (to which it is otherwise closely linked) to a peculiarly Israelite domestic situation—father and mother shared the responsibility for educating children. I am grateful to my colleague Peter Gentry for drawing this observation to my attention.

[156]Her role is clearly complementary to his, but she is not his competitor. She has her own personal faith (Prov 31:30), but she lacks egocentric ambition. Her energies are spent in securing the well-being of her children and her husband, as well as the needy in the neighborhood. Nor does she need to advertise her skill or her strength; her accomplishments speak for themselves and for her.

[157]In Gen 16:1-6 Sarai recognizes Abram as the head of the household, but in regard to Hagar and Ishmael Abraham listens to the voice of his wife. In Gen 21:8-21 Sarah demands that Abraham send Hagar and Ishmael away, and God affirms this action. In Gen 28 Rebekah assertively schemes to have her husband bless her favorite son. In 1 Sam 1 Hannah takes the initiative in praying for a son, and when the time comes to take Samuel to the tabernacle, Elkanah declares, "Do what seems best to you" (1 Sam 1:23). 1 Sam 19:11-17 has Michal taking the initiative and full responsibility for David's escape from her father Saul. In none of these or numerous other examples of husbands freely acceding to their wives' wishes/suggestions does the narrator express any surprise or displeasure over this fact, which contrasts sharply with Num 12, where Moses' sister (and brother) challenges Moses' unique authority within Israel.

Eighth, although women were excluded from official leadership roles in the community (priesthood, judgeships, elderships, military leadership[158] and the royal throne[159]), they were engaged by Yahweh in *ad hoc* prophetic roles[160] and apparently participated freely in many religious and cultic affairs.[161]

Indeed the picture of women at worship throughout the Old Testament presents a stark contrast to the misogynous attitudes that developed in the intertestamental period. Deuteronomy 12:12 invites the entire house-

---

[158]Deborah is commonly identified as one of the "savior" judges in the book of Judges, but a closer examination of the evidence makes it clear that her role in Judg 4—5 is exclusively prophetic. For a discussion of this issue, see Daniel I. Block, "Deborah Among the Judges: The Perspective of the Hebrew Historian," in *Faith, Tradition, and History: Old Testament Historiography in Its Near Eastern Context*, ed. Alan R. Millard et al. (Winona Lake, Ind.: Eisenbrauns, 1994), pp. 229-53; idem, *Judges/Ruth*, pp. 191-97.

[159]The Old Testament never applies the title *malkâ*, "queen," to any ruler of Israel or Judah, though it was applied to several foreign queens: Queen of Sheba (1 Kings 10; 2 Chron 9); Vashti (Esther 1) and Esther (Esther 2:22; 56:3; and others), both Persian queens. This did not stop Jezebel, the Tyrian wife of Ahab, from exerting considerable influence over him (1 Kings 18:4, 13, 19; 2 Kings 9), but as Mayer I. Gruber observes ("Women in the Ancient Levant," in *Women's Roles in Ancient Civilizations: A Reference Guide*, ed. Bella Vivante [Westport, Conn.: Greenwood, 1999], p. 141), her power probably derived from the strength of her personality rather than her official position. Her daughter, Athaliah, was married to Jehoram king of Judah. Upon the death of her son, Ahaziah, at the hands of Jehu, she seized control of the throne, ruthlessly attempted to eliminate all legitimate heirs to the throne and managed to rule in Jerusalem for seven years (2 Kings 11:1-20), but this was clearly an aberration from normal patterns of monarchic rule.

[160]Five women bear the title *nĕbî'â:* Miriam (Ex 15:20), Deborah (Judg 4:4), the unnamed wife of Isaiah (Is 8:3), Huldah (2 Kings 22:14) and Noadiah (Neh 6:14). To this list we should probably add Hannah, whose utterance in 1 Sam 2:2-10 bears the marks of a prophetic oracle.

[161]Presenting gifts for the construction of the tabernacle (Ex 35:20-29); composing and singing songs of celebration (Ex 15:1-21; Judg 5:1-31; 1 Sam 2:1-10); cultic and processional dance (Ex 15:20-21; Judg 21:19-21; Ps 68:26 [Eng. 25]; Jer 31:13; cf. women's participation in non-cultic celebrative dance: Judg 11:34; 1 Sam 18:6-7; 21:12; 29:5); cultic laments (2 Chron 35:26; Jer 9:16-17); playing musical instruments in the temple orchestra (1 Chron 25:5-7) and singing in the temple choir (Ezra 2:65; Neh 7:67); serving at the entrance to the tent of meeting (Ex 38:8; 1 Sam 2:22); participating in cultic meals (1 Sam 1:9); prayer (1 Sam 1:9-18); participating in family worship (Gen 35:1-7); celebrating the Passover (Ex 12:43-51); practicing Nazirite asceticism (Num 6:2; Judg 13:1-14); and making vows (Num 30:1-15). In addition to these legitimate religious practices, the Old Testament also reports a series of illegitimate female religious activities: false prophecy and magic (Ezek 13:17-23); necromancy (1 Sam 28); pagan/syncretistic lamentation in the temple over the death of Yahweh (Ezek 8:14-15); producing garments or decoration of pagan images (2 Kings 23:7); baking cakes and sacrificing to the "queen of heaven" (Jer 7:18; 44:15-19); and cultic prostitution (Deut 23:18-19 [Eng. 17-18]; Mic 1:7). Contrary to longstanding opinion, the last-named activity probably involved not prostitution at a sacred site as part of a fertility ritual but prostitution as a means to pay a vow. For discussion, see K. van der Toorn, "Cultic Prostitution," *ABD*, 5:510-13.

hold—parents, sons and daughters, male and female servants, and resident Levites—to rejoice before Yahweh at the place he would choose as his authorized place of worship. According to Nehemiah 8, the entire community of returnees from exile—men, women and children old enough to understand—attended the reading and exposition of the Torah and then participated in the holy festival that followed. Unlike the temple that Herod built to appease the Jews, which had separate courts for the women and Gentiles, respectively,[162] none of the Old Testament designs of structures for worship (tabernacle, Davidic temple, Ezekiel's temple) excluded women or even segregated them from men. And nowhere in the entire Old Testament do we read misogynous venom like that spewed out by Ben Sirach.[163]

In the light of all this evidence, the oft-repeated opinion that in ancient Israel women had no legal status and that they were merely personal property owned first by their fathers and then by their husbands is simplistic and erroneous. It is clear that when young girls married they transferred their accountability from their fathers to their husbands, but under normal or ideal circumstances, this was not an oppressive authority. On the contrary, a strong husband offered security and protection to one who otherwise would have been extremely vulnerable to economic and physical ruin.

Not that all women in ancient Israel were equally secure and equally loved. Apart from variations in the characters of their husbands, institutional factors contributing to a woman's insecurity included polygamy, divorce and widowhood. The first customary threat to a woman's security, polygamy—(simultaneous marriage to more than one wife, more precisely *polygyny*)—presented challenges to both husband and wives. Although the Old Testament appears to present monogamy (one husband, one wife) as the marital ideal (Gen 2:24-25), it contains no clear and unequivocal prescription for this marital pattern for the population in general.[164] To the contrary, biblical narratives report nu-

---

[162]For a diagram, see *EncJud*, 15:962.

[163]See Sir 25:13—26:12. For a brief discussion of this issue in Ben Sirach, see Collins, "Marriage, Divorce, and Family in Second Temple Judaism," pp. 143-45; for fuller treatment, see Warren C. Trenchard, *Ben Sira's View of Women: A Literary Analysis*, BJS 38 (Chico, Calif.: Scholars Press, 1982). A tone approaching this kind of spite is found in the Old Testament only in a few isolated Proverbs: 19:13; 21:9; 27:15.

[164]The use of the singular *'iššâ* in statements like that found in the Decalogue (Ex 20:17; Deut 5:21) implies but does not require monogamy, any more than the use of the singular *'āḥôt* in Lev 18:9 suggests that a person had only one sister. Remarkably, the Old Testament knows nothing of polyandry (simultaneous marriage to more than one husband).

merous polygamous examples.[165] But Elkanah is the only commoner noted to have been polygamous, from which one may conclude that the multiplication of wives was linked to a man's wealth and status within the community. Remarkably, the only person for whom the multiplication of wives was expressly prohibited was the king (Deut 17:17), and that for religious reasons—wives (presumably foreign wives acquired through dynastic marriage) would deflect him from wholehearted devotion to Yahweh.

Although polygamous marital arrangements may have presented certain advantages, the illustrations provided by the Old Testament clearly attest to the complications this form of marriage created for the operation of the household. Marriage to numerous wives may have provided sexual gratification for the husband, but it tended to rouse jealousy among the wives as they competed with each other for a night with their husband.[166] Marriage to numerous wives may have provided the husband with a symbol of status within the larger community, but it tended to increase the competition for status among the wives within the household[167] and increased the likelihood of frustration in the extended family.[168] Marriage to numerous wives may have increased the work force, but it led to competition and violence among the children[169] and injustices in the division of inheritances.[170] Marriages to numerous wives may have filled a man's "quiver" with children (Ps 127:3-5) and ensured for him life after death,[171] but the tensions among the children could make his earthly life miserable and send him to an early grave.[172] Of course the function/dysfunction of polygamous households varied greatly, depending upon the personalities and temperaments of husband and wives, the economic status of the household, the social status of the wives (whether they were originally free citizens or female servants elevated by marriage from the status of 'āmâ to 'iššâ).

---

[165]Lamech (Adah and Zillah, Gen 4:23), Abraham (Sarah, along with Hagar and Keturah, Gen 16; 25:1-2); Jacob (Leah and Rachel, not to mention their maidservants, Zilpah and Bilhah, respectively, who bore children for him, Gen 30), Esau (Judith, Basemath, Mahalath, Adah and Oholibamah, Gen 26:34; 28:9; 36:1-5), Gideon (many wives, including a Shechemite concubine, Judg 8:30-31), Elkanah (Hannah and Peninnah, 1 Sam 1:2), David (Michal, Abigail, Ahinoam, Maacah, Haggith, Abital and Eglah, 1 Sam 18:17-30; 25:38-43; 2 Sam 3:2-5), Solomon (a vast harem, 1 Kings 3:1; 11:3; 5:13; Song 6:8) and Rehoboam (eighteen wives and sixty concubines, 2 Chron 11:21).

[166]Gen 30:1-2, 15.

[167]Note Leah's and Peninnah's hunger for the love of their husbands, despite their fertility, in Gen 30:31-35 and 1 Sam 1:1-8, respectively.

[168]Gen 26:35.

[169]Judg 9:1-6; 2 Sam 13; 1 Kings 1—2.

[170]Deut 21:15-17.

[171]On the notion that fathers live on in their children, see further below.

[172]Gen 37, esp. vv. 29-36; 42:35-38; 43:11-14; 45:28.

A second major cause of female insecurity was widowhood,[173] being predeceased by a husband under whose wing a woman had previously found security (*měnuḥâ,* Ruth 1:9). As in our own day, in ancient Israel women tended to outlive their husbands,[174] a problem that became especially acute in wartime. The ancient clan system should have guaranteed security to every member of the extended family, including widows. However, since marriages were patrilocal, when the head of a household died, his widow's position within the household could be precarious. The fate of the widow of one of the "sons of the prophets" described in 2 Kings 4:1-7 illustrates the severity of the crisis precipitated by the death of one's husband, but her situation would be especially acute if she and her husband were members of a dysfunctional extended family. Even the levirate law, which was designed to provide a widow with a second husband, was driven not by concern for her well-being but by the need to preserve the male line and the patrimonial estate.[175]

The vulnerability of widows in ancient Israel is reflected in the fact that almost one-third of the occurrences of the word for "widow," *'almānâ,* occur in Mosaic legislation providing for the well being of other vulnerable groups, most notably orphans, aliens, and Levites.[176] Ordinarily a widow's care would have been the responsibility of either her sons or her father-in-law, or her husband's brothers. If these kinship ties were lacking, or if the men of her husband's clan refused to support her,[177] without the economic and physical protection of her husband she was vulnerable to exploitation and abuse,[178] and sometimes even murder.[179] At best she could resort to the dowry given her by her father at the time of her marriage, which occasionally might have included

---

[173]The problem of divorce has been discussed earlier. See above.

[174]The Old Testament knows of several men who were predeceased by their wives. In polygamous/bigamous situations (Abraham, Jacob) the grief would still be intense, but the widower's well-being within the household would still be secure. The most notable example of a widower in the Old Testament is Ezekiel, whose wife, "the delight of [his] eyes" *(maḥmad 'ênay),* Yahweh took as a sign of the coming grief in Jerusalem (Ezek 24:15-27). The term for widower, *'almān,* occurs only in Jer 51:5, in an awkwardly metaphorical sense, denoting the nation's abandonment by Yahweh in 586 B.C.

[175]On levirate marital institution, see further below.

[176]See *HALOT,* p. 58, for references.

[177]The prophets create the impression that this problem existed throughout much of Israel's history. Cf. Is 1:17, 23; 10:2; Jer 7:6; 22:3; Ezek 22:1, 25; Zech 7:10; Mal 3:5.

[178]Is 10:2; Jer 7:6; 22:3; Job 24:3, 21; Ps 94:6.

[179]Ps 94:6. This contrasts with Job's apologia in which he asserts that, contrary to the reproach of his "friends" (Job 22:9), he has indeed taken care of orphans and widows (Job 29:12-13; 31:16-17).

land,[180] but usually the widow would be dependent on others' charity,[181] and where this failed would be driven to sell herself or her children into debt slavery,[182] or to adopt the profession of a prostitute.[183]

The wife's responsibilities toward her husband. As noted above, according to the ideal presented in Genesis 1—2 ancient Israelites perceived a wife's role in a marriage to be threefold: (1) to aid her husband in fulfilling the blessing pronounced in Genesis 1:18, "Be fruitful and multiply and fill the earth"; (2) to fulfill the divine mandate of serving and keeping the garden, shorthand for governing the world on God's behalf; and (3) to provide companionship for her husband. I shall deal with each in turn.

First, whatever modern Westerners may think about the matter, the Old Testament witness is clear that for ancient Israelites the most important contribution a woman could make to a household was to present her husband with children. In ancient times people married that they might have children. Like Westerners until the eighteenth century, the Israelites believed that in the process of conception and fetal development a woman's womb merely functioned as the bed in which the seed of a male germinated and grew. Fathers lived on in their children. Accordingly, to bear a child was an act performed by a wife for her husband.[184] Indeed, the noblest contribution a woman could make to a household in general and her husband in particular was to bear a son for him. Through childbearing a woman earned her place in life and her share in the household. Conversely, failure to deliver on this obligation was viewed as a curse and a shameful disgrace.[185]

---

[180]See the case of Achsah in Judg 1:11-12. Female rights to land are also recognized in the case of Zelophahad's daughters (Num 36:1-9), but there too the primary concern is the preservation of the patrimonial estate.

[181]Job 31:16. Compare the vulnerability of the widow Ruth, whose well-being is dependent upon gleaning "among the ears of grain after one *in whose sight I may find grace*" (Ruth 2:2, author's translation; emphasis added).

[182]2 Kings 4:1-7.

[183]Note the rhetorical use of widowhood in prophetic threats that Yahweh will make Israel's widows more numerous than the sand of the seashore (Jer 15:8; cf. Jer 18:21; Lam 5:3), and the imprecatory psalmist's prayer that the wife of the wicked become a widow and his children orphans (Ps 109:9; cf. Job 27:15). At the same time, widowhood provides Yahweh with a powerful metaphor for his own benevolent character: He defends the rights of the widow (Ps 68:6 [Eng. 5], and he sustains her (Ps 146:9); he defends her property against encroachment and expropriation (Prov 15:25).

[184]From the Abrahamic narratives alone, note the following references: Gen 16:1, 16; 17:17, 19, 21; 21:2, 3, 5, 7, 9; 22:20, 23; 24:15, 24, 47; 25:2, 12.

[185]In Gen 30:1 Rachel vents her desperation to Jacob, "Give me children, or I shall die!" But later, at the birth of Joseph she expresses her relief, "God has removed my shame" (Gen 30:23 NLT). Female barrenness is a dominant motif in the patriarchal narratives, which begin with a redundant announcement of Sarai's/Sarah's barrenness in Gen 11:30, and the

Second, women played an important role in managing the household and contributing their labor to its maintenance. One may look upon each household as a microcosm of Eden, and the tasks of the husband and wife as being equivalent to that of Adam and Eve in the garden, viz., "to serve *('ābad)* and to protect *(šāmar)* it" as a sacred trust (cf. Gen 2:15). Depending on the economic status of the family, the wife's basic tasks in serving and guarding the household consisted of tending the garden, harvesting grain, cooking food and clothing the family.[186] In more complex households that included servants, the wife would supervise those involved in these domestic chores. Proverbs 31:10-31 provides the most complete picture in the entire Old Testament of the role of a wife in a typical middle-class family.[187]

[10]A good wife who can find?
   She is far more precious than jewels.
[11]The heart of her husband trusts in her,
and he will have no lack of gain.
[12]She does him good, and not harm,
   all the days of her life.
[13]She seeks wool and flax,
   and works with willing hands.
[14]She is like the ships of the merchant,
   she brings her food from afar.
[15] She rises while it is yet night
   and provides food for her household
   and tasks for her maidens.
[16]She considers a field and buys it;

---

problem is repeated in the life of Rebekah (25:21). In 1 Sam 1, Hannah the barren woman and Eli the priest share this perspective. After noting in 1 Sam 1:2 that Hannah has no children, and in 1 Sam 1:5-6 attributing the problem to Yahweh—he had closed her womb—the narrator notes that Yahweh remembered Hannah, and in the course of time she gives birth to a son (1 Sam 1:19-20; cf. v. 27). Eli also recognizes that conception is a divine act (1 Sam 1:17). For additional references to the involvement of Yahweh in the conception and birth of children, see Gen 18:9-15; 21:1-2; 25:21; 29:32, 33; 30:2, 6, 17, 22-24; Judg 13:3-7; Ruth 4:13-14.

[186]Although there appears to have been a general division of labor among the members of the household, the boundaries were not rigid and few of these domestic chores were restricted to women. Cain was a tiller of the soil (Gen 4:2); Abraham participated in preparing the meal for his heavenly visitors (Gen 18:1-8); Lot prepared a feast and baked unleavened bread for these same guests (19:3); Esau cooked a meal for his father (27:30-31); Gideon prepared a meal for his angelic visitor (Judg 6:19); and the Levite's father-in-law hosted him for three days (Judg 19:1-9).

[187]The heading suggests that the primary concern of this text is to assist a young man in finding a noble wife, but the acrostic form may suggest the incorporation of an independent literary unit, perhaps a catechism that women taught their daughters as they sought to prepare them for adulthood.

with the fruit of her hands she plants a vineyard.
[17] She girds her loins with strength
 and makes her arms strong.
[18]She perceives that her merchandise is profitable.
 Her lamp does not go out at night.
[19]She puts her hands to the distaff,
 and her hands hold the spindle.
[20]She opens her hand to the poor,
 and reaches out her hands to the needy.
[21]She is not afraid of snow for her household,
 for all her household are clothed in scarlet.
[22]She makes herself coverings;
 her clothing is fine linen and purple.
[23]Her husband is known in the gates,
 when he sits among the elders of the land.
[24]She makes linen garments and sells them;
 she delivers girdles to the merchant.
[25]Strength and dignity are her clothing,
 and she laughs at the time to come.
[26]She opens her mouth with wisdom,
 and the teaching of kindness is on her tongue.
[27]She looks well to the ways of her household,
 and does not eat the bread of idleness.
[28]Her children rise up and call her blessed;
 her husband also, and he praises her:
[29]"Many women have done excellently,
 but you surpass them all."
[30]Charm is deceitful, and beauty is vain,
 but a woman who fears the LORD is to be praised.
[31]Give her of the fruit of her hands,
 and let her works praise her in the gates. (RSV)

This biblical picture of mature feminine nobility is a far cry from the image of oppression and suppression that modern feminists associate with patriarchy. This woman finds her greatest delight in seeing to the well-being of her household. She is tireless in her service to husband and children, creative in her endeavors, self-effacing in her disposition, and compassionate in her actions. She serves and guards her piece of Eden well.

This is not to say that wives were not active outside the home. The activities of the woman described in Proverbs 31 were obviously not restricted to the house or the compound of the household, though they were all performed in the interests of the household. Accordingly, she shopped abroad for the resources needed to maintain the household, and the surplus goods produced by the household she sold. Some women were engaged outside the family. I have already noted the prophetic roles played by some women, such as Deborah, who performed her duties under the palm tree between Ramah and Bethel (Judg 4:4-5). The Old Testament evidence for other kinds of professional service outside the home is meager, but the discovery of several seals dating from the eighth to sixth centuries B.C. bearing the names of women demonstrate that women could occupy significant positions in the administration of government.[188]

Third, the wife provided companionship for her husband. Although a wife was legally subordinate to her husband, ideally she still functioned as his confidant and trusted friend.[189] The mutuality and equality, sympathy and love, commitment and compassion experienced in a healthy marriage are celebrated by the Shulammite in Song of Songs (my translation):

dôdî lî waʾănî lô	"My beloved is mine, and I am his" (Song 2:16)
ʾănî lĕdôdî wĕdôdî lî,	"I am my beloved's, and my beloved is mine" (Song 6:3)
ʾănî lĕdôdî wĕ ʿālay tĕšûqātô[190]	"I am my beloved's, and his claim is on me" (Song 7:11 [Eng. 10])

---

[188]Thirteen seals bearing the names of women who were authorized to seal legal documents have been discovered. Most of the women named are identified according to their fathers' names, "X daughter *[bt]* of Y," or according to their husband, "X wife *[ʾšt]* of Y." Of special interest is a late sixth-century B.C. seal bearing the inscription, *lšlmyt ʾmt ʾlntn phwʾ*, "(Belonging) to Shelomit maidservant of Elnathan the governor." Although this woman was obviously a subordinate to the governor, that she had her own seal attests to her official role. For further discussion of this and other seals, see Nahman Avigad, "The Contribution of Hebrew Seals to an Understanding of Israelite Religion and Society," in *Ancient Israelite Religion: Essays in Honor of Frank Moore Cross, Jr.*, ed. Patrick D. Hanson, Paul D. Miller Jr. and S. Dean McBride (Philadelphia: Fortress, 1987), pp. 205-6.

[189]Notions captured in Mal 2:11 by the Hebrew term *ḥăberet,* "consort," derived from *ḥābar,* "to ally oneself" (cf. LXX *koinōnos*). Cf. *HALOT,* pp. 287, 289.

[190]*Tĕšûqâ,* from *šûq,* "to urge, drive on, impel," and often translated "desire," occurs elsewhere only in Gen 3:16 (of the woman's post-Fall disposition toward her husband) and Gen 4:7 (of sin's disposition toward fallen humanity). Susan Foh ("What Is the Woman's Desire?" *WTJ* 37 [1975]: 376-83) argues that one of the effects of the Fall, hence the result of sin, is woman's desire to contend with man for leadership in the marriage relationship. According to Gen 3:16, the man responds with *māšal,* "to rule" (viz., to subordinate, exploit). Both represent perversions of the original pre-Fall ideal. If the Song of Songs is interpreted as a celebration of the relationship of man and woman in its Edenic innocence, the second line of this two-

This is not the lament of an oppressed woman in a patriarchal world but the celebration of satisfaction and security in a relationship of mutual love and commitment.

The mother's responsibilities toward her children. Proverbs 31:10-31, cited above, summarizes the basic responsibilities of wives in the daily care of their children: providing food, clothing and shelter. But as in our own time, there was much more to being a mother than these domestic functions. At a child's birth a mother exercised special care for her infant, carefully cutting the cord, bathing the child in clean water, massaging it with a special saline solution and wrapping it tightly in bands of cloth.[191] As noted earlier, mothers were often involved in the naming of their children. Since names generally expressed some aspect of the faith of the parent, one may see in the naming an attempt to pass on the faith to the next generation. During the child's first decade or so the nurture of the child was the special concern of the mother (though fathers were not uninvolved; cf. Hos 11:3-4). In Israel the home was the primary educational agency. In laying the foundations for civilized behavior, excellent performance and responsible decision-making,[192] the mother's role was as important as the father's. Once children reached adolescence, sons would spend more and more time with their fathers, learning the skills and developing the character required for responsible male adulthood, though appeals to sons to heed the instructions of their fathers *and mothers* in texts like Proverbs 1:8 and 6:20 suggest that mothers continued to teach adolescent sons as well. Meanwhile, mothers would train their daughters for their anticipated roles as wives and mothers in their own households.[193] Since marriages were patrilocal, this period of instruction was extremely important. Unlike a son, who typically set up his own household near his parents' home, a daughter had to be prepared to leave, and the need to adjust to new circumstances and new family dynamics required special and sensitive guidance.

But mothers' interest in their children naturally continued even after they

---

line text represents a sensitive rephrasing of line 1, and an acceptance of the ideals of Gen 2. The biblical writers view it as normal and natural for a man's "urge, drive, impulsion," to be for his wife, as an expression of loving responsibility, not in the sense of *māsal*, "to rule, dominate." Here the woman expresses complete contentment and security, knowing she belongs to her husband, and he assumes his rightful place as her protector.

[191]Ezek 16:3-4 provides the most complete description of the care of infants in the Old Testament. For a discussion of this passage, see Block, *Ezekiel 1-24*, pp. 473-76.

[192]Cf. William McKane, *Proverbs: A New Approach*, OTL (Philadelphia: Westminster Press, 1970), p. 268.

[193]As noted above, Prov 31:10-31 may have functioned as a sort of catechism for preparing young girls for adulthood.

were married. To witness the birth of grandchildren, and in some cases great-grandchildren, was deemed a special blessing (cf. Ruth 4:14-16). Within the context of the extended family, everyone bore responsibility for rearing the youngsters, but grandmothers played a special role. As for daughters who had left home, they were always welcomed back for a visit, and those who had lost their husbands through death or divorce could, if they chose, resort to the "mother's house" for refuge (Ruth 1:8).

The mother's responsibilities toward her servants. Obviously the primary obligations of a wife and mother were toward her husband and her children. However, the ubiquitous references to servants/slaves in both the Mosaic legislation and the narratives of the Old Testament attest to the widespread extension of the household to include non-kinsfolk, who were either hired as day laborers or owned as slaves. As expected in this patricentric culture, most of the legislation involving slaves is addressed to the heads of households. Since wives occupied the second rung in the social order of the household, the legislation calling for the humane treatment of slaves would have applied to them as well. But the pictures concerning mistresses' relationships with their servants in the narratives of the Old Testament often reflect the tension that often must have existed in these complex households. In the patriarchal narratives the stress points tend to revolve around issues of fertility and childbirth.[194]

---

[194]A fact reflected in Prov 30:21-23, which recognizes the intolerable situation of a maidservant *(šipḥâ)* supplanting her mistress *(gĕbîrâ)*. Gen 16:1-16 illustrates the problem. Hagar, Sarai's Egyptian *šipḥâ,* treated her barren mistress *(gĕbîrâ)* with contempt *(qālal,* Gen 16:4) after Abraham had taken Hagar as a wife *('iššâ,* Gen 16:3) and she had borne a child for him. Sarai responded to Hagar's triumphalism by "oppressing" *('ānâ)* her and convincing Abraham to send her away. The choice of *'ānâ* to describe a member of the chosen family abusing an Egyptian is both ironical (in Gen 15:13 and Ex 1:12, the same verb describes later Egyptian abuse of the Israelites) and judgmental, reflecting the narrator's negative disposition toward Sarai's action and signaling to the reader that such treatment of a maidservant violates Israel's ideals. The problem between mistress and slave woman recurs in Gen 21:8-21, which describes Abraham sending Hagar and her son away once and for all, at Sarah's demand and with the approval of God. Perhaps acknowledging the contradiction between this action and later legislation (Deut 21:15-17), the narrator tries to soften the reader's distress by (1) characterizing Ishmael as a *na'ar,* which in Genesis usually identifies a young man capable of taking care of himself (thus also Wenham, *Genesis 16-50,* p. 83); (2) highlighting God's concern for both child and mother by mentioning Hagar and referring to her as "your [Abraham's] maidservant"; (3) noting God's reassurance of Abraham that Ishmael's departure was necessary for the fulfillment of previous promises to Abraham and Sarah; (4) reminding Abraham that because Ishmael was his seed, God would guarantee him and his descendants nation status; (5) noting Abraham's careful attention to the needs of Hagar and Ishmael before he sends them off; (6) softening the expulsion by replacing Sarah's harsh *gārēš,* "to drive out," with the milder *šilléaḥ,* which is often used of sending an agent off to fulfill a mission. Westbrook ("The Female Slave," p. 228) interprets the verb as "he divorced her." For this usage, see Deut 22:19; 24:1, 3.

Genesis 29:21—30:13 provides a helpful illustration of the relationship between a wife and this type of female servant in an ancient Israelite household in several ways. First, when a rich man gave his daughter in marriage, the dowry could include slave-girls (*šipḥôt*, Gen 29:24, 29), who would serve the bride in her new home.[195] Second, the personal pronouns used throughout this text indicate that the slave girls were not merely subject to their mistresses; they belonged to them as property. Third, as in the case of Sarah and Hagar above, the mistresses took the initiative in suggesting that the husband have intercourse with the slave-girls.[196] In fact, the primary purpose of such arrangements was to provide progeny for the husband. Fourth, once the husband had intercourse with the slave-girl, she was considered his wife (*'iššâ*, Gen 30:4, 9), though in Genesis 35:22 the narrator explicitly recognizes at least Bilhah's secondary status by referring to her as Jacob's "concubine."[197] Fifth, as a concubine the slave-girl's legal position was divided. On the one hand, she satisfied the sexual needs of the head of the household and provided him with children; on the other, she remained the property of her mistress, who could order, discipline and sell her at will. However, once the concubine had borne a child for the man, the mistress's rights were restricted—she was prohibited from selling her, though she could reduce her status within the household.[198] Sixth, when a slave-girl bore a child, the mistress would adopt/legitimize the child as her own[199] and exercise her parental rights to the child by naming him (Gen 30:6, 8, 11, 13).

THE STATUS AND ROLES OF CHILDREN IN ANCIENT ISRAEL
The biblical vocabulary of progeny. The rich vocabulary for progeny

---

[195]For a discussion of the dowry and the place of slave-girls therein, see Westbrook, *Property and the Family in Biblical Law,* pp. 142-64.

[196]The narrator refers to Zilpah and Bilhah as slave-girls (*šipḥôt,* so also Gen 32:23 [Eng. 22]), but when Rachel proposes that Jacob take Bilhah as a concubine, she elevates her status by referring to her as an *'āmâ.*

[197]The meaning of *pîlegeš* remains unclear, though the quadraliteral form may point to a non-Semitic, perhaps Philistine, origin. According to usage, the term always identifies a female person whose primary function appears to be sexual, either for procreation (as in this context) or to gratify the desires of a man/husband. See further Chaim Rabin, "The Origin of the Hebrew Word *Pilegeš,*" *JJS* 25 (1974): 353-64; Manfred Görg, "*Piggul* und *pilaegeš*: Experimente zur Etymologie," *BN* 10 (1969): 10-11.

[198]For a full discussion of concubinage, see Westbrook, "The Female Slave," pp. 214-23.

[199]The physical gesture reflected in the idiom "to bear on the [mistress'] knees" *(tēled ʿal habberek),* which occurs only in Gen 30:3; 48:12; 50:23; Job 3:12, derives from the notion of the knee as the seat of procreative power. For further discussion and cognate Akkadian usage, see Nahum Sarna, *Genesis,* JPS Torah Commentary (Philadelphia: Jewish Publication Society, 1989), pp. 207-8. On Ruth 4:16, which employs a different idiom, see Block, *Judges/Ruth,* pp. 729-30.

in the Old Testament reflects the ancient Israelites' disposition toward children: The most common designations for children are *bēn*, "son," and its female etymological cognate *bat*, "daughter";[200] *yeled*, "fetus (Ex 22:21), male child, youth," and *yaldâ*, "female child";[201] and *zera⁽*, "seed." For votary purposes a text like Leviticus 27:1-7 recognizes the following as recognizable stages in people's lives: infancy (one month to five years), youth (five to twenty years), adulthood (twenty to sixty years) and old age (sixty years and above). But the Old Testament also has specific terms for stages of childhood. An infant is called *yônēq* (from *yānaq*) or *⁽ōlēl* and *⁽ûl*, both roots meaning "to suck, suckle." A weaned child is called a *gāmûl* (fem. *gĕmûlâ*, Is 11:8). *Ṭap*, from *ṭāpap*, "to take little steps," usually refers to little children, but according to Numbers 14:29-30 it could refer to anyone under twenty years of age, "little children."[202] The Old Testament uses several expressions for "adolescence": *⁽elem*, cognate to *⁽almâ*, a young woman of childbearing age;[203] *bĕtûlâ*, "an ostensibly reputable young girl who is past puberty and is, by default at least, still in the household of her father";[204] *bāḥûr*, "choice young man," the corresponding term for a young male (Amos 8:13); *na⁽ar* (fem. *na⁽ārâ*), which could refer to an unborn child (Judg 13:5-12), a newborn (1 Sam 4:21), a three-month-old infant (Ex 2:6), a nursing child (1 Sam 1:22), a weaned child (1 Sam 1:24), a seventeen-year-old youth (Gen 37:2) or a thirty-year-old adult (Gen 41:12). Since no married person is ever called a *na⁽ar*, some have suggested the term may refer to any young person from infancy to pre-

---

[200]With some 4,900 occurrences, *bēn* is the second most frequently used common noun in the Old Testament, exceeded only by *kōl*, "all." But if one includes *bat*, "daughter" (ca. 580x), even this exception is eliminated. For a tabulation of word frequencies, see *TLOT*, 3:1436.

[201]From *yālad*, "to bear." These expressions occur about ninety times. The abstract noun from the same root, *yaldût*, denotes "youth." See Eccles 11:9-10. Another word, *gōlem*, "embryo," also covers for "fetus" in Ps 139:16. Biblical Hebrew has special terms for specific kinds of children: *tô'ămîm*, "twins," from *tā'am*, "to bear twins" (Gen 25:24; 38:27); *yātôm*, "orphan, fatherless child"; and *mamzēr*, "mongrel, bastard," that is, a child born of an illegitimate union. The last word occurs only in Deut 23:3 and Zech 9:6 and is of uncertain derivation. For discussions, see Carol L. Meyers and Eric M. Meyers, *Zechariah 9-14: A New Translation with Introduction and Commentary*, AB 25C (New York: Doubleday, 1993), p. 106; Martin Rose, *5 Mose 12-25: Einführung und Gesetze*, ZBK (Zürich: Theologischer Verlag, 1994), p. 324.

[202]For the reading of the Torah, Deut 31:12 calls together four groups of people: men, women, children *(ṭap)* and aliens. For additional references, see *HALOT*, p. 378.

[203]In 1 Sam 17:56 David is classified as an *⁽elem*, "adolescent"; in 1 Sam 20:22, the word refers to the small boy (also *na⁽ar qāṭān*, "small lad," 1 Sam 20:35) who retrieved Jonathan's arrows. "Adolescence," the stage in life, is referred to by the abstraction *⁽alûmîm*. John Walton argues convincingly ("עֲלוּמִים," *NIDOTTE*, 3:415-19) that "a woman ceases to be an *⁽almâ* when she becomes a mother—not when she becomes a wife or a sexual partner."

[204]As defined by John Walton, "בְּתוּלָה," *NIDOTTE*, 1:780.

marital status,[205] one who has not assumed the role of a responsible adult in the community. The issue is complicated by the fact that *na'ar* often functions not as a designation for age but as a term for status, that is, a person in the service or employ of another.[206] But this is not merely menial service. John MacDonald has argued convincingly that the meaning of the Hebrew term *na'ar* is best captured in English by "squire," that is, "a young man of good birth."[207]

The high value ancient Israelites placed on children reflected in this breadth of juvenile vocabulary was based upon several pillars. First, every human being is created as an image of God and endowed with dignity in keeping with the divine charge to govern the world on God's behalf.[208] Therefore, to beget and bear children means more than mere procreation; it signifies co-creation—God involving father and mother in the creation of images of himself. Second, in a world languishing under the curse of death because of human sin, children—both male and female—represent the keys to the perpetuation of humanity[209] and the fulfillment of the divine mandate to populate the entire earth.[210] Third, although this prescientific world perceived conception as the implantation of male seed in the fertile soil of a female's womb,[211] children were viewed primarily as the product of divine action.[212] Conversely, whether due to barrenness or misfortune, childlessness was viewed as a curse.[213] As divine creations children were viewed as special treasures, blessings, gifts granted graciously to parents,[214] and the more children one had, the greater the sense of divine fa-

---

[205]Thus V. P. Hamilton, "נַעַר," *NIDOTTE,* 3:125. The stage in life, "youth," is referred to by the abstract noun *nĕ'ûrîm.*

[206]E.g., Gen 14:24; 18:7; Judg 8:20; 1 Sam 21:5-6; and so on.

[207]John MacDonald, "The Status and Role of the *na'ar* in Israelite Society," *JNES* 35 (1976): 147-70.

[208]Gen 1:28-30; Ps 8.

[209]Gen 5.

[210]Gen 1:26; 9:18-19.

[211]Note the references to semen as *zera',* "seed," in Lev 15:16, and to a son as *zera' 'ănāšîm,* "the seed of men," in 1 Sam 1:11. The only reference to the *zera'* of a woman occurs in Gen 3:15, a poetic text.

[212]Gen 15:3; 18:10-14; 21:1-2; 25:21; 29:31-35; 30:6, 17-22; Judg 13:1-7; Ruth 4:14.

[213]For the former see Gen 16:2; 20:18; 30:2; 1 Sam 1:5. For the latter see Lev 26:22; Deut 32:25; Ruth 1:1-5; Jer 15:7; Lam 1:20; Ezek 5:17; 36:12, 14; Hos 9:12. For a discussion of the root *skl,* "to bereave of children," see V. P. Hamilton, "שׁכל," *NIDOTTE,* 5:105-7.

[214]A disposition celebrated in common names like Jonathan, "Yahweh has given," and Jehoash, "Yahweh has bestowed." For a listing of additional names of this type and a discussion of their meanings, see Jeaneane D. Fowler, *Theophoric Personal Names in Ancient Hebrew: A Comparative Study,* JSOTSup 49 (Sheffield: JSOT Press, 1988), pp. 91-95.

vor.[215] This disposition is given poetic expression in Proverbs 17:6: "Grandchildren are the crown *[ʿateret]* of old men; and fathers are the glory *[tipʾeret]* of children" (my translation). Fourth, children were considered an important economic asset. As early as age five or six they could begin to contribute to the household economy, gathering fuel, watering the garden, picking produce, helping in food production and so on.[216] Fifth, in addition to sharing some of their neighbors' notions of life after death,[217] the Israelites also shared the idea that parents—particularly fathers—in a sense live on in their children. Accordingly, the worst fate one could experience was to have his "seed" cut off and his "name" destroyed from his father's household.[218] This conviction lies behind Jephthah's exclamation of grief

---

[215]Hence the blessing, "May the LORD bless you, and may you have many children," illustrated in the Adamic blessing (Gen 1:28), the Noachian blessing (Gen 9:1), the Abrahamic blessing/promise (Gen 15:1-6; 17:6; 22:17), and reiterated to Isaac (Gen 26:3-5, 24) and Jacob (Gen 28:13-15); the blessing pronounced by Rebekah's family upon her (Gen 24:60); Joseph's blessing of his grandsons (Gen 48:16); and the Bethlehemites' blessing of Ruth (Ruth 4:11-12). Note especially Ps 127:3-5 (my translation):

> See, children are a special grant *[naḥălâ]* of Yahweh;
> The fruit of the womb is a reward *[śākār]*.
> Like arrows in the hand of a mighty man,
> So are the children of one's youth.
> How blessed is the man
> whose quiver is full of them;
> They shall not be ashamed
> When they speak with their enemies in the gate.

And Ps 128:3-4 (my translation):

> Your wife shall be like a fruitful vine within your house;
> Your children like olive plants around your table.

[216]See further Meyers, "The Family in Early Israel," p. 27.

[217]See analysis of this issue in Daniel I. Block, "Beyond the Grave: Ezekiel's Vision of Death and Afterlife," *BBR* 2 (1992): 113-41.

[218]See Saul's plea with David not to do this to him in 1 Sam 24:22 (Eng. 21) and the widow's complaint in 2 Sam 14:7 that by executing her only son for murdering his brother, her townspeople "would put out the only burning coal I have left, leaving my husband neither name nor descendant on the face of the earth" (NIV). According to 2 Sam 18:18 Absalom set up a memorial for himself because he had no children to proclaim *(hazkîr)* his name after his death. See also Ps 37:28; Is 14:20-21. Reflecting this close association between an enduring seed and an enduring name, a related idiom spoke of annihilating one's "name" in place of "seed." In such cases the word *šēm,* "name," refers to one's reputation and honor, and serves metonymically for one's descendants, who provide one with a sort of posthumous existence. A series of related idioms refer to the total annihilation of a person, family, group or nation as the blotting out of the name: *hikrît,* "to cut off" (Josh 7:9; Is 14:22; Zech 1:4; Ruth 4:10 [Niphal]); *nigraʾ,* "to be withdrawn" (Num 27:4); *ʿābad,* "to perish" (Ps 41:6 [Qal]), "to obliterate" (Deut 12:3 [Piel], "to destroy" (Deut 7:24 [Hiphil]); *māḥâ,* "to blot out" (Deut 9:14; 2 Kings 14:27); *šāmad,* "to destroy" (Is 48:19 [Niphal]; 1 Sam 24:22 [Hiphil]); *hēsîr,* "to remove"

in Judges 11:35 at the sight of his daughter coming to meet him after he had won the victory over the Ammonites.[219]

Although all children were treasured as gifts from God, in Israelite families the firstborn played a special role. Hebrew has different expressions for a father's eldest child (*rēšît ʾôn,* "the first of [a father's procreative] strength")[220] and for a mother's firstborn (*peter reḥem,* "the one who opens the womb").[221] Closely associated with these expressions is the term *bĕkōr,* a word that occurs more than 120 times in the Old Testament. Although scholars usually translate *bĕkōr* as "firstborn,"[222] it is preferable to interpret the word as a designation for an honorific position in the family held by a male sibling and entitling him to preferential treatment.[223] Deuteronomy 21:15-17 specifies that the *bĕkōr* is en-

---

(Hos 2:19). For extrabiblical references to the same notion, see in particular VTE (Vassal Treaty of Esarhaddon) where the curse of "blotting out the name/memory" of the enemy occurs repeatedly: §§140, 161, 255, 315, 435, 524, 537, 663 (*ANET,* pp. 534-41). As in Hebrew, "name" (*šumu;* cf. Hebrew *šēm*) is closely linked with "seed" (*zarʾu;* cf. Hebrew *zeraʿ*).

[219]In the previous verse the narrator had noted emphatically "She was his only child; beside her he had neither son nor daughter" (Judg 11:34 RSV). In sacrificing his daughter he sacrificed himself! See Block, *Judges/Ruth,* pp. 372-74.

[220]This applies even in polygamous households: Gen 49:3; Deut 21:17; Ps 78:51; 105:36.

[221]Most often used of animals: Ex 13:12, 13, 15; 34:19, 20; Ezek 20:26; but also of a human firstborn: Ex 13:2; Num 3:12; 18:15.

[222]Thus *HALOT,* p. 131; *DCH,* 1:170; M. Tsevat, "בְּכוֹר *bĕkōr,*" *TDOT,* 2.121-27.

[223]The traditional interpretation may be questioned for etymological reasons and on the grounds of usage. In Arabic and Ethiopic the verb derived from the root *bkr* means "to get up early, to do something early." Cf. the derived Hebrew term *bikkûrâ,* which denotes "early figs," not "first figs" (*HALOT,* p. 172), which differs from later Syriac usage, "to be, to do something first" (cf. *HALOT,* p. 130; Tsevat, *TDOT,* 2:121). In Akkadian *bukru* occurs alongside *ašarēdu,* "foremost," and *rabû,* "great," in lexical texts related to inheritance, but the specific meaning "firstborn" for the term itself seems unlikely, especially in view of a series of poetic and mythological texts that suggest that some of the deities had several *bukru* (*CAD,* 2:309) and the fact that *bukru* itself could be modified with several superlative adjectives: *rēštu* ("best" *bukru*), *rabu* ("greatest" *bukru*), *ašarēdu* ("foremost" *bukru*). See further Frederick E. Greenspahn, *When Brothers Dwell Together: The Preeminence of Younger Siblings in the Hebrew Bible* (New York/Oxford: Oxford University Press, 1994), pp. 19, 27, 61-62. Several features of the usage of *bĕkōr* in the Old Testament also argue against "firstborn." First, the word occasionally applies to individuals and groups who are obviously not the firstborn: David (Ps 89:28), Israel (Ex 4:22; cf. Mal 2:10) and Ephraim (Jer 31:9). David was neither the firstborn of his earthly father (he was the youngest of Jesse's eight sons!) nor the firstborn of God his heavenly adoptive father. The fatherhood of God is recognized in numerous personal names that antedate or were contemporaneous with David but incorporate *ʿāb* as the theophore: Abiel (1 Sam 9:1; 14:51), Ebiasaph (1 Chron 6:8 [Eng. 23]), Abigail (1 Sam 25:3-42) and others. On these personal names, see Fowler, *Theophoric Personal Names,* passim. Yahweh's claim to Israel as his *bĕkōr* in Ex 4:22 or Ephraim in Jer 31:9 does not suggest that either of these is chronologically older than all the others (presumably the rest of the nations). Second, several texts speak of "making/designating" someone a *bĕkōr,* which suggests some legal procedure to achieve this goal (thus God with David in Ps 89:28). Deut 21:15-17 seeks to prevent bigamous/polygamous fathers from "bekoring" *(bikkēr)*

titled to a double portion of the inheritance, which is best interpreted as twice as much as the other heirs receive.[224] The aim of this law is to prevent a father from changing the rules of inheritance at the last moment on the basis of subjective preference for the son of a favored wife. If the son of the unloved wife is the designated *bĕkōr,* the double portion must go to him.[225] Accordingly, *bĕkōr* is best understood as a designation of rank, an indication of sociological rather than chronological priority.[226] The *bĕkōr* was the title of the privileged heir, the *primus inter fratres,* "first among brothers." Rather than making claims to Israel's antiquity, theological statements like "Israel is my son, my *bĕkōr*" (Ex 4:22), assert divine preference, analogous to Moses' statement in Deuteronomy 26:18-19: "Today Yahweh has declared you to be his people, a special treasure . . . and that he shall assign you a status higher *(ʿelyôn)* than all the nations that he has made—for praise, honor, and fame, and that you shall be a consecrated people to Yahweh your God."[227]

---

a younger son of a favored wife in place of the older son of the less favored wife who is "the first of his strength." Greenspahn notes correctly that this prohibition is not addressed to efforts "to eliminate a legal loophole whereby certain children were fictitiously designated firstborn in order to circumvent the rigidities of primogeniture" (*When Brothers Dwell Together,* p. 59). Third, since *bĕkōr* often occurs in the plural and since some texts speak of choosing a *rēšit* ("best, first") among the *bikkûrîm,* a meaning other than "first fruits" is required—there can only be one "first fruit." Fourth, Genesis and Chronicles use the derived abstract cognate noun *bĕkōrâ,* which denotes the rights associated with being the *bĕkōr,* as something that may be despised (*bāzâ,* Gen 25:32,34), sold (*mākar,* Gen 25:31, 33), taken away, expropriated (Gen 27:37), taken from the eldest and given *(nātan)* to another member of the family (1 Chron 5:1), or possessed by the second youngest member of the family (1 Chron 5:3). But the chronological priority involved in being the firstborn is a matter of historical record and cannot be changed or exchanged. This conclusion is not affected by the use of the feminine cognate *bĕkîrâ* to identify the "larger" of two daughters. The younger daughter is referred to as *šĕʿîrâ* (Gen 19:31) and *qĕtannâ* (1 Sam 14:49), both of which mean "small," rather than young.

[224]For discussion of the disputed phrase, *pî šĕnayim,* see Gershon Brin, *Studies in Biblical Law: From the Hebrew Bible and the Dead Sea Scrolls,* JSOTSup 176 (Sheffield: JSOT Press, 1994), pp. 240-47. The following represents the formula for calculating the *bĕkōr*'s portion according to Brin (n = number of sons):

$$\text{For an ordinary son: } \frac{1}{n+1} \qquad \text{For the } b\breve{e}k\bar{o}r\text{: } \frac{2}{n+1}$$

[225]A second potential injustice could have been incurred by giving the entire estate to the (younger) son of the favored wife. Precedent for this is found in Gen 25:5, according to which "Abraham gave all that he had to Isaac," leaving only gifts for the rest (Gen 25:6), despite the fact that Isaac was not the firstborn.

[226]My colleague Peter Gentry has kindly drawn my attention to André Feuillet's observation, based on the pre-Christian Leontopolis inscriptions, that like the Greek word *prōtotokos,* Hebrew *bĕkōr* does not necessarily imply the idea of "first in a series" and does not presuppose the existence of other children. See *Christologie paulinienne et tradition biblique* (Paris: Brouwer, 1972), p. 49.

[227]My translation; so also Greenspahn, *When Brothers Dwell Together,* p. 60.

In a society that was both patricentric and placed special value on the first son,[228] in the vast majority of cases the privileges of the *bĕkōr* would naturally have fallen to the oldest son.[229] But biblical texts also naturally qualify *bĕkōr* with explicit expressions for "firstborn." Instructions for the consecration of the firstborn define *bĕkōr* more closely as *peter reḥem,* "that which opens the womb" (Ex 13:11-15); instructions for the distribution of the inheritance qualify *bĕkōr* with *rē'šît 'ôn,* "the first of [procreative] strength" (Deut 21:17).[230] However, not every male *peter reḥem* qualified as a *bĕkōr.* Only one person could hold this position in any given household. In polygamous marriages this normally fell to the oldest son of the father and would not have been shared by the oldest son of each of the mothers.

In Israel the *bĕkōr* was not only favored by his father; he was also claimed by Yahweh. Although all children were viewed as gifts given by God to the parents, by means of a special ceremony[231] "firstborn" sons were ritually acknowledged as belonging to Yahweh and formally transferred to him.[232] In

---

[228]According to Meyer Fortes ("The First Born," *Journal of Child Psychology and Psychiatry and Allied Disciplines* 15 [1974]: 81-104), in the social and psychological system the oldest child is special because (1) with his birth, parenthood is confirmed as a fact; that is, his progenitor becomes a father; (2) with his birth, a new generation of sons is founded; and (3) he assumes the role of head over the group of brothers to follow. For a discussion of position of the firstborn from a sociological perspective, see Shuny Bendor, *The Social Structure of Ancient Israel,* JBS 7 (Jerusalem: Simor, 1996), pp. 175-88.

[229]When Joseph's brothers eat before him, he seats them in order from the oldest, referred to as *habbĕkōr kibkōrātô* (Reuben), to the youngest, referred to as *haṣṣā'îr kiṣ'îrātô* (Benjamin); Gen 43:33.

[230]Note also Gen 49:3; Ps 78:51; 105:36, where the expressions appear as a poetic parallel pair.

[231]Although Num 3:13 portrays Yahweh as consecrating the firstborn to himself, the experience of the child at the hands of his parents is expressed with a variety of verbs: he is "given to Yahweh" (*nātan lyhwh,* Ex 22:28-29), "transferred to Yahweh" (*he'ĕbîr lyhwh,* Ex 13:12), and "consecrated to Yahweh" (*hiqdîš lyhwh/qiddēš lyhwh,* Ex 13:2; Deut 15:19), and he "belongs to Yahweh/me" (*lyhwh hû or lî hû,* Ex 13:2; Lev 27:26). These statements are made of all kinds of firstborns: the firstborn of ceremonially clean animals were sacrificed as whole burnt offerings to Yahweh (Ex 13:15; Num 18:17-18; Deut 15:19-23); the firstborn of donkeys were redeemed with a lamb (Ex 13:13; 34:20) or by paying 120 percent of its value (Lev 27:26-27). For further discussion of the redemption of animals, see Brin, *Studies in Biblical Law,* pp. 196-208; of human beings, see ibid, pp. 215-26.

[232]The laws governing the consecration of the firstborn of animals call for the sacrifice of males (Ex 13:12, 15; 34:19; Deut 15:19), but the laws concerning the consecration of firstborn human beings do not specify the gender of the child. However, the evidence points strongly in the direction of male sons. (1) Elsewhere *bānay,* "my sons," could be interpreted inclusively as "my children," but in Ex 13:15 this is precluded by the fact that *bĕkōr,* which precedes this word, elsewhere always applies to males. (2) Speaking of the redemption of the firstborn by the Levites, Num 3:40-42 specifies the involvement of every male firstborn. (3) According to Num 18:16, the price for redeeming the firstborn is set at five shekels, which is identical to the valuation placed on a vowed male child, in contrast to a female child, who is valued at

contrast to the surrounding peoples, who believed that the first fruits of the soil and the womb were vested with intrinsic holiness, in Israel they became so by divine decree and were recognized as such through the human act of consecration.[233]

The status and roles of children in the home. A discussion of the status of children in ancient Israel may begin where children begin, in the actions of the parents that lead to the conception of the child. According to the Old Testament, not only do human beings express their humanity and their status as images of God within the context of heterosexual relationships,[234] but sexual activity itself has three functions: biological (procreation), social (physical expression of covenant commitment and intimacy) and aesthetic (for pleasure).[235] Within the context of marriage, sexual activity between husband and wife is purposeful, noble, sacred and necessary for the well-being of the family. Homosexuality,[236] premarital and extramarital sexual relations, and bestiality[237] are deemed abhorrent violations of the ethical and ritual order. Prostitution takes the sacrilege to another level, making commerce out of sexual activity and

---

three shekels (Lev 27:6). (4) The analogy of consecrated firstborn animals, which must be male (Ex 13:12, 15; 34:19; Deut 15:19), points to a male firstborn child. (5) Later biblical sources interpret Ex 13:2, 12 (which does not specify gender) as applying to males (Lk 2:23). For discussion of these considerations, see Brin, *Studies in Biblical Law*, pp. 213-15.

[233]Thus Sarna (*Exodus,* 65), who also observes that consecration rituals usually involved purification and induction rituals, the former involving washing one's entire body, laundering one's clothes and abstaining from ritually defiling contacts, and the latter involving a ceremony of investiture by a recognized priestly official. See Ex 19:10-11, 14-15, 22; 28:3, 41; 29:1, 33, 36, 44; 30:30; 40:13; Lev 8:12, 30; Num 8:6; 11:18; Josh 3:5; 7:13; 1 Sam 7:1; 16:5.

[234]Gen 1:27; cf. 2:24-25.

[235]As commended in Prov 5:15-23 and celebrated in the Song of Songs. Compare Sarah's sarcastic comment in the face of Yahweh's promise of a son next year in Gen 18:12, "Now that I am withered, am I to have enjoyment—with my husband so old?" (NJPS). For an insightful discussion of the contrast between the satisfying and fulfilling sexual relations within marriage and the empty and defiling experiences of prostitution, see Monford Harris, "Pre-marital Sexual Experience: A Covenantal Critique," *Judaism* 19 (1970): 134-44.

[236]The Old Testament characterizes homosexual relations as foolish and antisocial (*nābālâ,* Judg 19:23, a term used elsewhere of other gross sexual crimes: rape [Gen 34:7], premarital sex [Deut 22:21], gang rape of a woman [Deut 20:6, 10], incestuous rape [2 Sam 13:12-13] and adultery with a neighbor's wife [Jer 29:23]; cf. Magne Sæbø, "נָבָל, *nābāl* fool," *TLOT,* 2:710-14), morally shameful (*zimmâ,* Judg 20:6), wicked (*rāʿâ,* Gen 19:7; Judg 19:23) and abominable (*tôʿēbâ,* Lev 18:22; 20:13). Deut 22:5 also applies the last expression to transvestism. For a helpful summary statement of the Old Testament disposition toward homosexuality, see J. Glen Taylor, "The Bible and Homosexuality," *Them* 21.1 (1995): 4-9. On the biblical association of male homosexuality with Canaanite custom, see Baruch Levine, *Leviticus,* JPS Torah Commentary (Philadelphia: Jewish Publication Society, 1989), p. 123.

[237]Lev 18:23 repudiates bestiality as *tebel,* "perversion," and declares it a capital crime.

permitting males to abuse and defile women for their own gratification and pleasure.[238] Biblical prohibition of such deviations derived not only from the Israelites' high regard for patrilineal blood lines[239] but especially from Yahweh's demand for a holy nation, distinct in its ethic from the Canaanites.

With the exception of Samson's mother, who adopts a Nazirite's diet during her pregnancy,[240] the Old Testament is silent on how the period of waiting for the child was treated. With respect to the birth itself, experienced women of the household or the broader community served as midwives (mĕyallĕdōt),[241] who attended the birth of the child.[242] The midwife's tasks would have included cutting the umbilical cord, washing the child, massaging it with a saline solution and wrapping it tightly in cloths,[243] as well as

---

[238]The term zônâ applies to any woman who receives payment for her sexual favors. The Old Testament displays a generally tolerable disposition toward prostitutes themselves (Jer 3:3 is an exception), presumably because they were often driven to this "profession" by economic necessity, but it is explicit in its denunciation of cult prostitution (Deut 23:18 [Eng. 17]; though some treat qĕdēšâ here as a common prostitute who plies her trade at a cult center: E. A. Goodfriend, "Prostitution," ABD, 5:507-9; Mayer Gruber, "Hebrew qĕdēšâ and Her Canaanite and Akkadian Cognates," UF 18 [1986]: 133-48) and fathers filling the land with depravity (zimmâ) and defiling (ḥillēl) their daughters by having them serve as prostitutes (Lev 19:29). Deut 23:19 (Eng. 18) characterizes the presentation of funds received through prostitution at the house of Yahweh as tô 'ēbâ, "an abomination." The relatively greater culpability of males involved with prostitutes is evident also in Hebrew narratives. Dinah's brothers treated Hamor's violation of their sister as capital crime, accusing him of making a prostitute out of their sister (Deut 23:25-31). Judah is clearly stigmatized for resorting to Tamar (Gen 38:23), and even he recognized her relatively greater righteousness (Deut 23:26). The author of Judges treats Samson's fraternizing with prostitutes (Judg 16:1) as one of the evidences of Israel's degeneracy—doing evil in the sight of Yahweh.

[239]The paternity of a prostitute's child is difficult to prove. Tamar's feigned prostitution and her efforts to guarantee later exposure of Judah as the man who had fathered the child in her womb (Gen 38:12-26) were atypical. The same is probably true of Jephthah, for whom the name of the father is given (Gilead), though the name of his prostitute mother is unknown.

[240]Judg 13:7, 14.

[241]The word, a Piel participle form of yālad, "to give birth," occurs in Gen 35:17; 38:28; Ex 1:15, 17, 21.

[242]In Ex 1:16 Pharaoh instructs the midwives to "look upon the two stones" and make their decision whether a Hebrew child should live on the basis of what they saw. The word 'obnayim is usually understood as two bricks or stones over which the woman in labor squatted (Sarna, Exodus, p. 7), but the context favors understanding the reference to be to "testicles." See William H. C. Propp, Exodus: A New Translation with Introduction and Commentary, AB 2 (New York: Doubleday, 1998), p. 139; John I. Durham, Exodus, WBC 3 (Waco: Word, 1987), pp. 11-12. Unlike modern Western culture, which encourages fathers to attend the birth of a child, ancient Israelite standards of modesty precluded male involvement, even that of the father, except perhaps in emergency situations.

[243]Ezek 16:4; cf. Job 38:8-9.

assisting the mother in household tasks to speed her recovery. Undoubtedly a child's grandmother[244] and other members of the household also assumed responsibility for the care of children. Israelite tradition understood the pain of childbirth[245] to be a consequence of human sin, hence a constant reminder that human life continues only by the grace of God. In Israel children were named immediately after birth. As noted earlier, more often than not names were assigned by the infant's mother.[246] Personal names usually commemorated a significant personal or communal experience associated with the birth experience: the parents' gratitude to God (Jonathan, "Yahweh has granted"; Zechariah, "Yahweh has remembered"), their hope for the future (Jaazaniah, "May Yahweh give ear"), the pain of birth (Ben-oni, "son of my sorrow") or a contemporary event (Ichabod, "no glory").[247]

Of course, biological procreation was not the only means by which children entered a family. Adoption, the act whereby a person legally acknowledges another who is not his or her biological descendant, was widely practiced in the ancient Near East.[248] The Old Testament provides no regulations for and reports no explicitly identified cases of adoption, though several accounts have adoptive overtones.[249] Genesis 30:3-8 provides the most likely example, recounting that Rachel gave her maidservant to Jacob so she could bear children "on her knees." This interpretation is supported by the observation that Rachel named the progeny from this scheme (Dan, Naphtali) and Jacob incorporated them (along with the children of Leah's maidservant) into his family as *bona fide* sons, with rights to inheritance equal to

---

[244]According to Ruth 4:16-17, Naomi took Obed, her newborn grandson, held him to her bosom, and became his *'ōmenet,* "nanny," and laid him on her lap.

[245]Often used metaphorically by the prophets: Is 13:8; 21:3; 26:17; Jer 4:21; 6:24; 13:21; 22:23; 50:43.

[246]Gen 29:31—30:24; 35:18; Judg 13:24; 1 Sam 1:20. Examples of fathers naming their children are found in Gen 16:15; 17:19; Ex 2:22. In Ex 2:10 Moses is named by his adoptive mother, the princess of Egypt. Ruth 4:17 involves Naomi's neighbors in the naming her grandson, though it is doubtful their decision overrode that of Obed's parents. See Block, *Judges/Ruth,* p. 731. The Old Testament also attests several instances in which people are (re)named by God: he changes Isaac's name to Israel (Gen 32:28; 35:10); the *'almâ* of Is 7:14 is to name her child Immanuel; cf. the naming of Jesus in Matt 1:21.

[247]For studies of Israelite personal names, see Fowler, *Theophoric Personal Names;* Moshe Garsiel, *Biblical Names: A Literary Study of Midrashic Derivations and Puns,* trans. P. Hackett (Ramat Gan: Bar-Ilan University, 1991). See also de Vaux, *Ancient Israel,* pp. 43-46.

[248]See the discussion of adoption by de Vaux, *Ancient Israel,* pp. 51-52.

[249]Abraham's servant being designated his heir because he was childless (Gen 15:3); Moses being taken in by Pharaoh's daughter and treated as his son (she even named him! Ex 2:10); Genubath, the son of Hadad being raised in Pharaoh's house among his own sons (1 Kings 11:20); and Esther being taken in and raised by a relative Mordecai (Esther 2:7, 15).

the actual sons of Leah and Rachel,[250] except that these were physically the sons of Jacob, though not the sons of Rachel. The frequent reference to Yahweh's relationship with Israel as a father-son relationship[251] reinforces the impression that adoption must have been a relatively common experience—the metaphor would have been meaningless otherwise! Even more telling is Yahweh's bond with David and his descendants, which is expressed by what is commonly recognized as the adoption formula, "I will be his father, and he shall be my son."[252]

Unlike in the modern Western world, in ancient Israel children could nurse as long as three years after birth.[253] Customarily the infant was nursed by its mother,[254] though the practice of entrusting the child into the care of another nursing woman is well attested.[255] The case of Deborah, Rebekah's nurse,[256] demonstrates that a nurse could become an extremely significant member of a family. Apparently after Rebekah had been weaned the nurse continued to serve as her guardian and tutor,[257] and when the time came for her to marry, Rebekah's family sent the nurse along to provide continued companionship and assistance as she assumed a new role of wife and

---

[250]Note also Jacob's apparent adoption of Joseph's sons, Manasseh and Ephraim, by blessing them (Gen 48:8-22) and declaring that because of them Joseph was to receive a double portion of his inheritance, and Joseph's possible adoption of his great-grandsons, the sons of Machir, Manasseh's son, who were "born on Joseph's knees" (Gen 50:23). For a treatment of both these cases as adoptions by Joseph, see Greenspahn, *When Brothers Dwell Together,* pp. 121-22.

[251]Ex 4:22; Deut 32:6; Is 63:16; 64:7; Jer 3:19; 31:9; Hos 11:1.

[252]2 Sam 7:14; cf. Ps 89:27-28 (Eng. 26-27). For a discussion of ancient Near Eastern perceptions of a suzerain-vassal relationship as a relationship between father and adopted son, see Moshe Weinfeld, "The Covenant of Grant in the Old Testament and in the Ancient Near East," *JAOS* 90 (1970): 190-94; but note the recent cautionary response of Gary N. Knoppers, "Ancient Near Eastern Royal Grants and the Davidic Covenant: A Parallel?" *JAOS* 116 (1996): 681-84.

[253]1 Macc 7:27; cf. 1 Sam 1:20-23.

[254]Gen 21:7; 1 Sam 1:21-23; 1 Kings 3:21.

[255]Gen 24:29; 35:8; Ex 2:7-9; Num 11:12; 2 Sam 4:4; 2 Kings 11:2; Is 49:23; 2 Chron 22:11. Hebrew *mêneqet,* from the root *yānaq,* "to nurse, breastfeed," denotes "one who breastfeeds." Nowhere does the Old Testament indicate how a nurse was chosen, but she must have recently had a child of her own. With the high infant mortality rate, a person who had lost a child may have offered her breasts to someone else's newborn, or if she had sufficient milk she might breastfeed two children simultaneously. Alternatively, if the nurse was a household servant, a mistress who had just given birth may simply have commandeered her to perform this service.

[256]Gen 24:59; 35:8.

[257]Targum Jonathan renders *mêneqet* as *padgogthâ,* which is influenced by Greek *paidagōgos,* "tutor." This also accords with Mesopotamian custom according to which the *mušēniqtu,* "wet nurse," often also served as *tarbītu,* one who serves as guardian and tutor for a child.

mother. She became such an integral part of this family that, after the death of Rebekah, her one-time nursling and later her mistress, as an aged person continued to live and move about with the family of Rebekah's son Jacob. Gen 35:8 gives remarkable testimony to her significance, not only by remembering her name, but also by recounting the time and place of her death, which was memorialized in the naming of an oak near Bethel. Such honors were not even accorded her mistress![258]

The Hebrews were just one of many Semitic peoples who practiced circumcision.[259] In Israel circumcision was a religious rite, a mark of the covenant, performed on males on their eighth day.[260] Other than this ceremonial event, passages in a child's life were not clearly marked. Abraham celebrated the weaning of Isaac with a great feast,[261] undoubtedly reflective of the precarious nature of the life of an infant at the time, but there is no evidence of self-conscious awareness of childhood and adolescence as distinct phases of life.[262]

Cast as a manual for the instruction of a young man, the book of Proverbs offers a clear window into the ancient Israelite disposition toward youth. It is especially instructive to note the specific words used to refer to and characterize the person addressed.[263] (1) *Bēn* is an expression capable of a wide

---

[258]The place of Rebekah's burial in the family cave at Machpelah is noted in a later summary statement (Gen 49:31), but the narrative is silent on the time and circumstances of her death. Since she is never mentioned in later narratives, most assume that she had died by the time Jacob returned from Haran (cf. Gen 27:45).

[259]On circumcision in the ancient Near East, see Jack M. Sasson, "Circumcision in the Ancient Near East," *JBL* 85 (1966): 473-76; T. Lewis and C. Armerding, "Circumcision," *ISBE*, 1:700-702; R. G. Hall, "Circumcision," *ABD*, 1:1025-27. For discussion of the primary textual and iconographic evidence of circumcision in Egypt, see Frans Jonckheere, "La circoncision des anciens égyptiens," *Centaurus* 1 (1951): 212-34; Maurice Stracmans, "Encore un texte peu connue relatif à la circoncision des anciens égyptiens," *Archivo Internationale di Einografia e Preistoria* 2 (1959): 7-15; for an illustration, see *ANEP* §629. Cf. *ANET,* p. 326; Herodotus, *Histories* 2.104; Josephus, *Antiquities* 8.10.3.

[260]Gen 17. If circumcision in Egypt was reserved for a high caste, including the pharaoh, his priests, courtiers and other high standing servants, as Stracmans suggests ("Encore un texte peu connue relatif à la circoncision," p. 12), and if Israelite circumcision represents an adaptation of the Egyptian practice, inasmuch as all Israelite males were to be circumcised, it could be argued that in Israel nobility was democratized; all male citizens were acknowledged as courtiers of Yahweh (a suggestion raised by Peter Gentry in private conversation). But Sasson ("Circumcision in the Ancient Near East," p. 474), observes that it remains unclear whether the Egyptian practice was voluntary or imposed universally.

[261]Gen 21:8.

[262]This contrasts with the bar-mitsvah and bat-mitsvah and confirmation ceremonies in Judaism and many Christian denominations.

[263]For an excellent discussion of the terms for "foolish person" in the following list (3-8), see Michael V. Fox, "Words for Folly," *ZAH* 10 (1997): 4-15. I am grateful to Peter Gentry for alerting me to this article.

range of meanings, one of which was equivalent to "student," under the tutelage of a "teacher," referred to as his *ʾāb,* "father."[264] In Proverbs the word denotes a young man dependent on and accountable to mother and father. (2) *Naʿar* is a late adolescent in need of training as he prepares for adulthood.[265] (3) *Petî* (plural *pĕtāyim /pĕtaʾyim*), is from a root *pātâ,* "to be simple, open (minded)," hence a simpleton, a gullible person, one easily seduced or taken in by ideas of any kind, whose mind is untrained to discern truth from falsehood, hence in need of guidance.[266] (4) *Lîṣ/lēṣ* is a fundamentally flawed scoffer, mocker, who arrogantly displays his corruption by holding wisdom and instruction in derision and is in need of humbling.[267] (5) *Kĕsîl* is a shameless, stupid and insolent person, disinterested in wisdom and incorrigible in his ways.[268] (6) *Ḥăsēr lēb* is a mindless and heartless person, one who lacks sense and needs discipline.[269] (7) *ʾĔwîl* is an idiot, a morally stupid and thick-brained person, virtually indistinguishable from the *kĕsîl.* Both are characterized by *ʾiwwelet,* "moral corruption, folly," and both respond to discipline and correction with contempt.[270] (8) *Siklût/sākāl* means stupidity/ an obtuse and stupid person, without any necessary moral connotations.[271]

This vocabulary and the manner in which the words are used demonstrate that from an intellectual, moral and spiritual standpoint, Israelites believed persons in their youth were fundamentally flawed.[272] According to the opening thesis statement of Proverbs (1:2-7), the answer to this problem is

---

[264]Prov 1:8; 2:1; 3:1, 11, 21; 4:1, 10, 20; 5:1, 7; 6:1, 20; 7:1; 8:32; 10:1; et passim. The equivalent of *rab, rabbî,* in postbiblical Hebrew and Aramaic.

[265]Prov 1:4; et passim. See the excellent discussion by Ted Hildebrandt, "Proverbs 22:6a: Train Up a Child?" *GTJ* 9 (1988): 10-14.

[266]Prov 1:4, 32; 7:7; 8:5; 9:4, 16; 14:15, 18; 19:25; 21:11; 22:3; 27:12; See Chou-Wee Pan, "פתה," *NIDOTTE,* 3:714-16.

[267]The verb occurs in Prov 3:24; 9:12; 19:28; 24:9; the noun in Prov 1:22; 3:34; 9:7, 8; 13:1; 14:6; 15:12; 19:25, 29; 20:1; 21:11, 24; 22:10; 24:9. See further T. Powell, "ליץ," *NIDOTTE,* 2:798-800.

[268]The root occurs more than fifty times in Proverbs. E.g., Prov 3:35; 10:1; 13:20; 14:16, 24; 14:7, 33; 15:2, 7, 20; 21:20; 26:5; 29:11. See further Chou-Wee Pan, "כסל," *NIDOTTE,* 2:678-80.

[269]Prov 6:32; 7:7; 9:4, 16; 10:13; 11:12; 12:11; 15:21; 17:18; 24:30; cf. Prov 28:16. See further S. Meier, "חסר," *NIDOTTE,* 2:226.

[270]Prov 10:8, 10, 13-14, 18, 21; 12:16, 23; 13:16; 14:8, 24, 33; 15:2, 5, 14, 20; 16:22; 17:12, 28; 19:1; 20:3; 26:4, 5, 11; 27:3, 22; 29:11; and others. See further Chou-Wee Pan, "אויל," *NIDOTTE,* 1:306-9.

[271]*Siklût,* Eccles 1:17; 2:3, 12, 13; 7:25; 10:1, 13; *sākāl,* Eccles 2:19; 7:17; 10:3, 14. See further Chou-Wee Pan, "כל," *NIDOTTE,* 3:254-56.

[272]Youth was perceived as a rudimentary stage of life, devoid of understanding and sense (Prov 7:7). Children are naturally and fundamentally foolish (Prov 22:15). This is illustrated by Rehoboam who sent Solomon's kingdom to ruin by preferring the advice of "youngsters" (*yĕlādîm*) to that of the mature men (*zĕqēnîm,* 1 Kings 12:6-15).

reflected in a rich vocabulary of learning: *ḥokmâ,* "wisdom"; *mûsār,* "discipline, training"; *bînâ* (cognate to *tĕbûnâ* found elsewhere), "understanding"; *daʿat,* "knowledge"; *ʿormâ,* "cleverness, smarts"; *mĕzimmâ,* "discretion, prudence"; *leqaḥ,* "perception, insight"; and *taḥbulôt,* fundamentally "the art of steering a boat" but idiomatic for "leadership skill." Elsewhere one encounters the noun *śekel,* "insight, prudence,"[273] and a series of verbs for learning: *šāmaʿ,* "to listen," especially to fathers and instructors, and *hiṭṭeh ʿoznî,* "to incline the ear" to teachers (Prov 5:13); *lāmad,* "to learn" (Prov 30:3); *ḥānak,* "to initiate," that is, "bestow the status and responsibilities of adulthood."[274]

From the preamble and the book as a whole, it is evident that the goal of learning is not merely to produce an informed and intelligent adult but to prepare the young person for life. The dimensions of this learning are encompassed by the single word *ḥokmâ,* which at base means skill in a craft (Ex 35:30-35) but by extension refers to intellectual acumen (1 Kings 4:9-14 [Eng. 29-34]), shrewdness (Ex 1:10), literary appreciation (Prov 1:6),[275] ethical and moral integrity (Prov 1:3),[276] and an understanding of the mysteries of life (Prov 30:11-33). Accordingly, the book of Proverbs covers a wide range of practical and pragmatic subjects, including personal etiquette, discipline and self-control in the face of inevitable sexual temptation, the importance of hard work, the importance of right speech, and other social skills needed not only to get along with the rest of the household (Prov 6:16-19) but also to accept the responsibilities of adulthood in the broader community. To achieve these goals, stubborn wills needed to be broken, gullible minds needed to be given a framework for evaluating ideas, hard hearts needed to be softened, and self-centeredness needed to be replaced by a sense of membership in and obligation to the community. But underneath it all is a profound theological conviction that "The fear of Yahweh is the first principle of wisdom."[277] If a young person does not learn this, he or she remains a fool, and a society of fools cannot stand, let alone prosper. Accordingly, the task of training children and preparing them for mature adulthood fell not only to the child's parents but was deemed to be

---

[273]Prov 12:8; 16:22; 19:11. The cognate verb *haśkîl,* "to have insight, be prudent, achieve success," occurs in Prov 1:3.

[274]Thus Hildebrandt, "Proverbs 22:6a: Train Up a Child?" pp. 3-19.

[275]The verse speaks of understanding proverbs *(masāl),* figures of speech *(mĕlîṣâ),* wise words *(dibrê ḥokmâ)* and riddles *(ḥîdâ).*

[276]The verse refers to the ethical with a triad of stock expressions: *ṣedeq,* "righteousness"; *mišpāṭ,* "justice"; *mêšārîm,* "integrity, uprightness."

[277]Prov 1:7; 9:10; 15:33; Job 28:28; Ps 111:10; Eccles 12:13.

the responsibility of the community as a whole.

Children's responsibilities within the household. In the discussion of the status of children, the child/youth has been largely passive—the recipient of parental care and training. The expected response of the child would obviously change with time, but the first principle in a child's list of obligations was respect for parents. The importance of this injunction is highlighted in several ways. First, the vocabulary of respect involves verbs that elsewhere apply to Israel's required response to Yahweh: *kibbēd,* "to honor, ascribe glory to,"[278] and *yārē',* "to fear, revere."[279] Second, the command is built into the very constitution of the nation, being the first of the horizontal principles of covenant relationship cited in the Decalogue.[280] Third, the command to honor parents explicitly calls for the respect of both father and mother. Fourth, cast in apodictic form, the command provides no qualification, limitation or termination; respect from children is understood as an absolute parental right. Fifth, as Paul observes in Ephesians 6:1, in the context of a series of apodictic commands, this command is exceptional in being followed by a motive clause: individual Israelites' futures are dependent on their respect for the past. Sixth, in the catalogue of more than fifty injunctions outlining the dimensions of holiness in Leviticus 19 ("Be holy for I Yahweh your God am holy," Lev 19:2, my translation), pride of place goes to the command to honor mother and father (but note the reversed order: mother and father). Seventh, later legislation declares the treatment of parents with contempt as a capital offense.[281] Eighth, Ezekiel lists dishonoring parents among the crimes that characterized his generation and ultimately led to the fall of Jerusalem and the de-

---

[278]The verb appears with the following divine objects: (1) Yahweh: 1 Sam 2:30; Is 24:15; 25:3; 43:20, 23; Ps 22:24; Prov 3:9; (2) Adonai: Is 29:13; (3) Elohim: Ps 50:15; (4) Eloah: Ps 50:23; (5) El: Sir 7:31; (6) Creator: Prov 14:31; (7) Yahweh's envoy *(mal'āk):* Judg 13:17.

[279]As reflected in "The fear of Yahweh is the first principle of wisdom," cited above. The fear of Yahweh is also an important motif in Deuteronomy: 4:10; 5:29; 6:2, 13, 24; 8:6; 10:12, 20; 13:4; 14:23; 17:19; 25:18; 28:58; 31:12, 13. Significantly, in contrast to the surrounding peoples, for whom ancestor worship was a prominent feature of religious expression, the command intentionally stops short of worshiping one's "father and mother."

[280]Ex 20:12; Deut 5:16.

[281]Ex 21:17; Lev 20:9; cf. Deut 27:16; Prov 20:20. The verb *qillēl,* "to treat lightly, with contempt, as unimportant," though usually rendered "to curse," is the semantic antonym to *kibbēd,* "to honor, to treat with respect," not *bērēk,* "to bless." The procedure for dealing with an incorrigible and disobedient son is set out in Deut 21:18-21. His father and mother are to seize him and present him to the elders; after they have declared the charges against him, the whole community is to participate in the execution by stoning. The purpose of this harsh treatment is both cathartic (to rid the community of the evil) and prophylactic (to instill fear in all Israel).

struction of the temple in 586 B.C.[282] Indeed it could be argued that just as an individual's fear of Yahweh was measured by the degree to which he "walked in the ways of Yahweh,"[283] so children's respect for parents was measured by the extent to which they actually obeyed their parents.[284]

A second area of responsibility for the children in an ancient Israelite family involved the economy of the household. Five- and six-year-old boys and girls would begin to pick vegetables, gather fuel and clean up after a meal. The household would organize tasks according to gender by the time they reached adolescence, assigning the males labor that required greater strength and danger (hunting, handling domesticated livestock, and butchering cattle and sheep) and training females in the special skills needed to run a household (harvesting vegetables, preparing food, spinning yarn, knitting garments and caring for babies; cf. Prov 31:10-31). However, these divisions were not absolute; especially in harvest time men and women often worked side by side in the fields (Ruth 2).[285]

Third, each generation of children was obligated to guard the genealogical integrity of the family, particularly the lines of the males. This was to be achieved through a special institution, the levirate marriage.[286] By definition, a levirate marriage represented a legally sanctioned union between *yĕbāmâ,* a widow whose husband has died without having fathered any offspring, and the *yābām,* the brother of the deceased. While variations of this type of marriage are attested in second-millennium Ugaritic, Hittite and Middle Assyrian sources,[287] Deuteronomy 25:5-10 obligated an unmarried Israelite

---

[282]Ezek 22:7. Sarna cogently observes that the Torah assigns supreme importance "to the integrity of the family for the sake of the stability of society and generational continuity. Family life is the bedrock on which Jewish society stands" (*Exodus,* p. 113).

[283]Deut 10:12; 17:19; 31:12, my translation.

[284]Deut 20:18; Prov 1:8. Compare Jesus' rebuke of the Pharisees for their pseudospirituality in Mark 7:10-13, by which he disallows even the most pious excuse for failing to care for one's parents, for such invalidates the word of God.

[285]For an excellent discussion of the economic roles of children in premonarchic Israel, see Meyers, "The Family in Early Israel," pp. 25-32. Even with increased urbanization under the monarchies, these roles will not have changed much for most of the people, especially outside the capital cities of Jerusalem and Samaria.

[286]The institution has nothing to do with Levites. *Levir* is the Latin term for brother-in-law, corresponding to Hebrew *yābām.*

[287]For references, see Block, *Judges/Ruth,* pp. 675-76. For evaluation of the comparative extrabiblical evidence, see Westbrook, *Property and Family in Biblical Law,* pp. 87-89. Further bibliography and discussion is provided by Blenkinsopp, "The Family in First Temple Israel," in *Families in Ancient Israel,* ed. Leo G. Perdue et al. (Louisville: Westminster John Knox, 1997), pp. 63-64, 96; F. R. Ames, "Levirate Marriage," *NIDOTTE,* 4:902-5; Greenspahn, *When Brothers Dwell Together,* pp. 55-59.

male to "perform the duties of the *yābām*" by marrying his brother's widow. To prevent the name and family of the deceased from dying out, the first child born to this union was to assume the name of the deceased. If the *yābām* declined to fulfill his responsibility, in the presence of the elders the widow was to remove his sandal and humiliate him publicly by spitting in his face.[288]

Finally, in ancient Israel children provided a safety net for their parents in their old age, which means that beyond occasioning embarrassment and shame, childlessness produced great anxiety over what would happen to one in old age.[289] The absence of references to the elderly in Pentateuchal provisions for the care of other classes that were especially vulnerable (orphan, widow and alien) is striking and might suggest that their welfare was secured by existing structures. On the other hand, it is possible that the Deuteronomic prescription of a double portion of the inheritance for an eldest son may have had as much to do with responsibility as privilege (Deut 21:17), the extra portion serving as compensation for functioning as the *bĕkōr,* which included caring for elderly parents in their declining years.

However, the younger generation could not assume that they had fulfilled their obligations if they limited their expressions of respect to their own aging parents. Leviticus 19:32 calls upon the younger generation to rise up before the gray-headed (*śêbâ,* cf. Job 29:8) and honor *(hādar)* the face of the aged, without reference to one's own parents; in the same breath God calls upon them to revere *(yārē')* him; he is Yahweh, their God. Indeed Elihu's apologetic opening in Job 32:4 demonstrates that respect for the aged was not even limited to an Israelite's own people.[290] The report of two female bears killing a group of young lads for mocking Elisha in 2 Kings 2:23-25 illustrates the seriousness with which God dealt with contempt for elders in general and for an aged prophet in particular.[291]

---

[288]Old Testament narratives provide two illustrations of the custom at work: the story of Judah's sons who refused to fulfill their levirate obligations with their widowed sister-in-law Tamar (Gen 38) and the story of Boaz, who, through legal means, gained the right from the first in line to marry Ruth and thereby preserve the family and patrimonial estate of Elimelech (Ruth 4:1-12).

[289]The relief of Naomi, who had lost both her sons, is reflected in the blessing pronounced upon her at the birth of her grandson Obed in Ruth 4:14-15.

[290]Elihu's genealogy in Job 32:2 suggests he was an Israelite. Nonetheless, he had delayed responding to the debate between Job and his "friends," out of respect for their seniority (Job 32:4-7), though apparently none of these was a member of his ethnic community.

[291]The account obviously concerns respect for a prophet, but the words of the boys, "Go up you baldhead! Go up you baldhead!" (my translation) are taunting words with which good-for-nothings would attack the elderly.

THE STATUS AND ROLES OF THE ELDERLY IN ANCIENT ISRAEL

The status of the elderly. Old Testament authors referred to the elderly with several expressions. Whereas the term for "old age," *yāšēš/yāšîš*, occurs only four times,[292] this stage of life is often described literally in terms of days, as in "advanced in days" *(bāʾîm bayyāmîm)*,[293] or in a figurative sense, old age being referred to as *śêbâ*, literally "gray hair." The verb *śîb*, which occurs twice in the Old Testament,[294] means fundamentally "to grow white, become hoary," but in both texts it bears a derived sense of "to be old." The corresponding noun, *śêbâ* occurs nineteen times,[295] almost exclusively with the abstract sense "grayness," used metonymically for "old age,"[296] and often associated with death, as in "to die with gray hair."[297] The root is often paired with other terms for old age: *zāqēn*, "old";[298] *śêbâ yāmîm*, "sated of days";[299] *kabbîr yāmîm*, "abundant of days" (Job 15:10); *yāšîš*, "age" (Job 15:10). A more precise understanding of the term may be achieved by noting what kinds of terms occur as opposites. According to Deuteronomy 32:25, just as "young man" *(bāḥûr)* contrasts with "young woman" *(bĕtûlâ)*, so "nursling" *(yônēq)* contrasts with "old age" *(śêbâ)*.

Like that of their ancient Near Eastern neighbors, Israelite tradition held that during the antediluvian period people enjoyed extremely long lives and that the period after the flood witnessed a rapid decline in human life spans.[300] The patriarchal narratives have the founders of the Israelite nation

---

[292]Three of which are in Job. Job 15:10 naturally associates "old age" with "being gray-haired." In Job 32:6 Elihu contrasts himself as *ṣāʿîr lĕyāmîm*, "young of days," with the three friends who are *yĕšîšîm*. Job 29:8 contrasts *yĕšîšîm*, "old men," with *nĕʿārîm*, "young men." 2 Chron 36:17 treats "young man" *(bāḥûr)* and "young woman" *(bĕtûlâ)* as opposites, and *zāqēn*, "old," as a synonym to *yāšēš*, "aged."

[293]Gen 18:11; 24:1; Josh 13:1a, 1b; 23:1, 2; 1 Kings 1:1. Compare "to have long days" *(ʾārĕkû yāmîm,* Ex 20:12; Deut 5:16), "sated of days" *(śĕbaʿ yāmîm,* Gen 35:29; Job 42:17; 1 Chron 29:28; also simply *śābēaʿ,* Gen 25:8), "abundant of days" *(kabbîr yāmîm,* Job 15:10), "fullness of days" *(mĕlē yāmîm,* Jer 6:11) and "numerous of days" *(rōb yāmîm,* Zech 8:4).

[294]1 Sam 12:2; Job 15:10.

[295]Gen 15:15; 25:8; 42:38; 44:29, 31; Lev 19:32; Deut 32:25; Judg 8:32; Ruth 4:15; 1 Kings 2:6, 9; 1 Chron 29:28; Job 41:24; Ps 71:18; 92:15 (Eng. 14); Prov 16:31; 20:29; Is 46:4; Hos 7:9.

[296]In Prov 20:29 it comes close to the literal meaning: "The glory of young men is their strength; the honor of old men is their gray hair" (NASB).

[297]Gen 25:8; 1 Chron 29:28; Judg 8:32. Compare "to be buried with gray hair" (Gen 15:15; 25:8), but note especially the idiom "to bring down someone's gray hair to Sheol" (Gen 42:38 NASB; 44:29, 31; 1 Kings 2:6, 9), a euphemism for death.

[298]Gen 25:8; Lev 19:32; 1 Sam 12:2; Is 46:4; Ps 71:1-8.

[299]Gen 25:8; 1 Chron 29:28.

[300]Cf. Gen 5 and 11; "The Sumerian King List," *ANET*, pp. 265-66.

still living twice as long as we expect even in modern times,[301] but Psalm 90:10 reflects the more sober reality that "the days of our life are seventy years, or perhaps eighty, if we are strong." The Old Testament displays no consistency in the portrayal of the time at which one reaches old age. For votary purposes, the oldest category in Leviticus 27:1-7 involves persons more than sixty years old, but Samuel considered himself to be "old and gray" when he was only fifty-two (1 Sam 12:2). David was "very old" when he was seventy (1 Kings 1:15). If the life spans of the kings of Judah averaged forty-four years, as suggested in the books of Chronicles, common citizens must have generally died even younger, which suggests that a thirty-five-year-old person would have been viewed as a mature if not senior citizen.[302]

Ancient Israelite attitudes toward aging were ambivalent. On the one hand, there was the sober recognition of the debilitating effects of age, poignantly expressed by the venerable supporter of David, the octogenarian Barzillai in 2 Samuel 19:35-36 (Eng. 34-35):

> How many more years will I live, that I should go up to Jerusalem with the king? I am now eighty years old. Can I tell the difference between what is good and what is not? Can your servant taste what he eats and drinks? Can I still hear the voices of men and women singers? Why should your servant be an added burden to my lord the king? (NIV)

Elsewhere we read of old persons suffering from blindness,[303] obesity (1 Sam 4:18), the loss of circulation or hypothermia (1 Kings 1:1-4), disease of the feet (1 Kings 15:23),[304] infertility (Gen 18:11), loss of sexual pleasure (Gen 18:12) and failing strength (Ps 71:9). The author of Ecclesiastes has painted a powerful literary picture of aging in Ecclesiastes 12:2-7, which

---

[301]Abraham lived 175 years; Isaac, 180; Jacob, 147; Moses, 120.

[302]The rabbis identified the critical turning points of life as follows: five years of age, for the study of Scripture; ten years, for the study of the Mishnah; thirteen years, for becoming subject to the commandments; fifteen years, for the study of the Talmud; eighteen years, for the bridal canopy; twenty years, for pursuing (military service); thirty years, for full strength; forty years, for understanding; fifty years, for ability to give counsel; sixty years, for mature age *(ziqnâ);* seventy years, for a hoary head *(śêbâ);* eighty years, a sign of super-added strength; ninety years, the age of bending figure; and one hundred years, one is as one that is dead, having passed and ceased from the world *(Pirqe Aboth* 5:2-1). This compares with the ancient Babylonian view that "60 is maturity; 70 length of days; 80 old age; 90 extreme old age" (Sultan Tepe Tablet 400-45-49).

[303]Isaac, Gen 27:1; Jacob, Gen 48:10; Eli, 1 Sam 3:2; 4:15; Ahijah, 1 Kings 14:4.

[304]Godfrey R. Driver ("Ancient Lore and Modern Knowledge," in *Hommages à André Dupont-Sommer,* ed. André Caquot and Marc Philonenko [Paris: Adrien-Maissoneuve, 1971], pp. 283-84) interpreted *hel'â* as gangrene.

speaks in figurative terms of the loss of vision, vigor and teeth; increasing insomnia and anxiety; and waning ambition. But old age could also bring with it great emotional stress, especially if there were tensions in the family, as is reflected in the idiom "to bring *śêbâ* down to Sheol in sorrow" (Gen 42:38; 44:31) or distress (Gen 44:29). A violent death is described as "bringing *śêbâ* down to Sheol with blood" (1 Kings 2:9). Such calamities could be interpreted as signs of divine disfavor, the greatest fear of all, as expressed by the anxious psalmist in Psalm 71:9, but answered by the reassuring words of Yahweh in Isaiah 46:3-4.

Despite the tensions created by the onset of old age, growing old was viewed positively and affirmed as desirable. In contrast to the longing for the "fountain of youth" or the fruit that would keep one in a state of perpetual youth found in extrabiblical literature,[305] old age was the Israelite ideal, the time of fulfillment.[306] Nor would ancient Israelites have considered it rude to inquire directly about one's age, and in response to such inquiry to express pride in one's longevity.[307] On the other hand, it was axiomatic that the wicked died young.[308] To attain the "fullness of days," "a ripe old age," or "satiation of days" was interpreted as a sign of divine favor and a reward for faithfulness to Yahweh's covenant.[309] Zechariah sketches eschatological security and bliss picturesquely as a time when "Once again men and women of ripe old age will sit in the streets of Jerusalem, each with cane in hand because of age, and the city streets will be filled with boys and girls playing there" (Zech 8:4, my translation). According to Isaiah 65:20, in the ideal world of the new heaven and the new earth everyone will grow old, and those who fail to reach a hundred will be considered accursed. The last statement touches on a notion that surfaces elsewhere in the Old Testament. Among the most severe curses that one person might invoke upon another was that he would die

---

[305]Cf. Gilgamesh's discovery of the plant called "Man Becomes Young in Old Age," *ANET*, p. 96.

[306]Cf. Ps 21:5 (Eng. 4); 61:7 (Eng. 6). To this day in the Middle East old age is held in such high esteem that people will often exaggerate their age. Cf. Patai, *Family, Love and the Bible*, p. 207.

[307]Cf. Jacob's apparently modest answer to Pharaoh's question in Gen 47:9: "The days of the years of my sojourning are one hundred and thirty years; few and stressful have been the days of the years of my life; nor have they matched the days of the years of the life of my fathers in the days of their sojournings" (my translation).

[308]Job 36:6, 14; Ps 55:16, 24 (Eng. 15, 23).

[309]Ex 20:12; Deut 6:2; 22:7; 25:15. Cf. Prov 16:31, "A gray head is a crown of glory; it is found in the conduct of righteousness," and Prov 17:6, "Grandchildren are the crown of old men; the glory of sons is their fathers." Note also the idealization of old age in Ps 92:13-15 (Eng. 12-14) and Sir 25:6.

young.[310] Another form of the curse expressed a similarly malevolent intent: "Do not let his gray head go down to the grave in peace" (*šālôm*, 1 Kings 2:6 NIV).

The responsibilities of the elderly in the household. Obviously the waning of health in old age limited the economic contributions that senior members could make to a family unit. However, so long as they were able, aging females would assist in food preparation, making and mending clothes, and tending infants. As the energy of aging males diminished, they would stay closer to the house and provide assistance with the physical maintenance of the home. However, inasmuch as it was generally recognized that with increased years came increased wisdom, with age these persons' spiritual and pedagogical importance in the home actually increased. The Old Testament does indeed recognize that wisdom does not automatically come with old age,[311] but it was accepted that under normal circumstances this would be the case. Accordingly, younger women would drink deeply from the practical wisdom of the matriarchs in housekeeping and child-rearing issues. The counsel of grandmothers would be especially important for mothers with young children and adolescent girls preparing for marriage. Meanwhile the younger men would appeal to senior males for wisdom in managing the household work force, disciplining unruly children and relating to neighbors. The experience and wisdom of the elderly were especially sought in the gate, where the town council, consisting of "elders," would meet to discuss issues that affected the broader community and adjudicate legal cases among the citizens.[312]

As long as he was able, the senior male member of the household would function as the spiritual head of the family. Although both Israel and Judah

---

[310]This is concretely reflected in the curse and experience of Eli and his family for their contemptuous treatment of their sacred office in 1 Sam 2:30-33. Note also that when Samuel was brought back from the dead, he appeared in his aged form, rather than as a rejuvenated person (1 Sam 28:14).

[311]Solomon demonstrated that it is possible to be old but foolish (1 Kings 11:1-8). The author of Eccles 4:13 seems to have had him in mind: "Better is a poor but wise youth than an old but foolish king, who will no longer take advice." Compare also Elihu's response to the apparent folly of Job's three "friends" in Job 32:8-9. Ps 119:100 specifically asserts that obedience to the Torah, rather than years, is the measure of one's wisdom. This conviction received even more pointed expression in the rabbinic writings. For references, see "Age and the Aged," *EncJud*, 1:345.

[312]Cf. C. J. H. Wright, "Family," *ABD*, 2:768; J. Conrad, *TDOT*, 4:126-31. This respect for elders accounts for the force of the title "Ancient of Days" (*ʿattîq yômîn*), used of God holding cosmic court in Dan 7:9, 13, 22.

were officially Yahwist in faith,[313] it is doubtful that at any time in the nation's history the entire population, or even a majority thereof, was actually exclusively devoted to Yahweh, as called for by Moses in the Torah (Deut 4—6). The biblical picture of pervasive religious syncretism against which Israelite prophets and historians railed is currently being fleshed out by a variety of onomastic, inscriptional and iconographic archaeological evidence.[314] This appears to have been true especially in the villages away from Jerusalem.

Apart from leading the household in daily expressions of devotion, in syncretistic contexts the senior male member of the household would have played a leading role in the annual clan sacrifice and meal at the local *bāmâ,* "high place."[315] These religious activities played an important social function in affirming clan solidarity among the living and with the dead and in legitimating the social order based upon patrilineal descent. An important part of the ritual appears to have been the presentation of libations and sacrifices to deceased ancestors on the assumption that those already "gathered to their people/fathers" participated in the cult and that their disposition in the netherworld continued to have a bearing on the economic and physical well-being of the clan.[316] Attendance at these annual events seems to have been mandatory, at least for all males.

In orthodox Yahwistic households the role of the senior member in spiritual affairs was equally important, though it took different forms: supervising the seventh-day Sabbath, instructing the household in the Torah (Deut 6:4-9; 11:18-25); officiating at the Passover celebrations, which were originally celebrated at home (Ex 12:1-28, 43-51) but after the temple had been built were transferred to Jerusalem (Deut 16:1-8; 2 Chron 30:1-27; 35:1-19); leading the family, particularly the male members, to the central shrine for the annual pilgrimage festivals (Passover and Unleavened Bread, Festival of

---

[313]This is self-evident for Judah, whose religious leaders were custodians of the Torah and guardians of the official worship of Yahweh in Jerusalem, but according to Jeroboam's inaugural speech in 1 Kings 12:28, it was also true of the syncretistic northern forms of worship. In any case, the prophets all insisted that Yahweh alone was the God of all Israel, north and south. See 2 Kings 17:7-18.

[314]For discussion and bibliography, see Daniel I. Block, *The Gods of the Nations: Studies in Ancient Near Eastern National Theology,* 2nd ed., ETS Studies (Grand Rapids, Mich.: Baker, 2000), pp. 62-71.

[315]The account of Micah and the Levites in Judg 17—18 illustrates the importance of the family shrine and the leadership role played by the senior male member in a syncretistic household. This case involves three generations, Micah's mother, Micah, and his son, who is consecrated as priest. Apparently Micah's father was deceased.

[316]For detailed discussion of clan religion in Israel, see van der Toorn, *Family Religion,* pp.181-265.

Booths, Festival of Weeks; Ex 23:14-19; 34:18-26; Deut 16:1-17); instructing the younger generation in the theological and soteriological significance of Israel's cult observances (Deut 6:20-25); in general keeping alive the traditions of Yahweh's election of the ancestors, his deliverance of the nation from the bondage of Egypt, his establishment of his covenant with Israel and the revelation of the covenant stipulations at Sinai, his providential care for Israel in the desert, and the fulfillment of his promise to the ancestors in dispossessing the Canaanites and delivering their land into Israelite control.

In ancient Israel people responded to the death of a family member with emphatic verbal and nonverbal gestures of mourning: tearing one's garments, donning sackcloth, going barefoot, removing headgear, covering the beard, veiling the face, putting dust on the head, rolling in the dust, sitting on the ash heap, fasting and loud lamentation.[317] Mutilation of the body and shaving of heads and beards were condemned because of their association with pagan rites (Lev 19:27-28; Deut 14:1). In accordance with the Decalogic command, children continued to honor their deceased parents out of religious conviction, but the worship of the dead or any attempts to communicate with the deceased were strictly prohibited.[318]

When senior citizens died, they were buried in a family tomb. Proper burial was deemed important by Israelites not only to respect the bodies of deceased relatives but also to prevent the contamination of the land.[319] The worst fate one could experience was to be left unburied and exposed for scavenging jackals and buzzards.[320] For the majority of the population, who possessed modest means, a proper burial meant digging a shallow hole in the ground in a specially designated plot of land, depositing the body and covering it with soil. For people in higher socioeconomic strata, this involved tombs cut in the rock. The tombs of the latter were often complex, consisting of a front room, where the recently deceased members were laid to rest on benches complete with head rests, and side rooms, where the bones of the deceased were secondarily deposited after decomposition to

---

[317]See de Vaux, *Ancient Israel*, pp. 58-61, for references.

[318]Deut 18:11. Cf. Lev 20:6, 27; 1 Sam 28:3, 9; 2 Kings 8:19; Is 8:19.

[319]Cf. Ezek 39:12-16. On Israelite customs concerning the dead, see Klaas Spronk, *Beatific Afterlife in Ancient Israel and in the Ancient Near East*, AOAT 219 (Neukirchen-Vluyn: Neukirchener Verlag, 1985), pp. 238-44; Elizabeth Bloch-Smith, *Judahite Burial Practices and Beliefs About the Dead*, JSOTSup 123 (Sheffield: JSOT Press, 1992), pp. 25-61, 110-21.

[320]On the ignominy of being denied proper burial, see Deut 28:25-26; 1 Kings 13:22; 14:10-11; Jer 16:4. For a discussion of Hebrew views of death and afterlife, especially as portrayed by Ezekiel, see Daniel I. Block, "Beyond the Grave," pp. 113-41, esp. 120-29. See also Daniel I. Block, *The Book of Ezekiel 24-48*, NICOT (Grand Rapids: Eerdmans, 1998), pp. 373-74.

make a bench available for the body of a newly deceased member of the family. By being "gathered to one's people" (Gen 49:29) in a family tomb established by a founder of a new clan, the unity of the family was maintained even after death.

CONCLUSION

Many of the issues raised in this summary essay on ancient Israelite views of marriage and family call for much more thorough investigation and more detailed discussion. Limitations of space have precluded an exhaustive presentation of the evidence as well as a consideration of all or even most of the contemporary interpretations of the evidence. Scholars differ widely in their evaluation of the Old Testament as a witness to ancient Israelite realities and even more widely in their understanding of that witness. The Old Testament was not written in a day; the evidence it provides derives from more than a millennium of Israelite history. Nevertheless, given the conservative nature of ancient Near Eastern culture in general and the theological underpinnings of Israelite customs in particular, these conclusions would have applied to many if not most Israelites during the Old Testament period.

Ancient Israelite perceptions of family were grounded in the theological conviction that all human beings are created as images of God and that our humanity is expressed first and foremost in the context of community. No individual is an island. Vertically, the lives of children were perceived as extensions of the lives of their parents, and horizontally, all found their identity and security in society, whose basic building block was the household, the *bêt 'āb*. As the designation suggests, in this patricentric culture the focal point of the family was the father, who exercised authority over the entire household but more importantly carried the welfare of each of its members on his shoulders. In contrast to extrabiblical writings, the Old Testament is remarkably frank in its portrayal of many fathers in less than ideal light. Since the Old Testament is, for the most part, a witness to the moral and spiritual shortcomings of a rebellious people, we should not be surprised if it recounts the actions of fathers who wielded unreasonable and abusive power. But this does not necessarily discredit patricentrism as a fundamentally abusive system. The well-being of any group is dependent upon the moral character of its leaders, regardless of how they attain their leadership positions.

According to the Old Testament ideal, the members of the household lived in a symbiotic relationship with one another; each person had his/her contributions to make to the economic and spiritual health of the family as a whole and of fellow members in particular. The kind of individualism and emphasis on one's personal rights evident in modern Western culture would have been rejected as fundamentally inimical to the well-being of the family unit. This perspective underlies as basic a document as the Decalogue. Inasmuch as the individual declarations are addressed to would-be perpetrators of offenses against others, it may be viewed as an ancient Bill of Rights, not with one's own interests in mind but emphasizing the interests of the next person. This is how the members of the family were to view their roles. Fathers provided leadership in the interests of the household. Mothers stood at their sides supporting the economy of the household and providing and caring for the children who represented the key to the family's continued existence. Since people who are concerned primarily about their own interests are by definition immature, the aim of education, which was family based, was to prepare young men and women to assume responsibility for the welfare of the family and the community in their adulthood. Fundamentally this would involve spiritual nurture, ensuring that all members of the household loved and feared Yahweh, treasured the memory of his saving and covenant-making acts, and demonstrated their own covenant commitment by walking in the ways of Yahweh and serving him with undivided loyalty (Deut 10:12-22). But it would also involve training in technical skills necessary for the economic well-being of the household and in social skills indispensable to its operation as a family unit.

It is in these regards that an exploration of the family in ancient Israel offers the greatest potential for resolving family and marital issues of our own day. If it is impossible to return to the social and cultural conditions prevailing before the industrial revolution and the invention of the microchip, how much more unreasonable would it be to attempt to reconstruct the social realities of Old Testament Israel. Nevertheless, the rediscovery of one's own identity as a member of a larger community, the investment of personal energies for the well-being of all, and the rekindling of faith as the basis of family cohesion represent three general lessons to be learned from the Old Testament view of family. The extent to which more specific elements of ancient family life may be applied to the modern context beckons further investigation.[321]

---

[321]I am grateful to Professor Peter Gentry for his kind attention to this paper and his helpful bibliographic suggestions, and to Kenneth Turner and Gregory Smith for their assistance in stylistic matters.

3

Marriage and Family in Ancient Greek Society

S. M. BAUGH

In one sense, the Greek family is nothing special: a man, a wife, some children, and perhaps an aged parent living out his or her final few years. These aspects of the Greek family are common to families in all cultures and hardly worth extended treatment. What we want to know are the aspects of the Greek family that are, well, *Greek*—aspects that separate ancient Greek society from other peoples.

But this assumes that there was such a thing as a homogeneous Greek family. There were common features to families throughout the Greek world, but there were some very glaring anomalies as well—like the Spartans—which make the composition of a hypothetical "Greek family" somewhat problematic. Nevertheless, I will talk about a stable, unified "Greek family" as if it existed over the many centuries from the classical to the New Testament period. Though this raises technical problems, these will be ignored for now. In the end, I hope we find that the broad, generalizing description to follow will yield a faithful portrait, even if it is executed in a Monet-esque style. The approach in this essay will be rather simple: I will describe the family according to a natural progression as one would experience it from an adult viewpoint: from marriage to the bearing and raising of children to old age.

We will pause from time to time to consider topics or ancient sources of special interest. I have indulged in this essay in lengthy quotations of ancient sources out of conviction that none speak as powerfully as the ancients themselves; it is otherwise too easy to make cardboard cutouts out of the real people of that time.

SPARTA

Since I mentioned Sparta, it might be well to describe this curious society very briefly. Spartan organization drew extensive comment from contemporary Greeks and later generations of writers. As a way of coping with internal problems arising from their subjugation of a native people group called the *helots,* the Spartans evolved a unique society centering on the military service of their youths.

At age seven, a Spartan boy entered the *agoge,* or "public upbringing," which separated him from his family. He was enrolled in a rigorous program of self-denial and military training. There was hazing by the older youths, not unlike that found in military academies, and the boys lived in barracks or messes *(sysskania* or *pheiditia).* At age twenty, the boy could marry, but he also joined the army and—provided that he could pay the required supporting fee of produce from his family's private holding (worked by *helots)*—he joined one of the fifteen adult messes and its barracks life. It is thought that homosexual and pederast activities characterized life in the mess. In some ways this was encouraged; since the mess formed a military unit, these practices were thought to foster the camaraderie needed to stand fast in the phalanx when facing the spears of the enemy. In any event, family life for men in their military years was considerably restricted in Sparta, and the bearing and raising of children by the two or three thousand Spartan citizens was all geared toward this public military life.

In one sense, Spartan society was not essentially different from that in other Greek states: the rearing of male children was oriented toward the military needs of the state. An institution that survived long after the Greek states lost their independence to various imperial powers, including that of Rome, was a club for elite youths who were enrolled as *ephebes,* which served as a military training organization sponsored by the city-state. But the *ephebate* was first clearly attested in the Hellenistic era (though it survived for many centuries later), and it never shaped Greek societies the way that the Spartan barracks did Sparta.

FOUNDATION OF THE GREEK FAMILY

The ancient Greeks regarded Spartan society as a curiosity, though a much-admired one to be sure. Nevertheless, the family structure of Sparta illustrates three principles that characterize the Greek family in general and will come up again as we examine the details of the family in the Greek world. First, the Greek family was essentially utilitarian. It was not romantically idealized in general. Family for the Greeks was an institution that produced certain utilitarian benefits: (1) workers for the farm; (2) a new crop of recruits for the state's army; and (3) a source of provision and security in one's old age and continuity of the *oikos* (roughly "household"; but much broader at times) and its vital religious observance. The second and third principles belong together in ironic union: the Greeks were at once very conservative and quite innovative in their social structures, evidenced in the family. Greek families were the one stable component of an otherwise shifting political scene, yet the Greek city-state was always challenging the family's authority over its citizens and pushing the family to change. These three principles are basic elements of the Greek family, to which we now turn.

MARRIAGE

A Greek family began with the marriage of a Greek man to a Greek woman. Nothing surprising about that. But perhaps I should specify that at Athens—about which we know much more than we do about other Greek city-states—a law was passed in 451 B.C. to the effect that an Athenian family was to be composed of an *Athenian* man married to an *Athenian* woman. If the Athenian married a non-Athenian, no matter how *Greek* the non-Athenian wife or husband might be, the children could not be Athenian citizens.

If this seems blatantly chauvinistic, it was. Greeks typically dismissed foreigners as "barbarians," i.e., "non-Greek," and their loyalty to their city-states in the classical period knew no bounds. However, the motive for the move by the Athenians was said to have been to ensure that the poorer Athenian girls could find husbands. "For who would ever have taken to wife a non-dowered girl?" asked Demosthenes.[1] If Athenian men were allowed to produce legitimate, citizen children from foreign wives, not only would the pure Athenian blood be diluted—which was important because the Athenians believed that they had sprung from the Attic soil (they were "autochthonous")—but their ancestral religious practices would be compromised.

The case of Neaira in a law-court speech by Demosthenes (384-322 B.C.) is a case in point, so let us spend a little time with this interesting example of Greek marriage. Neaira was purchased as a young child by an amateur procurer who raised her and six other girls to become entertainer-prostitutes (*hetairai*). *Hetairai* were girls trained in music, dancing and conversational skills who would be contracted out to entertain and to provide sexual services at male banquets (*symposia*).

---

[1] Demosthenes *Against Neaira* 8; see *Against Neaira* 113, where Demosthenes mentions an Athenian law that provided dowries for poor girls "if nature has endowed her with even moderate comeliness." The translation here and for all classic literature is that given in the Loeb Classical Library (LCL) by Harvard University Press unless otherwise indicated, and all abbreviations are those used in the *Oxford Classical Dictionary (OCD)*.

After serving for some time with the procurer in Corinth, Neaira was purchased by two unmarried men who shared her services until the time came for them to marry. Neaira then purchased her freedom with the help of another of her lovers, and after a series of adventures, she attached herself to a roguish Athenian by the name of Stephanos. He brought Neaira to Athens and portrayed her to the world as his legitimate Athenian wife. In the meantime, he set her up privately as a *hetaira* as a source of income, sometimes seizing her clients as adulterers with his "wife" (a crime that carried the death penalty at Athens) and requiring large ransoms for their release.

Stephanos' legal problems began when he presented Neaira's daughter (conceived from some other father) as an Athenian citizen in marriage to an Athenian burgher named Phrastor. When Phrastor learned in due time that his wife, named Phano, was no citizen, he divorced her and refused to return her dowry. When Stephanos threatened litigation to get Phano's dowry back, Phrastor counter-threatened the charge that Stephanos had presented an alien woman to an Athenian as though an Athenian, the penalty of which if proven carried the forfeiture of citizenship and all property. But none of this went to court at that time, and later Phrastor adopted his son by Phano and tried unsuccessfully to have the boy enrolled as an Athenian citizen into his clan.

In the meantime, Phano, the daughter of Neaira, was somehow married off to Dionysos, the King Archon, one of the three highest officials in Athens, whose duties included supervision of the state's religious ceremonies.[2] This now brings Stephanos into deep trouble because, as wife of the King Archon, Phano participated in critical religious rites for the prosperity of the state, especially when she "offered on the city's behalf the sacrifices which none may name."[3] It was a most grave breach of law for an alien even to witness this unnamable rite and therefore the most heinous of crimes for an alien to participate in as a priestess. Divine vengeance upon the city must surely follow.

This ends the story of Neaira since Demosthenes' speech was the case for the prosecution and its outcome is not recorded. It is of interest that the punishment for the numerous crimes in the Neaira case included confiscation of

---

[2]It would be a mistake to underestimate the importance of these ceremonies and this office. This is not really like a United States president's attendance at a prayer breakfast. The official cults of a Greek state were taken very, very seriously because they were believed to give the state divine protection in a perilous world.

[3]Demosthenes *Against Neaira* 73.

property, heavy fines, and disenfranchisement for Stephanos and enslavement and public sale for Neaira and Phano. There are several elements operating in the background of the case of Neaira that are worth brief discussion for our understanding of Greek marriage and family.

First, we observe how the two young men who originally bought Neaira from the procurer had shared her services between them.[4] This does not seem to be unusual and is explained by the fact that Greek men were often married at around age thirty. Greek youths were not expected to remain celibate until the time of their marriage, and so they often utilized the services of *betairai* as mistresses. Witness in this connection the following passage from the only complete play by Menander (ca. 343-292 B.C.), *Dyskolos* ("Old Cantankerous"):

> [The hero of the play, Sostratos, falls in love with a free girl and tells his friend Chaireas ("a good friend, and a practical man, too") in order to help get her father to agree to the marriage (the father is the "old cantankerous" Knemon). Chaireas responds:] In such matters, Sostratos, my line is this. A friend asks me for help—he's in love with a call-girl *(betaira)*. I go straight into action, grab her, carry her off, get drunk, burn the door down, and deaf to all reason. Before even asking her name, the thing to do is to get her. Delay increases passion dangerously, but quick action produces quick relief. But if a friend is talking about marriage and a free girl, then I take a different line. I check on family, finance and character. For now I'm leaving my friend a permanent record of my professional efficiency.[5]

Hence, a liaison with a *betaira* is one thing—and common enough at that—but marriage to a free girl was quite another matter, for it required checking into the quality of the girl's family and the quantity of her dowry. So, first, this story makes the distinction between free and slave.

Second, the story of Neaira shows clearly that a father or other legal guardian *(kyrios)* married off a Greek girl. And I use the term *girl* here intentionally to convey an important point to keep in mind: Greek girls were typically married at age fourteen and sometimes earlier, even though their

---

[4] Cf. Acts 16:16-19 for another slave-girl owned by more than one master, in this case, a demon-possessed fortune-teller.

[5] *Menander Plays and Fragments,* trans. Norma Miller (London: Penguin, 1987), lines 58-67. I changed Miller's translation from "'nice' girl" in line 65 to "free girl" to be more precise to the Greek; cf. the Loeb rendering: "Say a man suggests marriage, a free girl." See also the first-century A.D. author Babrius, whose retelling of Aesop's fables include one of a middle-aged man with two mistresses who "was still spending his time on love affairs and carousals" (Babrius, Fable 22). It is clear that a middle-aged man was expected to have settled down by that time of life.

bridegrooms may have been much older, commonly about thirty.[6]

This early age of marriage explains why a girl was betrothed and married at the instigation of her father, who acted as her legal guardian *(kyrios)* and the provider of her dowry. It was very rare for a girl to choose her husband, though elopements do appear in ancient literature from time to time (e.g., Medea and Jason in the *Argonautika,* book 4). We often read of girls in Greek literature who, on their first venture into public—usually chaperoned—run headlong into either love or trouble (e.g., Chariton's Callirhoe). Respectable girls spent their earliest days in the women's quarters of the home (below), so they had little opportunity to fall in love before their betrothal to a stranger. They probably saw few men besides household members in their early years.

Third, the subject of the dowry appears in the Neaira story. The size of a girl's dowry often appears as a critical issue in the suitability of a Greek girl for marriage in our ancient sources, which was regarded by the Greeks as a merger of two families, not just the wedding of two individuals. W. K. Lacey writes in this connection:

> Nobody failed to give a dowry if he could help it; an uncle, it is said, guardian to four nieces and one nephew, would be sure to see that the girls were given dowries; friends gave dowries to the daughters of the poor; the daughters of *thetes,* the lowest financial class, who lacked brothers had by law to be given dowries by their relatives in accordance with their means; even the state stepped in very occasionally (in return for outstanding public services) to dower a man's daughters. . . . Dowries consisted of cash, or real-estate valued in cash. . . . Widows on their remarriage received dowries in exactly the same way as unmarried girls, and this is only natural since a woman's dowry was deemed to be her share of her paternal estate, a share set apart for her maintenance, and it is an unfailing principle of Athenian law that the head of the family who had a woman's dowry in his possession had to maintain her.[7]

Although a woman's dowry was in the control of her husband, it remained her property. If a man divorced his wife, he usually sent her back

---

[6]For instance, the girl in Menander's play is called a *pais eleuthera,* or *kore eleuthera,* "free girl." Importantly, the girl is never named in the play since she appears more as an object to be obtained than as a character in her own right. For the age of marriage in the Greek world, see Sarah B. Pomeroy, *Families in Classical and Hellenistic Greece: Representations and Realities* (Oxford: Clarendon, 1997), pp. 5-7; and Walter K. Lacey, *The Family in Classical Greece* (Ithaca, N.Y.: Cornell University Press, 1968), pp. 106-7.

[7]Lacey, *Family in Classical Greece,* p. 109; cf. Stephen C. Todd, *The Shape of Athenian Law* (Oxford: Clarendon, 1993), pp. 215-16.

to her father's household and had to return the dowry (as we saw in the case of Neaira's daughter). If the husband died, the widow's dowry provided for her maintenance (since she typically did not inherit her husband's property) and served as an inheritance for her children.

And finally, the Neaira case shows how state citizenship and marriage could be intertwined. In time the Greek city-states did create a kind of marriage reciprocity, so that a citizen of one state could have a spouse who was a citizen of the other state with reciprocal rights. The children would then be citizens of the state where the couple lived. And citizenship in the Greek states was a very important issue involving one's access to legal protections, ownership of property and involvement (and its perceived benefits) in the state cults.

One quickly gets the point that romantic ideals, like falling in love, were not always paramount in the issue of finding an appropriate spouse in the Greek world. In this connection the homey advice of Hesiod (ca. 700 B.C.) shows the utilitarian thrust of acquiring a wife in his agrarian society:

> Bring home a wife to your house when you are of the right age, while you are not far short of thirty years nor much above; this is the right age for marriage. Let your wife have been grown up four years, and marry her in the fifth. Marry a maiden, so that you can teach her careful ways, and especially marry one who lives near you, but look well about you and see that your marriage will not be a joke to your neighbours. For a man wins nothing better than a good wife, and, again, nothing worse than a bad one, a greedy soul who roasts her man without fire, strong though he may be, and brings him to a raw old age.[8]

BETROTHAL

Marriage legally began among the Greeks with betrothal, which was usually arranged between the husband-to-be and the bride's father or other legal guardian *(kyrios)* (her brothers, uncle or another male relative). In some cases a bride-gift was offered to the bride's father as incentive to accept the suitor (e.g., *Daphnis and Chloe* 3.25), though this was not strictly required.

For instance, in Menander's play, *Dyskolos,* mentioned earlier, the "old cantankerous" Knemon changes his spots after being rescued from falling down a well and turns over all his affairs to his son, Gorgias, then leaves the scene. Gorgias is now the legal guardian of his sister, so the hero Sostratos seizes his chance by asking Gorgias to betroth his sister to him. Gorgias says, "But these matters require your father's permission." Sostratos assures him

---

[8]Hesiod *Opera et dies* 695-705.

that his father will accede to his desires, so Gorgias recites the proper words: "Well then, I hereby betroth (her) to you in the sight of all the gods."[9] These words, although solemn enough and with the invocation of the gods and therefore legally binding, are missing an important customary ingredient: the specification of the dowry (which Gorgias adds later as one talent).[10] The play is not finished with betrothals since Sostratos plans to acquire Gorgias as husband for his sister. He finally persuades Gorgias of this, and Sostratos' father seals the bargain with the proper formula: "I hereby betroth to you my daughter now, young lad, for the harvest of legitimate children, and as dowry I bestow on her three talents".[11] (The legitimacy of the children refers to their proper Athenian citizenship status.) In none of these places is the bride-to-be consulted or even present during the betrothal; from other evidence this seems to be standard Greek practice.

With such a simple betrothal ceremony, often accompanied by a handshake before witnesses, two Greek families were now agreed to unite. It only remained to set the date of the marriage, which might be as early as later that day or within a day or two if the girl was of marriageable age—Demosthenes' sister was engaged at age five, so the wedding itself was sometimes some years off.

MARRIAGE RITES

The wedding ceremony itself ideally took place over a three-day period: the *proteleia* (pre-consummation) was a day of preparation and sacrifice; the wedding day (*proaulia,* "before the courtyard") itself culminated in the consummation of the marriage that night; and the day after was called the *epaulia* (after the courtyard). Each day had its special significance. This was the ideal Greek marriage sequence, though variations are known of course.[12]

The day before the wedding, the *proteleia,* was given over to sacrifices and other preparations for the wedding day itself. Theophrastus (ca. 370-286 B.C.), in his character sketches, says of the ungenerous man: "When he mar-

---

[9] *Dyskolos,* lines 762-763. Notice that even here the girl is not named.

[10] *Dyskolos,* line 845.

[11] *Dyskolos,* lines 842-844. The editor of the Loeb edition of *Dyskolos* adds the following note to this line: "The formula of betrothal, with its quaintly agricultural wording, seems to correspond with the one in use in contemporary Athens. The announcement about the dowry (whose size here is well above the comic norm . . .) was an integral part of the ceremony." Similar words of betrothal are found in another fragmentary play by Menaner (*Perikeiromene,* lines 1013-14).

[12] For what follows, see John Oakley and Rebecca Sinos, *The Wedding in Ancient Athens* (Madison: University of Wisconsin Press, 1993).

ries off his daughter, he sells the meat from the sacrifice except for the priests' share, and hires staff for the wedding feast who must bring their own dinners."[13] The meat sold here is from the preparatory sacrifice that the family has made to ensure the favor of the gods upon the couple.

Other ritual acts of preparation for marriage included baths for both bride and groom, though the bride's seems the more important ritual. For the groom, especially since he had normally passed already through boyhood into the adult stage, the transition represented in marriage was not as dramatic as it was for the bride, whose marriage usually represented the first stage of her entry into adulthood. Because of this, the rites for the bride included a bath with water usually drawn from some special sacred place, such as a particular spring, and carried in a special water jar in a procession. Many of these jars, called *loutrophoroi,* "bath-carriers," have been found adorned with paintings of the processions of which they were a part.[14]

Further preparatory rites for the bride included her dedication of the tokens of her childhood to a goddess, often to Artemis, the virgin goddess who watched over girls and women in childbirth. For instance, an anonymous epigram records just such a dedication:

Timarete, the daughter of Timaretos, before her wedding, has dedicated her tambourine, her pretty ball, the net that shielded her hair, her hair, and her girls' dresses to Artemis of the Lake, a girl to a girl, as is fit. You, daughter of Leto, hold your hand over the child Timarete, and protect the pure girl in a pure way.[15]

The reference to Timarete's purity here is a reference to her sexual purity or chastity, which was expected of Greek girls but not of their youths. Another epigram reads: "Alcibia dedicated to Hera the holy veil of her hair, when she entered into lawful wedlock."[16] Alcibia dedicated locks of her hair, which functioned for a girl as her "sacred head-covering" *(hiere kalyptre),* which is of interest for the interpretation of 1 Corinthians 11:5-6.

Not all Greek brides, of course, were young girls. Widows were often remarried in the Greek world.[17] This was especially likely since these women

---

[13]Theophrastus *Characteres* 22.4.

[14]There are many plates of these jars conveniently included by Oakley and Sinos in *The Wedding in Ancient Athens.*

[15]As cited in ibid., p. 14. The phrase "her girls' dresses" may actually refer to "her dolls' dresses."

[16]*Greek Anthology* 6.133. See also 6.207 (a dedication from several girls) and 6.276 (an unwed girl who had apparently passed the ordinary age for marriage offering the tokens of her childhood in hope of marriage and children).

[17]E.g., 1 Cor 7:8; 1 Tim 5:14; Hyperides *Lycophron* 6.

may have been married in their early teens and widowed while still in their twenties or thirties (not that marriage later in life is unheard of either). Marriage at such an early age for Greek women should be interpreted in the light of their average life expectancy of about thirty-six years (forty-two to forty-five years for men), caused especially by the high mortality rate of women during childbirth.[18]

Following the preparation, the second day of marriage was the wedding day itself (*proaulia; gamos* is the wedding proper). The preparatory sacrifices and dedications have been made, the house has been decorated with ribbons and greenery, and the wedding guests have been invited in preparation for this second day of festivities.

But where our Judeo-Christian heritage today (even in modern Greece) has a vow-taking ceremony officiated by a member of the clergy, the ancient Greeks had no equivalent. The only formal agreement involved in the Greek marriage had already taken place between the husband-to-be and the future father-in-law at the betrothal. That was the vow-taking as it were. This is not to say that the ancient Greeks regarded marriage as a secular event in the modern sense, quite the contrary; but the uniting of man and wife in ancient Greece was accomplished during the private sexual union on their wedding night.

If there was no "clergy ceremony" per se, it was because the Greek wedding day was a time of feasting and celebration among the family and family-connected community (both of which included the gods in their conception). A wedding was, as it were, a merger of two families. Indeed, one important ancient author, Plutarch (ca. A.D. 50-120) says this in passing, "The right guests for a banquet in honour of a political leader are public officials and civic leaders, if they are friends. At weddings and birthday parties, it is relatives, those who share in the worship of Zeus, Protector of the Family."[19] Here we see both that the relatives are directly involved as wedding guests because the wedding was a family event and that the worship of "Zeus, Protector of the Family" or even "Zeus the Family Member" (*homognios*) was what bound these people into a family unit.[20] The common wor-

---

[18]See Pomeroy, *Families in Classical and Hellenistic Greece,* pp. 6-7.

[19]Plutarch *Quaestiones convivialum libri IX* 5.5 (*Moralia* 679C-D).

[20]See Sophocles' play *Tereus,* in which a woman talks of the sweet life of a girl in her father's home until "when we reach puberty . . . we are thrust out and sold away from our ancestral gods and from our parents" in marriage to a stranger and his ancestral gods (Mary R. Lefkowitz and Maureen B. Fant, *Women's Life in Greece and Rome* [Baltimore: Johns Hopkins University Press, 1982], no. 32).

ship of certain gods in the Greek world, especially of ancestral gods, was often seen as a tie that bound a family or state together.

The wedding day, then, was a day filled with feasting and flowing wine among family and close friends. The size and cost of this gathering could overwhelm the resources of some families, causing it to become a topic of interest to the ancient Greeks. Plutarch again in his "Table-Talk" records a conversation on the subject at the wedding of his son, which reads in part:

> [One of the wedding guests by name of Senecio introduced the topic of the larger number of guests at weddings than at other parties:] For it is true, [Senecio] observed, that those lawgivers who have campaigned most vigorously against extravagance have particularly sought to limit the number of guests at weddings. . . . [And] the comic poets attack those who celebrate a wedding in a prodigal and ostentatious style, with splendid dinners and great outlay. . . . It is that of all the occasions for a banquet, none is more conspicuous or talked about than a wedding. When we offer sacrifice to the gods, or honour a friend on the eve of a journey, or entertain guests from abroad, it is possible to do so unnoticed by many of our intimates and relatives; but a wedding-feast betrays us by the loud marriage cry, the torch, and the shrill pipe, things which according to Homer even the women stand at their doors to watch and admire. Consequently, since no one is unaware that we are receiving guests and must have invited them, we include all our relatives, acquaintances, and connections of any degree, because we are afraid to leave anyone out.[21]

The passage in Plutarch contains many elements worth a bit of comment. First, the ostentatious size of the wedding feast was evidently a common topic of table conversation, treatment in comic plays, and even legislation designed to limit the extravagance.[22] Second, the wedding feast was a grand public event, and the families were "afraid to leave anyone out." Finally, Plutarch refers to "the loud marriage cry, the torch, and the shrill pipe, things which according to Homer even the women stand at their doors to watch and admire." The Homeric reference here is to the famous shield of Achilles emblazoned in part with the following scene by the craftsman god Hephaestos:

> Therein fashioned he also two cities of mortal men exceeding fair. In the one there were marriages and feastings, and by the light of the blazing torches they were leading the brides from their bowers through the city, and loud rose the bridal song *[hymenaios]*. And young men were whirling in the dance, and in

---

[21]Plutarch *Quaestiones convivialum libri IX* 4.2 (*Moralia* 666F-667A).
[22]Similarly, Roman officials sometimes tried to curb lavish expenditure in Greek state religious festivals during the imperial period.

their midst flutes and lyres sounded continually; and there the women stood each before her door and marvelled.[23]

The two passages from Homer and Plutarch are separated by eight or nine centuries, but both present the same essential elements of the wedding day. The wedding guests were treated to a grand feast and to the dancing of elaborate folk dances. To top off the day, the friends of the bride and others, in some cases under the supervision of the groom himself or of his deputy, would join in a procession to escort the bride to her bridal chamber *(thalamos),* which the groom had prepared.

The bridal procession often included the bride riding with the groom on an ox-cart or in a chariot surrounded by the revelers. The presence of the latter posed something of a danger, for it was not proper in the Greek world for respectable women to be in the company of drunken men. In one case of the Hellenistic orator Hyperides (389-322 B.C.), the defendant Lycophron was accused of propositioning the bride during her ride to her bridal chamber. He responds:

> There must have been attenders, gentlemen of the jury, with the carriage that conveyed the bride: first a muleteer and a guide, and then her escort of boys, and also Dioxippus. For he was in attendance, too, since she was a widow being given away in marriage. Was I then so utterly senseless, do you think, that with all those other people in the procession . . . I had the impudence to pass such comments on a free woman, in the hearing of everyone, and was not afraid of being strangled on the spot?[24]

The danger of "being strangled on the spot" was not overstatement, for Plutarch records a case of a merry-maker who suffered just such a fate after jumping onto the bridal chariot in drunken high spirits.[25]

The presence of torches was common in nocturnal processions of various sorts, but they appear again and again in our sources (including the many painted jars) as essential elements in the bridal procession. The marriage song or bridal song *(hymenaios)* also appears repeatedly as a part of the procession. Indeed, this traditional song was so identified with Greek marriage that it was used much like wedding bells might be used today. A sad epitaph in the *Greek Anthology* attributed to Erinna (350 B.C.?) mentions both the torches and bridal song:

---

[23]Homer *Iliad* 18.490-496.
[24]Hyperides *Lycophron* 4-5.
[25]Plutarch, "Bravery of Women," *Moralia* 244E.

I am the tomb of Baucis the bride, and as thou passest the much bewept pillar, say to Hades who dwells below "Hades, though art envious." To thee the fair letters thou seest on the stone will tell the most cruel fate of Bauco, how her bridegroom's father lighted her pyre with those very torches that had burnt while they sang the marriage hymn. And thou, Hymenaeus, didst change the tuneful song of wedding to the dismal voice of lamentation.[26]

At the end of the procession the bride had to be introduced into her new household "through the rite of *katachysmata,* the same rite as that by which newly acquired slaves were received into the house: when she first entered the house she was led to the hearth where nuts, figs, and other dried fruit and sweetmeats were showered over her and the bridegroom."[27] The hearth, its fire, and the attendant goddess, Hestia, were the symbolic center of the house, so that one commonly spoke of returning to one's "hearth" as even we might speak of "hearth and home" today.

The gods had been included in the marriage festivities all along, but as Plutarch mentions in his "Advice to Bride and Groom," there might be a special invocation of the goddess of fertility, Demeter, for the fertility of the couple: "Following close upon the time-honoured rites which the priestess of Demeter applied to you when you were retiring together to the bridal chamber, a discourse which equally touches both of you and swells the nuptial song will, I think, have a useful effect which will also accord with convention."[28]

At the end of all, however, was the bridal chamber and the marriage bed. Here, the wedding was consummated, and the Greek girl especially began her transition from girlhood to womanhood, which was not fully completed until she bore her first child.

The day after the wedding was the time for further rejoicing. The guests to the previous day's celebration were expected to appear with presents for the new couple. Theophrastus, again, writes of the "chiseler"—"When one of his friends is getting married, or marrying off a daughter, he leaves town some time before to avoid giving a present"[29]—so we cannot assume that everyone participated gladly in this aspect of the wedding! This was also the appropriate time for the father of the bride to bring the dowry, which was entrusted into the new husband's care as I mentioned above.

---

[26] *Greek Anthology* 7.712.
[27] "Marriage Ceremonies," *OCD*.
[28] Plutarch *Moralia* 138B.
[29] Theophrastus *Characteres* 30.19.

THE NEW COUPLE

Now that a Greek couple was married, their expectations for married life come into view. First, I should mention an important point assumed so far: Greek marriage was monogamous. The only cases of polygamy known among the Greeks occurred in severe, extended wartime when women were allowed to share a husband in order to raise children to restock the army. Otherwise, the Greeks were monogamous. This makes the references to "husband of one wife" (e.g., 1 Tim 3:2, 12; Tit 1:6) or "wife of one husband" (1 Tim 5:9) in the New Testament interesting and potentially misleading, because it makes it appear that polygamy was practiced then.

There are two options for understanding these statements about "husband of one wife" or "wife of one husband." The first is that the man or woman involved must not be divorced and remarried. Divorce in the Greek world was common enough as we shall see. The second option is that of concubinage, which was widespread and commonly accepted among both the Greeks and Romans.[30]

Adultery was conceived of by the Greeks as a sexual liaison of a free married woman with a man (married or not).[31] At Athens, a husband in such a case was forbidden to live with the adulteress on pain of disenfranchisement (the adulterer lost his life). The adulteress could no longer attend any public religious rites; if she did, she could be subjected to any punishment short of death with impunity for those who publicly shamed and abused her.[32]

However, it was not adultery per se for a Greek husband to have affairs with *hetairai* at dinner parties or to keep a mistress outside the home or to have one or more concubines among the slave-girls in his household[33] as we learn from Dio Chrysostom: "Do not many Athenian men have intercourse with their maidservants, some of them secretly, but others quite

---

[30]For the Romans, note how off-handedly Pliny the Younger mentions in *Epistles* 3.14 the concubines of a certain Roman killed by his slaves as just one example. For an important recent study related to this issue, see Jennifer A. Glancy, "Obstacles to Slaves' Participation in the Corinthian Church," *JBL* 117 (1998): 481-501.

[31]Adultery was conceived of as a sin against "the gods of her family . . . the gods to whom she swore to join with her own ancestors and her relatives in the sharing of life and the begetting of children according to law" (Lefkowitz and Fant, *Women's Life in Greece and Rome*, no. 107).

[32]Demosthenes *Against Neaira* 87.

[33]Relations of married Greek women with lovers among the household slaves does not seem to be as common.

openly?"[34] Other evidence for this practice is widespread.[35] In speaking of this in his advice to a new bride, Plutarch reasons that a wife should appreciate that the husband is preserving his wife's high character:

> If therefore a man in private life, who is incontinent and dissolute in regard to his pleasures, commit some peccadillo with a paramour [*hetaira*] or a maid-servant, his wedded wife ought not to be indignant or angry, but she should reason that it is respect for her which leads him to share his debauchery, licentiousness, and wantonness with another woman.[36]

This is curious reasoning, of course, but it represents the Greek attitude well. That this would be common in the Greek world makes sense when we recall that a Greek man who weds at age thirty was probably used to regular promiscuity at dinner parties *(symposia)* or perhaps with a *hetaira* he owned outright as in the case of Neaira. It would have marked a significant change of lifestyle for him to suddenly become faithful to one woman, especially when promiscuity with *hetairai* or slave-girls—as well as with boys[37]—was generally accepted practice for husbands in the Greek world.[38]

---

[34]*De servitute et libertate ii* (*Or.* 15) 5.

[35]For instance, a Greek fable tells of a man who fell in love with his one of his ill-bred slave girls and openly exhibited her so that "she, bedecked with golden ornaments and trailing a delicate crimson robe about her shanks, would take every occasion to quarrel with the mistress of the house" (Babrius, Fable 10). In Egypt, an impassioned letter thought to be from a slave concubine to her master, Apollonius, says, "I beg you, lord, if it please you, to send for me; if not, I die, because I don't see you day by day" (P.Giess. 17, in *Select Papyri*, ed. Arthur S. Hunt and Campbell C. Edgar, vol. 1, LCL [Cambridge, Mass.: Harvard University Press, 1988], n. 115). And in his advice on education, Plutarch begins his essay by saying as a matter of course that siring children through *hetairai* and concubines *(pollakai)* was less desirable than with one's wife ("The Education of Children," *Moralia* 1B); compare the gallant Megapenthes, who was borne to Menelaus by a slave (no name given) "when it was clear that he could hope for no other children from Helen" (Homer *Odyssey* 4, lines 11-12).

[36]Plutarch *Moralia* 140B.

[37]The subject of pederasty does not properly appear in an essay on marriage and the family, but this practice among the Greeks is widely attested in literary, epigraphic and material (art) evidence. However, that pederasty was not approved by all in the Greek world can also be shown. For instance, in his essay on the "Education of Children," Plutarch feels it necessary to comment on whether a father should discourage his son from associations with "the admirers of boys" (thereby showing how common this practice was). Plutarch himself is of two opinions but mentions that some fathers oppose the practice altogether (*Moralia* 11D-12D). Also in Longus's novel, *Daphnis and Chloe*, a pederast attracted to the youth Daphnis appears in a most unfavorable light (book 4).

[38]There are exceptions to this statement, of course. For instance, a marriage contract from Hellenistic Egypt (which seems to be where and when these originated) binds the husband not to keep a concubine or a boy (*P.Tebt.* 104 [92 B.C.], in *Select Papyri*, vol. 1).

We must also mention the issue of divorce. Divorce for the Greeks could be initiated by either party (or even by the wife's father) and was usually the result of some failure to provide the basic requirements of the implicit contract; for instance, house and board or legitimate children. Dio Chrysostom (ca. A.D. 40-110), for instance, clearly alludes to the latter in a dialogue on slavery when one of his characters says, "Yes, I know that freeborn women often palm off other persons' children as their own on account of their childlessness, when they are unable to conceive children themselves, because each one wishes to keep her own husband and her home."[39] It is clear that a Greek woman might fear divorce for childlessness. A man could also divorce his wife out of his obligation to marry a female heiress within his clan (*epikleros;* see below).[40]

There was really little form or legal procedure to divorce for the Greeks. The husband merely sent his wife and her dowry back to her father's household. The wife simply left and would either demand the dowry then or leave it to her legal *kyrios* to obtain for her.

But now, back to the ideal Greek couple. We possess a most illuminating treatise from Xenophon (b. 430 B.C.), called the *Oeconomicus,* on the subject of the proper (if idealized) functioning of a Greek household. In addition, written almost five hundred years later, Plutarch's advice to a newly married couple is also quite important. Let us look at both pieces *seriatim.*

Xenophon writes of a dialogue between Socrates and a wealthy Athenian by the name of Ischomachus, who appears as the head of a model Athenian household. The conversation turns quickly to the capability of Ischomachus' wife to manage things at home so that he can conduct his affairs, including the management of the family farm, outside the confines of the home. Socrates asks whether his wife came to him well prepared for her household management tasks or he had trained her. Ischomachus responds, "Why, what knowledge could she have had, Socrates, when I took her for my wife? She was not yet fifteen years old when she came to me, and up to that time she had lived in leading-strings, seeing, hearing and saying as little as possible."[41]

As Xenophon's dialogue proceeds, we find Ischomachus outlining the

---

[39] *De servitute et libertate ii (Or.* 15) 8.
[40] Cf. Lacey, *Family in Classical Greece,* pp. 108-9.
[41] *Oeconomicus* 7.5.

duties for his wife (who, typically, is not named in the piece[42]). In general, we are told, the divinely established order makes it more honorable for a woman to work inside the home and the man to work the fields (as well as to fight in the many Greek wars). In agrarian societies where 85 to 90 percent of all occupations outside the home were devoted to food production, this kind of division of labor is not uncommon.

The first duty of Ischomachus and his wife was to bear children for the propagation of the race as well as to support them in their old age.[43] Next, the wife's household management itself is detailed: she was to superintend the work of the household slaves and to care for them when ill, to spin and to weave wool (including teaching slave-girls the art), to manage and to inventory stores from the farm, and to manage the household accounts.[44] One can imagine how intimidating this might be for a fourteen-year-old girl at first, but Ischomachus assures his wife that their household is a partnership and that she is a vital part of their prosperity. In the end, the duties of the woman seem to go far beyond the picture one gets from such characters as Penelope in the *Odyssey* of a woman at leisure confined to the spinning of wool. It begins to resemble the picture painted in Proverbs 31 of a broad-ranging series of important responsibilities in household management.

This idea of partnership and of the idealized symbiotic relationship in marriage for the husband and wife with clearly defined roles also character-izes Plutarch's "Advice to Bride and Groom" (and other Greek sources), even though Plutarch's essay focuses more upon ethical behavior and the character of each marriage partner. Yet from Plutarch we glean a few other tidbits that illumine our picture of Greek marriage. One most notable is his advice to the bride not to use magical arts to capture her husband's love:

> Fishing with poison is a quick way to catch fish and an easy method of taking them, but it makes the fish inedible and bad. In the same way women who artfully employ love-potions and magic spells upon their husbands, and gain the mastery over them through pleasure, find themselves consorts of dull-wit-ted, degenerate fools.[45]

---

[42] We possess a number of Greek inscriptions stating that a donation is from a man, who is named, "and wife," e.g., "Publius Hordeonius Lollianus with wife and children . . . Tib. Clau-dius Metrodorus with wife and children . . . Hesperus son of Demetrius with his sons . . . Hierax son of Hermokratus with wife . . . " (Herman Wankel et al., eds., *Die Inschriften von Ephesus* [Bonn: Rudolf Habelt, 1979-1984], p. 20).

[43] *Oeconomicus* 7.19.

[44] See *Oeconomicus* 7.16-22 for an overview.

[45] *Moralia* 139A; see also 141C.

Instead, he says, "A wife, then, ought not to rely on her dowry or birth or beauty, but on things in which she gains the greatest hold on her husband, namely conversation, character, and comradeship."[46] To further this end:

> A wife ought not to make friends of her own, but to enjoy her husband's friends in common with him. The gods are the first and most important friends. Wherefore it is becoming for a wife to worship and to know only the gods that her husband believes in, and to shut the front door tight upon all queer rituals and outlandish superstitions. For with no god do stealthy and secret rites performed by a woman find any favour.[47]

Plutarch's advice to the bride to become a comrade for her husband should be tempered with what we have noted before about many Greek men seeking companionship outside the home or with mistresses *(hetairai)*. The symposium ("dinner-party"; see the works by Plato and Xenophon by this title) was a central male institution in the Greek world finding expression in home architecture. Though material remains for private dwellings are scant in Greece proper, enough remains to show that most homes had an *andron* ("male-room"), which was a formal dining room where a man could entertain guests at dinner. The man's wife did not participate in these affairs, which typically involved heavy drinking and often included entertainments by *hetairai*.

The free women of the Greek house occupied their own area, the "women's quarters" *(gynaikeia),* though not confined to a particular room or always on the second floor. An instance of this division is evident as early as Homer, where in the *Odyssey,* Penelope never attends the feasts of her suitors but is confined to her quarters as much as possible. Note the following passage in which Telemachos tells his mother Penelope to "go to your chamber *[oikos],* and busy yourself with your own tasks, the loom and the distaff, and bid your handmaids to ply their tasks; but speech shall be for men, for all, but most of all for me; since mine is the authority in the house."[48] Penelope's "chamber" would be her quarters or that part of the *oikos* reserved for her and her maids. The picture this presents, then, is one where a husband and wife might have a somewhat formally demarcated relationship in the home and easily dwell in somewhat different spheres.

The picture we have drawn of Greek conjugal relations so far is one that might seem excised of all romantic charm. Yet various sources also indicate

---

[46] *Moralia* 141A.
[47] *Moralia* 140D.
[48] Homer *Odyssey* 1.356-59 (LCL trans. altered); cf. *Odyssey* 21.350-353; *Iliad* 690-93.

that the Greeks were not so very utilitarian that all thoughts of romance in marriage were absent. Quite the contrary. Romance leading to marriage, whether through elopements or children prevailing upon parents to agree to a marriage, was a common theme in Greek novels of the first few centuries after Christ. Despite all odds after horrific adventures, the couples in these romances always live happily ever after in marital bliss. In addition, there are quite a few grave epitaphs like the following, which evidences real marital affection: "'Farewell, tomb of Melite; a good woman lies here. You loved your husband Onesimus; he loved you in return. You were the best, and so he laments your death, for you were a good woman.' 'And to you farewell, dearest of men; love my children.'"[49] The reliefs on such grave stones often show the departed being affectionately sent off by family members.

Nevertheless, the basic function of Greek marriage was predominantly the bearing of legitimate children. It is in this light that we must understand the famous passage in Demosthenes' speech against Neaira, which is often quoted. His purpose here is to point out the true function of marriage, as follows:

> For this is what living with a woman as one's wife means—to have children by her and to introduce the sons to the members of the clan and of the deme, and to betroth the daughters to husbands as one's own. Mistresses *[hetairai]* we keep for the sake of pleasure, concubines *[pallakai]* for the daily care of our persons, but wives to bear us legitimate children and to be faithful guardians of our households.[50]

CHILDREN

For the vast majority of ancient Greeks who carved a tenuous and often meager living from the soil, the coming of children meant both the introduction of helpers in the home (girls) and on the farm (boys) to help alongside the slave or two that even the poorest Greek family seemed to own. Sons in particular represented the only form of social security available to the Greek couple, for children were expected and in some cases required by law to support their parents in their old age.[51] Even the most wealthy of

---

[49]Lefkowitz and Fant, *Women's Life in Greece and Rome*, no. 26, p. 12; see also, for instance, the lovingly carved grave relief of Ampharete with her grandchild from the Hellenistic period; q.v. *Oxford History of Classical Art*, ed. John Boardman (Oxford: Oxford University Press, 1993), plate 126.

[50]Demosthenes *Against Neaira* 122.

[51]At Athens a man who neglected to provide for his parents would be disenfranchised; *Diogenes Laertius* 1.55.

city-dwellers were never so removed from the ravages of bad crops, through natural causes or through their willful destruction by enemy armies, that they could ignore the need for children to preserve them in their advanced years.[52]

Hence, the entrance of the child into the family was a major event, and one that was the object of many prayers for protection from the goddess Artemis—the virgin huntress whose bow and arrows were thought to slay children and mothers in childbirth—during the fearful pains of labor (the cause of many deaths in antiquity). We have several examples in the *Greek Anthology* of such prayers and dedications for safe delivery of children (whether these are school exercises or actual dedications makes no difference here). For example:

> Artemis, lady of Delos and lovely Ortygia, lay by thy stainless bow in the bosom of the Graces, wash thee clean in Inopus, and come to Locri to deliver Alcestis from the hard pangs of childbirth.[53]

> The head-kerchief and water-blue veil of Amphareta rest on thy head, Ilithyia; for them she vowed to thee when she prayed thee to keep dreadful death far away from her in her labour.[54]

> Artemis, the son of Cichesias dedicated the shoes to thee, and Themistodice the simple folds of her gown, because that coming in gentle guise without thy boy thou didst hold thy two hands over her in her labour. But Artemis, vouchsafe to see this baby boy of Leon's grow great and strong.[55]

> Goddess, saviour of children, blest Ilithyia, receive and keep as thy fee for delivering Tisis, who well remembers, from her pangs, this bridal brooch and the diadem from her glossy hair.[56]

The birth of a healthy child and a healthy mother were the cause of real rejoicing. Yet despite the repeated testimony that the bearing and raising of children in the Greek family was a primary purpose of marriage, when a child did come to the couple, it was not regarded as automatically a person and a member of the household until the father accepted it (as in the Roman

---

[52]Burning of fields was a common strategy in the Peloponnesian war.

[53]*Greek Anthology* 6.273.

[54]*Greek Anthology* 6.270.

[55]*Greek Anthology* 6.271.

[56]*Greek Anthology* 6.274. See also the Orphic hymn to Prothyraia (apparently a name for Artemis and Eileithyia), who is invoked as protectress of women in labor (Apostolos N. Athanassakis, ed. *The Orphic Hymns* [Atlanta: Scholars Press, 1977], p. 7: "Upon you alone pregnant women call, O comforter of souls, and in you alone there is relief from pains of labor").

familia as well). On the fifth day after the birth, the father would celebrate and initiate the child into the household in a ceremony called the *Amphidromia* (running-around). The father ran around the household hearth—the symbolic center of the *oikos*—with the child in his arms and thereby accepted him or her into the family. Then on the tenth day after birth, at the *Dekate* (tenth day), family and friends would celebrate a feast where the child would officially receive its name, often the name of a paternal grandparent or of a famous ancestor.[57]

Despite the provisions for the acceptance of a child into the family, there was also the grim, universal practice of infant exposure in the Greek (as well as the Roman) world. Before the child was accepted into the family by the father, it was not regarded as a person. If children were not accepted they would be exposed, meaning they were taken to a remote location, or even flung onto a dung heap, to die. There were ostensibly a number of reasons for this cruel practice, including spare resources (starvation in years of bad crops was a real threat to ancient families), unwillingness to leave an inheritance to more than one or two sons, birth of an illegitimate child to a *hetaira* or to a concubine, or the birth of a girl. (Girls needed dowries to get husbands and hence threatened the sometimes meager resources of the *oikos.*)

The exposure of infants in the Greek world was widespread, and evidence for the practice is likewise commonly encountered in a variety of sources. Sometimes the life of an exposed child who was picked up and raised by others was romanticized. Such children were called "foundlings" *(anairetoi).* In the Greek romance *Daphnis and Chloe,* both the hero and the heroine were foundlings raised by rustic foster parents. At the end of the story both children learn of their wealthy parents. In Greek mythology, an exposed child was sometimes raised by another couple as their own.[58]

But in reality, infant exposure gave rise to a disreputable industry in which exposed children were collected by slave dealers or others and set up to be raised by wet nurses until they could join a household as domestic slaves. As an example of this practice, the following contract preserved on an Egyptian papyrus is presented as poignant testimony:

---

[57]"Why, is not this the City's Tenth-day feast? I've just this instant given the child its name" (Aristophanes *Birds* 922-923). There were many other institutions of this sort involving the family and children; see Mark Golden, *Children and Childhood in Classical Athens* (Baltimore: Johns Hopkins University Press, 1990).

[58]E.g., the sons of Antiope; see *Apollodorus* 3.5.5.

To Protarchus from Isidora daughter of . . . and from Didyma daughter of Apollonius, Persian. . . . Didyma agrees to nurse and suckle, outside at her own home in the city, with her own milk pure and untainted, for a period of 16 months from Pharmouthi of the current 17th year of Caesar [13 B.C.], the foundling infant slave child . . . called . . . which Isidora has given out to her, receiving from her, Isidora, as wages for milk and nursing ten silver drachmae and two cotylae of oil every month. So long as she is duly paid she shall take proper care both of herself and of the child, not injuring her milk nor sleeping with a man nor becoming pregnant nor suckling another child . . . [the contract goes on with further specifications, including a 500 drachmae fine for damages should Didyma break the contract].[59]

Unlike the rosy picture in sources such as *Daphnis and Chloe,* life as a foundling undoubtedly held little romance. For instance, another papyrus document records the minutes of a legal proceeding that reads, in part, as follows:

[Introduction including the dating] Aristocles, advocate for Pesouris, said: "Pesouris, for whom I appear, in the 7th year of Tiberius Claudius Caesar the lord [A.D. 49] picked up from a rubbish-heap a male foundling[60] called Heraclas. This he entrusted to the defendant, and the nurse's contract which was made here referred to it as a son of Pesouris. She received her wages for the first year. The pay-day for the second year came round and again she received them. . . . As the foundling was being starved, Pesouris took it away. Subsequently, seizing an opportunity, she burst into the house of my client and carried the foundling off; and she seeks to obtain possession of the foundling as being her free-born child." . . . [The defendant counters:] "I weaned my own child and the foundling of these persons was entrusted to me. I received from them the whole eight staters. Subsequently the foundling died, [. . .] staters being still unearned. Now they seek to take away my own child."[61]

One can easily see here that the life of the Greek foundling held as little human comfort as that of an Oliver Twist in Dickensian England. Foundlings were usually brought up to be slaves. Indeed, we possess an inscription from Ephesus from around the time of Paul's sojourn there that speaks about public slaves who were themselves buying babies on the open market to raise as their own slaves.[62]

---

[59]BGU 1107, in Hunt and Edgar, *Select Papyri* 1, no. 16.
[60]The Greek word here is *somation,* the diminutive of *soma,* "body," a somewhat derogatory word for slaves. *Soma* in this sense is found in the New Testament only at Rev 18:13.
[61]P.Oxy. 37, in Hunt and Edgar, *Select Papyri* 1, no. 257.
[62]Herman Wandel et al., *Die Inschriften von Ephesos* 18.18-22. The market at Ephesus housed a wholesale slave market for distribution to other parts of the empire.

The alternative for a foundling, however, was a pitiless death by exposure. For girl babies especially, this seems to have been an all too common fate. One well-known source for this practice in the ancient world, a letter preserved on papyrus from an Egyptian recruit in the Roman army from 1 B.C., reads with startling frankness as follows:

> Hilarion to his sister Alis very many greetings, likewise to my lady Berous and Apollonarion. Know that we are still in Alexandria. Do not be anxious; if they really go home, I will remain in Alexandria. I beg and entreat you, take care of the little one, and as soon as we receive our pay I will send it up to you. If by chance you bear a child, if it is a boy, let it be, if it is a girl, cast it out. You have said to Aphrodisias "Do not forget me." How can I forget you? I beg you then not to be anxious.[63]

As today, abortion was another answer to unwanted children in antiquity. Both plant extracts and mechanical means were used, though doubtless with risk to the mother. Yet this practice was by no means universally accepted among the Greeks; witness the Hippocratic oath, which reads in part: "Neither will I administer a poison to anybody when asked to do so, nor will I suggest such a course. Similarly I will not give to a woman a pessary to cause abortion. But I will keep pure and holy both my life and my art."[64]

That abortion was not favored by all Greeks is also evidenced by a fascinating inscription from Lydian Philadelphia from the late second to early first century B.C.—which has broader implications for the Greek family as well. The inscription has been thought to represent a voluntary, private cult group, whose members came together from different families for worship. However, lately it has been persuasively interpreted as the rules for a single household *(oikos)* cult for the regulation of the cult of the man's wife, children, slaves and other free members attached to his *oikos*.[65] As such, this text has much to do with attitudes surrounding the Greek family, so most of the text is given as follows:

> May Good Fortune Prevail. For health and common salvation and the finest reputation the ordinances given to Dionysius in his sleep were written up, giving access into his *oikos* to men and women, free people and slaves. . . . When coming into this *oikos* let men and women, free people and slaves,

---

[63]P.Oxy. 744, in Hunt and Edgar, *Select Papyri* 2, no. 257.

[64]*Hippocrates,* LCC 1:300.

[65]See especially Stanley K. Stowers, "A Cult From Philadelphia: *Oikos* Religion or Cultic Association?" in *The Early Church in Its Context,* ed. Abraham Malherbe, Frederick Norris and James Thompson (Leiden: Brill, 1998), pp. 287-301.

swear by all the gods neither to know nor make use wittingly of any deceit against a man or a woman, neither poison harmful to men nor harmful spells. They are not themselves to make use of a love potion, abortifacient, contraceptive, or any other thing fatal to children; nor are they to recommend it to, nor connive at it with, another. They are not to refrain in any respect from being well-intentioned towards this *oikos*. If anyone performs or plots any of these things, they are neither to put up with it nor keep silent, but expose it and defend themselves. Apart from his own wife, a man is not to have sexual relations with another married woman, whether free or slave, nor with a boy nor a virgin girl; nor shall he recommend it to another. . . . A free woman is to be chaste and shall not know the bed of, nor have sexual intercourse with, another man except her own husband. But if she does have such knowledge, such a woman is not chaste, but defiled and full of endemic pollution, and unworthy to reverence this god whose holy things these are that have been set up. She is not to be present at the sacrifices, nor to strike against (?) the purifications and cleansings (?), nor to see the mysteries being performed. But if she does any of these things from the time the ordinances have come on to this inscription, she shall have evil curses from the gods for disregarding these ordinances.[66]

Several points in the text just cited are worthy of brief elaboration. First, we note in connection with the foregoing discussion on abortion that the giving of abortifacients, along with the use of poison, is explicitly forbidden in Dionysius' *oikos*. In isolation, we might assume that Dionysius prohibited the use of abortifacients because of a concern for the mother's health; however, in context we see that his concern was for the child since he excludes "any other thing fatal to children" as well. Furthermore, the use of magical potions was prohibited, attesting to just how common magic was in antiquity, especially as quasi-medical solutions to problems.

Granted the view that the Dionysius inscription represents the regulations for his *oikos* cult, it evidences a remarkable degree of control of the behavior within the household by the *kyrios* of the *oikos*. The exercise of this control was connected overtly to the family's worship, which was expected to conform to that of the *kyrios*.[67]

The code of conduct in this inscription, which appears to be quite strict

---

[66]The translation is that of Stephen C. Barton and Greg H. R. Horsley in "A Hellenistic Cult Group and the New Testament Churches," *JAC* 24 (1981): 9.

[67]Recall Plutarch's advice to a bride to worship her husband's gods, and note how this point bears on the conversion of whole households in the New Testament world. Cf. C. S. de Vos, "The Significance of the Change from ΟΙΚΟΣ to ΟΙΚΙΑ in Luke's Account of the Philippian Gaoler (Acts 16:30-4)," *NTS* 41 (1995): 292-96.

by ancient standards, focuses on sexual behavior. A married woman must have relations only with her husband, while a married man (note, it does not speak of unmarried youths) must not have relations with a married woman, boys or virgins. While relations of men with *hetairai* is not mentioned, all sexual relations outside of marriage might well be intended.[68] And note that illicit sexual relations carry divine sanction. This is interesting in light of the many adulterous affairs and rapes carried out by the Greek gods in the writings of their poets. Clearly Dionysius had a higher view of Zeus's morals than did Homer or Hesiod!

Finally, Dionysius' *oikos* appears to be quite large, including not just the immediate family but also slaves and free members of the extended family (such as widowed relatives and their children), to warrant an epigraphical record of these regulations. Powerful Greek households may have consisted of several hundred people when all were counted.

By no means, then, were children universally exposed or aborted in the Greek world. Quite the contrary![69] When children were born into a wealthy Greek household, they were carefully raised. Like today, handbooks on child rearing were common enough in the Greek world. Plutarch's essay called "The Education of Children" (*De liberis educandis*) is a good example of the type. Despite its literary character, we know that Plutarch was not speaking merely hypothetically, for he himself was the father of four boys (two of whom died in childhood) and at least one daughter (who died at age two). His letter of consolation to his wife, Timoxena, at the death of their infant daughter is filled with tender recollection of familial joys.[70]

Plutarch begins his essay on child rearing with what he considered a natural starting point: the child's parentage. Notable children will not come from cohabitation with *hetairai* or concubines, and a child might likely be a drunkard if conceived while the father is in his cups.[71] When the aristocratic child is born, Plutarch recommends that the mother do the nursing for a variety of practical reasons; yet if a wet-nurse should be used—i.e., a slave was often retained in the household for this purpose—she should be Greek for the sake of the child's character.[72] Other slaves who tend the child and serve as companions should also be Greek, "so that the children may not be

---

[68] So Barton and Horsley, "Hellenistic Cult Group," pp. 19-20 nn. 61-62.

[69] One woman boasts in her epitaph that she has borne twenty-nine children (*Greek Anthology* 7.743).

[70] "Consolation to His Wife," *Moralia* 608-11.

[71] *De liberis educandis* 2-3.

[72] Ibid., 5.

contaminated by barbarians and persons of low character, and so take on some of their commonness."[73]

Plutarch continues the same sort of advice about the child's *paidegogoi* (attendants; see Gal 3:24-25): they must be of good Greek character rather than enslaved war prisoners or barbarians. He says:

> Nowadays, the common practice of many persons is more than ridiculous; for some of their trustworthy slaves they appoint to manage their farms, others they make masters of their ships, others their factors, others they make house-stewards, and some even money-lenders; but any slave whom they find to be a wine-bibber and a glutton, and useless for any kind of business, to him they bring their sons and put them in his charge.[74]

Even more care must be taken in choosing the child's teachers, and one must not spare in payment of fees here. Plutarch supports this point with the quaint story of Aristippus, who, when asked by a father how much he required to tutor his son, replied 1,000 drachmas. At the father's outcry, "'Great Heaven! what an excessive demand! I can buy a slave for a thousand,' Aristippus retorted, 'Then you will have two slaves, your son and the one you buy.'"[75]

As Plutarch continues his essay, we see plainly that he commends the Greek father to direct his concern toward his son's character: piety toward his parents and the gods, chastity toward women, even-tempered, not dissolute, impulsive or brutish in temper, and so on.[76] The actual subjects of the education of the wealthy Greek son focus typically upon character development, elegant speech and moderate training in bodily exercise.[77] Plutarch concludes his advice with similar moral guidelines, characteristic of Greek philosophy, where "Observe due measure: and proportion is best in all things"[78] was an enduring maxim.

When Greek sons came of age, the family celebrated their initiation into manhood with the proper religious observances, including the boy's dedicating a lock of hair and his boyhood toys as tokens of his passing out of childhood. His father at that point would officially introduce him and register him with the clan or "brotherhood" *(phratry)* at a three-day festival called

---

[73]Ibid., 6.
[74]Ibid., 7.
[75]Ibid.
[76]Ibid., 10, 13.
[77]Ibid., 9, 11.
[78]Hesiod *Opera et dies* 694.

the *Apatouria,* which was held in the autumn. He was also initiated into the city-state *(demos)* in a separate rite. In his later teens, a citizen boy would participate in military training for a few years as an *ephebe,* which, in the Hellenistic and Roman periods, turned into an elite cultural club. When he was considered old enough, he would be betrothed to a suitable girl. As already mentioned, girls normally participated in their coming-of-age initiation at the same time as their marriage.

Now the idealized Greek family we have been tracing is complete: husband and wedded wife, sons who are beginning their participation in the state as citizen-soldiers and possibly budding statesmen, daughters ready to be given in marriage to members of families of equal station. ("One should, however," writes Plutarch, "betroth to his sons women who are not greatly above them either in birth or wealth . . . since those who take to wife women far above themselves unwittingly become not the husbands of their wives, but the slaves of their wives' dowries."[79])

The presence of slaves (some of whom might serve as concubines) and freedmen as members of the *oikos* was taken for granted—though I should mention that freeing slaves was much less common in the Greek era than in that of imperial Rome. Slaves were regarded as on the same level as minor children (cf. Gal 4). And slaves were everywhere in the Greek world, estimated as amounting to between one-third to as much as one-half of a Greek city's population.[80] Witness this grave inscription, for instance, where the final provision of a tomb was accorded to the slaves and freedmen of the *oikos:* "This tomb belongs to the Ephesian Aur. Alexander son of Apollonius and to his wife, Octavia Matrona, and to his brothers and his slaves and all his freedmen. It is unlawful for anyone to alienate this tomb."[81] This inscription comes from the later Roman period but shows the essential membership of the slaves and freedmen in the Greek *oikos.*

INHERITANCE

Ideally, the Greek couple looked forward to spending their later years surrounded by their grandchildren and eventually passing on into death at a good old age, leaving behind a good reputation and a solid Greek *oikos* for their sons to inherit and to carry on. The Greek focus on sons rather than

---

[79]*Moralia* 13F-14A.
[80]This would include publicly owned slaves, of course.
[81]Original in Dieter Knibbe and Bülent Iplikçioglu, "Neue Inschriften aus Ephesos VIII," *JÖAI* 53 (1981-1982) leaf #121 (p. 124); my translation.

daughters in their inheritance laws is commonly discussed.[82] We even read, for instance, the following line in Herodotus: "Cleomenes . . . died childless, leaving behind only a daughter."[83] While this may seem strange to us, that Cleomenes was *childless* with only a daughter, the statement must be understood in light of membership in the *oikos*. The daughter must have married and thereby passed out of Cleomenes' *oikos* and its *phratry* (clan) into that of her husband; hence, Cleomenes technically had no male heir.

The Greeks dealt with inheritance laws as directly as possible. Fathers were expected to leave their estates equally to their sons. If it was not sizable enough, no division was made, and some sons, like Xenophon and the famous ten thousand, became mercenary soldiers or colonists in other lands. The mother always retained her dowry, which provided for her in emergencies, as already mentioned.

If, for example, the father died leaving only a daughter as heir, she became an *epikleros,* which meant that one of the members of the clan would be obligated to marry her and thereby keep the vacant *oikos* in the clan (similar to a practice providing for widows in Old Covenant Israel). This situation produced marriages between, for instance, uncles and their nieces, which were otherwise not approved in Greek society.

The Greek ideal, however, was to live a full, moderate life and to depart in peace. Again, the epigrams in the *Greek Anthology*—perhaps literary exercises but still useful to perceive the ideal—illustrate:

> Find no fault with my fate, traveller, in passing my tomb; not even in death have I aught that calls for mourning. I left children's children, I enjoyed the company of one wife who grew old together with me. I married my three children, and many children sprung from these unions I lulled to sleep on my lap, never grieving for the illness or loss of one. They all, pouring their libations on my grave, sent me off on a painless journey to the home of the pious dead to sleep the sweet sleep.[84]

> I, the old woman who am now dust, was once the priestess of Demeter and again of the Cabiri and afterwards of Cybele. I was the patroness of many young women. I had two male children and closed my eyes at a goodly old age in their arms. Go in peace.[85]

---

[82]Gal 3:28 should be read in this light. For the law, see Todd, *Shape of Athenian Law,* pp. 216-31, and Ilias Annaoutoglou, *Ancient Greek Laws: A Source Book* (New York: Routledge, 1998), pp. 1-16.

[83]*Historiae* 5.48, my translation.

[84]*Greek Anthology,* 7.260.

[85]Ibid., 7.728.

As alluded to in the first epitaph, the funeral of a family member was accompanied by libations. Greek funerals were invariably cremations. The body was laid out on a bier and carried to its funeral pyre. Afterward, the ashes and any unburned bones were gathered and placed in an urn, which was put into a tomb. Sometimes the tomb was filled with objects such as a man's armor (as found in Philip of Macedon's tomb). In many cases, a shaft with a tube was cut into the rock of an underground tomb, into which family members would pour libations and ceremonial offerings on an annual remembrance of the day of death, either to appease the departed spirit or, more likely, to demonstrate that the departed was still a member of the *oikos*.

This completes the full cycle of the Greek family. We have seen its utilitarian side (though romance was certainly known as well), its focus on bearing heirs to carry on the *oikos* (despite the practice of exposure and abortion), and some of the most important rituals attending the wedding, children, and death. These institutions illustrate that the *oikos* was the most basic institution of the Greeks. It showed a remarkable resistance to substantive changes over the centuries—unlike, for instance, Greek democracy, which was very short lived. Some features of antique practices and structure are still in evidence in the modern Greek family.[86] Certainly, the Greek *oikos* formed a central institution at work in the New Testament world.

---

[86]Cf. Paul Sant Cassia and Constantina Bada, *The Making of the Modern Greek Family* (Cambridge: Cambridge University Press, 1991).

4

Marriage and Family in Roman Society

SUSAN TREGGIARI

G reek and Roman theorists saw marriage and the procreation of children as fundamental to human society.[1] According to Cicero (106-43 B.C.), the family was the seed-bed of the city (*De officiis* 1.54). It was so fundamental that the rules that shaped it were those of ancestral custom. Cicero also said,

> For the sake of life and the practice of living, a prescription has been made for recognised marriages, legitimate children, and the sacred homes of the household gods and family Lares, so that everyone should enjoy common and

---

[1]The reader who wants further information on topics touched on here will usually begin with recent English monographs on major subjects. On specific institutions and concepts and some individuals, *OCD* is a good starting point, with recent bibliography. For the family in general, see Keith R. Bradley, *Discovering the Roman Family: Studies in Roman Social History* (New York: Oxford University Press, 1991) and "Writing the History of the Roman Family," *CP* 88 (1993) 237-50; Suzanne Dixon, *The Roman Family* (Baltimore: Johns Hopkins University Press, 1992) and "Rewriting the Family: A Review Essay," *CJ* 89.4 (1994) 395-407. On the interaction of the family and law, see especially Jane F. Gardner, *Family and* Familia *in Roman Law and Life* (Oxford: Clarendon, 1998). On Roman marriage, Susan Treggiari, *Roman Marriage: Iusti coniuges from the Time of Cicero to the Time of Ulpian* (Oxford: Clarendon, 1991). There is also an excellent survey by Judith Evans Grubbs, "'Pagan' and 'Christian' Marriage: The State of the Question," *JECS* 2.4 (1994): 361-412. Stimulating essays on many topics will be found in the three volumes that derive from the Canberra conferences: Beryl Rawson, ed., *The Family in Ancient Rome: New Perspectives* (London: Croom Helm, 1986); *Marriage, Divorce and Children in Ancient Rome* (Oxford: Clarendon, 1991); and Beryl M. Rawson and Paul R. C. Weaver, eds., *The Roman Family in Italy: Status, Sentiment, Space* (Oxford: Clarendon, 1997). These were followed by a fourth conference at McMaster University in 2001. The proceedings are forthcoming in a volume edited by Michele George for Clarendon Press. There are also good recent papers in Suzanne Dixon, ed., *Childhood, Class and Kin in the Roman World* (London: Routledge, 2001); Päivi Setälä et al., *Women, Wealth and Power in the Roman Empire*, Acta Instituti Romani Finlandiae 25 (Rome: Institutum Romanum Finlandiae, 2002). On property, see Richard P. Saller, *Patriarchy, Property and Death in the Roman Family* (Cambridge: Cambridge University Press, 1994); for wills, Edward Champlin, *Final Judgments: Duty*

individual blessings. For living well is impossible without a good community and there is nothing happier than a well set-up polity.[2]

For centuries the family in Rome was scarcely affected by statute-law. But custom had the force of law and was far more sacred and basic than any recent statute on such matters as modifications to inheritance-practices or infringements of the sexual code.

Two points must be made at the outset. The first is that the world in which we attempt to isolate Roman ideas and practice was a complex and multicultural one. According to Roman legend, the City of Rome (traditionally said to have been founded in 753 B.C.) was an amalgam from the first (tracing its roots to intermarriage between male refugees from Troy and local Latin women and founded several centuries later, for Latin shepherds and men on the run, by Romulus, who then arranged for wives to be kidnapped from the neighboring Sabines). Archaeology also attests a cultural mix, though it cannot confirm, of course, the details of the literary account. A Latin city, sharing customs and rights with the other towns of the broad plain of Latium, Rome was from the start in touch with Etruscans on the other bank of the Tiber and with Sabines in the hills. As the population and power of the city expanded, so did contacts with more distant towns and tribes of Italy, with Greek colonists in southern Italy and Sicily and with Celts in the north. Foreigners were absorbed and enfranchised.

---

and Emotion in Roman Wills, 200 B.C.-A.D. 250 (Berkeley: University of California Press, 1991); David Johnston, *The Roman Law of Trusts* (Oxford: Clarendon, 1988). For demography, see Saller, *Patriarchy, Property and Death;* Tim G. Parkin, *Demography and Roman Society* (Baltimore: Johns Hopkins University Press, 1992). On sexual practices, see especially Thomas A. J. McGinn, *Prostitution and the Law* (New York: Oxford University Press, 1998). Elaine Fantham et al., *Women in the Classical World: Image and Text* (New York: Oxford University Press, 1994), is now the best general introduction to Roman women. For their relationship with children, see Suzanne Dixon, *The Roman Mother* (London: Croom Helm, 1988). For a rich collection of documents with explanatory comment, see Judith Evans Grubbs, *Women and the Law in the Roman Empire: A Sourcebook on Marriage, Divorce and Widowhood* (London: Routledge, 2002). The views I express here, for the most part, are argued more fully in my *Roman Marriage*.

Conventional periods of Roman history are as follows: Monarchy (753-510 B.C.), Republic (509-49 B.C.), Caesar's dictatorship and the Triumvirate (49-27 B.C.), and Principate (the period of the emperors, the "imperial period"; 27 B.C.-A.D. 284). I refer also to the "legendary period" (before ca fifth century B.C.), the "semilegendary period" (fifth to fourth centuries B.C.), the "historical period" (third century B.C. and after), the "central period" (c. 133 B.C.-A.D. 235), the "classical period of Roman law" (the first three centuries A.D.), the "Augustan period" (the principate of Augustus, 27 B.C.-A.D. 14) and the "Julio-Claudian period" (A.D. 14-68).

[2]*Republic* 5.7.

Old and new Roman citizens lived under Roman law, which included marriage customs. The pattern continued as Rome became the mistress of a Mediterranean empire. The expanded citizen-body, probably about 10 percent of the population of the empire in the late first century B.C., had many genetic roots, but even patrician families that could trace their male line (in theory) back to the earliest days of the city had absorbed much from non-Romans, especially the "high culture" of Greek literature and philosophy. An exclusively "Roman" regime of family and marriage is to some extent a theoretical construct.

On the other hand, Roman citizens were expected to live by Roman law. As citizenship continued to be extended in areas outside Italy, to Gallic tribesmen or Greeks or Jews, the new citizens had to adapt in some respects, while they retained much of their original culture. People who practiced marriage with half or full sisters, for example, would, when nearly all free people in the empire were enfranchised in the early third century A.D., find their unions invalid by Roman law. Of greater importance for individuals or groups enfranchised earlier was the fact that Roman law recognized only some "mixed marriages" between Roman citizen and non-Roman: there was severe discrimination (on the Roman side) against the children of an unrecognized "mixed marriage." Citizenship meant restrictions as well as privileges. So, despite cultural interaction over centuries, Roman marriage was sharply differentiated from the varied practices of coexisting cultures. At any given time, information of what it entailed might be sought from officials (annually elected *magistratus*) and from legal experts, and, as time went on, from a growing body of written material: statute-law, juristic interpretation and pronouncements of emperors. The rich written sources are unique in the ancient world. In what follows, *Roman* will refer to Roman citizens and the institutions and practices of citizens.

"PATRIARCHY": A MODERN MODEL OF THE EARLY SYSTEM

Early Rome has traditionally been regarded as a highly patriarchal society. Much of the scholarly reconstruction of how society was structured during the semilegendary period of monarchy (traditionally 753-510 B.C.) and Republic (509 B.C. onward) down to the third century B.C. depends on postulates about Indo-European cultures as a category and is thus highly speculative. Archaeological evidence cannot enlighten us here; relevant literary sources were all composed centuries later, and it is hard to pick out facts from all the material that idealizes and rationalizes institutions and customs.[3] Research therefore focuses on data on law, notably the fragments of the fifth-century *Twelve Tables* (learned by heart by schoolboys down to the time of Cicero [106-43 B.C.]) and the allusions to contemporary customs incorporated into Roman adaptations of Greek comedy by Plautus (produced c. 205-184 B.C.),[4] and on the Latin language itself.

In order to clarify the "patriarchal" elements in primitive Rome, let us describe a theoretical model. This will describe only one element in Roman society and must not be taken to approximate to a complex reality or to the experience of any individual.

The citizen body was divided into patricians *(patricii)* and plebeians *(plebeii;* collectively, the *plebs).* The patricians in early times alone supplied the senators *(patres,* fathers) and formed a restricted group. The rest of the citizens were plebeians. Membership in the group was transmitted in the male line. So was membership in a "clan" *(gens).* Membership in the small patrician *gentes* implied a common descent from one ancestor; it is likely that the larger, plebeian *gentes* were not restricted to blood-relations. The marker of clan membership was the name *(nomen, nomen gentile),* derived from the father. So a man's name, Claudius, or a woman's name, Claudia, denoted membership in the *gens Claudia* and descent through a line of male Claudii from the alleged common ancestor, the Sabine Attus Clausus. There are Roman stories of a whole patrician *gens* acting as a group, sending out all the adult males to fight as a unit (and be wiped out, with one survivor [the Fabii in 477 B.C.]), and there are modern conjectures about communal property. But, although family pride in the traditions of a whole patrician *gens* might have ideological importance, the clan did not operate as a group in the historical period, and membership is important only for some cult obligations, pride and the privileges that it might confer on individuals. There was no such thing as a clan chieftain (except presumably the founder of the line during the legendary period). Freed slaves took the *gentile* name of the former owner and were always plebeian.

In contrast, the household-head had great powers. Among several related and often overlapping connotations,[5] *familia* denotes the household, including children and slaves. The head of this group is the *paterfamilias.* He

---

[3]See, e.g., Dixon, *Roman Family,* p. 72.

[4]Cf., e.g., Alan Watson, *The Law of Persons in the Later Roman Republic* (Oxford: Clarendon, 1967); Myles McDonnell, "Divorce Initiated by Women in Rome: The Evidence of Plautus," *AJAH* 8 (1983): 54-80.

[5]Saller, *Patriarchy, Property and Death,* pp. 74-101.

is male and at least potentially a father *(pater)*. He must be independent of any male ascendant. He has "paternal power" *(patria potestas)* over his children born in lawful marriage, "children-in-power" *(filii/filiaefamilias)*, and, naturally, power over the slaves he owns, which need not concern us here. His paternal power may extend to subsequent generations: grandchildren born to his legally married sons as well as great-grandchildren through sons and grandsons. He can hardly hope to go further.

Patria potestas was removed by the father's death. The father could also release a child of any age by "emancipation" *(emancipatio,* a fictitious sale to a third party, who then freed the child, a ceremony repeated three times[6]). Daughters were also released by being transferred into the control, *manus,* literally "(the) hand," of a husband. Death or emancipation made the child legally independent, *sui iuris* (literally, of his or her own right). Imagine a *paterfamilias* who had three children in power, a married son age twenty-five with a son and daughter of his own (both in their grandfather's power), an unmarried daughter fifteen years of age and a younger son of ten. When the *paterfamilias* died, all three children became legally independent. The married son now had his two children in his own power. Guardians would be appointed (usually in the father's will) for the daughter (because she was a woman) and for the younger son (because he was a child under puberty), not to look after them, but to look after their property. However, all three were legally independent individuals and no one possessed paternal power over them. Adult elder brothers did not have legal power over sisters or minor brothers, though they might function as guardians. Mothers, because of their sex, could never hold paternal power. In practice, both mothers and brothers had moral authority and duty and might be much involved with the younger members of the family. Upon the father's death in our imaginary family, the two grandchildren, the son's children, came directly under their father's power. Suppose a different scenario: the eldest son predeceases his father. Then the grandchildren, like their aunt and uncle, also become independent, because they are freed from paternal power by the death of their grandfather and *paterfamilias.*

Originally, the power of the head of household was absolute.[7] He could

---

[6]Jane F. Gardner, *Being a Roman Citizen* (London: Routledge, 1992), pp. 60-72.

[7]See William V. Harris, "The Roman Father's Power of Life and Death," in *Studies in Roman Law in Memory of A. Arthur Schiller,* ed. Roger S. Bagnall and William V. Harris (Leiden: Brill, 1986), pp. 81-95; Gardner, *Being a Roman Citizen,* p. 55; Saller, *Patriarchy, Property and Death,* pp. 102-53.

legally put his children to death or sell them into slavery. Those under his power legally held no property: anything they acquired by their own efforts, gift, purchase or inheritance, became the property of the *paterfamilias*. Since they could do nothing in law on their own account, it was the father whose will was necessary for their marriage or divorce. On the other hand, the *paterfamilias* was, as it were, the trustee of the family property. When he died, those in his power, or *manus,* who became legally independent by his death (including daughters-in-power) stood to inherit, as *sui heredes,* "heirs to themselves."[8] The rules of intestacy meant that the property would be divided equally among them. If he made a will, he could vary this. He might also free children during his lifetime, by *emancipatio.*

What happened to women upon marriage? There were two systems. Both predate the law of the *Twelve Tables* in the mid-fifth century B.C. In one, which is generally regarded by scholars as the sole original system, a woman upon marriage entered into the control, *manus,* of her husband.[9] If she had a *paterfamilias,* he transferred her from his power to her husband's *manus.* If she was legally independent, she gave up her independence on entering *manus.* If her husband was himself a son-in-power, she came in effect under the control of his *paterfamilias.* According to the alternative system, a woman would not enter *manus* but would remain in her previous status, as daughter-in-power or independent woman.

Manus was created in three ways, logically distinct from the ceremonials that signified the inception of the marriage. Two of these methods might be used in conjunction with wedding ceremonies so that the beginning of *manus* and the beginning of marriage are associated and therefore easily confused. For patricians (perhaps exclusively), there was the religious ceremony of *confarreatio,* involving the sacramental use of a cake or loaf of a primitive form of wheat *(emmer):*

> Women come into *manus* by *farreum* (an emmer cake or loaf) through a type
> of sacrifice which is made to Jupiter Farreus. A loaf of emmer is used in this,
> and the name *confarreatio* derives from it. A number of acts and rituals take
> place in performing this procedure in due order. There are prescribed and

---

[8]Gaius *Institutes* 2.157; *Digest* 28.2.11, Iulius Paulus (fl. late second to early third century); William Warwick Buckland, *A Textbook of Roman Law from Augustus to Justinian,* 3rd ed., rev. Peter Stein (Oxford: Clarendon, 1963), p. 305. The *Digest of Justinian* is a compilation of extracts from earlier jurists (down to c. A.D. 300) made by a committee chaired by Tribonian at the orders of the emperor Justinian (ruled A.D. 527-65). It was promulaged A.D. 533. I have been selective in naming and dating the jurist who wrote the original extract (here, Paulus).
[9]See, recently, Gardner, *Being a Roman Citizen,* p. 211 n. 20.

solemn words and ten witnesses are present. This institution is still in existence today.[10]

The institution had survived to the time of Gaius's introductory textbook on
law in the second century A.D. because certain priests had to be born of a
confarreate marriage and married in this way themselves. But it survived in
attenuated form and had become rare by the first century A.D. It is of historical interest as a sacrament, almost certainly exclusively that of patricians,
from whom priests and priestesses were drawn, most notably the *flamen Dialis,* priest of Jupiter, and his wife, the *flaminica Dialis,* whose lives were
hedged with ancient taboos. There was a corresponding ceremony to remove the *manus* on divorce, *diffarreatio,* but this may not be ancient.

The second way of creating *manus* was open to plebeians and presumably commonly practiced. Here the ritual was nonreligious, a form of legal
sale and purchase, *coemptio,* literally, "buying together." This could take
place at any stage in a marriage, not just at the wedding.

> By *coemptio* they come into *manus* by mancipation, that is, by a kind of imag-
> inary sale. For in the presence of not fewer than five witnesses who are adult
> male Roman citizens, and of a scales-holder, the man into whose *manus* the
> woman passes buys her.[11]

In prehistoric times, the bride-price may have been a substantial sum to
buy a woman's reproductive powers for her new family.[12] But in classical
times the Romans knew nothing of this widespread human custom (which
comes into their customs with *donatio ante nuptias* in the late empire). Instead the piece of bronze (coinage had not yet been introduced) that was
handed over had purely symbolic value.[13] The woman was an agent, not an
object. Probably set words were spoken. The custom was similar to the formal manner of marking the sale of a slave, which would involve, parallel to
the ritual striking of the scale with a piece of bronze and the handing of it
to the vendor, a real exchange of a human being for something of value. But
the woman did not become a slave. By historic times, this was clearly a convenient way of putting the wife "in her husband's hand," *in manu mariti,* a
situation that conferred certain privileges as well as restrictions. Because it
involved property rights, an independent woman needed her guardian's

---

[10]Gaius (second century A.D.) *Institutes* 1.112.
[11]Ibid., 1.113.
[12]Geoffrey MacCormack, "*Coemptio* and Marriage by Purchase," *BIDR* 20 (1978): 179-99.
[13]Percy Ellwood Corbett, *The Roman Law of Marriage* (Aalen: Scientia Verlag, 1979 [1930]), pp.
78-85; Watson, *Law of Persons,* p. 24.

consent for *coemptio,* though not for marriage. We hear of a couple performing *coemptio* after the inception of a marriage, no doubt for economic reasons. Conversely, the husband might need to free his wife from his control, by *emancipatio,* for instance, in case of divorce.

The third method of creating *manus* lacked ritual. It is conventionally listed first, but that need not mean that our authorities thought it the most ancient. I keep it to the end because that seems simplest for the modern reader. Some modern scholars think it developed later than the two rituals.[14] This method required simply a year's cohabitation.

> A woman came into control if she remained married for a continuous year, because she was as it were acquired by usucapion because of the year's occupancy and went over into the family of the husband and obtained the position of a daughter.[15]

The parallel institution here is the acquisition of property: the *Twelve Tables* state that a person may obtain legal ownership of a piece of movable property if he "possesses" it uninterruptedly for one year, provided he has just cause and is acting in good faith. It took two years for immovables, such as land. This custom allowed vendor and buyer to do without the ritual transfer. Similarly, if a woman lived with a husband, or in his house, for a year, he became the legal holder of *manus.* The passage shows clearly that marriage and *manus* are distinguished and that acquisition of *manus* by this method antedates the fifth-century codification of law. There was no suggestion that the woman living in a man's house was not his wife from the beginning. The code also allows for the avoidance of *manus.*

> Therefore it was prescribed by the law of the *Twelve Tables* that if any woman did not wish to come into the husband's control in this manner, she should stay away for three nights each year and so break the *usus* of each year. But this rule has partly been abolished by statutes and partly wiped out by desuetude.[16]

Usus seems to have died out by the second century A.D. and perhaps was already uncommon in the first century B.C. *Coemptio* was perhaps the most convenient way of creating *manus* in the classical period. But *manus* itself seems to have been fairly rare by then.

Early Roman law developed in an agrarian society in which the family owned, worked and passed on land. Custom prescribed that when the *pa-*

---

[14]E.g., Gardner, *Being a Roman Citizen,* p. 211 n. 20.
[15]Gaius *Institutes* 1.111.
[16]Ibid.

terfamilias died, those who were freed from his power inherited equal shares. A wife *in manu mariti* had the same rights as a daughter-in-power. These rules about intestate succession embody the assumption of equal rights between the sexes. A wife who had joined a new family became a full member of it and was legally kin to her children.

Failing such heirs, the archaic system gave succession privileges to those most closely related through a male ascendant. Thus a man's sister might qualify, for she and he had the same father, but her children did not.[17] Archaic law visualized the family first as the group of husband, wife *(in manu)* and children (but for daughters only up to the time of marriage if they then went into *manus*) and second as *agnates,* relatives through males. This second, extended family shared a name, since names were derived from fathers. Of these, those whom we might expect to be effectively known as kin (apart from father and paternal grandfather and even his father) would be brothers, sisters, father's uncles, father's uncles' children, sisters' children, father's sisters, and a few remoter uncles, aunts and cousins in the male line. Male *agnates,* second in line to inherit, would become guardians to any underage children who lost their father. The legal structure dictates a lopsided view of the kin who matter.

But this primordial way of looking at things was modified over time, and shifts in the law must have been made because emotional ties with kin in the female line made themselves felt. The father's brother, who had a direct interest in a person's rights to property and who might become a guardian, was early stereotyped as a severe figure; the mother's brother, who had no material interest in a niece or nephew, was seen as a kindly uncle. There is also strong evidence for the family solidarity maintained by pairs of sisters and continuing into the next generation; consequently, the word for cousins who are the children of two sisters *(consobrini)* becomes the word in common use for cousins in general.

Interest in property also dictates more flexibility than the model allows. The father of an only daughter might consider whether he wanted to keep her in his power when she married so that she would inherit all his property automatically if he died without a will or if his will failed. Most propertied people would make a will, which would allow them to give to dependents and others specific or larger portions than the rules on intestacy allowed.

---

[17]For a detailed history of the development of rules of succession, see the lucid account in Gaius *Institutes* 3; Alan Watson, *The Law of Succession in the Later Roman Republic* (Oxford: Clarendon, 1971), p. 177.

Thus a peasant-farmer might well want to hand over the land intact to an eldest son (on or before his own death) and use livestock or produce or money to dower a daughter or give a start to a younger son. Our evidence suggests that the patriarchal system was subject to constant modification from very early (at least the fifth century B.C.). It provided a framework of rules and attitudes (such as the ideal of equal shares for all children, without regard to sex or age order). New legal ways of operating could develop out of it; social imperatives could alter. This flexibility allowed the institution of paternal power to continue right down to the late empire. This does not mean that the "right of life and death" was literally interpreted or that an adult son would have to ask his father every time he wanted to buy a sausage at the cookshop. It meant that law imposed a structure within which individuals and their families operated, as moral duty, emotional needs or economic advantage impelled them.

MARRIAGE AND THE FAMILY IN THE HISTORIC PERIOD C. 100 B.C.-A.D. 235

Sources. Our sources, especially literary and juristic texts and inscriptions (especially funerary), are comparatively rich for the "central" period of the late Republic (133-27 B.C.) and Principate (27 B.C.-ca. A.D. 235). It is therefore possible to attempt a synchronic sketch of both, though it is difficult to analyze continuity and change or to give a rounded picture for all classes of society, because different types of literature, extant for different periods, cast light on different facets of life. First, what section of society is illustrated? Literature was written by or for the upper classes; senators; the order immediately below them, called the *equites;* and the richer, educated classes of Italian or provincial towns, so it tends not to reflect the experience of small farmers or artisans. Jurists, too, came from this broad elite, and their thinking was no doubt shaped by the needs of the wealthier classes, though sometimes they—and the emperors—had to deal with queries from humbler folk. Tomb inscriptions give us our best evidence on sections of society below the elite, but the poorest of all could not afford such commemoration.

Second, what can we expect specific types of source to tell us? Let us think about two major contemporary literary sources for the late Republic, the late 60s to the 50s B.C. How much will the love poems of Catullus tell us of the *mores* of a young man of equestrian status from Verona in cultured senatorial/equestrian circles in the capital, and how much can we generalize about his contemporaries from his evidence? He writes touchingly of his affection for his brother (who died young) and for his home at Sirmione, vividly of parties with friends, and with equal passion of kissing lovers of either sex. Is any of this literary convention? Is it purely autobiographical or at least in part literary imagination? Such questions become important for our purposes when we seek to use as a historical source the apparently highly personal poems regarding a love affair with a lady who is (during at least part of the story) married to someone else and whom scholars (starting with Apuleius in the second century A.D.) identify with a patrician Clodia, possibly the one who was wife and then widow of the consul of 60 B.C. So how literally can we take a poet? On this point, we can adduce Cicero too, who has much to say on Clodia wife of Metellus. In his private letters he criticizes her behavior to her husband, and he repeats with glee the insults he traded with her brother, his political enemy, in which he implied an incestuous relationship between brother and sister. Later, when his hatred increased because Clodius had driven him into exile, Cicero, in a law-court speech in defense of his young friend Caelius, diverted the jurors from the point at issue by attacking Clodia, who, he asserted, was Caelius's discarded mistress and had instigated the trial out of spite. He exonerates Caelius by appealing to the double standard that allowed extramarital affairs with prostitutes to young men and by equating this noble and wealthy widow with an insatiable harlot. Cicero had an axe to grind; political debate and forensic argument allowed inventive invective. Do we believe in Clodia's succession of lovers? More important, do we believe these sources cast light on the marital and sexual behavior of a significant section of the upper classes in Rome of the late Republic? Probably no firm answer will ever be possible. Again and again, we must consider the nature of the literary genre and the prejudices or other limitations of the writer.

Similarly, the preoccupation of jurists is to explain the law, not to describe social facts (though they may incidentally cast light on these). Like writers of technical handbooks (on medicine or agriculture, for instance), they strive for objectivity, and they prescribe. On a tomb inscription, one may be concerned to pay a debt of gratitude to the dead; praise for what society considers virtue will be a major component; fashions for specifying age at death, family relationships, legal status (slave, freed or freeborn) or job may vary with time, place or class; or the inscription may consist of the bare name. Distinctive feelings or detailed biographies will unfortunately rarely appear. Such sources do not dovetail neatly to give us a complete picture.

We lack the letters, memoirs, legal documents (wills, inventories, marriage contracts) and administrative records (accounts, tax-records), and physical relics (house, furniture, clothing) from which we could draw a full picture of the life of any one individual from Roman times. At best we have such things as the nine hundred letters of Cicero (mostly *from* Cicero) spread over the latter part of his life (68-43 B.C.), a sample of those he wrote, which cover part of his private life. We have the relatively long funerary inscription that eulogizes a lady of unknown name who saved her husband during the proscriptions (the so-called *Laudatio Turiae*), or we can examine the historian Tacitus' tendentious and memorable reconstruction of the shortcomings of the governing class of the Julio-Claudian period (the *Annals,* covering A.D. 14 to 68, with gaps). Moderns make a sort of patchwork, taking all available data into account and balancing probabilities. In this short essay, it will not be possible to disentangle sources in any detail or justify hypotheses at length. I shall try to signal controversial points and suggest further reading.

By 100 B.C., social customs and statute law or the rulings of elected officials (chiefly the praetors) had allowed private law to evolve from its original rigidity. For instance, divorce, initially an option only for husbands and only in case of adultery or other serious fault on the wife's part, was later allowed without penalty to husbands for reasons that were not the wife's fault (her perceived sterility, a decision of ca. 230 B.C.). Subsequently the practice became much more common.

Demography. An understanding of demography is fundamental to the understanding of a given society. The consensus of modern scholars is that life expectancy in the Roman Empire as a whole in our period fell in the range of twenty-five to thirty years, comparable with that of other pre-industrial societies. There will have been variation in different areas and among different groups. For instance, the City of Rome, despite its water supply, baths, sewers and paved streets, was unhygienic, so infections and epidemics spread easily.[18] The wealthier classes and their servants lived on the hills and went to the country in the worst of the hot weather; the poor, in their crowded alleys and apartments, died of fever. Averaged out over the entire empire, twenty-five to thirty years seems about right for life expectancy at birth. This means that about half of the children born would be dead before ten years of age, about one-third (on the high estimate) by one year. About half of the survivors would have lost a father by the age of fifteen. For a woman to replace herself and her husband by leaving two children who grew up, she might need to have five or six babies. To put it more correctly, in a stationary population, if expectation of life at birth

---

[18]A. Scobie, "Slums, Sanitation and Mortality in the Roman World," *Klio* 68 (1986): 399-433.

is twenty-five years, women who survive until the age of fifty must produce on average 5.1 children.[19] It would be a common experience to lose a husband or wife by death and for a woman to die before the end of her childbearing years. Among citizens rich enough to afford to put up a grave monument with an epitaph, a woman tended to marry for the first time between about eighteen and twenty years of age,[20] and a man in his late twenties,[21] so that he was usually nine or ten years older than his bride. Originally, Roman male citizens from about eighteen to twenty-eight had been expected to spend the summer campaigning, and only after that would the future senator canvass for office in Rome and settle down to family life with a wife to give him children and her dowry to help launch him in politics. This strengthens the likelihood that a man will die before he has a chance to marry and beget a legitimate child. The theory for women was that they ought to marry as soon after puberty as possible, to guarantee their chastity and maximize their childbearing. In the senatorial class, this often seems to mean that they married younger than eighteen years. The legal minimum was in fact twelve, and some must have married as young as that. Augustus in his marriage legislation offered incentives and prescribed penalties that encouraged women to be mothers by twenty and men fathers by twenty-five. This may have had some effect on the propertied classes, in bringing down the age for men. In the light of this demographic picture, people might expect to experience the relatively early death of a husband or wife and their own remarriage, as well as the loss of siblings or children in babyhood or childhood. The gap in age between husband and wife is a social pattern that would affect their relationship. Besides, a woman at her first marriage might marry a man at his second, which would increase the probable gap. Conversely, a woman at her second marriage might be more likely to marry a man closer to her own age, as (probably) when Pomponia, Atticus's sister, married Quintus Cicero.

Theory. Roman thinkers, following Greek philosophers, see human behavior as a subset of animal behavior. The instinct to reproduce and to nurture children is a natural one. The state evolves from this state of nature: the family is the building block of the city.

---

[19]Saller, *Patriarchy, Property and Death,* p. 42.

[20]Brent D. Shaw, "The Age of Roman Girls at Marriage: Some Reconsiderations," *JRS* 77 (1987): 30-46.

[21]Richard P. Saller, "Men's Age at Marriage and Its Consequences in the Roman Family," *CP* 82 (1987): 21-34.

Because the urge to reproduce is an instinct common to all animals, society originally consists of the pair, next of the pair with their children, then one house and all things in common. This is the beginning of the city and the seed-bed of the state.[22]

The philosophers conceived of the household as a sort of constitutional monarchy. The father and husband might think about rules of behavior and might consult others, but those he consulted would be his opposite numbers from other households, not the subordinate members of his own household. He was answerable to the law and custom of his community and to public opinion but theoretically monarch within his own house. As Cicero's Scipio puts it to Laelius, "Isn't it true that no-one but you rules your entire house?"[23] We should not take such remarks to be literally true for all Roman households, but this neatly represents philosophical and legal theory.[24]

If he was *paterfamilias,* the father had power of life and death over his children. In practice the power seems to have been chiefly exercised at the time of a child's birth, when the father decided whether it should be reared. The autonomy of the *paterfamilias* was also circumscribed by the social expectation that he would consult a council of other heads of household, his relatives and his trusted friends before taking any important action and by the probable (though less approved) influence of his wife. Originally, perhaps the legal consent of *patresfamilias* sufficed to validate children's betrothal and marriage: in the classical period of law his consent was necessary as well as that of both bride and bridegroom. The withdrawal of the consent of the *paterfamilias* originally sufficed to break a marriage; later, emperors in the second century A.D. forebade fathers to break up a harmonious marriage and held that a father who initiated a divorce against his child's will merely ended his relationship as father-in-law and could not make the couple separate.[25] The third area of restriction is legal ownership by the *paterfamilias* of all property acquired by a child-in-power. In practice, it was usual to allow such a child to use and administer a personal fortune *(peculium).* Daughters needed a dowry: the father was expected to furnish or contribute to this, and the dowry was transferred to the husband for the duration of the marriage. All these paternal rights were softened by moral duty

---

[22]Cicero *De officiis* 1.54 (44 B.C.); cf. *Republic* 1.38.
[23]*Republic* 1.61; cf. Aristotle *Nicomachean Ethics* 1160b-1162a; David Konstan, *Friendship in the Classical World* (Cambridge: Cambridge University Press, 1997), pp. 70-72.
[24]See further on theories Treggiari, *Roman Marriage,* chaps. 6-7.
[25]Treggiari, *Roman Marriage,* p. 460.

and practical pressures that made them more flexible than a mere statement of his power suggests. In addition, the older the child, the more likely it was that the *paterfamilias* had died.

Theological significance. The Romans did not see each human marriage as an allegory. But each was an example of a natural animal mating. Marriage also existed on the divine plane, although the mythical adventures of gods and goddesses, with their many adulteries, were consciously rejected as models of human behavior. Nevertheless, the divine sister/wife and brother/husband, Juno and Jupiter, represented divine authority and protection for the institution of human marriage. This may be seen, for instance, in Plautus's *Amphitruo,* a retelling of the myth of Jupiter's fathering of Hercules. In order to consummate his love for the human Alcumena, the king of heaven must disguise himself as her husband, and in the end he must rescue her marriage to Amphitruo by making her innocence clear. The loving relationship of the human pair and the chastity and self-respect of Alcumena are dramatized. The humor is directed at the gods and at the misunderstandings they cause.

Juno was the most important divine protectress. As Juno Pronuba, represented by a sort of matron of honor, the *pronuba,* she presided at weddings. Diana, in various guises, was also a protectress of virginity, fertility and childbirth. Writers describe invocations of the god Hymen (who originates in Greek wedding hymns) during the wedding procession. Christian polemicists combed antiquarian writers to list numerous little gods who protected all stages of the beginning of a marriage, childbirth and the early lives of babies. It is not clear how much cult and belief in such beings existed in the historic period. At the time of engagement, well-wishers prayed that the marriage would turn out well; at weddings they wished the couple a long and harmonious union *(longa concordia).* Traditionally, the *paterfamilias* and his wife, the *materfamilias,* led the household cult. The father's *genius,* the "male spirit of a *gens*" (lineage) existing during his lifetime in the head of the family,[26] was a special protector of the *paterfamilias* and was associated with the marital bed.[27] The female equivalent of the *genius,* the Juno of the *materfamilias,* was also worshiped by household slaves.

The Greco-Roman gods of the major state cult had their individual histories in myth, but there was no orthodox theology. It would, however, be wrong to think that the gods were generally (except by Epicurean philoso-

---

[26]Cf. OCD.
[27]Juvenal *Satires* 6.22.

phers) thought to be uninterested in the moral behavior of human beings.

Definition. When in the sixth century Justinian's committee wanted to find a suitable excerpt to introduce the topic of marriage, they could find none earlier or more authoritative than Modestinus' (early third century A.D., died 244):

> Marriage is the joining together *[coniunctio]* of a male and a female, and a partnership for life in all areas of life *[consortium omnis vitae]*, a sharing in divine and human law *[divini et humani iuris communicatio]*.[28]

The Latin words *mas* and *femina* are used for male and female of animals, humans and divinities. In the very first paragraph of the *Digest*, on Justice and Law *(ius)*, we find the following passage of Ulpian (late second to early third century) on types of law:

> Natural law *[ius naturale]* is what Nature teaches all animals: for that law is not peculiar to the human race, but is common to all animals which are born on earth or in the sea and also to birds. From this derives the union of male and female, which we call marriage, from this comes the procreation of children and their rearing.[29]

This view goes back to Greek philosophy and is represented by Cicero in the quotation given more fully above in the discussion of demography. Cicero's words are also related to Modestinus's vague reference to sharing quoted above:

> The first sharing [*societas*] takes place in the actual mating of the pair, the next is that of the pair in their children. Then there is one house and all things in common.[30]

I have argued elsewhere that Modestinus's abstract *consortium omnis vitae* could include the intent of lifelong marriage,[31] which was part of the Roman ideal. But the idea of sharing is also a prominent part of the ideology, and that must certainly be denoted, as also in *communicatio*. The notably high-minded Stoic Musonius Rufus (born before A.D. 20, died before 101/2) says:

> The husband and wife . . . should come together for the purpose of making a life in common and of procreating children, and furthermore of regarding all

---

[28] *Digest* 23.2.1, Modestinus.
[29] *Digest* 1.1.1.3, Ulpian.
[30] Cicero *De officiis* 1.54.
[31] *Roman Marriage,* pp. 9-11.

things in common between them, and nothing peculiar or private to one or the other, not even their own bodies.[32]

We can add to this Greco-Roman theory the routine Latin phrases that described the purpose of legal marriage, *liberorum quaerundorum causa,* "for the sake of producing children," and cognates. This was familiar enough to be alluded to in jokes.[33] It reflects the husband's viewpoint: he married in order to create *liberi,* descendants. *Matrimonium* was an institution for making mothers *(matres).* Marriage was part of the ancient customary law of the people who became the Romans: statute law made some modifications, but there was little theorizing except for the argument that it derived from behavior shared with gods and animals and the views of moralists about the ideal relationship.

Some consideration was given to men unable to procreate. The rules fit oddly with the declared purpose of marriage. The broad term was *spado,* "eunuch," which included both congenital eunuchs and castrated males.[34] (The emperors repeatedly prohibited castration, but importation of castrated slaves was allowed.) A congenital eunuch could make a valid Roman marriage, but a castrated one could not.[35] It followed that a slave owner was allowed to free a woman in order to marry her, when he was under twenty or she under thirty (the minimum ages according to an Augustan law)—subject to the approval of a committee—even if he was a natural *spado* but not if he was a castrated male.[36] A congenital eunuch, but not a castrated man, could adopt.[37] Presumably the reason is that there was just a chance that the apparent natural *spado* would succeed in having a child.[38]

The vocabulary included *coniunx* (pl. *coniuges*) for either husband or wife; *uxor* for a wife; *mulier* for woman or wife; *maritus* for a husband; *vir* for man or husband. In an asymmetric set of usages, a man "led" *(ducere)* and received and kept a woman in marriage; a woman wedded a husband (*nubere,* with indirect object), came into and was in marriage with him.

Capacity. A couple legally capable of marriage had the reciprocal right to marry each other *(conubium).* Roman law ruled out marriage between ascendant and descendant (including adoptive relations) and between

---

[32]13A; trans. by Cora Lutz in "Musonius Rufus: The Roman Socrates," *YCS* 10 (1947): 89.
[33]Plautus *Pseudolus* 23.
[34]*Digest* 50.16.128.
[35]*Digest* 23.3.39.1, Ulpian.
[36]*Digest* 40.2.14.1, Marcion (later first half of third century).
[37]Justinian *Institutes* 1.11.9.
[38]Cf. *Digest* 28.2.6, *principium,* Ulpian: he is a man "who cannot easily procreate."

brother and sister. By the late Republic, marriage between first cousins was legal. A man might not marry the child of his sister down to the fourth generation, or his aunt, stepmother, stepdaughter, former mother-in-law or former daughter-in-law. When Claudius in A.D. 49 wanted to marry his brother's daughter, such marriages were legalized, but few followed his example. The rules for women followed the pre-Claudian pattern for men. Marriages that ignored the rules on affinity were incestuous and null and might be punished.

There were also rules about the minimum age: twelve for a girl. She had to be mature enough for intercourse, *viripotens*,[39] but, since the Romans held it improper to subject a girl to physical examination, the age qualification was what mattered to lawyers. A girl who "married" under twelve did not legally become a wife until her twelfth birthday when her status changed without further action. Moderns conjecture that *menarche* was, on average, at thirteen; this does not necessarily mean that the individual underage brides attested had not reached that early stage of puberty. Although some women of the imperial family, for dynastic reasons, are known to have been married very young (e.g., Agrippina the Younger, born in A.D. 15/16, was married in 28), even aristocrats seem more likely to marry in their midteens, and women of middling rank in their late teens.[40] Observable features of adolescence are mentioned as a social qualification. Similarly, boys had to be able to consummate the marriage. Fatherless boys were freed of guardianship either at fourteen or when judged by inspection to be physically mature (some lawyers demanded both qualifications). This might also indicate the legal qualification for marriage, but usually men married much later. The tomb inscriptions suggest the late twenties in society as a whole.[41] Men of senatorial or town-council rank married earlier to secure advantages under Augustan law, which privileged officeholders with children and encouraged men between twenty-five and sixty to be fathers. Emperors' destined heirs might marry earlier still. (Marcellus, born in 42 B.C., married Augustus's daughter in 25 B.C.; the future emperor Nero was about sixteen when he married Claudius's daughter.)

Citizen status was also a criterion. Roman citizens could normally form Roman marriages, as long as they were old enough and not closely related. The right of intermarriage *(conubium)* also existed with people of Latin sta-

---

[39]Justinian *Institutes* 1.10 *principium*.
[40]Shaw, "Age of Roman Girls at Marriage."
[41]Saller, "Men's Age at Marriage."

tus and certain citizens of other foreign communities. There could be no legal marriage between a citizen and a slave or between two slaves.[42] Some Roman citizens formed unions with foreigners, which might be recognized by the non-Roman community. A union involving at least one slave *(contubernium)* enjoyed no legal status.

Augustus's marriage laws of 18 B.C. and A.D. 9 introduced new restrictions. No freeborn male citizen was to marry a prostitute, procuress, freedwoman of a male or female procurer, woman taken in adultery or condemned by a public court, or former stage performer;[43] no senator or senator's child in the male line down to great-grandchildren was to marry or become engaged to a freedwoman, stage performer or daughter of a performer.[44] The rules for women must have corresponded. Marriage between freeborn and freed slave was otherwise encouraged.[45] At some point between Augustus (27 B.C.-A.D. 14) and Claudius (41-54), soldiers below a certain rank were forbidden to marry.[46]

The intention of the Augustan laws was to regulate and to encourage marriage and production of children.[47] The second statute, we are told, expected men between twenty-five and sixty and women between twenty and fifty to have children (and, it follows, to have entered a first marriage rather younger than twenty-five and twenty). An elaborate system of rewards and penalties was set up. Instead of offering family allowances, as modern states are able to do, Augustus was able to offer privileges to the officeholding classes and enhanced or restricted rights in private law. For example, a father was allowed to subtract one year for each child from the minimum age at which he could hold an office. A freeborn Roman woman with three living children or a freedwoman with four was allowed to be free of guardianship. This must have been a genuine benefit for lowerclass women, and no doubt was valued by all. Having children (numbers required varied in different contexts) exempted a man from serving as guardian. Being married or having children improved one's right to inherit from remote kin or friends. Conversely, the childless could only take half of such a bequest.

---

[42]*Tituli Ulpiani* (ca. A.D. 300) 5.3-5.

[43]Ibid., 13.2.

[44]*Digest* 23.3.44 *principium*, Paul.

[45]Ibid., 23.2.23, Celsus *Dio* 54.16.2.

[46]Sara Elise Phang, *The Marriage of Roman Soldiers (13 B.C.-A.D. 235)*, Columbia Studies in the Classical Tradition 24 (Leiden: Brill, 2001), shows the ban probably dates to 13 B.C.

[47]Beth Severy, *Reconceiving the* Res Publica: *Augustus, the Family and the Birth of the Roman Empire* (London: Routledge, forthcoming).

This was an unprecedented effort at social engineering, and the rules on inheritance were much resented by the wealthier classes, who were most affected. The whole complicated structure was swept away by early Christian emperors in the fourth and fifth centuries.

Betrothal. The upper classes sometimes arranged marriages well in advance, but in the classical period an engagement was unenforceable at law. The consent of future bride and bridegroom was legally necessary, as well as that of any *paterfamilias*.[48] The requirement that the consent of a daughter-in-power was legally necessary seems not to go back to the beginning: Ulpian says it could be assumed unless she made it clear she did not agree, and it was only proper for her to disagree if her *paterfamilias* had chosen a man of bad character.[49] A child might not be able to resist, but the prospect of girls being forced into distasteful marriages is softened by the fact that engagements were not actionable, that a *paterfamilias* might not survive until his daughter was marriageable, and that other family members might intervene. For whatever reasons, the theme of reluctant daughters is unexploited in Latin literature and Roman life. Reluctant sons, however, provide a literary *motif*. If we attach weight to the short excerpt from Ulpian, we must give equal weight to his contemporary Paulus's statement on the authority of a great Hadrianic lawyer: "But Julianus writes that a father is always understood to give his consent to a daughter, unless it is clear that he does not."[50]

There was no minimum age for betrothal, but jurists required a child to be able to understand what was going on: by the third century, this was understood to mean at least seven.[51] No special formalities were required and the engaged couple did not even need to be present,[52] but a party was no doubt usual. Politicians like Mark Antony and Octavian sometimes used their children as pawns: their daughters Antonia and Julia, born in 39, were betrothed, respectively, to L. Domitius Ahenobarbus and M. Antonius Antyllus in 37. Octavian also arranged the engagement of Vipsania, daughter of his great ally Agrippa, to his stepson (the future emperor Tiberius) when she was scarcely a year old.[53] Such betrothals of babies seem to have been unusual. Upperclass boys seem normally to have waited until they came of

---

[48]*Digest* 23.1.7.1, Paulus; 23.1.11, Julian (consul 149).
[49]Ibid., 23.1.12.
[50]Ibid., 23.1.7.1, Paulus.
[51]Ibid., 23.1.14, Modestinus.
[52]Ibid., 23.1.4.
[53]Nepos *Atticus* 19.4.

age and took the toga of manhood at age sixteen or seventeen. Since the
usual age gap at first marriage seems to have been nine or ten years, probably some girls were engaged as young as seven. We hear of long engagements with the marriage repeatedly postponed[54] and also of very short
ones. An engagement created a bond between the families: the vocabulary
of relationship by marriage *(affinitas)* was used, and a broken engagement
might be described as renunciation of a marriage relationship. But engagements were commonly broken, often for reasons of advantage, and there
were often no awkward side effects. If repudiation was thought to be mo-
tivated by perceived moral shortcomings, as the word implies (it is connected with the stem *pud,* implying shame), the reputation of the rejected
partner could suffer. But it must often have been clear that no blame attached and that the breaker of the engagement had merely found a richer,
better-born or better-looking candidate. No damages were payable, though
presents might be returned.

The qualities sought in a future husband or wife were generally agreed, to
judge by commonplaces in the literature: birth, wealth, family connections,
brains in a man, and beauty and virtue in a woman. What underlies this is the
purpose of producing children and giving them the best possible future. All
had to be judged relative to what the other partner could offer, and the ideal
package might not be available. We occasionally observe outsiders rating a
match by the conventional criteria. Fathers or other relations, or the future
bridegroom, or even the bride (not so much the young girl who was to be
married for the first time but widows and divorcees of a certain age), grap-
pling with reality, evaluated actual candidates. Negotiation and compromise
were often necessary. The ideology of love as the only or chief justification
for a match had not developed, though the happy endings of Greco-Roman
comedy featured the achievement of marriage by the young man who had
fallen in love with a girl who turned out to be virtuous and a freeborn citizen.
There are some real matches reported where attraction or affection seems to
have been a motive. For general recognition of such personal motivation, it is
sufficient to cite the Augustan rule that a male slave owner under the age of
twenty, who had to justify his wish to free a slave before a committee, had
good grounds if he wished to free a girl in order to marry her.[55]

Consent to marriage. "A marriage cannot exist unless everyone con-
sents, that is, those who come together and those in whose power they

---

[54]*Digest* 23.1.17.
[55]Gaius *Institutes* 1.18-19; *Tituli Ulpiani* 1.12-14.

are."[56] The rule about consent to marriage was the same as for betrothal. *Patresfamilias* had to give consent, as well as the man and woman. Consent was what constituted the marriage: "A marriage is made by consent, not by sexual intercourse."[57]

Too much paternal pressure might be counterproductive; a rhetorical school exercise allowed the student to produce the following thoughts:

> "You are to marry the wife I want you to marry," says my father. What is that to the point? Are you not aware that marriages are at our own choice? Our affections are not at your beck and call; you cannot order us to love or hate whom you want. Marriage is only eternal if it is a union brought about by mutual consent. When a wife is sought for me, the companion of my bed, the partner of my life, she must be chosen for all eternity. In any case, what is the good of compelling me against my will? If you do that, I will simply divorce her.[58]

Despite the conventions, individual choice and emotional motives played a part. We find one young man, Cicero's nephew Quintus, negotiating a marriage for himself with a woman not yet divorced, who, he said, had made the first move. Though he was presumably in his father's power, he negotiated without prior approval from his father.[59] The match came to nothing. When Cicero himself became eligible once more after divorcing Terentia, he rejected outright one candidate because of her looks. "I've never seen anything uglier," he said in private.[60] Philosophers would have regarded this reason as hopelessly frivolous.

When it came to a woman's second marriage, when she had been circulating in society for some time, she could claim more power of choice than when she was married for the first time. Cicero speaks of submitting candidates' names to Tullia for her approval, not of telling her whom to marry. In the end she, with support from her mother, chose her third husband.[61]

Weddings. What makes the marriage is the consent of the bride and bridegroom (as well as the *paterfamilias* of each, if he exists). Consent is a mental resolve to be married, each to the other. Each must express that resolve, in one form or another. There was no one necessary form of words, but the intention had to be clear. Various kinds of ceremony were practiced

---

[56]*Digest* 23.2.2, Paulus.
[57]Ibid., 50.17.30, Ulpian.
[58]Quintilian *Declamationes Minores* 376.2.
[59]Cicero *Ad Atticum* 15.29.2; 16.2.5.
[60]Ibid., 12.11 (46 B.C.).
[61]Treggiari, *Roman Marriage,* pp. 127-34.

and several verbal formulae are known to have occurred. Usually bride and bridegroom went through a ceremony in front of their family and friends. On the monuments and sarcophagi of married people, the most important moment of this is represented by the clasping of right hands, much as a modern wedding might be represented at the moment where a bridegroom, using his right hand, puts the ring on his bride's left hand (and sometimes vice versa). Often the bride marked her transition from her parents to her husband by going in procession to the bridegroom's house *(deductio)*. The day was marked by sacrifice, feasting, special dress and innumerable small customs. Some of those present had special ritual roles. Parents handed over the bride and expressed approval. But no priest or public official ratified the marriage, and no public register was signed. It was the couple who bilaterally made the marriage (with *patresfamilias,* if they existed). Nor was sexual consummation necessary to make the marriage valid, though it was expected to take place immediately.

Affectio maritalis. Marriage was founded on the intention of each of two people. How did each know what the other meant? How did any outsider know what they both meant? It could be quite tricky. For instance, people would usually expect married couples to live together, but impediments were common. Caesar spent most of his marriage to Calpurnia apart from her while he fought the Gallic war and then the civil war (from 58 until his death on 15 March 44 B.C.). They were never together for twelve consecutive months. Cicero was kept away from Terentia for a year or more at a time by exile, his provincial governorship or the civil war. A later lawyer, in the context of a rather odd rule that said that major gifts between husband and wife were invalid, raises the following question:

> If a wife and husband have lived apart for a long time but each reciprocally has honoured the marriage (something which we are aware has sometimes happened even between people of consular rank), then I think that gifts between them are not valid, on the grounds that the marriage is still in existence, for it is not cohabitation which makes a marriage, but conjugal attitude, *maritalis affectio.*[62]

Although our word *affection* derives from *affectio,* we must not translate the juristic phrase as "marital affection." An *affectio* of the mind may be a transitory mood, like irritation, anger, or love, says Cicero,[63] or "a more or less permanent mental . . . characteristic, a habitual state, disposition."[64] In the le-

---

[62]*Digest* 24.3.32.13, Ulpian.
[63]Cicero *De inventione rhetorica* 1.41; *Oxford Latin Dictionary,* s.v. 1.
[64]*Oxford Latin Dictionary,* s.v. 3.

gal texts it is particularly a purpose, intention, attitude or viewpoint.[65] A person can define even a small patch of ground as a farm, if he wants to: it is his *affectio* that makes it a farm.[66] If a man, when he checked his household stores, was in the habit of reckoning vinegar or beer or ale as wine, they could count as wine in his will too.[67] Thinking makes it so. So if you thought of a man as your husband, then he was—as long as he simultaneously thought of you as his wife and as long as there was no legal impediment.

Logically, if two Romans went through a marriage ceremony but did not intend to marry, the ceremony was meaningless. Quintilian says that even a sealed contract meant nothing if the intention to be married was absent.[68] Similarly, two people without capacity could not make a marriage. Conversely, if two eligible people regarded each other as husband and wife, they were married—even though they had no written document about property, no dowry had been handed over to the husband and there had been no celebration. This allowed the jurists to recognize that other sexual relationships might turn into marriage, without a public marking of the fact. If a man first lived with a woman as his concubine (an acknowledged mistress) and later they both began to regard each other as husband and wife, that is what they were. However, the date of the change might be hard for other people to establish.[69] Similarly a quasi-marriage between slaves could be transformed into legal marriage if they wished, once both of them were freed.

Outsiders, such as judges, were very often called upon to decide on the status of a relationship when one or both parties had died. The legitimacy of children and the transmission of property were probably at stake. How did they decide? Written documents would help—letters addressing the partner as wife or husband or tomb inscriptions paid for by the survivor would show how one person had viewed the other. Better still would be the registration of children (introduced by Augustus) by the father. A tomb inscription set up in the lifetime of both might make a joint claim to legal marriage. But very often the courts were reduced to finding out how the neighbors had regarded a couple. They looked at the relative social status of the couple and the way they behaved, their way of life.[70] Supposing legal Roman marriage was open to a couple, for instance neither was a slave, then it

---

[65]Ibid., s.v. 5.
[66]*Digest* 50.16.60, Ulpian.
[67]Ibid., 33.6.9, Ulpian.
[68]*Institutio oratoria* 5.11.32.
[69]*Digest* 39.5.31 *principium,* Papinian; cf. 24.1.3.1, Ulpian.
[70]Ibid., 39.5.31 *principium,* Papinian.

should usually be assumed that they were married. The only exception among the lower classes would be if the man was freeborn and the woman had been a prostitute because marriages between such people were invalid after Augustus's law.[71]

Divorce. By the time of Cicero a divorce could be brought about by either husband or wife and unilaterally. In theory, it was enough for one partner in the marriage to cease to regard the other as husband or wife. In practice, it was sensible and no doubt usual to inform the other partner. Cicero has a story from the late second century B.C.:

> What about what occurred in the living memory of our fathers, when a *paterfamilias* who had come from Spain to Rome, leaving his wife in the province pregnant, married another woman at Rome and did not send a notice of divorce to his previous wife? He then died intestate and each wife bore a son. It was not a trivial matter which was disputed, for an investigation was made about the civil rights of two citizens, both about the child born of the second wife and about his mother. She would have been reduced to the position of a concubine if judgment were given that divorce from an earlier wife takes place because of some fixed form of words, not because of a new marriage.
>
> In all these cases (sc. which Crassus cited) and in the case of the boy who was born from the second wife, when a message of divorce had not been sent to the first wife, there was an intense disagreement on points of law among experts.[72]

Although Augustus demanded that some divorces at least be properly witnessed, it remained in principle true that the partner's knowledge that she or he had been divorced was not *legally* necessary:

> Julian, in the eighteenth book of his *Digests* asks, whether a madwoman can send notice of repudiation or be repudiated. And he writes that a madwoman can be repudiated, because she is in the same position as a person who does not know: but neither she herself nor her curator can repudiate her husband, although her father can send notice of divorce.[73]

In practice, though, people were usually careful to ensure that their friends and families knew they had divorced, just as they made it known that they were married.

Divorce might happen because both husband and wife agreed on it. Such a consensual or bilateral divorce was expected to leave no bitterness or

---

[71]Ibid., 23.2.24, Modestinus.
[72]Cicero *De oratore* 1.183, 238.
[73]*Digest* 24.2.4, Ulpian.

blame and was said to happen *bona gratia,* "with a good grace." Again, the vital point about divorce is that no public authority had to ratify it. As in marriage, the *paterfamilias* of either husband or wife might be involved. In early law, he had probably been able to bring about a divorce of his son or daughter all by himself. But by the early Principate there were limits to his effectiveness. He could sue for return of dowry only if the daughter consented.[74] Eventually, in the second century, it was held that he could end the relationship of father-in-law and son-in-law but that he could not force his daughter to end the marriage.[75]

The theory that unites Roman thinking about marriage and about divorce is that both are free, a principle continued into modern law. In theory, no one could be compelled to marry. He or she could make a legal Roman marriage with any legally eligible person. No one could be compelled to remain married against his or her will. No one could be compelled to divorce. The pressure that might be exercised by families and the state's attempts to persuade and blackmail people into marrying so that they produced children are irrelevant to this principle. What makes a marriage is the joint consent of two qualified individuals. The marriage lasts as long as both continue to consent. If one withdraws consent, there is a divorce.

At the period when either party could legally divorce the other at will, people expressed the ideal of a loyalty that lasted as long as both lived.[76] We have no statistics on divorce, although moralists held that it happened too often. Some members of the upper classes divorced several times, for instance, Pompey and the future emperor Augustus; political motives seem to have been important. Similarly, divorce, remarriage and adoption were instruments of dynastic policy in the imperial family, particularly for Augustus. Others divorced for incompatibility (often early on) or because relations had become inharmonious after years of relative contentment. Some marriages were amicably dissolved bilaterally, when both decided they should not continue: "It often happens that because of a priesthood or even sterility, or old age or ill health or military service it is inconvenient to maintain a marriage, and therefore the marriage is dissolved with good will."[77]

A famous eulogy to a dead wife (*Laudatio Turiae*) portrays her as suggesting divorce after many years of marriage, so that her husband might

---

[74]Ibid., 24.3.34, Africanus (mid-second century); *Tituli Ulpiani* 6.6.

[75]*Digest* 24.1.32.19-20; *Codex Justiniani* 5.17.5.

[76]*Laudatio Turiae* 1.27.

[77]*Digest* 24.1.60.1-62 *principium.*

have descendants. The husband's explosion of feeling is a classic passage
on the ideology of marriage.

> When you despaired of your ability to bear children and grieved over my
> childlessness, you became anxious lest by retaining you in marriage I might
> lose all hope of having children and be distressed for that reason. So you pro-
> posed a divorce outright. I must admit that I flared up so that I almost lost con-
> trol of myself; so horrified was I by what you had tried to do that I found it
> difficult to retrieve my composure. To think that separation should be consid-
> ered between us before fate had so ordained, to think that you had been able
> to conceive in your mind the idea that you might cease to be my wife while I
> was still alive, although you had been utterly faithful to me when I was exiled
> and practically dead![78]

Despite the legal option, individual wives are rarely attested as taking
the initiative and divorcing unilaterally. But women in general are severely
criticized for doing such things.[79] We have no information on the lower
classes.

After a divorce, husbands remained legally responsible for children, who
were essential for the continuance of the male line. This does not mean,
however, that mothers lost touch. Scribonia, for instance, divorced by the
future Augustus on the day she bore Julia in 39 B.C., accompanied her into
exile in 2 B.C. Divorced wives might have the children living with them.
However, a young mother would be expected to remarry, and lawyers and
others were concerned that she might neglect the children of the first marriage. There was also a phobia about the stepmother who married a man
with children from an earlier marriage. There is, however, no criticism of the
upbringing that Livia and Augustus gave to the sons of her first marriage,
who came to her when their divorced father died. Similarly, the single stepmother Octavia is not criticized for her care of the children of Antony (by
Fulvia and by Cleopatra), who had divorced her.

To divorce a wife because of adultery (or behavior likely to lead to adultery) was probably legal from the beginning. In such circumstances, the husband could mulct the dowry. In the historic period, no cause need be
alleged. The blame for divorce lay with the person who gave cause (this includes a husband's blatant sexual misconduct) or who initiated the divorce

---

[78]*Laudatio Turiae* 1.31-33, 40-43; translation from Erik Wistrand, ed., *The So-called Laudatio Turiae,* Studia Graeca et Latina Gothoburgensia 34 (Göteborg: University of Göteborg, 1976).
[79]Seneca *De beneficiis* 3.16.2; Martial *Epigrams* 6.7, 10.41; Juvenal *Satires* 6.224-30.; Tertullian *Apologia* 6.6.

when the other had not committed a fault. There were some legal penalties involving dowry. A man might be criticized for divorcing the mother of his children or a wife of long standing.

Christian emperors (not necessarily because they were Christian) restricted the right to divorce unilaterally. Constantine allowed wives to divorce only a husband who committed murder, prepared poisons or violated tombs, while a husband could divorce for adultery, preparation of poison or procuring.[80] Further refinements followed. It was not until Justinian that consensual divorce was penalized.[81]

Dowry. It is striking that dowry is the topic connected with marriage that most concerned the Roman jurists. They theorized little about the nature of marriage, which had developed with minimal intervention from lawgivers. Divorce attracted more attention, but most of their energy was devoted to the complicated consequences of divorce as it affected property, and particularly the dowry that a woman normally brought into a marriage.

When a woman entered *manus,* everything she owned became the husband's. By the first century B.C., this seems to have been equated with dowry. For the majority who, in historical times, did not enter *manus,* it was usual to bring a dowry into the marriage. Dowry was not legally essential, but it was customary for a woman to bring it to her new family. A woman without a dowry might have difficulty marrying. An increased dowry might compensate for diminished attractions in other respects (being past one's youth, apparently infertile, having been repudiated by a previous husband and so on). Poor women and even slaves seem to have tried to produce some kind of dowry. The richer classes might constitute a dowry that included land, houses, cash, slaves, livestock, and valuables such as plate and jewels or consumer items such as textiles.

During the marriage, the dowry belonged to the husband, but it was in theory separable from his own property. Late classical jurists tend to stress that it was only temporarily in his possession, as long as the marriage lasted, and might have to be restored: "Although the dowry is among the husband's goods, yet it is the wife's."[82] Non-lawyers in the central period already saw things this way. But the husband administered the dotal property and enjoyed the income from it. He could sell items (except that Augustus limited

[80]Judith Evans Grubbs, *Law and Family in Late Antiquity: The Emperor Constantine's Marriage Legislation* (Oxford: Clarendon, 1995), pp. 228-32, 242-60.

[81]Ibid., pp. 232-41; Antti Arjava, *Women and Law in Late Antiquity* (Oxford: Clarendon, 1996), pp. 177-92.

[82]*Digest* 23.3.75, Tryphoninus.

his right to sell dotal land in Italy; land was the securest ancient investment) or invest cash. He was responsible for careful and honest administration. When the dowry was transferred to him, it might be valued: it was to the wife's advantage if this were done, for the husband would then be liable for return of the full value of items that might have depreciated, such as clothes or animals.[83] The revenues from dowry seem to have been expected to balance the additional expenditures needed to support a wife and probably to contribute toward the maintenance of any children of the marriage.[84]

Variant arrangements were possible; for instance, the wife might promise to pay her own expenses (including the support of her servants) and the husband allow her the revenues of the dowry from which to do this. The wealthier classes negotiated all sorts of financial arrangements as it suited them. There was possibility for friction: as early as the comedies of Plautus the richly dowered wife and the demands she makes on her husband in her pursuit of a fashionable lifestyle are a literary commonplace.[85] From the husband's point of view, his desire for the biggest possible dowry had to be counterbalanced by his fear that it would give his wife leverage to use against him. The bigger the dowry, the more difficult it was to divorce a wife, at least in the opinion of satirists and moralists.

The size of dowry was expected to be appropriate to the standing of the two parties. The lawyers talk of fixing it in the light of the resources and status of the bride's family and the status of the bridegroom.[86] It was clearly very distressing for an elite family if a financial crisis threatened their ability to dower their daughters. To give dowries to poor and respectable women was one of the recognized benefactions appropriate for wealthy women, the Senate or the emperor. Private friends might also step in. During the imperial period, the minimum capital required of a senator was one million sesterces. Consequently, this was the amount he would need to pass on to any son who was to qualify for the Senate; this was also the sum conventionally mentioned as a suitable dowry for his daughter[87] or a very big dowry.[88] Many senators possessed property worth much more than this minimum. (The largest fortunes cited for the early Principate are of 400 million. This ex-

---

[83]Ibid., 23.3.10 *principium*, Ulpian.

[84]François Dumont, "Les revenues de la dot en droit romain," *Revue historique de droit français et étranger* 1 (1943): 1-43; Treggiari, *Roman Marriage,* pp. 332-40.

[85]E.g., Plautus *Menaechmi* 120-22.

[86]E.g., *Digest* 32.43, Celsus.

[87]Tacitus *Annals* 2.86.

[88]Seneca *Ad Helviam* 12.6; Juvenal *Satires* 6.137; 10.335; and others.

cludes the emperor himself.) So the figure is not incredible, though we must take it only as a ballpark figure of what our sources thought possible.[89] This dowry minimum had allegedly already been exceeded in the second century B.C. by the daughters of Scipio, with approximately 1,250,000 sesterces each. In the imperial period, we are told by Apuleius in his tendentious speech in his own defense, that his wife, a prosperous North African but not of senatorial family, had capital of four million sesterces and gave him a dowry worth 300,000: she was protecting the interest of the sons of her first marriage.[90] It has been persuasively argued by Saller that the need to provide a dowry was not such a crushing responsibility as it later became in European societies.[91] However, it could stretch resources when the timing of a marriage was inconvenient, and fathers could worry about it.[92]

Dowry, though a cash figure might be put on it, was, at least for the upper classes, often a package of various sorts of property. If cash, it would normally be paid in three annual installments, starting one year after the wedding. Friends and family, especially a mother, might contribute. However, the primary responsibility fell on the father, if he was alive, or the bride herself, acting with the approval of her guardian, *tutor,* if she was fatherless.

The rules, which developed gradually, about what happened to dowry when a marriage ended, depended on the provenance of the dowry and how the marriage came to an end. If the wife died and the dowry had come from her father or grandfather (this was called *dos profecticia*), it returned to him. But if, as was quite likely, the male ascendant had died before the wife, the husband retained it. If the dowry came from anyone else *(dos adventicia),* the husband kept it, unless the donor had made a legal stipulation for its return. If it was the husband who died, the widow could reclaim her dowry, and his heirs (who might be her children) could make no deductions.

If the marriage ended in divorce, the wife and her *paterfamilias* had the right to sue her husband for the return of the dowry. The type of action was based on equity and seems to go back to the early second century B.C. The husband was allowed to deduct fractions of the dowry because of children or because of the wife's immorality or to repay expenses or gifts or property that she took away. The fractions may have changed over time: we hear of a deduction of one-sixth for the wife's adultery and one-eighth for lesser

---

[89]Walter Scheidel, "Finances, Figures and Fiction," CQ 46 (1996): 222-38; Saller, *Patriarchy, Property and Death*, pp. 204-24, esp. 217.
[90]*Apologia* 71, 77, 91, 92.
[91]Saller, *Patriarchy, Property and Death*, p. 212.
[92]E.g., Cicero *Paradoxa Stoicorum* 44; Suetonius *Gaius Caligula* 42.1.

faults.[93] These retentions were all abolished by Justinian in the sixth century. A husband whose misconduct caused a divorce was compelled to restore any cash component of the dowry in six months (rather than by three annual installments).

If the marriage had produced children, a widower could keep one-fifth of the dowry for each child. In the case of divorce, the divorced husband, if the divorce was initiated from the wife's side and he had committed no fault, could keep one-sixth for each of three children. This did not apply if he had initiated the divorce.[94]

There were detailed rules on deductions that the husband might make to take account of his expenditure on dotal property. These might be defined as necessary (to preserve the property's value, for example, stopping a building falling down), useful (intended to make the property more profitable, for instance, creating a vineyard), or for pleasure (for instance, adding wall-paintings). There were also complicated calculations about the income in a year when a divorce took place.

Many people seem to have made contracts that defined in advance what should happen to dowry at the end of the marriage: this might avoid litigation. Saint John Chrysostom, Bishop of Constantinople 398-403, introduced the congregation's preoccupation with this kind of thing into a sermon:

> When you are on the point of taking a wife you run after alien lawyers with great eagerness, sit beside them, and meticulously explore the question of what will happen if your wife dies without issue, and what will happen if she has a child, or two, or three, and how she will enjoy her property if her father is alive, or if he is not, and what part of her share will go to her brothers and what to her husband, and in what circumstances will the husband take control of all her property, so that he does not have to give up any of it to anyone, and when he will lose possession of it entirely. And you busy yourself about many such things and you keep asking them questions, searching round and about and up and down to make sure that in no way can any of the wife's property go back to any of her relations.[95]

But here we are thinking about the total picture of the impact of death on the wife's property rights and not just of where the dowry would go.

Property. It was expected that a wealthy woman would (if she was not a daughter in power) have personal property that was greater than the

---

[93] *Tituli Ulpiani* 6.9.
[94] Ibid., 6.3, 10.
[95] PG 51:226-227.

dowry transferred to her husband. Unlike women in some societies, Roman women could own every kind of property, including land.[96] The only peculiarity was that any woman independent of a *paterfamilias* needed to have a guardian to validate certain property transactions. Women until the age of twelve were in "guardianship of prepubertal children" and thereafter in "guardianship of women" *(tutela mulierum)*. Additional protection was added under the emperors for those under twenty-five years of age. Under the Principate, exemption from the requirement for a guardian could be won. But in any case, the guardian's approval seems to have been a "rubber stamp" (except for a freedwoman, whose guardian was usually her ex-owner, who had an interest in controlling her property).

In classical Roman law, there was no expectation that the husband would make a premarital settlement on the wife. There are rare known instances of the husband making a gift to enable her to give him a dowry. But the custom of a substantial premarital gift from the husband's side, *donatio ante nuptias*, was introduced only during the fifth and sixth centuries.

Most wives, not entering *manus*, continued to be members of their natal family. Lawyers were preoccupied with keeping family property intact and clearly separate, so a custom arose of discouraging gifts between husband and wife.

> It is accepted by custom among us that gifts between husband and wife are invalid. The reason for this practice is to prevent them being plundered reciprocally because of their mutual love, by not being moderate in gift-giving but by extravagant generosity towards each other.[97]

The date of the custom is unknown, but it is probably pre-Augustan and certainly current in Augustus' time. Other juristic passages add the possibility that gifts would discourage interest in children, would make it possible for one to put pressure on the other, would enrich the poorer and impoverish the richer, and would corrupt the harmony that should be seen to exist.[98] What the lawyers wanted to avoid was gifts that enriched husband or wife at the expense of the other. The rule never applied to ordinary birthday presents. Nor does it seem to have stopped husbands and wives from giving each other property, such as land. But such gifts could be revoked during

---

[96] In 169 B.C. the Voconian Law tried to prevent men in the richest class from leaving their entire property to a woman, for instance an only daughter or a wife, but there were no restrictions on the type of property.

[97] *Digest* 24.1.1, Ulpian.

[98] Ibid., 24.1.2; 24.1.3 *principium*-1.

one's life or after one's death if not confirmed in the will. In A.D. 206, Severus and Caracalla changed this, allowing gifts if the donor showed no signs of changing his or her mind and the will did not specifically revoke them. However, if it was the recipient who died or the marriage was ended by divorce, such gifts continued to be revocable as before.[99] The system was more flexible than the jurists suggest when they speak of "invalid" gifts.

The ideology of sharing and the practicalities of a joint household pushed in opposite directions. The husband expected the wife to run the household and give orders to his slaves when necessary. He might provide her with personal staff and equipment for her needs. It was generally expected that he would provide the matrimonial home, but it was not uncommon for the wife to own it. Either might administer the other's financial affairs. Often they were joint owners of property such as slaves: this seems to have been especially typical of the poorer classes, who owned few slaves. Some husbands became their wives' legal guardians, often nominated by their fathers.

A wife's right to inherit her husband's property on his death if he had not made a will (and vice versa) came after that of blood relations, unless she was *in manu* or a close relative herself. Even if a Roman made a will, some imperfection might invalidate it. Then the rules on intestacy would come back into play. The rules also show the ancient preference for kin, especially in the male line. There were further restrictions imposed by various statutes on the rights of *coniuges* to inherit under wills.

By the Voconian Law (169 B.C.) male or female testators with the highest census rating could not make a woman heir and executor, *heres*. Nor could legacies be bigger than the share the *heres* took. There were no problems under this law with a wife in this class making her husband her heir. The Augustan marriage legislation allowed husbands and wives to leave each other 10 percent of their estates by virtue of being married, but the whole if they had one child. In practice, people tried to dispose of their property in many different ways. A husband might leave his wife the estate in trust for their children or make a son heir but leave her, as legacy, the enjoyment of a house and revenue for her lifetime. Or wife and children might be coheirs. A woman might leave property to her son in his father's power, on condition that the father emancipate him so that he would own the property independently. Specific items of property might be transmitted as legacies. A husband might leave property to his wife for her to take once she succeeded in having children in a subsequent marriage, thus fulfilling the Au-

---

[99]Ibid., 24.1.3 *principium;* 24.1.32.

gustan requirement. Legacies to wives, which required more discussion by lawyers than did those to husbands, included legacy of her dowry (which saved her time and trouble in getting it back), of consumer durables that he had provided for her, of valuables and accessories such as jewelry and the expensive toilet sets like the silver ones that are such prominent exhibits in museums, of stores such as food, and of annual allowances for her support. For lack of systematic records, we cannot say whether husbands and wives tended to give each other priority over children or children over each other. We can see that all sorts of plans were possible. It is also apparent that both testators and legal theorists were anxious to protect the offspring of earlier marriages, posthumous children and the interests of a surviving *coniunx*.[100]

Adultery. Roman society required women of respectable class to be chaste, whether married or not. During the Republic, with some encouragement from aediles and censors, families policed the behavior of women and young sons. Adultery by the wife was presumably always grounds for divorce. She might also be punished by a council of her kin. The husband who divorced his wife for adultery might (through judicial action) take monetary compensation from the dowry; he might also seek damages from the lover. It was a literary commonplace that husbands would enjoy various imaginative forms of physical reprisal against a man they caught in their house.

The Augustan adultery law (most often called by scholars the *Lex Iulia de adulteriis*), which bore the emperor's own name and was passed in 18 B.C. or soon after, "protected" married women, unmarried girls *(virgines)* and women who had been married but were now single *(viduae:* widows and divorcees). They could be prosecuted on a criminal charge for extramarital sexual intercourse. If the woman was married, that counted as *adulterium* (the word is related to *alter,* "another man"). Otherwise, it was *stuprum,* illicit intercourse in general, which also denoted illicit intercourse between males.[101] If a woman had an extramarital relationship with a man of low socio-legal or moral status, such as a slave or a pimp or an actor, that would only make it worse. A slave could be prosecuted for committing adultery with a respectable woman. Freeborn boys had already been protected by an earlier law; homosexual *stupra* with them were also targeted by Augustus.

---

[100]See recently Janne Pölönen, "The Division of Wealth Between Men and Women in Roman Succession," in *Women, Wealth and Power in the Roman Empire,* ed. Päivi Setälä et al., Acta Instituti Romani Finlandiae 25 (Rome: Institutum Romanum Finlandiae, 2002), pp. 147-79.

[101]See R. Elaine Fantham, "*Stuprum:* Public Attitudes and Penalties for Sexual Offences in Republican Rome," *EMC* 10 (1991): 267-91, esp. 269-71.

Protection was not extended to slaves as sex objects. A man's sexual access to his own slaves of either sex is as old as Homer. They were his property. The slave was not dishonored or regarded as acting immorally. There is a sad and funny passage in the Elder Seneca's book about rhetorical exercises and oratory, on how Haterius inadvertently used a word with sexual connotations.

> Haterius wanted to say everything in a polished and splendid style, so he often accidentally chose expressions which could not escape mockery. I remember that when he was defending an ex-slave, against whom it was alleged that he had been the *concubinus* [sleeping-partner] of his ex-owner, he said "unchastity in a freeborn man is grounds of accusation, in a slave constraint, in a freedman a dutiful and friendly service *[officium]*." This gave rise to jokes: "you aren't doing your *officium*" to me," "A is much involved in *officia* for B." For some time afterwards unchaste and obscene men were called "dutiful."[102]

Haterius was probably right to say that slaves had no choice. Freedmen in general were supposed to show respect and perform certain personal services to their ex-owners; *officia* were also proper between friends, family members and status equals. *A fortiori,* slave women were not expected to refuse if asked. To seduce another man's slaves, in contrast, was, in legal terms, corruption ("spoiling" a slave) for which damages might be claimed. In terms of etiquette, it was also appalling bad manners that might cause great offense.[103] Similarly prostitutes, who were often slaves or freed slaves or free noncitizens, were available. Prostitution and procuring were legal, though the practitioners suffered civil disabilities. Prostitutes were defined as those who openly offered sexual services to all comers at a price.[104] Women in various other professions that brought them into contact with a male clientele were equated with prostitutes. Intercourse with such women did not expose a man to prosecution under Augustus's law. Slaves and prostitutes did not count.[105]

Only the most idealistic, for instance, the Stoic Musonius Rufus, objected to the double standard and the sexual exploitation of slaves.[106] Dio of Prusa expresses the worry that brothel keepers degraded women and children and that the infection might spread, so that women and children of higher status

---

[102]Elder Seneca *Controversiae* 4 *preface* 10; cf. J. N. Adams, *The Latin Sexual Vocabulary* (Baltimore: Johns Hopkins University Press, 1982), pp. 163-64.
[103]Horace *Epistulae* 18.72-75; cf. C. Gracchus ap. Gellius 15.12.3.
[104]*Digest* 23.2.43.
[105]McGinn, *Prostitution,* esp. pp. 197-98.
[106]Lutz, "Musonius Rufus," pp. 87-89.

would be attacked.[107] The prevalent view seems to be that later expressed by Augustine, that prostitutes contained male lust.[108] To go to brothels and frequent street walkers might be vulgar and show lack of discrimination, but these activities were venial, at least in a young unmarried man, as long as he did not make a habit of it or waste the family's money.[109]

Under Augustus's innovative law, illicit intercourse with women of respectable socio-legal status laid a man open to prosecution for *stuprum* or, if the woman was married, *adulterium*. The man's marital status was irrelevant. There were no public prosecutor and no police force in the modern sense. Prosecutions, in criminal as in civil cases, were brought by private citizens, who would be rewarded by a share in the fine if they won the case. If they lost, they might risk being prosecuted in turn for bringing a frivolous charge. There is very detailed juristic commentary on the adultery law so that we know a great deal about procedure. The quantity of information is one piece of evidence for the law having been enforced. The focus is on adultery, not *stuprum*. We hear of adultery charges against a number of high-placed women in the Julio-Claudian period, often linked with a treason charge. It is important to stress that the crime had to be committed knowingly and with criminal intent. Rape victims or women who mistakenly "married" a man who was already married were innocent.

Proving adultery can be a difficult matter. The law distinguished sharply between a person caught in the act and others against whom there was other evidence. If a woman's father who was her *paterfamilias* or who had transferred her to the control of her husband found her in the act of adultery in his house or her husband's, he might punish the offense at once, by killing both daughter and adulterer.[110] But he must at least attempt to kill both, "almost with one blow and in one onslaught"[111] if he was to avoid the risk of being himself charged with murder and perhaps convicted. The husband in similar circumstances might kill the man if he was of low status or a family freedman or slave, but the husband was forbidden to kill his wife.[112] If the husband had this irrefutable evidence of adultery, he was to divorce his

---

[107]*Euboicus* 133-138.

[108]*De ordine* 2.14.12.

[109]Cicero *Pro Caelio* 48-50; Horace *Satires* 1.2.31-35 are examples of the commonplace on broadmindedness, balanced in the orator's repertoire by an equally lively set of arguments deploring the decadence of the times.

[110]*Collatio* 4.2.3.

[111]*Digest* 48.5.24.4.

[112]*Digest* 48.5.25 *principium; Collatio* 4.3.1.

wife, with citizen witnesses. After such a divorce, the husband or the father
had sixty days in which he might prosecute the woman. Failing that, an outsider might bring a prosecution, within the next four months. If the woman
remained married, or was divorced and remarried without receiving notice
of prosecution, the alleged adulterer had to be prosecuted first. Otherwise,
the prosecutor could choose which to prosecute but could not prosecute
both at once. Only if the man was condemned could a charge be brought
against a married woman: "As long as a marriage lasts, . . . a woman cannot
be accused of adultery: for a third party ought not to disturb and trouble a
wife approved by her husband."[113]

The penalties were severe: banishment to an island and confiscation of
half a man's property, half a woman's dowry and one-third of her property.
A convicted adulteress could not make a new valid marriage. A husband
who had evidence proving his wife's adultery could be prosecuted for con-
niving and pay the same penalty, as could anyone who facilitated adultery.
The machinery was elaborate.

The legislator's motivation was no doubt complex. He may have reacted
to concerns about perceived laxity, especially in the ruling class of which he
was himself an example, concerns that were rendered pressing by the experience of civil war. He may have judged it proper to be seen to be taking
action. The law might also be used to coerce and control the senators with
whom he necessarily had to work in the government of the empire. Confiscation would swell the exchequer.

Did this law deter adultery? From time to time later emperors intervened
personally, encouraged prosecutions, imposed more stringent punishments
or passed further subsidiary laws, often signs that a statute was perceived
not to work properly. There were some notorious prosecutions. We cannot
tell how common extramarital sexual activity was either before or after. Although the law did not stop Ovid from publishing erotic verses that (despite
his denials) include married women as objects of pursuit, that kind of light-
hearted literature dried up: possible evidence that the law had an effect and
possible evidence of a change of fashion, like the revival of old-fashioned
moral standards, which Tacitus claims came about after the extravagances
of the Julio-Claudian period.[114]

Eventually, Constantine restricted the right of prosecution to the husband

---

[113]*Digest* 48.5.27 *principium.*

[114]Tacitus *Annals* 3.55, with A. J. Woodman and R. H. Martin, eds., *The Annals of Tacitus: Book 3,* CCTC (New York: Cambridge University Press, 1996).

and near relatives of the alleged adulteress.[115] Further modifications were introduced by Justinian in the sixth century.[116]

Polygamy. By definition, a marriage was formed by two people of opposite sex. Roman law did not envisage the possibility that a person could regard more than one other person as husband or wife, so bigamy, polygyny and polyandry were logically impossible. A person who apparently took a second wife without divorcing the first was entering a relationship that was legally null. For Cicero the second "wife" was merely a concubine, unless divorce had taken place (see discussion of divorce above). She was blameless. He, if the woman was of respectable status, had (after the Adultery Law) committed *stuprum.* Any children would be illegitimate. The Romans disapproved of polygamy. Sallust is contemptuous of polygamous societies in which no wife has the position of an equal partner but all are held equally cheap.[117]

Concubinage. Apart from casual sex, a man might properly take a concubine, but not while he was married. It seems that the normal periods of life in which such a sexual union was tolerated were youth and old age, roughly the ages at which the Augustan marriage law did not expect a man to have a child (before twenty-five and over sixty). A *concubina* was usually of lower social status than the man, with whom she lived in a stable relationship as long as he wished. It was a unilateral arrangement, so there is no noun to describe him. She was often his freedwoman. She might have a respected position in his household and perhaps entertain his male guests.[118] The classic instance in the central period is Antonia Caenis, freedwoman and secretary to Antonia the Younger (daughter of Antony and niece of Augustus, wife of his stepson and mother of the future emperor Claudius).[119] Caenis became the mistress of the future emperor Vespasian when he was an up-and-coming new man, before his marriage and the birth of his three children. When he became a widower, she became his concubine again. They were an elderly and affectionate couple. Vespasian's sons were expected to greet her with a kiss.

The concubine and her partner would not be charged with *stuprum.*

---

[115]*Codex of Theodosius* 9.72; for the context and later developments, see Evans Grubbs, *Law and Family in Late Antiquity,* pp. 205-25.

[116]Evans Grubbs, *Law and Family in Late Antiquity,* p. 215.

[117]*Bellum Jugurthinum* 80.6.

[118]Susan Treggiari, "*Concubinae*," *PBSR* 49 (1981): 59-81; Thomas A. J. McGinn, "Concubinage and the *Lex Julia* on Adultery," *TAPA* 121 (1991): 335-75.

[119]Suetonius *Vespasian* 3, 21; *Domitian* 12.3.

There were no legal obligations, but men might give a concubine enough property to ensure that she would be comfortable after the relationship ended (in separation or his death). These social rules of the game are those recognized by the jurists. They also took into account the possibility that the man's attitude to the relationship might change and that he might start regarding his concubine as his wife.[120] If this happened and there was no legal obstacle, then the union was changed into marriage without any further action, which might make it hard for third parties to know of the change.

A powerful man, such as the emperor, might break the social rules by having a recognized mistress despite being married. So Antony allegedly flaunted his actress-"wife" Volumnia Cytheris although he was married to Fulvia. Nero also had an official *concubina*, the freedwoman Acte, while he was married to Octavia. In invective, dissolute Roman men are often accused of keeping large numbers of *concubini/concubinae* (sexual partners of both sexes) for their enjoyment. Such people would not have merited the unique and accepted position that the lawyers consider, in which the concubine fulfills some of the functions of a wife. Even Vespasian had two such women to share his siesta after Caenis died.

Contubernium. In concubinage the man's intention to be married, *maritalis affectio*, was absent. In *contubernium,* another extralegal union, legal capacity was lacking, since at least one of the two partners was a slave: "There is no right of marriage *[conubium]* with slaves."[121] "Between slaves and free persons marriage cannot be contracted but *contubernium* can."[122]

Contubernium between two slaves of the household (both his own or, e.g., one belonging to him and one to his wife) might be recognized and indeed fostered by a slave owner. The children would be born slaves of the owner of the woman slave. The union was not protected by law. This type of quasi-marriage might also involve two slaves from different households or a free person and a slave. It frequently happened that male slaves who worked for the emperor in administrative posts and whose prospects were excellent had as *contubernales* freeborn women, especially the daughters of freed slaves of the emperor (who had earlier held similar administrative posts). The children of a male slave and a free woman were born free by ordinary human law *(ius gentium),* though re-

---

[120] *Digest* 39.5.31 *principium.*
[121] *Tituli Ulpiani* 5.5.
[122] Paul *Sententiae* 2.19.6.

strictions were introduced in the time of Claudius.[123]

If the couple started out as fellow slaves, one might be freed before the other. Supposing the man were manumitted first, he might then try to buy and free his quasi-wife (and perhaps the children) or persuade the owner to free her. Once both were free, they had the legal capacity to be husband and wife in Roman law. Supposing both of them wished to be married, *contubernium* automatically became Roman marriage. Any subsequent children would be freeborn and legitimate. Because so many people outside the upper classes were unable to form a valid Roman marriage, "illegitimacy" seems not to have been much of a social handicap in the lower classes, though it affected succession rights to the father.[124] Legitimacy was, nevertheless, preferable. We can see this in an epigraph to a successful freedman on a second-century tomb monument from Budapest:

> To the spirits of the departed. Titus Flavius Felicio, Augustalis of the colony of Aquincum, set this inscription up during his lifetime to himself and to Flavia Secundina formerly (= now dead) his fellow-freedwoman and wife who lived fifty-five years, and to T. Flavius Felicissimus formerly his natural son who lived twenty-three years, and to T. Flavius Ingenuus his legitimate son, and to T. Flavius Felix his natural son and to Flavia Felicula his natural daughter, and to Flavia Felicissima his grand-daughter, all still alive. T. Flavius Felicio saw to the erection of this monument for his family and himself.[125]

The parents had been slaves of the same owner. Felicissimus, Felix and Felicula were natural children (not legitimate). The youngest child was born free after his parents' union and thus was legitimate; his name Ingenuus means "freeborn." We may assume, because of his name, that the elder three were born slaves, before the mother was freed. The biological connection with their father is pointedly marked by their names. Perhaps the parents were freed simultaneously (probably from the imperial service): there is no child in this epitaph, born free but illegitimate, who would prove that the mother was freed first. We can guess that they perhaps acquired and manumitted the elder children. Ingenuus is a source of pride, but natural children are freely acknowledged.

Other extramarital sexual activity. Gender roles have been inten-

---

[123]On this category of slave civil servants see Paul R. C. Weaver, Familia Caesaris: *A Social Study of the Emperor's Freedmen and Slaves* (Cambridge: Cambridge University Press, 1972).

[124]Beryl M. Rawson, "*Spurii* and the Roman View of Illegitimacy," *Antichthon* 23 (1989): 10-41.

[125]*Année Épigraphique: Revue des publications épigraphiques relatives à l'antiquité romaine* (Paris: Presses Universitaires de France, 1939), #10.

sively studied.[126] The word *homosexuality* (notoriously a Greek/Latin hybrid of modern invention) has no Greek or Latin equivalent. The same may be said of *heterosexuality*. Sexual acts were of course performed by Roman (or Greek) men with men, or women with women. It has become an orthodoxy among recent scholars that Greeks and Romans defined sexual acts in terms of who did what to whom. It was acceptable in general for a man to insert his penis into a woman's vagina or a man's anus, and acceptable for a woman to be penetrated. For a woman to desire to penetrate another or for a man to desire to be penetrated was not acceptable. The arguments depend on ideas of gender roles. It was seen as proper for a man to be active and a woman to be passive, for the man to take the initiative and the woman to submit.

We have seen already that such general freedom was severely circumscribed by social and legal constraints. A woman, other than a slave (who had no free will) or a prostitute (who offered her body to give sexual gratification to anyone who paid), or a woman classified with prostitutes, was not morally free to be penetrated by anyone other than her husband. The Augustan Law made such penetration a criminal act for both agents, if woman and penetrator acted deliberately.[127] A woman who performed an active role with another woman is rarely mentioned, but where our male sources write of such an act (usually in fictional contexts) it is with scorn or mockery. Still less is said of women who took a "passive" role with other women. The act was not illegal. Though homosexual acts with slave boys or male prostitutes were (up to a point) allowable to men who took the active part, the same act (whether rape or seduction) with a freeborn Roman boy was punished by fathers, by the aediles and other officials, by army officers and under the ill-documented Scantinian Law of 149 B.C. The Augustan Adultery law also penalized *stuprum* between males. The reputation of the boy would suffer. Although the Romans unfairly pretended that they learned homosexual practices from the Greeks, their attitudes toward sexual acts between adult males and adolescent boys were far less

---

[126]See, recently, David Halperin, "Homosexuality," *OCD*, pp. 720-23; Judith P. Hallett and Marilyn B. Skinner, eds., *Roman Sexualities* (Princeton, N.J.: Princeton University Press, 1997); Craig Williams, *Roman Homosexuality: Ideologies of Masculinity in Classical Antiquity* (Oxford: Oxford University Press, 1999); Sara Elise Phang, *The Marriage of Roman Soldiers (13 B.C.-A.D. 235)*, Columbia Studies in the Classical Tradition 24 (Leiden: Brill, 2001), pp. 229-95. These volumes also provide further bibliography.

[127]Susan Treggiari, "Caught in the Act: *In Filia Deprehendere* in the *Lex Iulia de Adulteriis*," in *Vertis in Usum: Studiens in Honor of Edward Courtney*, ed. Cynthia Damon, John F. Miller and K. Sara Myers (München: Sauer, 2002), pp. 243-49.

tolerant than those current in certain circles in Greek cities. If a Roman boy lost "the flower of his youth" (the equivalent of virginity) or his sexual integrity *(pudicitia)*, his reputation was gravely compromised.[128] A virtuous young soldier would, it was thought, kill his would-be lover sooner than submit.[129] Allegations of adolescent unchastity form raw material for much political and forensic invective in the late Republic—evidence for the preoccupations of the ruling class if not the behavior of the individuals named. To be a man's passive partner was evidence of insufficient self-control and self-respect (disqualifying one from political leadership) and of improper desires (he enjoyed it) or of mercenary motives (he got money or advantage out of it). Promiscuity was bad; so was a prolonged relationship with an identified lover.

Homosexual relations between two grown men are rarely represented in literature or art of the Roman period. Thel typical couple in the various literary genres comprises a boy whose cheeks show down, but not a beard, and a youth who is bearded but not yet of an age to marry. Because homosexual activity was thought of as belonging to phases in youth (first as the passive and then as the active agent, though heterosexual activity is also attributed to very young men), a man attacked for an immoral sex life with other men is often portrayed as sexually voracious with women too. Mark Antony is a classic example. Cicero makes him first the equivalent of a male prostitute and then of a "wife" who led young Curio astray. In the very same invective, he portrays Antony in maturity as first the adulterer and then the overuxorious husband of Fulvia. He also accuses Antony of trying to push another of his lovers, a mime-actress, into the society of respectable women and public figures.[130]

It has been difficult for scholars to disentangle reality from diverse literary genres, including erotic verse and the novel *Satirica* (where amours with low-class youths are part of the material), invective and historiography, where "unmasculine" behavior (e.g., taking a female sexual role, *muliebria pati*)[131] is attacked. The poet Catullus can write tender poems about kissing a boy or a woman;[132] he can threaten oral or anal rape against a couple of

---

[128]E.g., Catullus 62.46; Cicero *Pro Rabirio Perduellionis Reo* 8; *Orationes philippicae* 2.3, 15, 3.15; Suetonius *Divus Julius* 49; Valerius Maximus 6.1 *preface,* 5, 6, 9, 10; Fantham, "*Stuprum,*" pp. 273-82.

[129]Cicero *Pro Milone* 8; Valerius Maximus 6.1.12, cf. 11; Plutarch *Marius* 14.3.

[130]*Orationes philippicae* 2.

[131]Adams, *Latin Sexual Vocabulary,* pp. 189-90.

[132]Catullus 5, 7, 48, 99.

men of his own class;[133] he can also attack the most prominent men of his day as enjoying the passive role with other men.[134]

Men who chose to have sexual intercourse only with men (homosexual men as a social group in our contemporary sense) are hard to find in Roman sources, though some scholars detect voluntary pathics, *cinaedi,* as a cultural group. Homosexual behavior had little direct impact on marriage and the family. Though some men had sexual experiences with other men, this did not usually mean any extra reluctance to marry and procreate. Casual sexual intercourse between men of the slave-owning classes and their slave women was inevitable, which does not mean that it happened between all slaves and masters. But if it led to an emotional relationship, complications might ensue. In the classical period a Roman wife had always, in legal theory, the option of divorce.

Celibacy and remarriage. Women were expected to marry, and lifelong celibacy is practically unexampled. Even the six Vestal Virgins could retire after thirty years. Nor was first marriage long postponed. Men were often seen as reluctant to marry: some, such as the poets Virgil and Horace, were apparently life-long bachelors. But the Augustan marriage-legislation (and earlier, the censors) penalized those who were unmarried or childless at the moment when they might otherwise have reaped some benefit, such as an inheritance from a person not closely related by blood. For a man in the elite classes never to have married was probably exceptional, though some, like Atticus, waited until middle age.

Viduae, single women, widows and divorcees who did not remarry, were, however, a feature of Roman society, particularly because husbands frequently predeceased wives, and divorcees of advanced years or tarnished reputation were unattractive to potential husbands. There was also an idealization of the woman who married only once, the *univira (vel sim.),* who was considered fortunate and alone qualified to act as *pronuba* at weddings, when the participants wished a long and happy marriage to the couple. The women given the title on their tombstones had often predeceased their husbands. But young women whose marriage ended usually remarried. Antonia, the niece of Augustus (36 B.C.-A.D. 37), was unusual: she married rather late (16 B.C.), bore three children, was widowed in 9 B.C. and never remarried.[135] Having had only one wife was scarcely ever a moral distinction for

---

[133]Ibid., 16.
[134]Ibid., 29, 57.
[135]Nikos Kokkinos, *Antonia Augusta: Portrait of a Great Roman Lady* (London: Routledge, 1992).

a man, though he might be regarded as lucky if he had a long and happy marriage. If he had what he or the law considered enough children, a divorced man or widower might abstain from marrying again, as the emperor Tiberius did (divorced 2 B.C., died A.D. 37). Serial marriage was a common phenomenon in the upper classes.[136] Pompey (106-48 B.C.) first married Antistia and then divorced her in 82 to marry the pregnant Aemilia, whose own divorce was arranged by her stepfather Sulla, who was in control of Rome at the time. The advantage of the new match was destroyed by the bride's death. Then, from ca. 80, he was for years the husband of Mucia, who gave him several children. He divorced her in late 62, alleging her adultery with Caesar (she remarried), and in 59 married Caesar's daughter, Julia, to cement a new political alliance. He was devoted to her until her death in childbirth in 54. In 52 he married Cornelia, widowed in 53 and daughter of a new ally, and seems also to have been devoted to her, until his own death in 48. Pompey (like Augustus) was exceptional in his manipulation of marriage and divorce, but his record illustrates the range of possibilities, for both men and women of the upper class.

Contraception, deliberate abortion, abandonment of children and infanticide. Their comparative ignorance of human biology meant that the Romans could not know when conception was most likely to occur or draw a sharp line between contraception and procured abortion. Some wanted to limit the number of their children.[137] Various charms or amulets were recommended; so were pessaries, which had some efficacy.[138] Women had access to traditional knowledge of plants that prevented or checked conception.[139] Some provoked abortion by drugs or surgery, both dangerous. Romans deplored abortion when it deprived a man of fatherhood; abortionists might be prosecuted for murdering the woman if things went wrong. Abortion was not regarded as murder of the fetus. It was conventionally held that people abandoned babies in times of crisis, and the poor when they could not feed them. Such children, often left in places of public resort, might be fostered, often treated as slaves (this was theoretically illegal if they were freeborn, but almost impossible to stop). They might die. Deliberate infanticide also occurred and was one of the rights of the *paterfamilias*. It was not considered murder if he did it at once, instead of indicating that he intended to rear the newborn baby,

[136]Bradley, *Discovering the Roman Family,* p. 129.

[137]Tacitus *Germania* 19.5.

[138]M. Keith Hopkins, "Contraception in the Roman Empire," *CSSH* 8 (1965): 124-51.

[139]John M. Riddle, "Oral Contraceptives and Early-Term Abortifacients During Classical Antiquity and the Middle Ages," *Past & Present* 132 (1991): 3-32.

though otherwise it was. The legal situation changed with later emperors: infanticide became equivalent to parricide in A.D. 374.[140]

CHILDREN

Our less tendentious sources portray the upper classes as more interested in procreation than in limiting their families.[141] They do not seem to have succeeded in producing the average of five children per woman of completed fertility necessary for replacement. Despite the accepted fragility of young lives, there is plenty of evidence for warm attachment to babies.[142] Children are sympathetically portrayed in art and literature.[143]

Adoption. The Romans could be flexible in shaping their families.[144] Such flexibility was important in a regime where the early death of wife, husband or child was always possible. Property could be disposed of in many ways. The availability of divorce allowed serial marriage. If a man wanted a son to continue his line, he could adopt a male, often adult. He had two options. First, he could persuade his *paterfamilias* to transfer him *(adoptio)*. This is what Augustus did when he adopted the two young sons of Agrippa and Julia, his own daughter. Gaius (born 20 B.C.) and Lucius (born 17) thus became the adoptive sons of their maternal grandfather. Second, a Roman could convince an independent head of household to give up his own name and family cults and become a son-in-power *(adrogatio)*. There is a good example of this in A.D. 4 (after Gaius and Lucius had died), when Augustus's stepson Tiberius Claudius Nero was adopted by the emperor and became Tiberius Julius Caesar. The surviving grandson, Agrippa Postumus, was also adopted. In turn, although Tiberius had a son of his own, he adopted his own nephew Germanicus. This gave Augustus two adoptive sons (clearly distinguishable in age and experience) and two adoptive grandsons, thus marked out for succession not only to his property but to his power. Females could also be transferred by *adop-*

---

[140]See in general William V. Harris, "Child-Exposure in the Roman Empire," *JRS* 84 (1994): 1-22; "Demography, Geography and the Sources of Roman Slaves," *JRS* 89 (1999): 62-75; Walter Scheidel, "Quantifying the Sources of Slaves in the Roman Empire," *JRS* 87 (1997): 159-69; Mireille Corbier, "Child Exposure and Abandonment," in *Childhood, Class and Kin in the Roman World,* ed. Suzanne Dixon (London: Routledge, 2001), pp. 52-73.

[141]Evans Grubbs, *Law and Family in Late Antiquity,* pp. 107-8.

[142]Mark Golden, "Did the Ancients Care When Their Children Died?" *GR* 35 (1988): 152-63.

[143]Beryl M. Rawson, "Children in the Roman *Familia,*" in *The Family in Ancient Rome: New Perspectives,* ed. Beryl M. Rawson (London: Croom Helm, 1986), pp. 170-200.

[144]Mireille Corbier, "Divorce and Adoption as Roman Familial Strategies *(Le Divorce et l'Adoption 'en Plus')*" in *Marriage, Divorce and Children in Ancient Rome,* ed. Beryl Rawson (Oxford: Clarendon, 1991), pp. 47-78.

tio. Later emperors allowed women to adopt and be adrogated. *Adoptio* also allowed fathers of several children to enhance their prospects by transferring one or more into childless families. Sometimes a testator would make it a condition that the heir take his or her name. It was this custom that turned the young C. Octavius into C. Julius Caesar in 44 B.C. Others might bring up foundlings *(alumni)* and treat them with affection.[145] Or freedmen and freedwomen might be substitutes for children and inherit family property.

Roles and ideology. The conventional list of a man's most precious possessions named wife, house, children and country, sometimes friends as well. So Crassus praised Cicero for having saved everything he held dear: "every time he beheld his wife, his home, his country, he beheld a gift from me."[146] For a wife, her husband, home, children and country make the corresponding foursome.

Lucretius (ca. 94-55 B.C.) criticizes the conventional attitude, what people would say when someone died:

> "Now your happy home will not receive you any more nor your excellent wife nor will your sweet children run to meet you and snatch the first kiss and touch your heart with silent sweetness. You will not be able to enjoy your prosperity and be a protection to your family. Poor wretch wretchedly" they say "one cruel day has taken from you so many rewards of living." But they don't add this "and no longing for those things shall weigh you down."[147]

But Horace (65-9 B.C.) gives eloquent testimony to the normal reaction: "You must leave the earth and your home and your pleasing wife, nor of these trees which you tend will any one follow their temporary owner except the hateful cypresses."[148]

The joys of family affection were also linked to more practical considerations. The wife should be a helpmate:

> But if a chaste woman does her part to help the house and dear children, like a Sabine or the suntanned wife of an agile Apulian, and piles up the sacred hearth with seasoned wood before her man comes home tired, shutting the happy flock in with hurdles, she drains the swollen udders, and bringing out this year's wine from the sweet jar she prepares unbought feasts.[149]

---

[145]Beryl M. Rawson and Jane Bellemore, *"Alumni:* The Italian Evidence," *ZPE* 83 (1990): 1-19.
[146]Cicero *Epistulae ad Atticum* 1.14.3 (61 B.C.).
[147]Lucretius 3.894-901.
[148]Horace *Odes* 2.14.21-24.
[149]Horace *Epodes* 2.39-48.

Dio (early third century A.D.) thinks Augustus would have addressed the upper classes like this, when encouraging them to marry:

> For is there anything better than a wife who is chaste, domestic, a good house-keeper, a rearer of children; one to gladden you in health, to tend you in sickness, to be your partner in good fortune, to console you in misfortune; to restrain the mad passion of youth and to temper the unseasonable harshness of old age? And is it not a delight to acknowledge a child who shows the endowments of both parents?[150]

Such ideals are echoed in real life. When, under Tiberius, the Senate held a debate on whether provincial governors should be allowed to take their wives with them, the emperor's son Drusus made a speech in defense of this recent practice. In Tacitus's version, he claims that a husband would not like to be parted for long from his dearest wife and their children. Besides, long absence was like a divorce and gave the wife opportunity to misbehave. So indeed might the husband. Much better for him to have a wife to relax with after work.[151] Germanicus (Drusus' elder brother by adoption) had already illustrated this uxoriousness when he took his wife and some of the children to Egypt during his eastern mission. He made a fuss in his speech about the pain of separation from other members of the family:

> I, who have been sent, as I said, by my adoptive father to regulate the overseas provinces, I have a most difficult assignment, first because of the sea-voyage and due to having been separated from my (adopted) father [Tiberius] and grandmother [Livia] and mother [Antonia] and siblings [Claudius, Livilla; adoptive brother Drusus] and children [only Nero Caesar, Drusus Caesar, the younger Agrippina and Drusilla] and intimate friends."[152]

The Roman ideal was a partnership. Musonius, continuing the passage quoted above in the discussion of the definition of marriage, gives lofty expression to this idea:

> In marriage there must be above all perfect companionship [*symbiosis*] and mutual love [*kedemonia*] of husband and wife, both in health and in sickness and under all conditions, since it was with desire for this as well as for having children that both entered upon marriage. Where, then, this love for each other is perfect and the two share it completely, each striving to outdo the

---

[150]Cassius Dio 56.3.3-4 (LCL translation).
[151]Tacitus *Annals* 3.34.
[152]Translated by Kokkinos an *Antonia Augusta,* p. 82.

other in devotion, the marriage is ideal and worthy of envy, for such a union is beautiful. But where each looks only to his own interests and neglects the other, or, what is worse, when one is so minded and lives in the same house but fixes his attention elsewhere and is not willing to pull together with his yoke-mate nor to agree, then the union is doomed to disaster and though they live together, yet their common interests fare badly; eventually they separate entirely or they remain together and suffer what is worse than loneliness.[153]

That ordinary people had a high ideal of marriage is confirmed by some examples we have of people who divorced, not for reasons perceived as sensible, such as the need to have children, but because they were unhappy. According to an anecdote, Aemilius Paullus divorced a wife everyone else thought was ideal. But he said he was the only one who knew where his shoe pinched.[154] There are two apparent paradoxes here. One is that the theoretical availability of divorce, whatever its actual frequency, could be an incentive for each partner to try to make the other happy. The other is that divorcing because of unhappiness is evidence for the ideal of happy family life.

What moral characteristics secured family happiness? What were members of the family expected to do for each other? We hear most about what makes a good wife. But the surprise is that many of the qualities attributed to the good wife are also praised in husbands. As Saller has proved in investigating the relations of *pietas* (dutifulness), the traffic was supposed to run two ways, for instance between parent and child. There was a demand for reciprocal performance of duty between all family members.[155]

The most famous eulogy of all, the so-called *Laudatio Turiae,* says that the wife shared with all married ladies of good repute her woolworking, observance of religion, quiet way of dressing,[156] equal care for her own relatives and his, and four abstract virtues: *pudicitia, obsequium, comitas* and *facilitas.* The first is the virtue that implies all others in Roman thinking about women. "Chastity" is an unsatisfactory translation, for abstinence is not involved. *Pudicitia* connotes sexual integrity (as in Valerius Maximus's listing of both boys and women). In a married woman, it means exclusive loyalty to the husband and implies love.

First of all, *pudicitia* must be kept, for when that is lost all virtue collapses. This is the chief virtue of women. This recommends a poor woman, extols a rich one,

---

[153]Musonius 13A: "What is the chief end of marriage?" translated by Lutz in "Musonius Rufus," p. 89.
[154]Plutarch *Aemilius Paullus* 5.1.
[155]*Patriarchy, Property and Death,* pp. 102-14.
[156]Cf. Pliny the Younger *Panegyric* 83.7.

redeems an ugly one, adorns a lovely one; (a chaste woman) deserves well of her ancestors, since she does not pollute their blood with illegitimate offspring; she deserves well of her children, who have no need to blush for their mother or doubt their father, and well especially of herself, because she defends herself from the insult of another man's body. The worst disaster in being a prisoner of war is to be prey to a stranger's lust. Men are made illustrious by consulships, eloquence raises them to immortal fame, military glory and the triumph of a new family hallow them; there are many things which in themselves ennoble glorious abilities. The peculiar virtue of women is *pudicitia*. This made Lucretia the equal of Brutus or perhaps put her above him, since it was from a woman that Brutus learned to be incapable of being a slave. This made Cornelia the equal of Gracchus, and Porcia of the second Brutus. Tanaquil is more famous than her husband: he, among the many names of kings, has been hidden by antiquity, she, by her rare virtue among women has been enshrined so deep in the memory of all the ages that she cannot be shaken loose.[157]

The last two of the qualities of the *Laudatio*—*comitas* and *facilitas,* being considerate or gracious and easygoing—are qualities attributed by Tacitus to Livia in his damning obituary:

She ran her household with oldfashioned morality, she was more *gracious* than women in the old days thought proper, she was an ambitious mother, an *easy-going* wife and one well adapted to the craft of her husband and the hypocrisy of her son.[158]

These qualities made a marriage run smoothly and were equally appropriate for a husband to show to his wife.[159] *Facilitas,* being easygoing, was a valued quality in friends or husbands and wives, though it could easily slide into laxity and (perhaps for this reason) is not the sort of quality often mentioned in the grave wording of tombstones. *Obsequium,* the second quality, was also a virtue for both partners. This means dutiful behavior or cooperativeness. Both *coniuges* also owed each other reverence because of the nature of the marriage bond.[160] The duty of husband and wife could be summed up as mutual faith, *fides,* which was stressed in all kinds of reciprocal relationships, including the political and economic. It is *fides* when a wife rescues her proscribed husband; it is *fides* when the anonymous hero-

---

[157]Seneca (mid-first century A.D.), quoted by Jerome (ca. A.D. 348-420), *Adversus Jovinianum libri II* 1.49=319C-320B.

[158]Tacitus *Annals* 5.1.

[159]Cicero *Epistulae ad Atticum* 6.6.1, with *obsequium;* Horace *Epistulae* 2.2.133; Livy *Roman History* 33.21.4.

[160]Pliny the Younger *Epistulae* 8.5; cf. Columella *De Re Rustica* 12 *preface* 7; *Digest* 25.2.3.2.

ine's husband refuses to divorce her for sterility.[161] A husband shows faith in the strict administration of the dowry, the wife in looking after the house.[162] This is faith not in the sense of believing in someone but in the sense of acting justly and fairly, in accordance with the demands of the bond, which are greater for marriage than for ordinary commercial partnerships. *Pietas,* which Saller characterizes as an "affectionate devotion among all family members,"[163] perhaps goes further still and becomes more emotional. Romans might classify under *pietas* the self-sacrifice of a husband who chose to die instead of his younger wife or the one who pined to death for love.[164]

Duties between parents and children were similarly defined. Reciprocal *obsequium* and reverence were prescribed between parent and child.[165] Indulgence, *indulgentia,* was expected chiefly from parent to child, but also reciprocally between husband and wife, or from mistress to lover.[166] The wife's role was to look after the house and guard the family property. The Christian Tertullian, criticizing the sexual motives that lead men to make second marriages, says they pretend they need someone to run the house, organize the staff, keep the keys, manage the spinning, provide meals and share the husband's anxieties.[167] Working wool to supply the household with clothes and blankets symbolizes the virtuous wife. A Roman senator would think these sensible reasons for remarriage. The wife would look after young children. Lower-class women helped the husband in the shop or worked independently, for instance as midwives or merchants, making a contribution to the budget. Upper-class women helped a husband's political career and entertained his friends.

Tacitus portrays one senator making a pathetic speech about the emperor Claudius (whose previous wife had been executed):

> The gruelling work by which the emperor rules the world requires supporters, so that he may be free from domestic worry and able to take counsel for the common good. What could be a more honourable relief for a man with the mind of a censor than to take a wife, his partner in prosperity and adversity,

[161]Valerius Maximus *Memorable Deeds* 2.1.4; *Laudatio Turiae* 2.45.

[162]Treggiari, *Roman Marriage,* p. 238.

[163]*Patriarchy, Property and Death,* p. 131.

[164]Ibid., p. 108, citing Pliny the Elder, *Naturalis historia* 7.121-122.

[165]Cicero *Epistulae ad Quintum fratrem* 1.3.3; Terence *Hauton timorumenos* 152; *Corpus Inscriptionum Latinarum* 6.3150, 10853, 10620, 28888.

[166]Treggiari, *Roman Marriage,* p. 242.

[167]*De exhortatione castitatis* 12.1.

to whom he may confide his innermost thoughts and entrust his little children, when he is a man not accustomed to luxury and sensuous pleasures, but one who has from his earliest youth obeyed the laws?[168]

Ideally, a wife acted as companion and confidante, listened to her husband's anxieties, kept his secrets, and offered him counsel.[169] Everyday couples were expected to show their approval of each other by leaving property in their wills or by putting up epitaphs. Self-sacrifice was praised. Roman literature is full of admirable women who stood by their husbands in time of disaster, accompanying them into exile or staying in Rome to work for their return, or committing suicide with them. Harmony, *concordia,* was the characteristic most admired in an ideal marriage. The companionship of wife and husband is well expressed in the epitaphs of quite humble people:

> Here lies my wife Urbanilla, full of modesty, at Rome companion and partner in my business, rooted in parsimony. When all our business had been successfully completed and she was returning to our country with me, Ah, Carthage snatched my unhappy partner from me. I have no hope of living without such a wife. She kept my house, she helped me with counsel. Deprived of light, unhappy, she rests closed in marble. I, your husband Lucius, have covered you in marble here. This is the fate which fate has given us when we are given to the light.[170]

> To the spirits of the departed and the eternal memory of Blandinia Martiola, that most innocent girl, who lived 18 years 9 months and 5 days, Pompeius Catussa a Sequanian citizen, plasterer, to his incomparable wife, most kind to him, who lived with me 5 years, 6 months and 18 days without any taint of accusation. He saw to the setting up of this epitaph during his lifetime to himself and his wife and dedicated it under the trowel. You who read go to the baths of Apollo to bathe. I did that with my wife and wish I still could.[171]

> Laughter and luxury I always delighted in, in the company of my dear friends, but such a life after the death of my chaste lady Valeria I did not find; while I could I had an enjoyable life with my holy wife.[172]

Marriage, ideally, was a lasting, faithful and happy commitment.

---

[168]Tacitus *Annals* 12.5.

[169]Treggiari, *Roman Marriage,* pp. 244-45.

[170]*Corpus Inscriptionum Latinarum* 8.152; *Carmina Epigraphica* 516 (near Capsa in North Africa).

[171]*Corpus Inscriptionum Latinarum* 13.1983 (Lyon in Gaul, third century A.D.).

[172]*Corpus Inscriptionum Latinarum* 8.7156; *Carmina Epigraphica* 498 (monument of a silversmith from Cirta in North Africa).

5

Marriage and Family
in Second Temple Judaism

DAVID W. CHAPMAN

Listen to me your father, O children; and act accordingly,

   that you may be kept in safety.

For the Lord honored the father above the children,

   and he confirmed the right of the mother over her sons.

Whoever honors his father atones for sins,

   and whoever glorifies his mother is like one who lays up treasure.

Whoever honors his father will be gladdened by his own children,

   and when he prays he will be heard.

Sirach 3:1-5 RSV

For most Jewish people in the Second Temple period, family formed the central social institution in their lives. While a minority considered celibacy a worthy alternative, certainly the large majority of Jewish people in Palestine and in the Diaspora believed that marriage and the procreation of children were required of them. However, this is not to say that Jewish communities of the period were agreed on all matters of marriage and family.

Current study of Judaism in this period recognizes the diverse cultural contexts that are involved. The era of the Second Temple begins with the return of the captives to Jerusalem as reported in Ezra/Nehemiah, and it concludes with the destruction of the Jerusalem temple six hundred years later. Aside from the obvious breadth of time in the materials, the study of this era must also recognize the diversity of locales from Judea and Galilee to such Diaspora Jewish communities as those in Egypt, Cyrene, Rome, Greece, Asia Minor and Babylonia. Even in one particular region such as Judea there were often different groups active (e.g., the Pharisees, Sadducees and Essenes) as well as known disputes within those groups (e.g., between the Houses of Shammai and Hillel). Thus, many factors encourage the student of this era to look for diversity. On the other hand, aside from race, there were uniting factors among otherwise diverse Jewish communities—such as a shared history and ancestral religion. Hence, this brief study will seek to develop areas of continuity and discontinuity in beliefs about and practices within the family by evaluating the existing evidence from the Second Temple period.

This study examines Jewish concepts of family prior to the fall of the Second Temple (A.D. 70) and focuses on Jewish literature and artifacts outside of the canonical Old Testament.[1] A complication arises in that rabbinic writings, which contain some of the most detailed material concerning marriage and family in early Judaism, actually were written during a later era and likely represent the discussions of a single fairly cohesive group. This serves as a caution to the overuse of these materials.[2] However, rabbinic literature also conveys on its surface a desire for preserving older traditions—evidenced, for example, in the attribution of historical names to certain sayings. Optimally, rabbinic traditions that have some claim to antiquity should be corroborated by other writings from within the Second Temple period itself.

MARRIAGE

Jewish marriage in this period consisted of the formal union of a man and a woman. It was generally preceded by betrothal and often vouchsafed by a marriage contract obligating certain financial arrangements. Marriage resulted in the act of procreation, which was widely viewed as permissible only in marriage. However, even aside from the death of a spouse, marriage did not necessarily guarantee a lifetime relationship since divorce was com-

---

[1]Some key literature from this period is of disputed Jewish provenance. My general practice is to follow scholarly consensus and to note when disputed literature is employed. For a defense of the Jewish origins of Pseudo-Phocylides in particular, see Pieter W. van der Horst, *The Sentences of Pseudo-Phocylides: With Introduction and Commentary,* SVTP 4 (Leiden: Brill, 1978), pp. 70-76, 81-83; more concisely argued in van der Horst's translation of the text in *The Old Testament Pseudepigrapha,* ed. James H. Charlesworth (New York: Doubleday, 1983-1985), 2:565-68.

[2]Furthermore, the number of marriageable men in Palestine would have been drastically reduced as a consequence of the Jewish wars against Rome, an observation made by Isaiah M. Gafni, "The Institution of Marriage in Rabbinic Times," in *The Jewish Family: Metaphor and Memory,* ed. David Kraemer (Oxford: Oxford University Press, 1989), p. 15. This may have affected post-70 rabbinic teaching on marriage, thus heightening the possibility of discontinuity between rabbinic literature and the situation during the Second Temple period.

monly permitted. Further, in different sectors within Judaism there were debates concerning the limitations on who could wed, the number of wives allowed, and even whether marriage itself was a necessary duty.

Central legal aspects. Many of our written sources from this era treat marriage from a legal perspective. Certainly, extant marriage and divorce certificates present such a viewpoint. Also rabbinic writings often focus on application of marriage law, as do the most extensive sections on marriage in the Dead Sea Scrolls and in authors such as Josephus and Philo. It is thus reasonable to begin our discussion with the central legal aspects of marriage, even if ultimately marriage in Jewish antiquity was not merely a legal construct.

Betrothal. Traditionally, prior to marriage there was an act of betrothal. Betrothal constituted a formal commitment to marriage and often involved an exchange of something of value to signify that commitment. Already there were biblical examples of betrothal,[3] and there was biblical legislation that assumed betrothal concerning matters of war[4] or unchastity.[5] However, none of these texts spelled out the legal and procedural aspects of betrothal itself, which quite probably were so well known in the society that they did not require codification.

Second Temple sources continue to represent certain biblical narratives as betrothal accounts, as in Isaac and Rebekah.[6] The expanded romance of Joseph and Aseneth metaphorically states these biblical figures to have been betrothed beforehand in eternity and contrasts their eternal connection to the villain's misunderstanding of betrothal.[7] Furthermore, concerning both unchastity[8] and war,[9] Jewish literature repeats biblical legislation that assumes betrothal.

Josephus provides several examples of betrothal before marriage among the Jewish royal family during the Second Temple period, including Herod himself,[10] Pheroras,[11] Herod's grandsons,[12] and Mariamne and Archelaus.[13] It ap-

---

[3]Gen 29:21; 2 Sam 3:14; Joel 1:8; as a metaphor in Hos 2:19-20; possibly in Gen 19:14.
[4]Deut 20:7.
[5]Deut 22:23-27; contrast Ex 22:16-17; Deut 22:28-29.
[6]Josephus *Ant.* 1.242-245.
[7]*Jos. Asen.* 21:3; 23:3; cf. 1:8.
[8]Josephus *Ant.* 4.251-52; *Ag. Ap.* 2.201; Ps.-Phoc. 198.
[9]E.g., Josephus *Ant.* 4.298, where Josephus indicates that both the betrothed as in Deut 20:7 and the recently married as in Deut 24:5 are free from military service.
[10]Josephus *Ant.* 14.300, 351, 467; cf. *J.W.* 1.344.
[11]Josephus *Ant.* 16.194.
[12]Josephus *J.W.* 1.556-558, 560, 565; *Ant.* 17.14.
[13]Josephus *Ant.* 20.140. Likely betrothal is also represented in *Ant.* 16.194-196.

pears from Josephus and other sources that betrothal caused a change of status, so that Hyrcanus could be called Herod's familial relation during betrothal, even while the marriage was some time off.[14] This change of status during betrothal is similarly found in the expansive retelling of the Joseph narratives, in which a betrothed woman is already called her future husband's "wife."[15]

The length of betrothal likely varied. Rabbinic sources indicate a year as a sufficient time for a virgin to prepare to wed after her future husband asks for her,[16] but this clock likely begins after the girl is considered of age—typically in her twelfth year (cf. *m. Nid.* 5:6-8). Even then these rabbinic sources allow more time to pass before the formal marriage, though the future husband then has some obligation to provide for her. Further, betrothals could be made long before the boy and girl are "of age."[17] Though timings are not typically mentioned in our historical sources, a quick calculation would imply that a considerable period of betrothal passed before Herod married Mariamne.[18]

The scant inscriptional evidence points to females marrying between twelve and eighteen years of age.[19] Later rabbis debated the age at which a young man should wed, and opinions vary between fourteen and roughly twenty-four years of age, though the discussion suggests an earlier age is generally preferred.[20] However, the Qumran sect in one document indicates

---

[14]Josephus *Ant.* 14.467; *J.W.* 1.344. Note the term κηδεστής in *Ant.* 14.325; cf. *J.W.* 1.240-241.

[15]*Jos. Asen.* 21:1; 23:3.

[16]See *m. Ketub.* 5:2; cf. *m. Ned.* 10:5; thirty days are granted to a widow to prepare for remarriage.

[17]Thus rabbis (even in the first century A.D.) discuss a female minor's "right of refusal" to consummate her betrothal in marriage (*m. Yebam.* 13:1-5; *t. Yebam.* 13:1-5).

[18]Josephus *Ant.* 14.300, 467.

[19]Pieter W. van der Horst, *Ancient Jewish Epitaphs: An Introductory Survey of a Millennium of Jewish Funerary Epigraphy (300 B.C.E.-700 C.E.)*, CBET 2 (Kampen: Kok Pharos, 1991), pp. 103-4. Horsley notes a broader age range of twelve to twenty-six years of age, and he admits that the bulk of the evidence comes from Rome, which may affect its reliability for circles outside Italy (especially Palestine). See G. H. R. Horsley, *New Documents Illustrating Early Christianity: A Review of the Greek Inscriptions and Papyri Published in 1979* [*New Docs* 4] (Marrickville: Macquarie University, 1987), pp. 222-27 (esp. summary on p. 226). However, some later rabbinic traditions allow girls to be married even at the age of three (*b. Nid.* 45a)!

[20]In *b. Qidd.* 29b-30a. This passage associates with the second-century A.D. school of R. Ishmael in naming the age of twenty as the latest a son should be married. In *m. 'Abot* 5:21 the age of eighteen is suggested for men by a Tannaitic authority. See discussion in S. Safrai, "Home and Family," in *The Jewish People in the First Century: Historical Geography, Political History, Social, Cultural and Religious Life and Institutions*, ed. S. Safrai and M. Stern, CRINT 1.2 (Philadelphia: Fortress, 1976), 2:755 n. Later rabbinic texts are adduced in David Kraemer, "Images of Childhood and Adolescence in Talmudic Literature," in *The Jewish Family: Metaphor and Memory*, ed. David Kraemer (Oxford: Oxford University Press, 1989), pp. 72-74.

that men should not have sexual intercourse—requiring marriage—until the age of twenty.[21]

Rabbinic literature allows for three methods of cementing a betrothal: by exchange of money (a fairly small amount is required), by a writ of betrothal or by sexual intercourse with the intent of betrothal[22]—the last being the only way to cement levirate marriage.[23] However, other Jewish literature implies that virgin betrothed couples should not have intercourse until after the wedding (*Jos. Asen.* 21:1). The importance of proving the wife's virginity on the wedding night (discussed below) indicates that sexual intercourse was likely avoided as the method of cementing a betrothal with a virgin.

There are occasional hints of a betrothal ceremony in the literature. Josephus's description at one point implies that children who are being betrothed as part of the betrothal ceremony joined their right hands together.[24] A brief mention of a betrothal meal is found in the Mishnah (*m. Pesaḥ.* 3:7).

Biblical legislation at times treats betrothed couples with the same degree of legal responsibility as married couples.[25] Already we have noted in Second Temple literature that betrothed couples could be addressed as husband and wife.[26] It is not surprising then that the cessation of betrothal can resemble the end of a marriage, though this is most prevalent in rabbinic texts. If a betrothed man dies, the woman is regarded as if she were a widow,[27] though she is still considered a virgin when it comes to remarriage.[28] If both parties are alive, then the breaking of a betrothal can be treated like divorce,[29] though the girl returns to her father's control.[30] The rabbis prescribe a substantial monetary penalty on the man for the breaking of betrothal, which for some rabbinic figures was equal to the penalty for divorce in a marriage.[31] Josephus

---

[21] 1QSa = 1Q28a I, 9-11.

[22] See *m. Qidd.* 1:1; *m. Ketub.* 4:4; *t. Qidd.* 1:1-4. Sexual intercourse during betrothal seems to have been more acceptable in Judea (cf. *m. Ketub.* 1:5; *m. Yebam.* 4:10).

[23] See *m. Qidd.* 1:1; *m. Nid.* 5:4; *Sifre Deut.* 288.

[24] Josephus, *J.W.* 1.559. Note the relationship between the verb used for joining hands (συναρ-μόζω), which itself can be used of joining in wedlock, and the verb ἁρμόζω, often used for betrothal.

[25] Compare Deut 20:7 and Deut 24:5 concerning military service. The penalty for sexual intercourse with a betrothed girl (death by stoning) is the same as for adultery (Deut 22:23-27—especially v. 24 where she is called "the wife of his neighbor").

[26] See Ze'ev W. Falk, *Introduction to Jewish Law of the Second Commonwealth,* AGJU 11 (Leiden: Brill, 1972-1978), 2:289-90.

[27] See *m. Yebam.* 4:10; 6:4.

[28] In *m. Ketub.* 1:2.

[29] See *m. Git.* 6:2; *m. Yebam.* 2:6-7.

[30] In *m. Ketub.* 4:2.

[31] E.g., *m. Ketub.* 5:1.

does in fact indicate that some royal betrothals were broken,[32] though he does not report whether a monetary penalty had to be paid in these instances. In light of the rabbinic teaching on betrothal requiring divorce and remuneration, Joseph's desire to "put away" Mary "secretly" (Mt 1:19) upon learning of her pregnancy would likely have required an act of divorce.[33]

Marriage contract. Frequently, written documents were produced to ratify a marriage. Such a certificate, termed a *ketubah* in rabbinic Hebrew, primarily stipulated the financial terms of the marriage. Though known from early ancient Near Eastern literature, there is debate on whether such documents were employed in the biblical period.[34] Nonetheless, multiple examples of such documents can indeed be found throughout the Second Temple period, and references to marriage papers appear in some Jewish literature. The book of Tobit indicates that the marriage of Tobias and Sarah was formalized not just by the giving of the bride by her father (Tob 7:12-13) but also by a sealed written contract (Tob 7:14).[35] There is also ample rabbinic teaching on the matter from shortly after the Second Temple period.[36] Nonetheless, the form of these documents and their contents varied over the centuries.

Seven Aramaic Jewish marriage contracts were discovered at Elephantine, and several others exist from Dead Sea manuscripts (both in Aramaic and Greek). An examination of the least fragmentary documents from Elephantine indicate a basic pattern in this fifth-century B.C. Jewish colony in Egypt.[37]

---

[32]Josephus *J.W.* 1.565; *Ant.* 16.228; also *Ant.* 17.18.

[33]On this passage, see the helpful analysis in Raymond E. Brown, *The Birth of the Messiah: A Commentary on the Infancy Narratives in the Gospels of Matthew and Luke,* new updated ed., ABRL (New York: Doubleday, 1993), pp. 125-28. Keener's argument that this would entail Joseph's forfeiture of the dowry is not sufficiently supported by the text he cites (*m. Ketub.* 7:6), though the suggestion is worth further study; see Craig S. Keener, "Marriage," *DNTB,* p. 685.

[34]See John J. Collins, "Marriage, Divorce, and Family in Second Temple Judaism," in *Families in Ancient Israel,* ed. Leo G. Perdue et al. (Louisville: Westminster John Knox, 1997), pp. 109-10.

[35]The "sealing" of the contract is found in MSS Vaticanus and Alexandrinus as well as the Old Latin and Semitic MSS. Sinaiticus omits it. See Carey A. Moore, *Tobit: A New Translation with Introduction and Commentary,* AB 40a (New York: Doubleday, 1996), pp. 216 n. 224.

[36]E.g., *m. Ketub.* 4:7-12.

[37]The least fragmentary are papyri C 15, K 2 and K 7 (= B2.6, B3.3 and B3.8). The papyri are gathered in A. Cowley, *Aramaic Papyri of the Fifth Century B.C.* (Oxford: Clarendon, 1923), pp. 44-50, 54-56, 131-32, 153 (= C 15, C 18, C 36 and C 48); and in Emil G. Kraeling, *The Brooklyn Museum Aramaic Papyri: New Documents of the Fifth Century B.C. from the Jewish Colony at Elephantine* (New Haven, Conn.: Yale University Press, 1953), pp. 139-50, 199-222, 291-96 (= K 2, K 7 and K 14). For a more recent edition, see Bezalel Porten and Ada Yardeni, *Textbook of Aramaic Documents from Ancient Egypt* (Winona Lake, Ind.: Eisenbrauns, 1986-1993), 2:30-33, 60-63, 78-83, 131-40 (= B2.6, B3.3, B3.8 and B6.1-4). The most fragmentary contracts are also available in Bezalel Porten, "Five Fragmentary Aramaic Marriage Documents:

Such certificates begin by listing the date and identifying the parties. They typically have the bridegroom speaking in first person to the male head of the bride's household—this head of the house is usually the father, but he can also be a brother or the owner of a slave girl. The groom announces, "She is my wife and I her husband from this day forever."[38] A *mohar* price is recorded as paid from the bridegroom to the male head of the bride's household. Then follows a listing of items the bride brings into the marriage (her dowry), the monetary worth of which is then totaled. If either party dies before the couple has children, provisions are made for the surviving spouse to control all;[39] and the penalty for divorce is stipulated if either party (the husband or the wife) initiates a divorce. These agreements close with naming the scribe and listing the witnesses to the contract.

Having mentioned the similarities, there are also some differences between these Elephantine contracts. In one document (K 2), the man (Ananiah b. Azariah) marries a handmaiden named Tamut who is owned by Meshullam and who already has a son.[40] This certificate follows the basic pattern above (with Meshullam as master naturally serving as the male head of the household), except that a *mohar* payment is not mentioned and additional provisions are made to account for the slave woman's son. In some other contracts a substantial monetary penalty is invoked on the husband should he put away his wife without divorce or should he commit polygamy.[41] Some of these legal instruments also specify that the dowry granted to the wife by her own family is an irrevocable gift.[42]

New Collations and Restorations," *AbrN* 27 (1989): 80-105. For sake of simplicity, below only the Cowley and Kraeling numbering will be followed.

[38]This exact wording is found in K 2 lines 3-4, but it can also be seen with mild variations in K 7 line 4; K 14 line 4; C 15 line 4.

[39]Some have suggested that the husband "inherits" the property (for his lifetime and for his descendants) whereas the wife "has power over it" (possibly just for her lifetime); but such an argument must contend with the way that Mibtahiah's sons inherit her former husband's land. See Bezalel Porten, *Archives from Elephantine: The Life of an Ancient Jewish Military Colony* (Berkeley: University of California Press, 1968), pp. 256-57.

[40]A synthetic reading of this text with other documents concerning Ananiah b. Azariah can be found in Porten, *Archives from Elephantine*, pp. 200-13.

[41]C 15 lines 29-36; K 7 lines 30-32, 36-37. A deed of divorce is also mentioned at the beginning of the small portion that is extant of C 18. K 7 mentions that if the wife cohabits with another man after being "put away," then she will receive merely the benefits of a divorce (lines 33-34; see Kraeling, *Brooklyn Museum Aramaic Papyri*, p. 218). A further aspect of K 7 is its prohibition forbidding either the husband or the wife to go to court against his or her spouse with two other people of the spouse's sex (lines 37-40).

[42]C 18 lines 1-3; K 7 lines 40-42.

In contrast to the fifth-century date of these early Elephantine texts, the Judean desert marriage certificates originate from the second century A.D. These include Jewish agreements written in Aramaic or in Greek. The Aramaic contracts differ from their Greek counterparts in several respects.

Beginning with the extant Aramaic marriage certificates from the Judean desert,[43] one notes that they are addressed from the husband directly to the wife in the second person.[44] This contrasts both with the Elephantine documents (which are addressed to the male guardian of the bride) and with the Greek Judean contracts (which are written in the third person). These certificates are all "double documents," where the text of the contract is repeated twice, with the upper text being folded and sealed in case the unsealed lower text needed to be confirmed.[45] Though in some places these Aramaic contracts are quite fragmentary, they likely all began with a statement of the parties involved and a date. The husband announced "you will be my wife according to the law of Moses," and he probably promised to feed and clothe his wife.[46] The husband then declared the monetary amount of the *ketubah* payment which he, or his estate, owes the wife on the dissolution of marriage.[47] Then follows a series of promises from the husband. Though again the texts are fragmentary, these assurances likely included: the promise to redeem the wife if she was taken captive, the promise that their male children would inherit the *ketubah* in addition to their regular inheritance, the promise that upon the wife's death their female children would still be supported by the husband until they were married, and the prom-

---

[43]P.Yadin 10; Mur 20; Mur 21.

[44]The two **Murabba'at** texts can be found in P. Benoit, J. T. Milik and Roland de Vaux, *Les Grottes de Murabba'at*, DJD 2 (Oxford: Clarendon, 1961), pp. 109-17; text and English translation in Léonie J. Archer, *Her Price Is Beyond Rubies: The Jewish Woman in Graeco-Roman Palestine*, JSOTSup 60 (Sheffield: Sheffield Academic Press, 1990), pp. 290-94. Having been mentioned by Yadin in earlier publications, the text of P.Yadin 10 (= 5/6Hev 10) appeared in a full edition in Yigael Yadin, Jonas C. Greenfield and Ada Yardeni, "Babatha's *Ketubba*," *IEJ* 44 (1994): 75-101. That edition has now been revised in Yigael Yadin et al., eds., *The Documents from the Bar Kokhba Period in the Cave of Letters: Hebrew, Aramaic and Nabatean-Aramaic Papyri,* JDS (Jerusalem: Israel Exploration Society, 2002), pp. 118-41.

[45]Sometimes the lower text is more expansive (Mur 21). The upper text of P.Yadin 10 is no longer extant.

[46]The reference to the law of Moses is likely in Mur 20 recto I line 3; and P.Yadin 10 recto line 5. The feeding and clothing section is quite fragmentary in all manuscripts, though likely in P.Yadin 10 recto line 5.

[47]P.Yadin 10 lines 11, 16; Mur 21 recto II, lines 10, 13, 16.

ise that upon the husband's death his heirs would either provide for her or return her *ketubah*.[48] The documents concluded with an acceptance of these terms, and witnesses signed the contract. Strikingly these details, especially the promises (and likely also the *ketubah* payments), align well with early rabbinic teaching and with later extant Jewish marriage contracts.[49]

Second-century Jewish marriage documents written in Greek express some variation within themselves.[50] So Mur 115 is actually a certificate of remarriage, in which the two parties (Salome and Eleaios) had divorced but were subsequently marrying one another again. P.Yadin 18 concludes with the bride's father and the husband signing the document in Aramaic, whereas this section is not extant in other contracts.[51] Fur-

---

[48]Again, the fragmentary nature of the documents makes perfect identification difficult here, but it is probable that the promises are found in the following lines: (1) redeem wife (P.Yadin 10 recto lines 10-11; Mur 20 recto I line 6[?]; possibly in missing Mur 21 recto II line 9); (2) sons inherit *ketubah* (Mur 20 recto I lines 7-8[?]; Mur 21 recto II lines 13-14; not in P.Yadin 10 but possibly in the missing recto lines 12-13); (3) daughters supported (P.Yadin 10 recto line 14; Mur 20 recto I lines 8-9; Mur 21 recto II lines 10-12); and (4) provision for widowhood (P.Yadin 10 recto lines 14-16; Mur 20 recto I lines 9-11; Mur 21 recto II lines 14-16). The first promise is clearly present in P.Yadin 10, whereas the original editors of Mur 20 and 21, which are both highly fragmentary at this crucial spot, thought that this point in those documents was a divorce clause. In light of the evidence of P.Yadin 10 (as well as later Cairo Genizah texts) the argument can be advanced that there was not a divorce provision in the Murabbaʿat texts (at least at this junction), but rather a promise to redeem the wife if she is captured (which is certainly a possible reconstruction in Mur 20 based on the readable Aramaic letters in line 6). On this, see Yadin et al., "Babatha's *Ketubba*," p. 93.

[49]On the *ketubah* and the promises, see *m. Ketub.* 4:7-12. These are found in tenth- and eleventh-century marriage documents from the Cairo Genizah; see Mordechai Akiva Friedman, *Jewish Marriage in Palestine: A Cairo Geniza Study*, (Tel-Aviv: Tel-Aviv University and the Jewish Theological Seminary of America, 1980), esp. 1:239-88, 347-91, 427-43.

[50]The two Greek marriage documents from Murabbaʿat (Mur 115 and Mur 116) may be found in P. Benoit et al., *Les Grottes de Murabbaʿat*, pp. 243-56; text and English translation in Archer, *Her Price Is Beyond Rubies*, pp. 294-97. P.Yadin 18 and P.Yadin 37 are in Naphtali Lewis, Yigael Yadin and Jonas C. Greenfield, eds., *The Documents from the Bar Kokhba Period in the Cave of Letters: Greek Papyri*, JDS (Jerusalem: Israel Exploration Society, 1989), pp. 76-82, 130-33. The first major report on XHev/Se 69 (= XHev/Se Gr. 2) is that of Hannah Cotton, "A Cancelled Marriage Contract from the Judaean Desert (XHev/Se Gr. 2)," *JRelS* 84 (1994): 64-86. Further, XHev/Se 69 (= XHev/Se Gr. 2) and P.Yadin 37 (renamed XHev/Se 65 and considered a receipt of dowry rather than a marriage contract) are granted newer editions in Hannah M. Cotton and Ada Yardeni, *Aramaic, Hebrew and Greek Documentary Texts from Naḥal Ḥever and Other Sites*, DJD 27 (Oxford: Clarendon, 1997), pp. 224-37, 250-74.

[51]Cotton suggests that XHev/Se Gr. 2 originally ended with the scribe writing (in Greek) in place of the bride's mother because of her illiteracy; see Cotton, "Cancelled Marriage Contract," p. 77n.

ther, in one document it appears that the mother of the bride gave away her daughter.[52]

Nonetheless, there is marked continuity on several points between these Greek contracts. All were double documents written in the third person. Each began with a place and date—the dating connected to the names of the Roman authorities in power. The monetary value of the dowry was then stated, and some documents indicate that the husband added to the dowry.[53] Promises were made to feed and clothe the wife and to provide for their children. Witnesses signed the verso. The Judean Greek documents varied from the corresponding Aramaic certificates by the use of the Greco-Roman form of stating the date, the use of third person and the focus on the woman's dowry as opposed to a *ketubah* promise from the husband. Further, they do not refer to the marriage being "according to the law of Moses." These distinctives were almost certainly influenced by Hellenistic legal procedures. The issue is whether these differences result from Jewish cultural assimilation to Hellenistic values or from a simple desire to write a contract that could stand in a (Hellenistic) court of law. Perhaps both motives could be deduced.[54]

Despite the widespread evidence for the use of marriage certificates in Second Temple Judaism, these texts should not be taken to prove that everyone went to the time and expense of having a contract drafted. Thus, the rabbis allow for legal crises arising from circumstances where there is no legal marital document and for improperly written documents, implicitly recognizing that not every married couple had such legal notices, despite the exchange of monies.[55]

---

[52]So Cotton, "Cancelled Marriage Contract," pp. 77-78; Cotton and Yardeni, *Aramaic, Hebrew and Greek Documentary Texts,* pp. 265-66. Not only is such a practice found in Egyptian papyri; Cotton also points out that in rabbinic teaching the mother could give away an underage fatherless daughter (*m. Ketub.* 6:6).

[53]On the dowry, see discussion below in the next section. Such a dowry addition (three hundred denarii) is found among the Judean contracts only in P.Yadin 18 lines 13-14, 47.

[54]On P.Yadin 18 observe the debate between Wasserstein and Katzoff, both of whom ultimately grant significant Greek and Roman influence in this contract. A. Wasserstein, "A Marriage Contract from the Province of Arabia Nova: Notes on Papyrus Yadin 18," *JQR* 80 (1989): 105-30; Ranon Katzoff, "Papyrus Yadin 18 Again: A Rejoinder," *JQR* 82 (1991): 171-76. Cotton ("Cancelled Marriage Contract," pp. 81-85) broadens this discussion to other Greek contracts.

[55]See *m. Ketub.* 4:7; *m. Ketub.* 4:8-11. Though the reconstruction of the text is at issue, further support might be alleged from XHev/Se 65 (= P.Yadin 37), where the document can be understood to formalize the financial arrangements in a preexisting unwritten marriage. So the response to Lewis and to Ilan in Cotton and Yardeni, *Aramaic, Hebrew and Greek Documentary Texts,* pp. 227-29. Lewis suggests that the couple had been living together since betrothal; see Lewis et al., *Documents,* p. 130. Ilan argues they had been cohabiting prior to a legal marriage in keeping with accepted Judean practice; see Tal Ilan, "Premarital Cohabitation in Ancient Judea: The Evidence of the Babatha Archive and the Mishnah (*Ketubbot* 1.4)," *HTR* 86 (1993): 247-64.

Exchange of monies. As was noted above, property or money was exchanged at the inception of marriage. The woman came with a dowry, but in various ways down through history the man also was expected to compensate for the woman. The dowry is well represented in documents throughout this period, but compensation paid by the husband presents some complex shifts in antiquity.

Beginning with the dowry, certain Old Testament texts illustrate such a gift from the father to his married daughter for her to take into married life.[56] The intertestamental book of Tobit likely represents this concept when the father Raguel gives half of all his possessions to the bridegroom of his only daughter (Tob 8:21).[57] Josephus reports substantial dowries (one hundred talents) given to members of the royal house.[58] The plight of those girls who have inadequate dowries is noted, and persons outside the family can help underwrite the dowries of those in need.[59] While it may be recognized that a good dowry is important in marrying off one's daughter, conversely men are warned to beware of seeking wealthy women with good dowries—advice that Josephus even attributes to Jewish law.[60]

Several ancient Jewish marriage contracts record the possessions that the wife has upon entering into marriage (i.e., her dowry). In the fifth century B.C. one learns of a handmaiden who entered into marriage with just a woolen garment, a mirror and a bit of ointment—the value totaling just over seven shekels.[61] On the other hand, from the same period, Yehoyishma came into marriage with a long list of household items and money totaling nearly eighty shekels.[62] The Elephantine documents also in two instances testify to substantial gifts of land from the bride's father to the

---

[56]Most clearly of land from Pharaoh to his daughter (Solomon's wife; 1 Kings 9:16); also servants in Gen 29:24 and likely Gen 24:59, 61. An expansion in a Second Temple Greek translation of Joshua (Josh 16:10 LXX) appears to be influenced by 1 Kings 9:16.

[57]Moore, *Tobit,* pp. 246-47. Another apocryphal book indicates Jewish awareness of pagan ceremonial royal "marriages" to goddesses. In these marriages a human king would pledge himself to a goddess, and in return the temple of the goddess was expected to pay the royal figure a "dowry" (2 Macc 1:14).

[58]*Ant.* 16.228; see also *Ant.* 13.82. A similar substantial dowry (one hundred talents) is mentioned in *T. Jos.* 18:3 (Jewish provenance debated).

[59]Philo *Spec. Laws* 2.124; *Flight* 29.

[60]Ps.-Phoc. 199-203; cf. Sir 25:21; Josephus *Ag. Ap.* 2:200. Further evidence of this warning can be found in *T. Jud.* 13:4-8 (Jewish provenance debated).

[61]Kraeling, *Brooklyn Museum Aramaic Papyri,* p. 143 (= K 2 lines 4-7).

[62]K 7 lines 5-17. Additional items are also listed on lines 17-21. The above total assumes that one karsh = ten shekels. Fragmentary dowry lists are also known from Elephantine, e.g., K 14 and C 36.

bride for use by both the bride and her husband, though these are formally transferred in additional legal papers.[63] The Jewish Greek marriage certificates from the second century A.D. also refer to dowries. In these later texts the dowry can be expressed solely in the form of money (gold and silver totaling five hundred denarii in XHev/Se 69 or two hundred denarii in the remarriage contract Mur 115) or in goods for the wife's use, which are then evaluated (two hundred denarii in P.Yadin 18; ninety-six denarii in P.Yadin 37).[64] Rabbinic sources indicate that a father can marry his daughter without a dowry (literally, he can "marry her naked"), but this must be negotiated ahead of time or he must pay a minimum dowry of fifty denarii.[65]

Typically in antiquity the dowry reverted to the wife if the marriage ended (either through divorce or death of a spouse).[66] However, at some points in history the dowry was technically under the control of the husband while they remain married,[67] whereas the wife may have exercised greater authority in other contexts.[68] Nevertheless, as noted above, the dowry often consisted of property that would be most used by the wife, such as jewelry, clothing or pottery.

Traditionally the term for the property/money a man paid for marriage to

---

[63]See K 6 for the gift of a house to Yehoyishma—a gift associated with her marriage in K 10 line 7 and in K 12 line 18; note the discussion in Kraeling, *Brooklyn Museum Aramaic Papyri,* pp. 191-97. For the gift of property to Mibtahiah, see C 8 (Cowley, *Aramaic Papyri,* pp. 21-25). This latter gift was not totally under Mibtahiah's control in that her children took possession of the land should she be divorced; cf. C 9 (Cowley, *Aramaic Papyri,* pp. 25-29), and see Porten, *Archives from Elephantine,* pp. 240-45.

[64]These dowries are conveniently noted in Cotton and Yardeni, *Aramaic, Hebrew and Greek Documentary Texts,* pp. 266-68.

[65]The Hebrew is fifty *zuz* (= denarii); see *m. Ketub.* 6:5. The amount is five *selas* (= approx. twenty denarii) in *t. Ketub.* 6:4.

[66]The dowry stays with the wife if the marriage ends in divorce initiated by either party according to the Elephantine papyri K 2 lines 8-10; and K 7 lines 21-28. If considered a dowry addition, then C 15 lines 22-29 would be exceptional because the money originated from the husband and thus reverted to him upon divorce. The marriage certificate Mur 116 (lines 5-6) from the Judean desert indicates that the dowry is passed on to the wife's sons on her death rather than remaining in the husband's possession.

[67]Thus the husband is recorded as acknowledging his receiving of the dowry and his contentment with it in Elephantine marriage contracts.

[68]In the Jewish Greek text P.Yadin 18, the wife or her delegate appears to have executive control over the dowry. The complex interplay of who controlled the dowry (husband or wife) may here mirror complexities in Greco-Roman society; cf. the description in Susan Treggiari, *Roman Marriage: Iusti Coniuges from the Time of Cicero to the Time of Ulpian* (Oxford: Clarendon, 1991), pp. 327-31.

his wife was *mohar*. The term itself is found in Scripture,[69] and the concept is implied in other biblical passages.[70] In these texts the bride's father or male head of the household receives the *mohar*.

The *mohar* is present in Aramaic marriage contracts from Elephantine (fifth-century Egypt), though its price here is nominal (five shekels) in comparison with the dowry.[71] In one instance (C 15) the *mohar* is paid to the bride's father; in another (K 7) it is paid to the bride's brother acting as head of the house. Though the Aramaic of the text is debated, one document at Elephantine may imply that at this time the groom could also add gifts to the wife's dowry, primarily in the form of household possessions.[72] A related addition to the wife's dowry is found in the second-century A.D. document from the Babatha archive (P.Yadin 18 lines 13-14, 47)[73]; however, in P.Yadin 18 the money remains the property of the wife upon her asking.

---

[69]E.g., Gen 34:12; Ex 22:15-16 [Eng. 22:16-17]; 1 Sam 18:25. It is unfortunate that several English translations render *mohar* as "dowry" in these passages (e.g., KJV, NASB) since a dowry is most properly the property a woman brings with her into the marriage. However, it should be noted that the dowry interpretation was present as early as the LXX (so φερνή in Gen 34:12; Ex 22:15-16) and later in Philo (*Spec. Laws* 3.70-71, with interesting developments). Cf. Elias Bickerman, "Two Legal Interpretations of the Septuagint," in *Studies in Jewish and Christian History,* ed. Elias Bickerman, AGJU 9.1 (Leiden: Brill, 1976), 1:210-11. It has been pointed out that the translation "bride-price" (e.g., NIV) is also unfortunate in that it may connote that the woman is being treated primarily as a commodity (cf. Collins, "Marriage, Divorce, and Family," p. 113).

[70]Gen 24:53; 29:18-20; Deut 22:28-29.

[71]C 15 lines 4-6: "I have given you, as the price of your daughter Miphtahiah *the sum* of 5 shekels, royal weight. It has been received by you and your heart is content therewith" (translation by Cowley, *Aramaic Papyri,* p. 46, italics indicate reconstructed text; similar in Porten and Yardeni, *Textbook of Aramaic Documents,* 2:33). That a *mohar* payment to the father is in view is evidenced not only by the term *mohar* itself in line 4 but also by the references to the father by second-person possessive pronouns throughout (cf. "your daughter" in lines 3 and 5). While this marriage likely concerns an Egyptian man marrying a Jewish woman, a *mohar* payment is also in view in K 7 lines 4-5 (this papyri is fragmentary at the word mentioning the amount; Kraeling argues the amount here is 1 karsh = 10 shekels; see Kraeling, *Brooklyn Museum Aramaic Papyri,* p. 209).

[72]C 15 (= B2.6) lines 6-14. Porten and Yardeni (*Textbook of Aramaic Documents,* 2:30-33) reconstruct the text as a straightforward dowry by interpreting lines 6 and 7 as property that Mibtahiah brought to Ashor (twice reading לי). On the other hand, Cowley contends that the Aramaic verb in line 6 is best interpreted in light of line 14 (which totals the *mohar* money into the dowry addition), indicating that the gifts in lines 6-14 were given from the husband to the wife (see Cowley, *Aramaic Papyri,* comments on lines 6 and 14, pp. 47-48). If one considers this a dowry addition, then it is distinct from the *mohar* since the gifts are effectively given to the woman for her use as part of the dowry rather than given to the male head of the wife's household. However, on the theory that the husband himself provides this dowry addition, it would naturally revert to the husband upon divorce, unlike a standard dowry (C 15 lines 22-29).

[73]A dowry addition is also found in the fifth-century A.D. marriage contract from Antinoopolis (lines 20-23) published in Colette Sirat et al., *La Ketouba de Cologne: Un contrat de mariage juif à Antinoopolis,* PapCol 12 (Opladen: Westdeutscher, 1986), pp. 20-22.

By the rabbinic period there are sparse late references to a *mohar* concept.[74] Instead, focus is on a payment known as the *ketubah* (a term identical to that for the marriage contract itself) which is a payment the man must make if he divorces his wife or which is due a husband's widow upon his death. The *ketubah* is explicitly set in the Mishnah as two hundred denarii for a virgin or one hundred denarii for a widow, though it is permissible to exceed these amounts.[75] An expanded payment appears to be in view in the marriage contract P.Yadin 10, where the contracted amount is set at four hundred *zuzin* (= four hundred denarii).[76]

Key rabbinic sources locate the origin of the *ketubah* payment (as a payment retained by the husband until the marriage ends and thereafter owed to the wife) as the invention of the famous first-century B.C. rabbinic forerunner Simeon ben Shetach.[77] This literature claims that Simeon's innovation entails dictating that a payment regularly owed to the bride's father at the inception of marriage be instead paid only at its dissolution. In these sources the motives for such change are variously said to have been to make marriage easier (property/money is not required up front) and/or to make divorce harder (since the man would have to pay the woman if he divorces her). Based on this evidence, many interpreters have suggested that the *ketubah* is a refashioning of the *mohar* under the influence of Simeon ben Shetach. A more complex read under the influence of *b. Ketub.* 82b and the Elephantine marriage documents (mentioned above) is to suggest a threefold development through the Second Temple period from (1) the *mohar* being paid to the male head

---

[74]See Michael L. Satlow, *Jewish Marriage in Antiquity* (Princeton, N.J.: Princeton University Press, 2001), pp. 203-4, 349 nn. 39-42. By the second century A.D. the meaning of the term *mohar* had apparently shifted in some West Semitic contexts to mean a payment from the bride's family to the husband, as can be seen in references to *mohar* in the Nabatean debenture P.Yadin 1 (= 5/6Hev 1) line 18; note comments on this text in Yadin et al., *Documents: Hebrew, Aramaic*, pp. 171-72.

[75]See *m. Ketub.* 1:2; *m. Ketub.* 5:1.

[76]P.Yadin 10 recto lines 6 and 8. The text records the price in both places as four hundred *zuzin* which equal one hundred *sil'in*. Originally the editors suggested that this number one hundred was equal to the amount specified in the Mishnah for widows (cf. *m. Ketub.* 1:2; 4:7; 5:1) and argued that this must be Babatha's second marriage; see Yadin et al., "Babatha's *Ketubba*," p. 77. However, this has been challenged by Friedman, who points out that the Mishnah specifies one hundred *zuzin* for the widow, and here the one hundred *sil'in* clearly equal four hundred *zuzin* (four times the standard *ketubah* for a widow); see Mordechai A. Friedman, "Babatha's *Ketubba*: Some Preliminary Observations," *IEJ* 46, no. 1-2 (1996), pp. 56-61. Friedman's point (also made in a separate Hebrew publication by Safrai) has been accepted by the new editors; see Yadin et al., *Documents: Hebrew Aramaic,* p. 119. The term *zuzin* is also found in Mur 20 (recto col. 1 line 5), though unfortunately the amount has been lost.

[77]See *t. Ketub.* 12:1; *y. Ketub.* 8.32b-c; *b. Ketub.* 82b.

of the household, to (2) a dowry supplement paid directly to the wife, to (3) a promissory amount due upon divorce or widowhood.[78]

However, Michael Satlow has recently challenged the reliability of the Simeon ben Shetach references.[79] While he acknowledges ample evidence for the dowry in early Judaism, Satlow notes that the concept of the *ketubah* payment is not mentioned in prerabbinic published literary sources from the Second Temple period itself. Further, the vast majority of extant marriage contracts from the period do not explicitly mention a *ketubah* payment. And he contends that, where the term *ketubah* is found in earliest marriage contracts (e.g., Mur 21), it refers to a dowry. Granted, there are dowry additions and divorce penalties in the Elephantine papyri, but these are not true *ketuboth*. Thus Satlow argues that there is a paucity of real evidence for early use of the *ketubah*. Combine this with the rabbinic tendency to attribute legendary material to Simeon ben Shetach and with the way that the rabbinic *ketubah* requirements (e.g., two hundred denarii) line up with standard dowry payments that the wife brought into the marriage (especially in the Qumran marriage contracts), and Satlow contends that the rabbinic *ketubah* payment is actually a late first-century A.D. development.

Satlow is right to notice the limited evidence outside rabbinic traditions. But perhaps he is too quick to cast aspersions on some rabbinic references that indicate that a well-developed *ketubah* concept already lay behind first-century A.D. debates between the schools of Hillel and Shammai.[80] Further,

---

[78]The three-stage interpretation is supported by Collins, "Marriage, Divorce, and Family," pp. 113-14. Four stages are envisioned by Archer, *Her Price Is Beyond Rubies,* pp. 159-63. An argument for (a basically two-stage) development in continuity with a switch from Mesopotamian to Ptolemaic Egyptian practices is found in Markham J. Geller, "New Sources for the Origins of the Rabbinic Ketubah," *HUCA* 49 (1978): 227-45.

[79]Michael Satlow, "Reconsidering the Rabbinic *ketubah* Payment," in *The Jewish Family in Antiquity,* ed. Shaye J. D. Cohen, BJS 289 (Atlanta: Scholars Press, 1993), pp. 133-51. Summarized in Satlow, *Jewish Marriage,* pp. 213-16.

[80]In *m. Yebam.* 4:3; *m. Ketub.* 8:6; *m. B. Bat.* 9:8-9 (9:10 includes comments of R. Akiba and Ben Azzai). Satlow's response is to attempt to diffuse these pre-Yavneh references to *ketubah* by contending that they view *ketubah* as a subset of the dowry—the subset portion that is wholly at the husband's disposal during marriage ("Reconsidering," pp. 142-43). This would require a highly technical definition of the term *ketubah,* though for his argument to work Satlow elsewhere claims that this term is actually most often "ambiguous." Satlow's contention, that in these passages *ketubah* is a technical term for a subset of the dowry, is at variance with the natural reading of these rabbinic sayings since the nature of the *ketubah* as a promissory payment (rather than a dowry) is elsewhere clearly defined in the overall context of these tractates. Further, Satlow's own attempt at mitigating the force of the evidence in Mur 21 by saying that *ketubah* in Mur 21 refers to the whole dowry is at odds with his claim that the *ketubah* is only a portion of the dowry in other literature. More telling is the similar shift

though the evidence is fragmentary, there are at least two marriage contract papyri that likely refer to a *ketubah* payment.[81] Finally, remember that rabbinic teaching likely did not have a universal impact on early Judaism despite its strong sway in later Jewish communities. Thus it is entirely possible that the lack of widespread corroboration in fragmentary documents and in nonrabbinic literature may be less an indication that the *ketubah* had not yet been founded in rabbinic circles and more an indication that it was not yet pervasive throughout all Jewish societies.[82] Thus it seems possible that the rabbinic traditions themselves could record with some accuracy the development of the *ketubah* payment within rabbinic Judaism.[83] More confidently one can note that at some stage in the later Second Temple period the practice of a *ketubah* payment became the primary contribution of the husband at the inception of marriage.

Acceptable marriage partners. Which Jewish marriages were legally permissible? Biblical law in several locations limits the kinds of permissible marriages. Hence when sexual relations are prohibited with close family members in Leviticus 18:6-18, this effectively disallows incestuous mar-

---

in argumentation found within Satlow's paragraph on the Hillel/Shammai evidence when he defines *ketubah* as a mere portion of the dowry and then a few sentences later as the (whole) dowry.

[81]P.Yadin 10 lines 11, 16; Mur 21 recto II, lines 10, 13, 16. P.Yadin 10 (= 5/6Hev 10) lines 10-11 concurs well with rabbinic teaching about the need to redeem a wife who was taken captive without subtracting the cost of redemption from her *ketubah* (*m. Ketub.* 4:9). While some reconstruction is required, line 16 of P.Yadin 10 most likely mentions that the *ketubah* is due the wife if, upon the husband's death, his heirs send her away—again cohering with rabbinic teaching on the *ketubah* (e.g., *m. Ketub.* 4:12). Although P.Yadin 10 was published after Satlow's 1993 article, Satlow did respond in his later book—arguing that, if the term *ketubah* in P.Yadin 10 refers to the rabbinic concept of an obligation from the husband's resources, then these texts would not contain a reference to the dowry. Since he considers the omission of a dowry record unlikely, he believes that they must actually be references to the dowry, which was at this stage called a *ketubah* (see Satlow, *Jewish Marriage*, pp. 201-2). However, this overlooks the continuity mentioned above between these documents and rabbinic legislation concerning the *ketubah*. Friedman suggests that the practice of registering the dowry in Palestinian marriage contracts had not yet become widespread; see Friedman, *Jewish Marriage*, pp. 292-93.

[82]If the fifth-century A.D. Antinoopolis marriage contract (see Sirat et al., *La Ketouba de Cologne*, esp. pp. 12-15, 20-22, 42-56) should be seen to contain a dowry and a dowry addition (totalled together as a *ketubah*), then the variation from rabbinic teaching serves to show just how slow an impact rabbinic teaching may have had (especially in Egypt), for rabbinic teaching on the *ketubah* payment had been around for centuries by the time of this contract.

[83]Satlow himself appears willing to allow that the rabbis may be absorbing a practice that is testified elsewhere in a limited way in the papyri (Satlow, *Jewish Marriage*, p. 216); but the difficulty here is assessing whether the innovation is coming into rabbinic thought from practices outside the movement, or the influence went primarily the other direction.

riages.[84] Elsewhere the Pentateuch recognizes, and apparently permits, Jewish marriages to war captives as well as to slaves.[85] Priests have special rules requiring that they not marry a divorcee or a harlot.[86] Beyond that, the high priest must marry a virgin—widows, divorcees and harlots are specifically disallowed—and she must be of Hebrew stock.[87] I will discuss in a later section how this creates potential difficulties for the high priest in levirate marriages.

Comparing these biblical laws with later Jewish teachings, one notes that the incestuous sexual relations continue to be strongly prohibited,[88] though the list is also condensed in some literature. Pseudo-Phocylides speaks against intercourse with a father's second wife, a father's concubines, one's sister or a wife of one's brother.[89] Josephus lists illegal sexual relations with a mother, stepmother, aunt, sister or daughter-in-law.[90] It is likely that Josephus's complaint against Herodias—that she "flouted the way of the fathers"—has to do with her marrying her husband's brother while both brothers are still alive.[91] This same complaint against Herodias was made by John the Baptist according to Mark 6:17-18 (also Mt 14:3-4; Lk 3:19).

Some Second Temple authors legislate beyond the biblical incest injunctions. The Damascus Document goes further than the biblical listing of prohibited intercourse by noting that the prohibitions that the law writes for males "apply equally to females," thus rendering forbidden relations between an uncle and his niece.[92] However, Safrai notes that later rabbinic literature considered the marriage of a sister's daughter a pious act.[93]

While the biblical incest injunctions appear to be very much in force, it

---

[84]Also Lev 20:14, 17, 19-21; Deut 22:30; 27:20, 22-23.

[85]Deut 21:10-14; Ex 21:7-11.

[86]Lev 21:7; cf. Ezek 44:22. The Leviticus text apparently mentions two classes of people: (1) a woman defiled by harlotry (a natural way to read the pairing of the Hebrew participle and adjective *zōnâ waḥălālâ*, and also the likely interpretation of the LXX), and (2) a divorcee (cf. NASB, NIV). However, it is possible, though unlikely, that the first class should be divided in order to create three total classes—namely "a harlot or a defiled woman or a divorcee" (cf. RSV). Note below that Josephus apparently expands on what constitutes a "defiled woman."

[87]Lev 21:13-15.

[88]E.g., Sir 23:16-21; cf. *Pss. Sol.* 8:9.

[89]Ps.-Phoc. 179-83.

[90]Josephus *Ant.* 3.274.

[91]Josephus *Ant.* 18.136. Thus contravening Lev 20:21. Whiston's translation implies that the concern is her divorce of her first husband (and thus many author's follow him), but the Greek focuses more on the remarriage while both brothers are living (so also the LCL translation).

[92]CD V, 7-11; cf. 11QTemple LXVI, 12-17. See discussion in Yigael Yadin, *The Temple Scroll,* 3 vols. (Jerusalem: Israel Exploration Society, 1977-1983), 1:371-72.

[93]Safrai, "Home and Family," 754.

is also the case that marrying within one's own smaller "tribe" or family clan was promoted in some sectors of Judaism. This is present in some places in the Old Testament.[94] The practice is clear in the book of Tobit,[95] where Tobit himself lists Noah, Abraham, Isaac and Jacob as exemplars of this ideal (Tob 4:12). Indeed, Tobit implies that a death sentence awaited anyone who married his daughter outside their tribe and whose inheritance was to fall to that daughter (Tob 6:12).[96] The book of Judith notes that its widowed heroine had previously married within her tribe and family (Jdt 8:2). *Jubilees,* in recounting biblical history, repeatedly notes those who took the daughter of a relative as wife.[97] The ideal of marrying within one's tribe is also found in marriages permitted the king by the Qumran sect.[98]

The biblical laws limiting priestly marriages are also repeated in Second Temple literature. Following the biblical text, Josephus affirms that the high priest may not marry a widow. However, Josephus actually expands the list of prohibited priestly marriages, in addition to harlots and divorcees, to include slaves, prisoners of war and women whose occupations are suspect (hawking or innkeeping).[99]

Going beyond clear biblical injunctions, Josephus forbids all men the right to marry female slaves; and he later presents as indecent Pheroras's inability to constrain his love for a slave woman.[100] Josephus also says men should not marry prostitutes, even though this is only forbidden to priests in Leviticus 21:7—the two issues being that prostitutes cannot make acceptable nuptial sacrifices and that the children of such a union would not grow up in virtue.[101]

A major point of discussion has to do with the need to marry a fellow Hebrew. Jewish law proscribes marriage with Canaanites, while the sons of Moabites and Ammonites are not admitted into the assembly of the Lord for

---

[94]Esp. Num 36:5-9, 11; also cf. the marriages of Isaac and Jacob.

[95]E.g., Tob 1:9; 3:15; 4:12-13; 6:10-12.

[96]Briefly discussed in Will Soll, "The Family as Scriptural and Social Construct in Tobit," in *The Function of Scripture in Early Jewish and Christian Tradition,* ed. Craig A. Evans and James A. Sanders, JSNTSup 154 (Sheffield: Sheffield Academic Press, 1998), pp. 170-75.

[97]*Jub.* 4:15, 16, 20, 27, 28, 33; 8:6; 11:7, 14. So Safrai, "Home and Family," p. 754. See the note on *Jub.* 4:15 by O. S. Wintermute in *OTP,* 2:61 n.

[98]11QTemple LVII, 15-19. For rabbinic examples, see Joachim Jeremias, *Jerusalem in the Time of Jesus: An Investigation into Economic and Social Conditions During the New Testament Period,* trans. F. H. and C. H. Cave (Philadelphia: Fortress, 1969), pp. 365-66.

[99]See Josephus *Ant.* 3.276-277. See the note in H. St. J. Thackeray et al., *Josephus,* LCL (Cambridge, Mass.: Harvard University Press, 1926-1965), 4:450-51.

[100]Josephus *Ant.* 4.244; *Ant.* 16.194.

[101]Josephus *Ant.* 4.245.

ten generations and Edomites for three generations.[102] Outside the law, marriage to fellow Jews was encouraged in the Old Testament,[103] sometimes even demanded—especially at the inception of the Second Temple period in Judea.[104] Significant problems in the Old Testament narrative are created by Israelite men being attracted to foreign women—especially from Moab and Philistia. However, the Old Testament also recognizes marriages to captives from wars;[105] and key Jewish exemplars are married to non-Jews in Scripture (e.g., Joseph, Samson, Boaz and Esther).

The fear of mingling the Jewish race with others continues in the Second Temple period even after the time of Ezra-Nehemiah. This is quite evident in rewritings of biblical law where additions are made forbidding intermarriage with other races, even to the point of death.[106] In Pseudo-Philo's retelling of biblical narrative there is repeated mention of the abhorrence of sexual intercourse with Gentiles.[107] The Greek expansive translation of Esther describes this key female exemplar of Jewish intermarriage asserting in her apocryphal prayer that she "abhors the bed of the uncircumcised and of every foreigner."[108] One also sees opposition to foreign marriage in the threatened apocalyptic punishment of Jews who marry foreigners.[109] Further opposition to intermarriage may be found in the Jewish testament tradition and in narrative.[110] The Qumran Temple Scroll requires that the king of Israel take a Jewish wife from his own family, an apparent addition to the laws of Deuteronomy 17.[111] In this same vein Josephus argues that Solomon failed as a king because he transgressed the law of Moses that required him to marry only from his own people.[112] An early second-century A.D. Aramaic

---

[102]Deut 7:3; 23:3, 8; cf. Ex 34:11-16.

[103]E.g., Gen 24:3, 37; 28:1; Num 36:8; Judg 14:3.

[104]Ezra 9:2; 10:2-4, 11-44; Neh 13:23-29; cf. the metaphor in Mal 2:11.

[105]Deut 21:10-14.

[106]Philo *Spec. Laws* 3.29; *Jub.* 30:7-17. The context of this expansion in *Jubilees* is a reading of Gen 34:1-17 (the rape of Dinah and the death of the men of Shechem). See also the rewritten biblical narratives in *Jub.* 20:4; 22:20-21; and esp. 25:5, 9.

[107]Esp. *L.A.B.* 9:5; 43:5; 44:7; also 18:13; 21:1; 30:1.

[108]Add Esth C 26 = 4:17u = 14:15. Differences in word order exist between the A and B recensions of Greek Esther, but the effect is the same. See Robert Hanhart, ed., *Esther*, Septuaginta 8.3 (Göttingen: Vandenhoeck & Ruprecht, 1966), p. 167.

[109]E.g., *2 Bar.* 42:4.

[110]Thus *T. Job* 45:3. A similar ideology can be found in *Jos. Asen.* 8:5, though with more receptivity to speaking to Gentile virgins (cf. *Jos. Asen.* 7:4-6) and allowing the possibility of marriage after conversion (see below). See also (with, in my opinion, likely Jewish influence) *T. Levi* 9:9-10; 14:6. Further, note the references to marrying within one's own tribe below.

[111]11QTemple LVII, 15-17. Yadin, *Temple Scroll*, 1:353-55.

[112]Josephus *Ant.* 8.191-92.

divorce certificate from **Murabba'at** allows the divorced wife to remarry any *Jewish* man.[113] And even some pagan authors recognized Jewish refusal to have intercourse with non-Jews.[114]

Nevertheless, the Old Testament law permitting marriage to war captives (e.g., Deut 21:10-14) continues to be passed down in Judaism.[115] Also transmitted is the teaching concerning the Ammonites, Moabites and Edomites—according to rabbinic literature the first two are forbidden for all time, but the last is permissible after three generations (e.g., *m. Yebam.* 8:3). It is also interesting to examine how biblical examples of intermarriage are developed in the Second Temple era.[116] When Samson marries a Philistine, the reticence of the parents to allow such a non-Hebrew marriage is played up in Josephus, though God's hand is recognized.[117] However in Pseudo-Philo, when Samson marries Delilah, the condemnation is more pronounced.[118]

The most fascinating developments in the treatment of a biblical exemplar concern Joseph, who married Asenath the daughter of Potiphera priest of On.[119] The information on Asenath's father would imply that she was a Gentile, even a daughter of an Egyptian pagan priest. In contrast with these likely implications in the biblical text, Pseudo-Philo calls Joseph a "crown for his brothers" because he did *not* afflict his seed (with a foreign wife) unlike Samson.[120] However, in a lovely romantic book from the late Second Temple period (possibly early rabbinic period), the relationship between Joseph and Asenath is developed in great detail. Aseneth (note the slight change in her name) is indeed represented as a non-Jewish native of Egypt[121] who must be converted.[122] Yet, after her repentance, fasting and conversion, an angel announces her acceptance before God,[123] allowing

---

[113]Mur 19 lines 7, 19.

[114]So Manetho in Josephus *Ag. Ap.* 1.239. See Menahem Stern, *Greek and Latin Authors on Jews and Judaism* (Jerusalem: Israel Academy of Sciences and Humanities, 1974-1984), 1:79, 82, 85 n. Also Tacitus *Historiae* 5.5.2 (Stern, *Greek and Latin Authors*, 2:19, 26, 40n.).

[115]E.g., Philo *Virtues* 110-115; Josephus *Ant.* 4.257-259; *Sifre Deut.* 211-214 (the *Sifre* clearly labels such women as Gentiles).

[116]As a further example, Er and Onan are singled out in *T. Jud.* 10:1-6 as Judah's descendants who, at the encouragement of their mother, refuse intercourse with their Aramaean wife Tamar; because of this God puts them both to death (cf. *Jub.* 41:2).

[117]Josephus *Ant.* 5.286; cf. Judg 14:2-3.

[118]*L.A.B.* 44:5.

[119]Gen 41:45, 50; 46:20.

[120]*L.A.B.* 44:5.

[121]E.g., *Jos. Asen.* 4:9; 9:1.

[122]*Jos. Asen.* 8:5-9.

[123]*Jos. Asen.* 9:1—13:15; 14:1—17:10.

Aseneth and Joseph to wed.[124] It would appear that *Joseph and Aseneth* solves the problem of Aseneth's Gentile roots by making her a convert to Judaism.

Indeed there is a theme in Second Temple Jewish literature of Jew-Gentile marriage requiring the conversion of the future Gentile spouse to Judaism and (if male) undergoing circumcision.[125] So Josephus reports instances of men converting to Judaism and being circumcised in order to marry Jewish women.[126] Josephus even reports that Sylleus the Arab refuses marriage to Salome because it would have necessitated his coming over to Judaism—a price he was unwilling to pay.[127] In rabbinic teaching proselytes remain acceptable spouses for non-priests, though it takes many generations of proselyte women to achieve the status of an Israelite woman.[128]

However, it is not always the case that Jew-Gentile marriages were predicated upon true conversion.[129] While at the beginning of the Second Temple period Ezra-Nehemiah drastically opposed intermarriage with foreign women (and the corresponding lure to worship foreign gods), this situation also proves that just such relationships were accepted by some Jews, even in Palestine. A few decades later we have in documents from Elephantine Egypt an example of a Jewish woman who was married in her second and third marriages to two different Egyptian men (C 14, C 15). Before the first Egyptian husband would release her property after their divorce, he required her to swear by an Egyptian goddess, showing that he had certainly not become a fervent proselyte. Her second Egyptian husband (her third husband overall) may have become a proselyte[130]; in any case their offspring were considered Jewish (see C 20 lines 3-4). Even more striking is the case

---

[124]*Jos. Asen.* 18:1—21:9.

[125]It is a fascinating conundrum to compare this to Gen 34:14-17.

[126]Josephus *Ant.* 20.139, 145. Interestingly, when Drusilla divorces her husband to marry Felix the procurator, Josephus says she has transgressed the ancestral laws (*Ant.* 20.143). It is unclear which law is involved: (1) she possibly could have committed adultery (so Whiston in his translation note on *J.W.* 2.247) although this is not the most natural way to read the Greek syntax; (2) it could be that the divorce itself was unlawful; (3) it could be that Felix had not converted to Judaism (on Drusilla's Jewishness, cf. Acts 24:24).

[127]Josephus *Ant.* 16.225. However, this report differs from that in *J.W.* 1.566, where Herod compels an end to this possible marriage. Regardless of how one synthesizes these two accounts, Josephus could only have expected his readers to believe the *Antiquities* version if in fact Gentile conversion could be considered a prerequisite to marrying a Jew.

[128]See *m. Qidd.* 4:1, 7; cf. *m. Ketub.* 1:4.

[129]So Polemo forsakes Jewish customs once Bernice has left him (Josephus, *Ant.* 20.146).

[130]For discussion of Mibtahiah's intermarriages with Egyptian men, see Porten, *Archives from Elephantine*, pp. 245-62. Cowley (*Aramaic Papyri*, p. 47) allows that her third husband may have ultimately become a proselyte and changed his name to Nathan.

from Elephantine of the Jewish priest Ananiah marrying an Egyptian slave girl, whose right to wed he obtains from her master (K 2).[131]

In summary, incestuous marriages continue to be legislated against in Second Temple literature, and some voices even extend the biblical prohibitions to uncle and niece. Nonetheless, marriage within one's own family tribe was encouraged in many sectors of early Judaism. A preponderance of sources call for Jews to marry within the race, but intermarriage appears to be practiced by some, especially (but not exclusively) subsequent to conversion.[132]

Arrangement of marriages. Who typically arranged Jewish marriages? In Old Testament texts, primarily the parents orchestrate marriages. Often this is done by the man's father, occasionally at the request of his marrying son; sometimes it is coordinated by his mother or the wife's father.[133] Where a father is not living or active, a brother as family patriarch can assume this role (e.g., Gen 24:51). But in many places the future husband himself initiates an agreement with the wife's parents.[134] In some places it is clear that the future wife's wishes are taken into account (Gen 24:58). As many royal marriages during the monarchy show, politics can play a role in the selection of royal spouses (cf. the parable in 1 Kings 14:9).

Nearly all these patterns have some analogy in Second Temple Judaism. Political marriages are frequently reported, especially among those aspiring to royalty, even when these are multiethnic.[135] Certainly the biblical narratives are retold in literature from the era, sometimes with interesting changes. For example, in Josephus, Rebekah calls her brother Laban the "guardian of my virginity."[136] From this statement one can see both the importance of virginity and that the male head of the household could be responsible for the maintenance of this.

Josephus explicitly states that Jewish law requires one to ask for a wife in marriage from her male guardian.[137] Such a procedure is witnessed in Jewish

---

[131]For an analysis of this relationship, see Porten, *Archives from Elephantine,* pp. 200-234 (esp. pp. 200-202 on the priesthood of Ananiah and pp. 205-13 on the marriage contract).

[132]Feldman has argued that the actual number of intermarriages must have been low; see Louis H. Feldman, *Jew and Gentile in the Ancient World: Attitudes and Interactions from Alexander to Justinian* (Princeton, N.J.: Princeton University Press, 1993), pp. 77-79.

[133]Father: Gen 24:51; 38:6; son: Gen 34:4; Judg 14:2; mother: Gen 21:21; wife's father: 1 Sam 18:21; less clearly the widow's mother-in-law in Ruth 3:1.

[134]Multiple times with David and Solomon; Esau as a negative example in Gen 26:34-35.

[135]E.g., Josephus *Ant.* 13:80-82; also note examples above in discussion of betrothals.

[136]Josephus *Ant.* 1.248; cf. Gen 24:51.

[137]Josephus *Ag. Ap.* 2.200.

romance narratives, though a royal figure can act in lieu of the direct male guardian.[138] The extant Elephantine marriage contracts are all addressed to the male guardian and not to the bride herself, even when the bride is remarrying.[139] The rabbis insist on the father's control over the betrothal process.[140] Nonetheless, certain texts presuppose that women have the right to reject a marriage proposal.[141] And rabbinic literature indicates that, after a certain age, the woman has some say concerning whom to marry.[142]

The marriage ceremony. Custom provided guidance in the conduct of the marriage ceremony, but no one ancient text informs fully about how such ceremonies were conducted. Descriptions of wedding ceremonies appear in different works of narrative literature. A reasonable outline can be seen in *Joseph and Aseneth* where, after the father figure (Pharaoh) places his hands on the head of the couple, he invokes the Lord's blessing on them, turns them to one another to kiss and then calls for a seven-day-long marriage feast.[143] Also of importance in this tale is the consummation of the marriage in sexual union.[144]

Other details are mentioned in the book of Tobit. Binding oaths are made between the husband and the bride's father and formalized in written contract; then a bridechamber is made up for consummation of the marriage. The feasting lasts for fourteen days.[145] A major subplot in Tobit revolves around the important act of marital consummation, for narrative tension is created in asking whether Tobias will survive the night in the bridal cham-

---

[138]Tob 7:11-12; *Jos. Asen.* 20:8-9; 21:2-7.

[139]So K 2; K 7; K 14; C 48; remarriage: C 15.

[140]See *m. Ketub.* 4:4.

[141]Ps.-Phoc. 204.

[142]The "right of refusal" granted young girls the right to break betrothals (even marriages, according to the school of Hillel) under certain circumstances (*m. Yebam.* 13:1-3; *t. Yebam.* 13:1-2). See further Judith Romney Wegner, *Chattel or Person? The Status of Women in the Mishnah* (Oxford: Oxford University Press, 1988), pp. 117-19.

[143]*Jos. Asen.* 21:5-8. I have omitted some details that may appear only because of the royal nature of this wedding, such as the use of gold crowns, though crowns with gold thread are known in rabbinic law. See Archer, *Her Price Is Beyond Rubies,* pp. 193-94.

[144]*Jos. Asen.* 21:9.

[145]Tob 7:11, 14, 16; 8:4-9, 19. The figure of fourteen days may intentionally double the standard seven days for narrative effect. That the inception of the feast awaited the consummation of the marriage is here due to the expectation of Raguel that Tobias would not survive the night (given previous events in the book; cf. Tob 8:9-18). The nature of Tobit's portrayal of family and the degree to which its marital practices are standard for Judaism in this period are discussed in Moore, *Tobit,* pp. 224-33, esp. 232-33. For brief comments on the wedding ceremony, see Will Soll, "The Book of Tobit as a Window on the Hellenistic Jewish Family," in *Passion, Vitality, and Foment: The Dynamics of Second Temple Judaism,* ed. Lamontte M. Luker (Harrisburg, Penn.: Trinity Press International, 2001), pp. 263-67.

ber, since seven men have previously been killed by a demon in the attempt. Concern over this possibility of demonic intervention leads to prayer.[146] Though without a similar stated concern about demonic intervention, prayer to the divine during wedding festivities can also be found in Josephus's assumption that the wife will engage in the custom of offering nuptial sacrifices to God (*Ant.* 4.245).

Safrai summarizes rabbinic teaching on the marriage ceremony as a fourfold process.[147] First, the bride prepared by bathing, perfuming and adorning herself. Second, she was conveyed from her father's house to the groom's in a carriage with a wreath while people sang and danced—often this occurred in the evening with a torch processional. Third, the groom went out to receive the bride into his house (or into the *chuppah* structure inside the house). Fourth, the festival in the home consisted of blessings (requiring ten men present) and a week-long feast. Rabbinic tradition indicates that differences did occur between Judean marriage and those ceremonies in Galilee, most notably the ceremony involved less privacy for the couple in Judea in order to ascertain the proof of virginity required.[148]

Throughout Second Temple literature, sexual consummation of the marriage forms an important aspect of the marriage. Among other things, from this event the virginity of the wife is proved. Biblical law permitted a newly wed husband to charge the wife with not being a virgin (a capital offense); and evidence of her virginity came from the wedding night (Deut 22:13-21). Such a law was repeated in Qumran texts and in Josephus.[149] This law had a special concern to protect the wife from a false claim against her virginity.[150] Rabbinic law indicated that the marriage of virgins should occur on a Wednesday night in case a charge was to be lodged afterwards since the courts sat in session on Thursday.[151]

Roles and relationships. In discussing the roles men and women played in marriage, it should certainly be acknowledged that our literary sources predominately (if not entirely) come from the hands of men. This is certainly a limitation, but in itself it tells something about the society in which marriage took place. The general perspective these sources provide

---

[146]Tob 3:7-9; 8:4-8.

[147]Safrai, "Home and Family," pp. 757-60. See also Archer, *Her Price Is Beyond Rubies,* pp. 189-206.

[148]See *t. Ketub.* 1:4.

[149]11QTemple LXV, 7-15; Josephus *Ant.* 4.246-248.

[150]Cf. *t. Ketub.* 1:5 where these penalties are heightened.

[151]See *m. Ketub.* 1:1.

could be fairly deemed patriarchal, though the husband also has obligations to his wife.

Domestic life requires both husband and wife to contribute to the up-keep of the family. This is illustrated in rabbinic views of household roles, which are undoubtedly idealized but nonetheless likely widespread. According to the Mishnah, the wife must grind flour, bake bread, wash clothes, cook food, nurse their children, ready her husband's bed and work in wool. Women who come into marriage with servants can charge some of these duties to the servants. The husband must provide food, clothing and a bed for his wife.[152]

Beyond these respective domestic duties, there is substantial evidence of the ideal of male leadership in the household. So Josephus says the Law indicates that wives are inferior to men in all things.[153] God has given authority to the man, thus the woman must be submissive. However, Josephus also notes this is to result not in her humiliation but in her being properly led. Rabbinic writings grant the husband significant control over the household; however, he also has obligations to his wife, and his control is limited in some other respects.[154] A wisdom text from Qumran associates the dominion of the husband over the wife with reference to the opening chapters of Genesis.[155] This wisdom writing spells out that such dominion is solely the husband's prerogative (and no other man's), requiring that she "walk in accordance with your desire and not add [any-thing]".[156] Yet, even here we should note that this Qumran text appeals to the wife as a "helper"[157] so the concept of dominion is not the only focus of this text.

One aspect of the husband's dominion in the context of 4Q416 is the husband's authority to annul the vows of his wife.[158] The concept arises

---

[152]See *m. Ketub.* 5:5, 8. The Mishnaic rights of the wife are well discussed in Wegner, *Chattel or Person?* pp. 71-80.

[153]Josephus *Ag. Ap.* 2.201. Josephus does not clearly indicate the portion of the Law to which he is referring. Elsewhere in this section he makes reference to legal teachings also not clearly found in the Old Testament (e.g., sexuality is only for procreation, *Ag. Ap.* 2.199). Perhaps in both instances we are dealing with an interpretive tradition that has grown out of Genesis (as Thackeray suggests in his translation).

[154]See especially Wegner, *Chattel or Person?* pp. 40-96.

[155]4Q416 2 III, 20—IV, 7 = 4Q418 10.3-9. The context refers to the "leave and cleave" section of Gen 2:24, as well as the "helper" concept of Gen 2:18, 20. It is possible that the concept of dominion has been developed from Gen 3:16.

[156]4Q416 2 IV, 7.

[157]4Q416 2 III, 21; cf. Gen 2:18, 20.

[158]4Q416 2 IV, 7-10 (= 4Q418 10.9-10).

from Numbers 30:6-16 and is repeated in the Damascus Document,[159] with the stipulation that vows are to be annulled by the husband only if he knows that they ought not be kept (i.e., when they violate the covenant).[160] Philo repeats the legislation concerning vows without such a limitation.[161] Rabbinic traditions also developed significant teaching about annulling vows.[162]

The ability to annul vows speaks of the husband's authority in marriage and additional legal responsibility. In fact, in rabbinic literature men bear more legal obligations than women in many aspects of the law.[163] These additional responsibilities, nevertheless, are generally recognized as placing men in a privileged position,[164] as testified in the famous statement of Rabbi Judah: "Three benedictions a man must bless every day: Blessed [are you, Lord,] who did not make me a gentile. Blessed [are you, Lord,] who did not make me a woman. Blessed [are you, Lord,] who did not make me an uncultured person."[165] The explanations given in the Tosefta for each of these three blessings are tied to each group's status with respect to the law. In particular, a man gives thanks that he is not a woman because "a woman is not bound by [all] the commandments."[166]

If the attribution to Rabbi Judah bar Ilai is correct, then these three

---

[159]CD XVI,10-12.

[160]Also repeated in 11QTemple LIV,2-3.

[161]Philo *Spec. Laws.* 2.24-25; cf. *Alleg. Interp.* 2.63.

[162]E.g., *m. Ned.* 10:1-11:12.

[163]See, for example, *m. Qidd.* 1:7-8; *m. Ber.* 3:3. However, the actual picture of what laws were performed by women during this period may be more complex; see Tal Ilan, *Jewish Women in Greco-Roman Palestine* (Peabody, Mass.: Hendrickson, 1996), pp. 176-84.

[164]So Wegner, *Chattel or Person?* p. 153.

[165]*t. Ber.* 7:18 (translation mine). The text followed here is that of Karl Heinrich Rengstorf, ed., *Die Tosefta: Seder I: Zeraim*, Rabbinische Texte 1.1 (Stuttgart: W. Kohlhammer, 1983), p. 52. Tzvee Zahavy's English translation follows the Vienna manuscript in reversing the order of benedictions two and three; see Jacob Neusner and Richard S. Sarason, eds., *The Tosefta: Translated from the Hebrew* (New York: Ktav, 1986), 1:40 (under *t. Ber.* 6:18). The Jerusalem Talmud also reverses the order of these benedictions in *y. Ber.* 9:2 (13b); see text and translation in Heinrich W. Guggenheimer, *The Jerusalem Talmud: first order Zeraïm; tractate Berakhot*, SJ 18 (Berlin: Walter de Gruyter, 2000), pp. 622-23; further English translation available by Tzvee Zahavy in Jacob Neusner, ed., *The Talmud of the Land of Israel: A Preliminary Translation and Explanation* (Chicago: University of Chicago Press, 1982-1994), 1:318 (under *y. Ber.* 9:1).

[166]The same explanation is found both in *t. Ber.* 7:18 and *y. Ber.* 9:2 (13b). The commandments which women are not required to keep are likely the kind mentioned in *m. Qidd.* 1:7-8; but Guggenheimer argues that in the context of the Yerushalmi this would refer to women not needing to say other required benedictions (see Guggenheimer, *Jerusalem Talmud: Berakhot*, p. 623).

benedictions likely originated in the middle of the second century A.D.,[167] and the degree to which R. Judah's daily saying of these benedictions was actually representative of rabbinic practice in an earlier era is debatable.[168] In any case, the statement does illustrate a rabbinic tendency to recognize a more limited legal status for women, and to consequently associate females (both married and unmarried) with groups less privileged than Jewish males.[169]

Among Second Temple authors, Ben Sira and Philo are frequently singled out for their strong statements about women in general and, more specifically, about male authority in marriage.[170] In the Philonic passage mentioned earlier on the authority of a husband over a wife's vows, the

---

[167]The same statement is attributed instead to Rabbi Meir in some (but not all) manuscripts of *b. Menah.* 43b. Since the testimony of both the Tosefta and the Yerushalmi predate the Bavli (and since some manuscripts of the Bavli support the R. Judah reading), the attribution to R. Judah is more probable (although it is conceivable that both rabbis made similar statements). In any case, R. Meir also taught during the middle of the second century.

[168]R. Judah's statement does not appear in the Mishnah, which is an earlier codification of rabbinic law. Nor is there any indication that these benedictions were said daily as part of the required daily prayers known as the *Shema* and the *Shemoneh Esreh* (on which see Schürer, *HJPAJC,* 2:454-63). The existence of similar benedictions in later Jewish prayer books even through modern times need not imply the antiquity of the tradition before R. Judah (contra Leonard Swidler, *Women in Judaism: The Status of Women in Formative Judaism* [Metuchen, N.J.: Scarecrow, 1976], p. 81). The fact that these benedictions appear in three rabbinic works (the Tosefta, Yerushalmi and Bavli) also need not imply widespread acceptance at an early date, since rabbinic traditions in the Tosefta often make their way directly into the later compendiums of the Talmuds. The Talmuds do not necessarily testify to independent traditions, and the continuance of the Tosefta saying in later rabbinic writing does not strongly imply a widespread (and widely practiced) earlier tradition. For opposing views on this (with little argumentation) see Johannes Leipoldt, *Die Frau in der antiken Welt und im Urchristentum,* 2nd ed. (Leipzig: Koehler & Amelang, 1955), p. 86; Swidler, *Women in Judaism,* p. 81 (who calls them "three separate direct quotations"); and Paul K. Jewett, *Man as Male and Female: A Study in Sexual Relationships from a Theological Point of View* (Grand Rapids, Mich.: Eerdmans, 1975), pp. 92-93 (dependent on Leipoldt's opinion). On the other hand, the influence of R. Judah in late second and early third century Judaism is significant; and R. Judah could be voicing a sentiment that existed before him. Subsequent use of these benedictions is implied for the later Amoraic period (several generations after R. Judah) in the reported comments by R. Aha b. Jacob in *b. Menah.* 43b-44a.

[169]However, direct application to the background of Gal 3:28 is unlikely given the lack of mention of slavery in any early extant versions of the R. Judah benedictions, and also recognizing that R. Judah himself would have uttered this pronouncement in the mid-second century. For attempts to apply this to Gal 3:28 see, e.g., Madeleine Boucher, "Some Unexplored Parallels to 1 Cor 11,11-12 and Gal 3,28: The NT on the Role of Women," *CBQ* 31 (1969): 53; and Swidler, *Women in Judaism,* p. 81.

[170]See the treatments, both concluding women are held by these authors to be inferior, in Warren C. Trenchard, *Ben Sira's View of Women: A Literary Analysis,* BJS 38 (Chico, Calif.: Scholars Press, 1982); Dorothy Sly, *Philo's Perception of Women,* BJS 209 (Atlanta: Scholars Press, 1990).

husband is called her "lord."[171] Meanwhile, Ben Sira pens harsh warnings about the "evil wife," including his famous statement that from a woman was the beginning of sin and the cause of death. The husband is thus told that if his wife does not follow his guiding hand, he should divorce her.[172]

Despite the insistence in these authors that the leadership of the household belongs to men, there is evidence that such roles of authority were not always followed. Negative evidence comes from the practical acknowledgment of the converse as Ben Sira speaks of the woman who can rule over a man.[173] Pseudo-Phocylides knows the man who is a slave to his wealthy wife.[174] Accounts of powerful women could be multiplied in rabbinical literature and in other authors, especially in Josephus's account of women in Jewish royal families. If there was a strongly patriarchal orientation to marriage in the literature of this period, that is not to say that every household imitated this order.

Moreover, while it is tempting to read this literature purely with a view to the dynamics of authority in marriage, we do well to keep in mind the marks of real affection and tenderness in marriage that are often mentioned. Even Ben Sira, who makes strong (almost misogynistic) statements, can speak of the gladness that comes from a woman's beauty, of the privilege of a man with a kind and humble spouse, of the help and support a wife can provide, and of the longing of an unmarried man for marriage.[175] Pseudo-Phocylides admonishes men to love their own wives, not to be overcome by destructive eros but to be mutually and kindly disposed toward one another through old age without strife.[176]

Beyond the explicit teaching of Second Temple figures, one also sees evidence of deep mutual affection between husbands and wives in some ex-

---

[171]Philo *Spec. Laws* 2.24.

[172]Sir 25:13-26, esp. vv. 24, 26.

[173]E.g., Sir 33:19; 47:19.

[174]Ps.-Phoc. 199-200; cf. Sir 25:21-22.

[175]Sir 36:22-25. In some enumerations this is Sir 36:27-30. Cf. Sir 7:19; 25:1; 26:1-4, 13-18; 40:23. It has well been observed that Sirach in 36:22-25 maintains his husband-centered focus (see Swidler, *Women in Judaism,* pp. 39-40; Trenchard, *Ben Sira's View,* pp. 19-26), but his earnest appreciation of a good wife still appears heartfelt.

[176]Ps.-Phoc. 193-197. This may have special reference to sexual restraint, concerning which Pseudo-Phocylides also commands men not to outrage their wives with "shameful ways of intercourse" (Ps.-Phoc. 189). Though the exact meaning of this phrase is difficult, it is clear that the man has sexual responsibilities to his wife that ought to lead to a long-lasting and unified life together. See Van der Horst, *Sentences of Pseudo-Phocylides,* p. 237.

tant Jewish funerary inscriptions. This evidence lies not only in the epithets and memorials employed in speaking of a deceased spouse[177] but also in the length of some of the marriages.[178] For example: "Publius (?) Alfius Juda the *archon* (and) *archisynagogos,* who lived 70 years 7 months 10 days. Alfia Soteris, with whom he lived 48 years, made (the monument) for her incomparable, well-deserving husband."[179]

Celibacy. Sufficient evidence exists to suggest that at least some Jewish people practiced celibacy. In *On the Contemplative Life* Philo describes in detail the lives of a Jewish ascetic sect he calls the Therapeutae, which is found in many places but especially near Alexandria, Egypt.[180] The Therapeutae include both men and women, and they have in their midst older female virgins, who have maintained their virginity out of a love of wisdom.[181] It should be noted that Philo himself retells this evidence of celibacy in the Therapeutae in the most glowing of terms.

Nevertheless, of Jewish ascetic sects, the Essenes are more famous.[182] Philo and Pliny indicate that the Essenes were strictly celibate. Pliny says they are "without women" and renounce love.[183] Philo remarks that the Essenes live in many areas of Judea, and consist of men and no children.[184] In addition to describing the harmonious asceticism of the Essenes, Philo says they repudiate marriage because women are selfish and jealous creatures who, among other things, trick men by their charms into marital slavery.[185] It has been noted that this clearly misogynistic argument for a celibate lifestyle is lacking in Philo's description of the Ther-

---

[177]So (perhaps slightly overstated) in Harry J. Leon, *The Jews of Ancient Rome* (Philadelphia: Jewish Publication Society of America, 1960), pp. 129-34, 232.

[178]E.g., note the age and sentiments expressed in David Noy, *Jewish Inscriptions of Western Europe* (Cambridge: Cambridge University Press, 1993-1995), vol. 2, no. 103 (twenty-one years; = *CIJ* 476), no. 584 (thirty-four years; = *CIJ* 537); vol. 1, no. 11 (twenty-five years; = *CIJ* 636), no. 20 (forty-eight years; = *CIJ* 553). All these are from the second to fourth centuries A.D.

[179]Ibid., vol. 1, no. 20 (=*CIJ* 553).

[180]Philo *Contempl. Life* 21-22.

[181]Ibid., 68.

[182]Some identify the Essenes and the Therapeutae as a single group, but there are significant nuanced differences between the two. See Emil Schürer, *The History of the Jewish People in the Age of Jesus Christ (175 B.C.-A.D. 135),* ed. Geza Vermes et al., rev. English ed. (Edinburgh: T. & T. Clark, 1973-1987), 2:591-97; Geza Vermes and Martin D. Goodman, *The Essenes According to the Classical Sources,* Oxford Centre Textbooks 1 (Sheffield: Sheffield Academic Press, 1989), pp. 15-17. The Vermes-Goodman volume also provides text and translation of the Pliny, Philo and Josephus texts cited in this paragraph.

[183]*Nat.* 5.17.4.

[184]Philo *Hypothetica* 11.1-3 in Eusebius *Praep. ev.* 8.11.1-3.

[185]Philo *Hypothetica* 11.14-17.

apeutae mentioned above,[186] which may imply that such a misogynic assertion was not the only motive for celibacy among various Jewish sectarians.

Josephus, in his more extensive and nuanced treatment of the Essenes, also reports a low view of women as an Essene motive for avoiding marriage, for they believed that females were lascivious and unfaithful and that wives caused domestic quarrels.[187] However, Josephus designates two "orders" of Essenes who differ primarily over whether to remain celibate or to marry.[188] According to Josephus the former group recruits other people's children in order to maintain their sect; yet even these celibate Essenes do not completely deny that others should marry, recognizing that procreation is necessary.[189] Among the latter group of marrying Essenes, there is a strong focus on procreation as the reason for marriage, to the extent that women are apparently tested for their likely childbearing abilities prior to marriage.[190]

The Dead Sea Scrolls from Qumran are commonly identified with the Essene sect, even though there are multiple passages in the Qumran scrolls that indicate that at least some members of the sect were in fact married.[191] And the Damascus Document from the Cairo Genizah, manuscripts of which have been found at Qumran, also assumes married couples and children in its sect.[192] The question is: Are there any Qumran passages that imply that some members of the group practiced a celibate lifestyle? Recent authors have noted that, although the Damascus Document clearly permits married adherents of the sect into certain "camps," it also assumes unmarried mem-

---

[186]Joseph M. Baumgarten, "Celibacy," in *Encyclopedia of the Dead Sea Scrolls,* ed. Lawrence H. Schiffman and James C. Vanderkam (Oxford: Oxford University Press, 2000), 1:123.

[187]Josephus *J.W.* 2.121; *Ant.* 18.21.

[188]Josephus *J.W.* 2.120, 160-161.

[189]Josephus *J.W.* 2.120-121.

[190]Josephus *J.W.* 2.161.

[191]Some key examples: men of the community may not have intercourse with a woman (i.e., be married) until twenty (1QSa = 1Q28a I, 9-11); women and children are included in community gatherings (1QSa = 1Q28a I, 4); men must cleanse themselves from sexual relations before entering the city of the temple (11Temple XLV, 11-12). Whether 4Q502 is considered a marriage ritual or an affirmation of elderly members, reconstructions of the text agree on the presence of female members in the celebratory community. See the edition of 4Q502 in Maurice Baillet, *Qumran Cave 4 III (4Q482-4Q520),* DJD 7 (Oxford: Clarendon, 1982), pp. 81-105 (arguing it is a marriage ritual on p. 81). Similar acknowledgment of the presence of female members, though discounting the claim that 4Q502 is a marriage ritual, in Joseph M. Baumgarten, "4Q502, Marriage or Golden Age Ritual?" *JJS* 34 (1983): 125-35. See further Eileen Schuller, "Women in the Dead Sea Scrolls," in *The Dead Sea Scrolls After Fifty Years: A Comprehensive Assessment,* ed. Peter W. Flint and James C. Vanderkam (Leiden: Brill, 1999), 2:123-39.

[192]E.g CD VII, 6-9 (= CD-B XIX, 2-5); CD XV, 5-6; CD XII, 1-2 (= 4Q271 5 I, 17-18). The Qumran copies have additional passages of interest, e.g., 4Q270 7 I, 12-14.

bers.[193] The *Rule of the Community* (1QS) does not mention women members of the sect, and the communal lifestyle would appear to preclude separate families within the community; but this rule does not explicitly advocate celibacy.[194] Further, another text that appears alongside this *Rule* in the most extensive manuscript is among those texts apparently allowing marriage.[195]

How then can one account for the lack of clear celibacy requirements in the Qumran scrolls? Basically there have been three answers: (1) deny that Pliny, Philo and Josephus provide accurate accounts of the Essenes; (2) deny that the Qumran scrolls represent an Essene sect; or (3) follow Josephus and assert that there were two groups of Essenes (one celibate and one married), even if Josephus, Pliny and Philo overemphasized the importance of the celibate group.

Negotiating among these three options demands more focus on the Qumran documents than can rightly be spent in this brief space, but some quick comments should be made. Concerning the first option, certainly Pliny and Philo were geographically distant from the Essene community, and thus their accounts must be followed with some caution. Philo, however, does present a significant level of detail, which may indicate access to oral or written sources. Moreover, Josephus purports to have considered becoming an Essene[196] and writes with even greater detail than does Philo. It would be unwise to quickly discount such testimony. Concerning the second option, outside the single issue of celibacy there are multiple points of contact with the sectarian documents of Qumran and the Philo, Pliny and Josephus descriptions of the Essene movement; therefore, despite some serious recent challenges, the difficult identification of Essenism with Qumran still remains a viable option.[197]

---

[193]Notice the conditional ("if") in CD VII, 6-7: "And if they reside in camps in accordance with the rule of the land, and take women and beget children"; translation in Florentino García Martínez and Eibert J. C. Tigchelaar, eds., *The Dead Sea Scrolls Study Edition* (Leiden: Brill, 1997-1998), 1:561. See Joseph M. Baumgarten, "The Qumran-Essene Restraints on Marriage," in *Archaeology and History in the Dead Sea Scrolls*, ed. Lawrence H. Schiffman, JSPSup 8 (Sheffield: Sheffield Academic Press, 1990), pp. 18-19; Elisha Qimron, "Celibacy in the Dead Sea Scrolls and the Two Kinds of Sectarians," in *The Madrid Qumran Congress: Proceedings of the International Congress on the Dead Sea Scrolls Madrid, 18-21 March 1991*, ed. Julio Trebolle Barrera and Luis Vegas Montaner, STDJ 11.1 (Leiden: Brill, 1992), 1:289-91.

[194]Such a reading requires that "fruitful offspring" in 1QS IV, 7 be considered figurative language.

[195]1QSa = 1Q28a I, 9-11.

[196]Josephus *Life* 1.10-11.

[197]Even if one were to resolve that the Qumran documents are not from the Essene sect, the conclusion reached below (that Essenes had both celibate and married components) could still be affirmed on the basis of Josephus alone (whose veracity is generally assumed by those

The third view, then, is perhaps best, indicating that the Essene sect had both celibate and married orders, each represented in different Qumran documents.[198] Supporters of this third view also point to the overwhelming number of male skeletons in the Qumran cemetery when compared with the few female and child burials in extensions to the cemetery.[199] In this view, the Rule of the Community in its core describes the celibate community, but other texts of this rule have been adapted for married sectarians.[200] Difficulties linger because the preponderance of texts found at Qumran do assume marriage, and the existing documents do not contain clearly articulated reasons for celibacy along the lines of those misogynist arguments that Philo and Josephus say the celibate Essenes promoted. Nevertheless, there is some cause to affirm the practice of celibate communal monasticism within the Qumran documents themselves. And certainly other authors recognized a celibate Jewish sect in Judea during the close of the Second Temple period.

In summary, sufficient evidence exists to affirm that some sectarians in Second Temple Judaism practiced celibacy as part of their ascetic lifestyle. For some sects the reasons for celibacy could reportedly extend into misogynist devaluation of women, but certainly not for all. Further, a celibate lifestyle could also be appreciated even by those Jewish people who themselves were married. Thus, for example, the accounts in Philo and Josephus (who were themselves married) are largely sympathetic to Essene celibacy; and presumably also the married Essenes affirmed and valued their celibate brothers. Even some nonsectarian literature is at pains to affirm the validity of celibate choices in certain circumstances. For example, the Wisdom of Solomon acknowledges the righteousness of a barren woman whose barrenness results from her refusal to engage in unlawful marital unions (Wis 3:13).

Nonetheless, while there are some (primarily sectarian) traditions favoring celibacy, there are also strong tendencies to the contrary in this period. As

---

who argue that the Essenes did not author Qumran literature). The point is that some Jewish sectarians in this period advocated celibacy, and this argument does not rest solely on Qumran being an Essene site.

[198]Recently supported using an innovative rationale in Qimron, "Celibacy," pp. 287-94. Cf. Todd S. Beall, *Josephus' Description of the Essenes Illustrated by the Dead Sea Scrolls,* SNTSMS 58 (Cambridge: Cambridge University Press, 1988), pp. 38-39, 111-12.

[199]Though it is reasonable to take this into account, nevertheless, caution must be exercised with this evidence since there has been insufficient archaeological work on the cemeteries to reach decisive conclusions. See Schuller, "Women in the Dead Sea Scrolls," pp. 139-41.

[200]E.g., see Joseph A. Fitzmyer, "Marriage and Divorce," in *Encyclopedia of the Dead Sea Scrolls,* ed. Lawrence H. Schiffman and James C. Vanderkam (Oxford: Oxford University Press, 2000), 1:511-12.

noted above, Josephus indicates that even one order of the Essenes differs from the rest of the Essenes principally on the issue of marriage, arguing that it is necessary to marry in order to continue the human race.[201] Indeed, during the Second Temple period the default assumption outside some sectarian groups is that marriage and family are duties for most Jewish people.[202]

Widows. The apocryphal book of Judith provides a sensitive account of widowhood. After her husband's death, Judith's grief is evident in that she lived for over three years in a widow's tent on the roof of her house, fasting on non-festival days and wearing the clothes of widowhood (Jdt 8:4-8). Yet she was amply provided for by her husband's legacy in gold, silver, slaves, cattle and fields—an estate that she maintained. Her righteousness is well known, and she is widely respected in Judea for her wisdom (Jdt 8:8-31). While some of these details are likely played up for narrative effect, in order for the reader to engage the story, there must have been some correspondence to reality in the description of widowhood.

Upon the death of her husband a woman entered into the legal status of widow. The requirements of the Torah concerning widows were continued in later Jewish law. Widows were responsible to keep their own vows, for they had no husband who could invalidate such vows.[203] Widows could not marry a high priest.[204] Yet widows were among the special class of individuals whom the community was obligated to support and whom the Lord helped.[205]

In a patriarchal society the loss of a husband was keenly felt, beyond the emotional toll. Certainly a widow could be a woman of independent means, but often she was dependent on others. Most marriage contracts noted earlier have some section that concerns the widow's rights. The Elephantine contracts (fifth-century B.C. Egypt) grant the wife full control over her husband's estate only if they have no children. The Aramaic texts from the Dead Sea appear to follow rabbinic tradition in that the husband's family is obligated to care for his widow or to give her *ketubah* to her.[206] Judith's recep-

---

[201]Josephus *J.W.* 2.160.

[202]E.g., Pseudo-Phocylides mandates both marriage and procreation, arguing that one must continue one's name and return to nature the gift of one's own life (Ps.-Phoc. 175-76). See further evidence below under "Sexuality in Marriage."

[203]Num 30:9; cf. 11QTemple LIV, 4-5; Philo *Spec. Laws* 2.25.

[204]Lev 21:14; cf. Ezek 44:22; Philo *Spec. Laws* 1.105-107; *m. Yebam.* 6:4.

[205]Deut 10:18; 14:29; 24:17-22; 26:12-13; cf. Is 1:17; Jer 22:3; see Philo, *Spec. Laws* 4.176-178. Widows are also singled out as needing to avoid sexual intercourse in 4Q269 9.5-6; 4Q270 5.19; 4Q271 3.12.

[206]Cf. *m. Ketub.* 4:12; 11:1-4; 12:3-4.

tion of her husband's estate provides further expression of this legal possibility in Judea (Jdt 8:7).

One way of caring for widows in Jewish society could be to follow the practice of levirate marriage prescribed in Deuteronomy 25:5-10. In that passage a widow who has no sons to take care of her (notice the assumption that males must provide for females) is required to be married to the brother of her deceased husband. The practice of levirate marriage was certainly remembered in at least one sector in the Second Temple era, for it is paraphrased in Josephus and legislated in rabbinic literature.[207] The Josephus paraphrase omits the scriptural detail that the brothers should be living together, and it explains the reason for the procedure by noting that this prolongs hereditary lines and takes care of the widow.

Deuteronomy requires that, should the brother refuse the marriage to his widowed sister-in-law, she should bring him to the elders, and there, should he persist in his refusal, she is to pull his sandal off, spit in his face and speak words of disdain (Deut 25:7-10). The rabbis called this *halitzah*. Josephus, in referring to *halitzah*, adds that this procedure is performed whether the brother-in-law's reasons for refusal are "slight or serious."[208] Josephus supplements the biblical account by stating that the widow is to say that her brother-in-law has outraged the memory of his deceased brother by not marrying her, and he asserts that the woman is then free to marry again.

That the biblical text itself (Deut 25:7-10) does not mention exceptions to the law of *halitzah* likely led Josephus to say that *halitzah* must be performed whether the grounds for refusal are slight or serious. So too rabbinic literature meditates on who must perform *halitzah* because their grounds for not marrying are exceedingly serious[209]—e.g., they are high priests who cannot marry a widow.[210] One wonders if the mandating of *halitzah* in cases where the grounds are serious reduced the impact of it in cases where the brother-in-law had no foundational objection. The lack of corroborating evidence outside of Josephus and the rabbis may indicate that discussions of levirate marriage were limited to some sectors of Judaism in this period (e.g., Phar-

---

[207] Josephus *Ant.* 4.254-56. Much of the Mishnaic tractate *Yebamot* assumes the practice of levirate marriage.

[208] Josephus *Ant.* 4.255.

[209] E.g., *m. Yebam.* 2:3-4.

[210] See *m. Yebam.* 6:4. Some grounds (such as avoidance of incest) are so clear that even the act of *halitzah* need not be performed (*m. Yebam.* 1:1; 2:3; *Sifre Deut.* 288-289).

isees in Palestine).[211] Levirate marriage is assumed for the sake of argument in the Sadducees' questioning of Jesus concerning the resurrection in Matthew 22:23-28 (= Mk 12:18-23; Lk 20:27-33).

Polygamy. While the earliest marriages in the Old Testament are monogamous, there are nonetheless many famous examples of polygamy in Old Testament narrative (e.g., Jacob, David and Solomon). More properly this could be deemed polygyny, since they involve one man marrying two or more women. Old Testament law in one place actually assumes the practice of polygyny, laying out laws of inheritance in such circumstances (Deut 21:15-17).

Josephus reiterates such a law in the first century A.D.[212] Further, he records some actual narratives of polygamy in the Second Temple period, at least in the royal family.[213] Indeed, Josephus excuses these multiple marriages by saying that such unions have from ancient times been permitted.[214] These passages from Josephus also illustrate the strife that was a natural result between competing royal wives (and their sons). Ben Sira recognized the problems of disharmony between spouses that come from multiple wives.[215] Also, second-century Christians could cast aspersions on Judaism for its acceptance of the practice of polygamy.[216]

Early rabbinic writings postulate multiple wives for the sake of legal dis-

---

[211]Satlow notes both the lack of clear teaching on levirate marriage in Philo and Qumran literature and the way that Josephus appears to mimic Greek *epiklerate* teaching over biblical levirate marriage. Based on this he holds out the possibility that the institution of levirate marriage was altogether ignored in the Second Temple period (see Satlow, *Jewish Marriage,* p. 186). However, Satlow underplays the way that Josephus clearly linked his understanding of such marriages to the biblical text. And Satlow himself admits that the same tendency to associate levirate marriage with the Greek *epiklerate* exists in the rabbis (*Jewish Marriage,* p. 187), who also are clearly speaking of the biblical levirate marriage. Finally, at least some of the rabbinic material is attributed to the first century A.D. (e.g., *m. Yebam.* 1:4; 4:3; *t. Yebam.* 1:10), and some examples of early levirate marriage are passed down in rabbinic writings (see Jeremias, *Jerusalem in the Time of Jesus,* p. 372 n.). It seems best then to acknowledge that levirate marriage was at least being discussed in light of similar Greek concepts (and possibly even practiced) in first-century Palestine.

[212]Josephus *Ant.* 4.249-250.

[213]E.g., Herod in Josephus *Ant.* 14.300; *J.W.* 1.477, 562.

[214]Josephus *J.W.* 1.477; cf. *Ant.* 17.14.

[215]Sir 26:6; cf. Sir 37:11 (and possibly Sir 25:14-15). According to Trenchard, *Ben Sira's View,* pp. 232-33, the passage likely refers to polygamy. See a similar opinion with less argumentation in Patrick W. Skehan and Alexander A. Di Lella, *The Wisdom of Ben Sira,* AB 39 (New York: Doubleday, 1987), pp. 347, 349, 432. Snaith suggests that it may instead refer to a wife's rival who is not married to the man; see John G. Snaith, *Ecclesiasticus or the Wisdom of Jesus son of Sirach,* CBC (Cambridge: Cambridge University Press, 1974), p. 133.

[216]Justin *Dialogue with Trypho* 141.

cussion;[217] and they permit the king eighteen wives, apparently basing the calculation on three times King David's allotment.[218] Rabbinic traditions also pass down some examples of polygyny among the priestly families during the Second Temple period.[219] However many rabbinic rulings appear to assume monogamous marriages. It thus appears that rabbinic authorities may have had differing positions on polygamy, especially after the Second Temple period. Indeed Gafni has argued that Palestinian rabbinic authorities were swayed by Greco-Roman culture to disavow polygamy, while Babylonian rabbis were not under the same cultural pressure.[220]

On the other hand, while Philo acknowledged that the law of Deuteronomy 21 permits polygyny, he nevertheless believed the law was given because it was impossible to cure a man of such lusts. Philo was indeed quite disparaging of any husband who would lustfully take another wife and thus show hatred to the first wife and her offspring.[221]

Certain passages from this era do seem to disavow polygamy outright. So, following the biblical legislation in Deuteronomy 17:17, the king must remain monogamous in the view of the sectarian Qumran scrolls, only being permitted remarriage on the event of his wife's death.[222] Indeed, the Damascus Document contends that, to avoid fornication, monogamy is required of all, based on Genesis 1:27 ("male and female he created them"), on the pairing of animals in Noah's ark, and on the example of the king's monogamy.[223]

More disputed is Pseudo-Phocylides ("Add not marriage to marriage, calamity to calamity," Ps.-Phoc. 205). Does this forbid polygamy or remarriage? The case can certainly be made for polygamy being disallowed.[224] And, even

---

[217]E.g., *m. Ketub.* 10:1-6; *m. Ker.* 3:7; *t. Yebam.* 1:10; cf. *Sifre Deut.* 215.

[218]See *m. Sanh.* 2:4; cf. *Tg. Ps.-J.* Deut 17:17. For discussion of King David and the number eighteen, see Herbert Danby, *The Mishnah* (London: Oxford University Press, 1933), p. 384 n.

[219]E.g., *t. Yebam.* 1:10. See further Safrai, "Home and Family," p. 749 n.

[220]Gafni, "Institution of Marriage," pp. 21-25.

[221]Philo *Spec. Laws* 2.135-139. More often Philo focuses on an allegorical exposition of this law (*Alleg. Interp.* 2.48; *Sacrifices* 19-33; *Sobriety* 21-25; *Heir* 47-49). However, there is a surprising vividness to the description of a man with two wives in *Virtues* 115.

[222]11QTemple LVII, 17-18; cf. CD V, 1-6. A claim to widespread application of this Temple Scroll passage beyond the king may need to be tempered if one follows the editor's suggestion that the fragmentary beginning of column LXIV of that scroll quotes Deut 21:14-17; see Yadin, *Temple Scroll,* 2:421. The Damascus Document excuses King David's offense against the biblical injunction for royal monogamy by saying that he had not seen the sealed book of the law (CD V, 2-6).

[223]CD IV, 20-V, 2. Cf. Geza Vermes, "Sectarian Matrimonial Halakhah in the Damascus Rule," *JJS* 25 (1974): 199-201.

[224]Van Der Horst, *Sentences of Pseudo-Phocylides,* 245-47. He also however notes the possibility that Ps.-Phoc. 205 refers to remarriage.

if one were to contend that this forbids remarriage, it would be hard to envision the author of an injunction against remarriage conversely approving of polygamy.

Two extant marriage contracts from fifth-century B.C. Elephantine contain clauses prohibiting the husband from marrying an additional wife and from acknowledging another (preexisting?) marriage.[225] In the less fragmentary text the penalty for such an action is substantial (two hundred shekels in C 15 line 34).[226] These texts bespeak opposition to polygyny among Jews in Egypt, but they also testify to a possibility that had to be curtailed with threats of loss of property.

Finally, there exists possible documentary evidence for Jewish polygamy from two second-century A.D. documents in the Palestinian Babatha archive.[227] After her husband Judah's death, Babatha was engaged in a property dispute with Miriam. In the ensuing exchange Babatha and Miriam both refer to Judah as "my and your late husband." Napthali Lewis has argued that this phrase must indicate that both ladies were married to Judah at the time of his death.[228] Katzoff counters that this instead implies serial monogamy (Judah having divorced Miriam before marrying Babatha).[229] Lewis's explanation is ultimately the simpler of the two, though it must be admitted that the evidence is slight. If granted as an instance of polygyny, then these texts illustrate that polygamy could occur among non-royalty, albeit amid people with some economic means.

In sum, it appears that some Jewish people in this era actually practiced polygamy, while many others opposed the custom. The location of various Jewish communities and the surrounding culture likely influenced acceptance or rejection of polygyny. Where polygamy was practiced, the evidence most clearly indicates that it involved royalty or families of some economic means. Further, literary sources note the disharmony that could potentially result from multiple marriages.

Sexuality. In legal descriptions, sexual intercourse is reserved for marriage between a man and his wife. The purpose of sexuality is widely thought to be procreation, though the pleasure of the sexual act appears to

---

[225] C 15 lines 31-36; K 7 lines 36-37.

[226] Although the text is highly fragmentary at the crucial point of naming the penalty, the editor of K 7 translates the penalty for polygamy in this text as an automatic divorce (see Kraeling, *Brooklyn Museum Aramaic Papyri*, pp. 207, 219).

[227] P.Yadin 26; P.Yadin 34.

[228] Lewis et al., *Documents,* pp. 22-24; Naphtali Lewis, "Judah's Bigamy," *ZPE* 116 (1997): 152.

[229] Ranon Katzoff, "Polygamy in P.Yadin?" *ZPE* 109 (1995):128-32.

be recognized and legitimized by some. However, the widespread need for sexual legislation, as well as the occasional steamy story in Josephus or the rabbis, indicates that not all followed the law. Certain means of birth control were recognized for legitimate unions, but abortion and infanticide were soundly condemned.

Sexuality in marriage. As noted, sexual intercourse was reserved for marriage. Indeed, some sources indicate that sex in marriage was permissible only for the purpose of procreation. Josephus himself affirms this view, and he singles out the order of Essenes, whose marriage practices demonstrate their focus on procreation.[230] The assumption that procreation is the purpose of marriage and intercourse is evident in Philo's statement that those who marry women who have already proven to be barren are impiously looking for fleshly enjoyment like boars and goats; they are thus enemies of God.[231] Similar injunctions against marrying a barren woman are found among the rabbis, though without Philo's intense rhetoric.[232] If a marriage failed to produce children after ten years, then rabbinic teaching calls on the man to divorce his wife in favor of one who might produce a child.[233]

Nonetheless, there is also a strong strand in rabbinic literature that recognizes the legitimate sexual desires of a spouse in marriage without mention of procreation as a result.[234] Thus, according to the Mishnah, in the first century A.D. the houses of Hillel and Shammai debated how long a man may vow to go without providing intercourse to his wife—the period being one to two weeks.[235] Other Tannaitic statements indicate that most couples were expected to copulate at least once a week unless the husband's business took him away on lengthy trips. The husband can fine the wife for failing to meet this obligation, and so too can the wife fine the husband.[236]

Concerning other legal matters, key sources agree that men are not to

---

[230]Josephus *Ag. Ap.* 2.199; *J.W.* 2.161.

[231]Philo *Spec. Laws* 3.36; cf. 3.32-35.

[232]E.g., *t. Yebam.* 8:4.

[233]E.g., *m. Yebam.* 6:6; *t. Yebam.* 8:5-6.

[234]So the argument in *Mekilta Neziqin* 3: "And as to sexual relations? You may propose the following argument *a fortiori:* if things for which, to begin with, you have not entered into marriage, you are not permitted to withhold from her [i.e., food and clothing in Ex 21:10], things for which, to begin with, you enter into marriage [i.e., sexual relations], you surely should not have the right to withhold from her." Translation from Jacob Neusner, *Mekhilta According to Rabbi Ishmael: An Analytical Translation,* BJS 154 (Atlanta: Scholars Press, 1988), 2:126.

[235]See *m. Ketub.* 5:6; cf. Ex 21:10.

[236]See *m. Ketub.* 5:6-7.

have intercourse with a woman in her menstrual period.[237] Further, some authors contend that sexual intercourse is to be avoided with a pregnant wife.[238] However, an unattributed later rabbinic tradition actually states benefits to intercourse for the woman and child in later stages of pregnancy.[239]

A purification washing is required after sexual intercourse in biblical law (Lev 15:18)—the period of uncleanness lasting until the evening. This is repeated in Second Temple literature, even in explicating and defending the law to Gentile readers.[240] Such a biblical law has received a substantial expansion in an interesting requirement from the Qumran sectarian texts that men who have intercourse with their wives not enter the "city of the Temple" for three days.[241] The context implies that the impurity of sexual intercourse must be cleansed before entering the holy city.[242]

Sexuality outside of marriage. Biblical law often legislates against adultery[243] and Old Testament prophetic and Wisdom texts continue this warning. Second Temple literature frequently affirms biblical commands against adultery, especially in relation to the Decalogue.[244] Josephus argues the correctness of the law on this point, since it is in the interest of the state and the family to have legitimate children. Josephus further reiterates the biblical pun-

---

[237]Josephus *Ant.* 3.275; following Lev 20:18; see also CD V, 6-7; Philo *Spec. Laws* 3.32-34. Leviticus forbids intercourse with a woman during her menstrual period (Lev 18:19), and the context is one of sins that merit execution; however, elsewhere in Leviticus the man who does this must be considered unclean for seven days (Lev 15:24), with no hint of further punishment. Apparently, Josephus believes this warrants the death penalty (*Ant.* 3.275), though this is less clear in the biblical text. It is likely that this is one of the prohibited times of sexual intercourse with one's wife that is considered "fornication" in 4Q270 7 I, 12-13 (also fragmentary in 4Q267 9 VI, 4-5).

[238]Josephus *Ag. Ap.* 2.202; Ps.-Phoc. 186. It appears from *Ag. Ap.* 2.202 that Josephus fears this will cause the death of the child, but in another place Josephus indicates that Essenes avoid intercourse during pregnancy because they recognize that conjugal relations are solely for the purposes of procreation (*J.W.* 2.161).

[239]See *b. Nid.* 31a. See further under "Birth Control" below.

[240]E.g., Josephus *Ag. Ap.* 2.198, 203. The rationale Josephus gives for such absolutions is that the sexual act causes part of the soul to go to another place (*Ag. Ap.* 2.203).

[241]11QTemple XLV, 11-12; cf. CD XII, 1-2; 4Q271 5 I, 17-18. This law may have been expanded in accordance with the three days men were to abstain from intercourse with their wives before the theophanic meeting at Mount Sinai (Ex 19:15). So Fitzmyer, "Marriage and Divorce," p. 512.

[242]The extension of Old Testament law is both in applying the purity legislation to not defiling the city and in requiring an extended period of three days exceeding the biblical law of a single day. Purity is mentioned in the context beginning with 11QTemple XLV, 5 and continuing through the next column. Note that a man with a nocturnal emission receives a similar command (11QTemple XLV, 7-10), which is worth comparing to Lev 15:16-17.

[243]E.g., Ex 20:14; Lev 20:10; Deut 5:18; 22:22.

[244]E.g., Ps.-Phoc. 3; Philo *Spec. Laws* 3.8-9; *L.A.B.* 44:6.

ishment of death against a man who commits adultery with a married wife or with a betrothed virgin.[245] Jewish wisdom texts also warn against adultery, for adulterers are said to be likely to lose their unlawful children—indeed, such children will have no honor and face eschatological judgment.[246]

The focus in most antiadultery texts is on men not having intercourse with married or betrothed women. The biblical penalties are less for a man who seduces an unmarried woman, and this influences Second Temple thought.[247] This could lead to speculation that fornication with unmarried women was not highly disdained. However, indications abound that for men any sexual relations outside of marriage were viewed as prohibited.[248] And other sources suggest the importance of the man being a virgin going into marriage.[249] From this teaching it is natural that Jewish literature views with great dismay the sexual violence of rape[250] and the selling of oneself or others into prostitution,[251] even if these crimes were still found in society.[252]

As discussed above with regard to the marriage ceremony, virginity was very important for a woman entering into marriage and was to be evidenced on the wedding night.[253] The rabbis even required a higher *ketubah* (two hundred denarii) payment for a virgin than for a previously married woman (one hundred denarii).[254] Josephus instructs young men to marry virgins, though as an alternative he somewhat grudgingly permits them to wed unmarried free women.[255] As a further illustration of the importance of virginity in marriage, one need only read the first two chapters of the romantic story of *Joseph and Aseneth;* there the righteousness of the two central characters is testified by their virginity prior to marriage.

Hence early Judaism was concerned that daughters remain virgins in their father's house until they marry and depart to their husbands. Manuscripts of the Damascus Document found at Qumran warn concerning a young woman who has "done the act" while in her father's house, or one who has had a "bad reputation during maidenhood"[256]—the latter is to be examined

---

[245]Josephus *Ant.* 3.274; *Ag. Ap.* 2.201; also *Ant.* 4.251-52; also see 11QTemple LXV, 1-8.
[246]Wis 3:16-19; cf. Sir 23:22-27.
[247]Deut 22:28-29; cf. Ex 22:16-17; for the Second Temple era, cf., e.g., 11QTemple LXVI, 8-11.
[248]So Josephus *Ag. Ap.* 2.199; a possible inference as well from the Greek in *Ag. Ap.* 2.201.
[249]E.g., *Jos. Asen.* 4:7; 7:3-4.
[250]E.g., 11QTemple LXVI, 1-11; Josephus *Ant.* 4.252; cf. Deut 22:23-29.
[251]E.g., Ps.-Phoc. 177-78; Josephus *Ant.* 4.206; cf. Lev 19:29.
[252]*Pss. Sol.* 2:11-13.
[253]See, e.g., Deut 22:13-21; 11QTemple LXV, 7-15; Josephus *Ant.* 4.246-248; *m. Ketub.* 1:1.
[254]See *m. Ketub.* 1:1-4.
[255]Josephus *Ant.* 4.244.
[256]4Q269 9.4-7; 4Q270 5.17-20; 4Q271 3.10-15.

by trustworthy women. And one of the most caustic sections in Sirach states the anxiety of a father for his daughter—especially that she maintain her virginity while still in his house.[257]

The importance of maintaining a woman's virginity until the time of marriage has led to the recommendation that she be cloistered.[258] This practice is highlighted in the Jewish romance *Joseph and Aseneth* where Aseneth's virginity is protected by her cloistering in a tower where no man can see her.[259] Second Maccabees implies that virgin women were normally kept indoors.[260] Nonetheless, there were special festival days that were set aside for the "daughters of Zion" to join in public celebration.[261] On a broader level, since modesty was an important concern for women, at least some sectors of Second Temple Judaism expected all free women to remain in the house. Thus Philo asserts that women should take care of the house and remain at home unless they are going to the temple; virgins inhabit the innermost part of the house, and married women stay inside the outer courts.[262] While it is difficult to analyze how widespread cloistering was in this period in Judaism, it is clear such seclusion was taught and practiced by many.[263]

Homosexuality and other illicit behaviors. Homosexuality, which is prohibited in Leviticus 18:22 (and merits the death penalty in Lev 20:13), also is soundly condemned in Jewish literature of this period. While some Greco-Roman authors likewise oppose homosexual activity, Jewish rejection of homosexuality most often was at odds with the prevailing culture.[264]

Jewish opposition to homosexual practice is especially evident in literature from the Diaspora. Jewish sections in the Sibylline Oracles portray homosexuality as a prophetic indictment of Hellenistic culture,[265] which the pious race of Jews will not imitate.[266] Philo, in a passage reminiscent of Romans 1:26-27, portrays the decline of sexual morality in Sodom into homo-

---

[257]Sir 42:10; cf. vv. 9-14.

[258]Ps.-Phoc. 215-217.

[259]Esp. *Jos. Asen.* 2:1-9.

[260]2 Macc 3:19; cf. 3 Macc 1:18.

[261]See *m. Ta'an.* 4:8. See further discussion, especially of rabbinic sources, in Louis M. Epstein, *Sex Laws and Customs in Judaism* (New York: Ktav, 1967), pp. 68-75.

[262]Philo *Spec. Laws* 3.169-171.

[263]On the modesty expected from women in public, and the practice of cloistering, see Jeremias, *Jerusalem in the Time of Jesus,* pp. 359-63. See further Archer, *Her Price Is Beyond Rubies,* pp. 101-22, 239-50; Ilan, *Jewish Women,* pp. 128-34.

[264]*Letter of Aristeas* 152.

[265]*Sib. Or.* 3:185-187; later against Rome in *Sib. Or.* 5:166-167, 387.

[266]*Sib. Or.* 3:594-600, 764; 4:34; 5:430.

sexual behavior, resulting in an effeminate culture.[267] Philo follows the Pentateuch in prescribing the death penalty for homosexuality,[268] which he claims is deserved because homosexuality does not allow for the propagation of the human race and because the sin produces disgrace and effeminacy. Philo also, though he is one to study and incorporate Greek philosophy, nevertheless severely criticizes Plato's famous dialogue *Symposium* for its focus on homosexual love.[269] Josephus likewise disallows sodomy and reiterates the Old Testament death-penalty command.[270] Pseudo-Phocylides at several junctions opposes homosexual practice, including both gay and lesbian relations.[271] Further, Pseudo-Phocylides advises parents to guard their young sons from homosexual relations with a man.[272] It is in this context that the author of Pseudo-Phocylides instructs parents to prevent boys from appearing in feminine hairstyles, presumably to prevent them from attracting older men.[273] A similar opposition to homosexuality was paralleled in the early Christian church.[274]

Homosexuality, incest and bestiality were legislated against alongside one another in the Old Testament (e.g., Lev 18:6-23). This has influenced the connected treatments of these in early Jewish literature.[275] Jewish opposition to incest was discussed above under permissible marriages. Bestiality is forbidden in the Old Testament upon pain of death, and further condemned in later Jewish literature.[276] In an interesting, if scientifically unlikely, explanation of biblical opposition to bestiality, Philo alleges that Moses gave this law partly to prevent the birth of strange half-human animals such as the legendary Minotaur.[277]

Birth control, abortion and infanticide. It is worth noting again the frequent teaching about sexual intercourse as purposed solely for procreation.[278] With this conceptual framework, birth control makes little sense.

---

[267]Philo *Abraham* 135-137. See also *Spec. Laws* 2.50.

[268]Philo *Spec. Laws* 3.38-39; cf. 37-42; *Hypothetica* 7.1 in Eusebius *Praep. ev.* 8.7.1.

[269]Philo *Contempl. Life* 57-63.

[270]Josephus *Ant.* 3.275; *Ag. Ap.* 2.199. One could possibly also note evidence in the long recension of 2 *Enoch* 34:2.

[271]E.g., Ps.-Phoc. 3 (cf. *Sib. Or.* 2:73); Ps.-Phoc. 190-192.

[272]Ps.-Phoc. 213-214.

[273]Ps.-Phoc. 210-212. See Van der Horst, *Sentences of Pseudo-Phocylides,* pp. 249-51.

[274]Rom 1:26-27; 1 Cor 6:9; 1 Tim 1:10; *T. Jac.* 7:19-20.

[275]E.g., Josephus *Ant.* 3.274-275.

[276]Ex 22:19; Lev 18:23; 20:15; Deut 27:21; Philo *Spec. Laws* 3.43-50 (cf. possibly *Hypothetica* 7.7); Ps.-Phoc. 188-189; Josephus, *Ant.* 3.275; *Sib. Or.* 5.393.

[277]Philo *Spec. Laws* 3.44-45.

[278]E.g., Ps.-Phoc. 175-176.

However, there is another strain of teaching noted above that conceives of intercourse outside of the sheer desire to produce children, and this would allow notions of birth control to arise. The sources that directly address this issue are primarily rabbinic and thus later than the destruction of the temple, though it is worth noting that there was probably not much technical innovation in birth control from the early first century to the end of that era. Rabbinic sources speak of at least three methods of birth control: spilling of seed, the *mokh* and a cup of roots.

The principal Old Testament exemplar who "spilled his seed" is Onan (Gen 38:6-10). He is not viewed positively for his action in the Torah, though this is probably because of his unwillingness to obey his father and provide Tamar with a child (similar to the later levirate marriage laws).[279] Nevertheless, Philo condemns him for practicing *coitus interruptus* because, Philo says, he transgressed by falling into an irrational desire for self-centered pleasure and thus broke the social code governing all of society.[280] This is naturally in keeping with Philo's insistence that intercourse be reserved for procreation lest the seeking of pleasure overwhelm one's rational mind. On the other hand, Rabbi Eliezer permits the spilling of seed during intercourse with a pregnant spouse, though other rabbis reject this.[281] Rabbinic law has thus rejected such a method of birth control, though reportedly not without some early dissension.

According to one Tannaitic rabbi, a *mokh* (likely an absorbent material inserted in the woman) could be used to prevent fertilization during marital intercourse with a wife who is a minor (and might die in pregnancy), who is pregnant (on the theory that intercourse may damage the fetus) or who is nursing (since another pregnancy would inhibit lactation).[282] While the rabbinic majority does not agree with him, this tradition reveals one birth-control technique known in early Judaism, and it indicates that some Jewish people recognized certain circumstances in which birth control was necessary. Another well-known technique that some Jewish people may have employed is evidenced in the blanket rabbinic condemnation of men or

---

[279]A similar evaluation can be found in *T. Jud.* 10.1-6 which indicates that the sin of Onan (and also his brother Er) consisted in their desire not to have children by Tamar. Also cf. *Jub.* 41:4-5.

[280]Philo *Posterity* 180-181; *Unchangeable* 16-19; cf. *Hypothetica* 7.7.

[281]In *b. Yebam.* 34b (cf. *t. Nid.* 2:6). See David M. Feldman, *Birth Control in Jewish Law* (Westport, Conn.: Greenwood, 1968), p. 187.

[282]In *b. Yebam.* 12b; 100b; *b. Ketub.* 39a; *b. Nid.* 45a. Cf. *t. Nid.* 2:6. See further Feldman, *Birth Control*, pp. 169-98.

women drinking a "cup of roots" to prevent pregnancy.[283]

While there is only sparse evidence concerning birth control in this literature, abortion and infanticide as means of limiting children in a family are firmly rejected in a wide swath of literary texts, even though these practices were prevalent in Hellenistic and Roman societies. Both abortion and infanticide are repudiated in Pseudo-Phocylides and in a Jewish section from the *Sibylline Oracles*.[284] Philo, in an extensive passionate argument, draws upon both Exodus 21:22 and natural law to argue against infanticide and the exposure of infants.[285] Philo also states that "no one shall cause the offspring of women to be abortive by means of miscarriage, or by any other contrivance."[286] Josephus claims that the Law forbids abortion, noting that the punishment on the mother for abortion is the same as that for infanticide—both cases destroy a human soul and decrease the human race.[287] Such pagan authors as Hecataeus and Tacitus recognized the distinctive Jewish obligation to raise their children (as opposed to abandoning or destroying them), both noting that this had increased the numbers of Jews.[288]

A key passage concerning the status of a child during pregnancy is found in Exodus 21:22. The Hebrew text likely implies that if a woman is struck and gives premature birth, a fine is incurred if she gives birth to a healthy child; otherwise *lex talionis* is mandated (presumably for injury to the baby or to the mother). However, the Septuagint translators interpreted the text to the effect that *lex talionis* only applies to the man who violently causes a woman to give birth to a *fully formed* baby—injury to those fetuses not fully formed merits a fine.[289] Philo's exposition follows the Septuagint.[290] Josephus, however, interprets *lex talionis* to apply only in the event of the death

---

[283]In *t. Yebam.* 8:4. For an instance of actual use (by the wife of the famous R. Hiyya), see *b. Yebam.* 65b-66a. Later Jewish traditions about the "cup of roots" may be found in Feldman, *Birth Control,* pp. 235-36, 239-41.

[284]Ps.-Phoc. 184-185; *Sib. Or.* 3.765-766. Possibly compare *Sib. Or.* 2.281-282 (though of much more disputed Jewish provenance).

[285]*Spec. Laws* 3.110-119; cf. *Virtues* 131-133.

[286]*Hypothetica* 7.7 in Eusebius *Praep ev.* 8.7.7; translation by C. D. Yonge. In Greek this passage, while mentioning two means of causing abortion, clearly forbids such actions.

[287]Josephus *Ag. Ap.* 2.202.

[288]For an account of this, see Stern, *Greek and Latin Authors,* 1:27, 29 (on Hecataeus in Diodorus 40.3.8); 2:19, 26 (on Tacitus *Historiae* 5.5.3); see also Stern's informative note in *Greek and Latin Authors,* 1:33-34.

[289]The formation of the fetus is also discussed in rabbinic tradition (see *b. Nid.* 30b). Elon notes that abortion was prohibited among talmudic sages even if it was not deemed a capital crime; see Menachem Elon, "Abortion," *EncJud,* 2:99.

[290]Philo *Spec. Laws* 3.108-109.

of the mother.[291] Some allude to this implying Jewish acceptance of abortion at an early stage of fetus development.[292] However, in the LXX, Philo and Josephus, there remains a fine for causing the miscarriage, showing some opposition to the act. Moreover, both Philo and Josephus clearly teach against abortion (along with other authors mentioned earlier).[293]

Though not strictly a means of birth control, perhaps it should be mentioned here that there is significant opposition to castration in Jewish sources from this period.[294] Yet here the Wisdom of Solomon provides some hope to faithful law-abiding eunuchs (Wis 3:14-15).

Divorce and remarriage. Deuteronomy 24:1-4 permits a husband to give his wife a writ of divorce if she "finds no favor in his eyes because he finds in her some indecency" (lit. "he finds in her a nakedness of thing"). She is then free to remarry, but the former husband may not marry her ever again after she marries another. A "writ of divorce" was also common enough to be used as a metaphor in Jeremiah 3:8 and Isaiah 50:1.

A famous rabbinic passage details legal discussion about Deuteronomy 24:

> The School of Shammai say: A man may not divorce his wife unless he has found unchastity in her, for it is written, *Because he hath found in her* indecency *in anything.* And the School of Hillel say: [He may divorce her] even if she spoiled a dish for him, for it is written, *Because he hath found in her indecency in* anything. R. Akiba says: Even if he found another fairer than she, for it is written, *And it shall be if she find no favour in his eyes.*[295]

Such a debate between the houses of Hillel and Shammai would have occurred in the first century A.D. Some scholars are skeptical about such attributions, but even a cautious approach has grounds for believing that a significant debate over what constituted a permissible divorce was brewing in some sectors in Judaism at this time.[296] This would help explain why Josephus states that the Mosaic law allows divorce for "whatsoever

---

[291]Josephus *Ant.* 4.278. See the helpful comments in Louis H. Feldman, *Judean Antiquities 1-4,* vol. 3 of *Flavius Josephus: Translation and Commentary,* ed. Steve Mason (Leiden: Brill, 2001), pp. 448-89. The later rabbinic work *Mekhilta* (*Neziqin* 8) considers only harm to the mother in exacting *lex talionis.*

[292]See the insinuation to that effect in Feldman, *Birth Control,* pp. 257-62, esp. 257-59.

[293]Philo *Hypothetica* 7.7; Josephus *Ag. Ap.* 2.202.

[294]Ps.-Phoc. 187; Philo *Hypothetica* 7.7; Josephus *Ant.* 4.290.

[295]In *m. Giṭ.* 9:10. Translation in Danby, *Mishnah,* p. 321. Also see the strange circumstances mentioned in *m. Ketub.* 5:5; 7:1-5.

[296]A fine summary of other rabbinic data can be found in David Instone-Brewer, *Divorce and Remarriage in the Bible: The Social and Literary Context* (Grand Rapids, Mich.: Eerdmans, 2002), pp. 85-117.

cause,"[297] noting further that there are many such causes.[298] Josephus at the end of the first century A.D. appears to follow the Hillel line of the argument. With a similar ease, Ben Sira instructs men to divorce their wives if they will not accept their husband's control.[299] This ease of divorce in some circles helps explain the form of the question from the Pharisees to Jesus in Matthew 19:3: "Is it lawful for a man to divorce his wife for any cause at all?" (NASB).

However, Qumran sectarians apparently placed severe limitations on divorce in the case of a Jewish king, for he is not permitted to take another wife unless his spouse dies.[300] Some argue that, since the Qumran sectarians require common people to keep the same rules as the king, this text implies that the sectarians would rule against any divorce.[301] Nevertheless, earlier in the Temple Scroll it legislates for the female divorcee alongside the widow: both are responsible to keep their vows since they have no husband or father who can annul them.[302]

The actual presence of divorce in society is witnessed in several passages in Josephus, some predicated on adulterous behavior,[303] but most requiring a fairly loose interpretation of Deuteronomy 24:1 to be lawful, if that was a concern.[304] Notably, all these divorces made it possible for the person to marry another (more desirable) spouse.

In the fifth-century B.C. Elephantine papyri, three marriage documents

---

[297]καφ' ἀσδηποτοῦν αἰτίας, translation from Thackeray in *Josephus,* 4:597; a similar phrase occurs in *Ant.* 3.276. On ἀσδηποτοῦν, see LSJ, δήποτε s.v. and p. 1260a.

[298]Josephus *Ant.* 4.253; cf. Philo *Spec. Laws* 3.30.

[299]Sir 25:26; contrast 7:26; 28:15.

[300]11QTemple LVII, 17-19.

[301]Fitzmyer, "Marriage and Divorce," p. 512. Defended more fully in Joseph A. Fitzmyer, "The Matthean Divorce Texts and Some New Palestinian Evidence," in *To Advance the Gospel,* ed. Joseph A. Fitzmyer, 2nd ed. (Grand Rapids, Mich.: Eerdmans, 1998), p. 93 [originally in *TS* 37 (1976): 197-226]; idem, "Divorce Among First-Century Palestinian Jews," *ErIsr* 14 (1978): 105.

[302]11QTemple LIV, 4-5; see Num 30:9. Cf. further Gershon Brin, "Divorce at Qumran," in *Legal Texts and Legal Issues,* ed. Moshe Bernstein, Florentino García Martínez and John Kampen (Leiden: Brill, 1997), pp. 231-44.

[303]As threatened in Josephus *J.W.* 1.508-9.

[304]See Pheroras in *Ant.* 16.198; Archelaus in *J.W.* 2.115 and *Ant.* 17.350; Mariamne in *Ant.* 20.147; and Josephus himself in *Life* 426. This was at least Josephus's second marriage (cf. *Life* 414-415). The vagueness of the charge against Josephus's wife in *Life* 426 ("being unpleased with her behavior"), while it may be an indirect charge of lasciviousness, is more likely to be a broad indictment. On this text, see Steve Mason, *Life of Josephus,* vol. 9 of *Flavius Josephus: Translation and Commentary,* ed. Steve Mason (Leiden: Brill, 2001), p. 170. Pheroras divorces his former slave wife to please Herod; Archelaus the ethnarch divorces Mariamne because of love for Glaphyra; Mariamne divorces Julius Archelaus to marry Demetrius. In a similar category but of less direct import is Vashti's divorce in *Ant.* 11.194-195.

contain divorce provisions that are still extant. Remarkably, each of these assumes that the wife can initiate a divorce.[305] In these documents the penalty for the man divorcing is forfeiture of the *mohar*[306] or the cost of a "divorce payment" where there was no original *mohar*.[307] If the wife divorces him then she pays a set divorce payment of seven and a half shekels.[308] Such a penalty is literally, in Aramaic, the "silver of hatred." Divorce is achieved by the man or the woman saying, "I divorce [literally 'hate'] you." Apparently this was said publicly "in the congregation."[309] If either party initiates a divorce, the wife is allowed to leave with the possessions she brought into the marriage: her dowry, if she supplied one.[310] One important text from Elephantine indicates that at least one Jewish lady (Mibtahiah) was indeed divorced from her Egyptian husband and left with considerable possessions, though it is not clear who initiated the divorce.[311]

Manuscripts from the early second century A.D. display the continuing practice of divorce; and, though these are slightly later than our period, they evidence a marked continuity with the practices noted above. A divorce certificate from Wadi Murabba'at (ca. A.D. 111) records Joseph divorcing Miriam; it specifies that she may remarry any Jewish man and that her dowry will be returned (including damaged goods restored).[312] A few years later (ca. A.D. 134-135) another Aramaic document, though not itself a writ of divorce, references the divorce certificate of Shelamzion and confirms that the former husband owes her nothing.[313] It is possible that a Jewish marriage contract in Greek from A.D. 130, in which there are diagonal pen strokes across the original document, was cancelled because of divorce.[314] Finally, a Greek

---

[305]C 15 lines 22-26; K 7 lines 24-28.

[306]C 15 line 27; also apparently K 7 line 22.

[307]K 2 lines 7-8.

[308]C 15 lines 23-24; K 2 line 10; K 7 line 26.

[309]C 15 lines 22, 26.

[310]K 2 lines 8-10; K 7 lines 22-24, 26-28. Above it is noted that if one holds C 15 to provide an example of a dowry addition (as per Cowley, contra Yardeni and Porten), then the wife leaves with none of the items listed in C 15 (lines 6-14; cf. lines 27-28) because these were originally given her by the groom.

[311]C 14.

[312]Mur 19 (text and French translation in Benoit et al., *Les Grottes de Murabba'at,* pp. 104-9; English translation in Archer, *Her Price Is Beyond Rubies,* pp. 297-99).

[313]XHev/Se 13 line 7. The purpose of this document itself has been debated, as has whether it portrays the wife writing a divorce document to her husband. See the text and editors' comments in Cotton and Yardeni, *Aramaic, Hebrew and Greek Documentary Texts,* pp. 65-70.

[314]XHev/Se 69 (formerly XHev/Se Gr. 2). Death of one of the members is also a possibility, though the present editors appear to prefer cancellation due to divorce; see Cotton and Yardeni, *Aramaic, Hebrew and Greek Documentary Texts,* p. 250.

marriage document from A.D. 124 reports the remarriage of Eleaios and Salome, indicating a reconciliation between a formerly divorced couple.[315]

One important debatable issue concerns whether a woman could divorce her Jewish husband. This issue is often framed by asking whether Mark 10:12 (which acknowledges wife-initiated divorces) accurately portrays first-century Palestine. As was noted above, Elephantine marriage contracts contain reciprocal divorce provisions, implying that the wife was free to put away her husband.[316] With regard to the later social context of Mediterranean Judaism, it is clear that over time Roman law increasingly permitted divorce initiated by the wife (or at least by her father), and this practice was well established by the first century A.D.[317] Josephus reports some royal divorces initiated by the wife.[318] However, Josephus himself says that such a writ of divorce from a wife was "not according to Jewish laws."[319] Nevertheless, Josephus implies that a wife can leave her husband, but she may not remarry unless the former husband "puts her away"; she must ask him to write her the writ of divorce and thus divorce her.[320] Therefore, in Josephus's estimation the wife has the right to ask for a divorce, but she does not possess the power to enact it of her own accord. Nevertheless, it is possible that the divorce reported in the Judean second-century text XHev/Se 13 was initiated by the wife, although this is disputed.[321] Even if one ignores this disputed text, there remains cause

---

[315]Mur 115 (text/translation in Benoit et al., *Les Grottes de Murabba'at,* pp. 243-54; English translation in Archer, *Her Price Is Beyond Rubies,* pp. 295-96).

[316]The importance of the Elephantine papyri for this question is highlighted in Ernst Bammel, "Markus 10 11f. und das jüdische Eherecht," *ZNW* 61 (1970): 95-101.

[317]See Treggiari, *Roman Marriage,* pp. 441-46. It is possible that the ability for the wife to divorce lies behind Philo *Spec. Laws* 3.30, but this passage is not definitive here.

[318]So Salome in *Ant.* 15.259-260; Herodias in *Ant.* 18.136; Mariamne in *Ant.* 20.147; and possibly Drusilla in *Ant.* 20.141-143.

[319]Josephus *Ant.* 15.259.

[320]Ibid.

[321]Tal Ilan contends that the document is a divorce certificate initiated by the wife; see Tal Ilan, "Notes and Observations on a Newly Published Divorce Bill from the Judaean Desert," *HTR* 89 (1996): 195-202. Schremer responds that there was a divorce initiated by the husband, but that this document is not the divorce certificate; see Adiel Schremer, "Divorce in Papyrus Se'elim 13 Once Again: A Reply to Tal Ilan," *HTR* 91 (1998): 193-202. An ideological rejoinder is made in Tal Ilan, "The Provocative Approach Once Again: A Response to Adiel Schremer," *HTR* 91 (1998): 203-4. Fitzmyer repudiates the claim that this is a divorce document, though he allows that it mentions a divorce initiated by the husband; see Joseph A. Fitzmyer, "The So-Called Aramaic Divorce Text from Wadi Seiyal," *ErIsr* 26 (1999): 16-22 (English pagination). Cotton and Qimron agree that it is not a divorce certificate, but they still believe that it indicates the wife had earlier initiated a divorce; see Hannah M. Cotton and Elisha Qimron, "XHev/Se ar 13 of 134 or 135 c.e.: A Wife's Renunciation of Claims," *JJS* 49 (1998): 108-18. Instone Brewer suggests that it is a divorce certificate from the wife to the husband, but that at some points

for asserting that some Jewish people in antiquity believed a wife could divorce her husband, though others (such as Josephus) concluded that a wife's request for divorce had to be ratified by her husband.[322]

Remarriage is apparently permitted in Deuteronomy 24:1-4, and Second Temple literature clearly expects the wife to be able to remarry upon divorce.[323] The key element in a divorce certificate from a husband to a wife according to the rabbis was the phrase "you are free to marry any man."[324] Such a phrase could receive some stipulations as in the case of the Judean divorce certificate Mur 19, "you are free on your part to go and become the wife of any *Jewish* man that you wish,"[325] but freedom to remarry is still assumed. Only two Second Temple texts might possibly disallow remarriage, but it is more likely that they argue against polygamy.[326]

While remarriage is widely permitted, there remains the question under which circumstances one could remarry a former spouse. Deuteronomy 24 forbids remarriage when there has been an intervening marriage to another person after the original divorce. Working from this clear rule, remarriage to one's own spouse after an extended separation was permitted by rabbinical authorities in certain circumstances.[327] As mentioned earlier, contract Mur 115 witnesses just such a remarriage. But it appears that King Herod violated biblical law when he remarried (or at least readmitted to his bed) Doris after executing his intervening wife.[328]

FAMILY

Jewish families in antiquity often lived in close proximity to their parents, making for extended family networks. Patriarchal leadership was assumed, and authority over family affairs was vested in the father or eldest son. Otherwise, a widow could have significant control over her own affairs and those of her younger children. Children were expected to honor and obey their parents (both father and mother), and the parents were to care

---

the scribe chose to write in third person; see David Instone Brewer, "Jewish Women Divorcing Their Husbands in Early Judaism: The Background to Papyrus Ṣe'elim 13," *HTR* 92 (1999): 349-57.

[322]See further Friedman, *Jewish Marriage*, pp. 312-46.

[323]E.g., Josephus *Ant.* 4.253.

[324]See *m. Giṭ.* 9:1-3.

[325]Cf. m. *Giṭ.* 9:2. Translation from Archer, *Her Price Is Beyond Rubies*, p. 298.

[326]So CD IV, 20—V, 2; Ps.-Phoc. 205. On these see "Polygamy" above, and note especially Vermes, "Sectarian Matrimonial Halakhah," pp. 197-202.

[327]See m. *Giṭ.* 4:7-8; *m. Yebam.* 13:6; t. *Yebam.* 6:4; 13:5.

[328]Josephus *J.W.* 1.451; *Ant.* 16.85. For these texts I am indebted to Ilan, "Premarital Cohabitation," p. 250 n. Cf. also *J.W.* 1.590.

for, discipline and educate the children. Slaves could be part of a family household, and Wisdom literature places restraints on the treatment of slaves. Property was generally under the control of the family patriarch, though women and children could be granted property. Marriage documents evidence a careful system of providing during widowhood for surviving spouses and children.

Household and family leadership. While housing construction varied throughout various regions of the Mediterranean, there is evidence that extended Jewish families often lived close to one another. For example, in fifth-century Elephantine, Mibtahiah's father gives her housing property from his own land.[329] Elsewhere, Palestinian courtyard, multistory architecture allowed additions built for family members.[330] In such household conditions a person must relate frequently to his or her extended family. This elevated the need to show love to kinsmen and reverence to elder members of the family.[331]

Second Temple literature indicates that the leadership of the family was generally vested in a male figure—often the father or eldest son. Earlier we noted that the male leader was in charge of marrying daughters and providing dowries; further, he controlled all family property (unless it was legally deeded to the wife). Also above (under "Roles and Relationships"), it was noted that there is substantial evidence for the ideal of male leadership in marriage. However, in this same section, we remarked that many Second Temple authors do speak of marriages where this ideal was not the *de facto* situation. Furthermore, widows at various points in Jewish history could exercise some control over even large inheritances (e.g., Judith).

Children. Given the significance placed on procreation (see "Sexuality in Marriage" above) and the sheer joy of begetting a child, children were a welcome blessing from the Lord.[332] While numerical requirements for procreation are not often found in Second Temple literature, there is the report of a rabbinic debate between the first-century A.D. houses of Hillel and Shammai over the number of children required in order to fulfill the biblical requirement to "be fruitful and multiply." Both schools expected at least two children—the house of Shammai required two boys; the house of Hillel, a

---

[329]See Porten, *Archives from Elephantine*, pp. 240-45.

[330]Safrai, "Home and Family," pp. 730-35. A variety of structures is mentioned in Santiago Guijarro, "The Family in First-Century Galilee," in *Constructing Early Christian Families: Family as Social Reality and Metaphor*, ed. Halvor Moxnes (London: Routledge, 1997), pp. 49-61.

[331]E.g., Ps.-Phoc. 219-222.

[332]Celebrations after a child's birth are limited by Josephus (*Ag. Ap.* 2.204), but this is principally because of his opposition to drunkenness.

boy and a girl.[333] The very same Mishnah that discusses the number of children required for married couples also mentions divorce of a barren wife after ten years.[334] Thus a childless woman could be in a grave predicament, as Ben Sira fears (Sir 42:10). Nevertheless, some authors seek to provide comfort to the righteous barren woman (Wis 3:13-14).

Childbirth could be dangerous for the wife—evidence of this may be observed in inscriptions that mention the death of women while giving birth.[335] On the other hand, children also suffered from a very high rate of mortality before they were of marriageable age.[336]

Beyond merely food and clothing, parents provided for their children the monies needed for marriage. And parents also were responsible for the discipline and education of their children. The Decalogue requires children to honor their fathers and mothers (Ex 20:12; Deut 5:16), and this is repeated in later Jewish literature.[337] Ben Sira writes that it is God's will for the father to be honored and for the mother's rights to be recognized by their children (Sir 3:2). Respect for a father even atones for sins and permits one's prayers to be heard (Sir 3:3-5, 14-16)! Pseudo-Phocylides says, "Honour God first and foremost, and thereafter your parents."[338] Josephus pens a similar sentiment, which he attributes to the Law.[339] A wisdom text from Qumran instructs children to honor father and mother, "for like God is to a man so is his father, and as masters are to a male so is his mother."[340] This comparison of the father to God is quite striking, and no less so the respect accorded

---

[333]See *m. Yebam.* 6:6; variant tradition in *t. Yebam.* 8:4.

[334]See *m. Yebam.* 6:6; required in *t. Yebam.* 8:5.

[335]E.g., William Horbury and David Noy, *Jewish Inscriptions of Graeco-Roman Egypt* (Cambridge: Cambridge University Press, 1992), nos. 85 (= *CIJ* 1515), 99 (= *CIJ* 1530b), 106 (= *CIJ* 1481). E.g., "In the 23rd year, Pharmouthi 30, there died Kleopas, wife of Petos, in childbirth, the loved one. Weep for me, all men, for I died at 25 (?) years old" (no. 99, translated in ibid., p. 175).

[336]Van der Horst estimates that less than half would reach adulthood (see *Ancient Jewish Epitaphs*, pp. 83-84; cf. pp. 73-74).

[337]E.g., Philo *Decalogue* 165-166; *Spec. Laws* 2.224-233. See Adele Reinhartz, "Parents and Children: A Philonic Perspective," in *The Jewish Family in Antiquity*, ed. Shaye J. D. Cohen, BJS 289 (Atlanta: Scholars Press, 1993), pp. 66-69.

[338]Ps.-Phoc. 8 (translation in Van der Horst, *Sentences of Pseudo-Phocylides*, 116).

[339]Josephus *Ag. Ap.* 2.206.

[340]4Q416 2 III, 15-16 (= 4Q418 9.17-18), translation mine. The phrase "like God" (Hebrew כאל), which is present in 4Q418, is actually "like a father" (Hebrew כאב) in 4Q416—the difference being a single letter in Hebrew. One text must be the result of scribal error or intentional change. The 4Q416 reading certainly appears mistaken, lest the text read "like a father is to a man so is his father"; the multiple use of "father" in the context may have produced a scribal mistake. A similar view is held by the editors; see John Strugnell, Daniel J. Harrington and Torleif Elgvin, *Qumran Cave 4 XXIV: Sapiential Texts, Part 2,* DJD 34 (Oxford: Clarendon, 1999), p. 120. Cf. Philo *Spec. Laws* 2.233.

the mother. This Qumran text contends that honoring parents produces glory for oneself as well as the biblical length of days.

While instructing children to honor their parents, this literature also seeks to encourage the parents to discipline their children. Partially this is done through moral and practical instruction, but it also must include prevention from foolish commitments and correction from errors. For example, daughters in the Old Testament may have their vows annulled by their fathers (Num 30:3-5), and this legislation is repeated in Second Temple literature.[341]

Physical discipline was likely widely practiced. Ben Sira goes beyond even Proverbs (13:24; 23:13-14) in encouraging the loving father to whip his son often (Sir 30:1, 12-13). He further instructs the man not to pamper his boy with tender care, laughter or playing together (Sir 30:7-10). On the other hand, Pseudo-Phocylides charges parents not to be harsh with their children.[342]

The development of early Jewish interpretations on Deuteronomy 21:18-21 forms a fascinating study. In this Old Testament text parents with a rebellious son are told, after a failed attempt to chastise him, to bring their son before the city leaders in order to stone him. While this passage is simply retold in some texts,[343] often in more interpretive contexts its impact is weakened by making it difficult to meet the conditions for invoking the death penalty. Josephus recounts the law but adds a lengthy parental speech addressed to the child in hopes of changing his ways.[344] Philo requires an escalated series of punishments prior to the death penalty: the parents must first make verbal threats, then beat their son and then have him imprisoned—only then can parents ask for his execution, assuming they are both in complete agreement.[345] Pseudo-Phocylides (208) alters the Deuteronomic teaching in three ways: first the *mother* is told to discipline the son, second the problem is referred to the "elders of the family" or "the chiefs of the people" (allowing for two different interpretations of the Deuteronomic "elders of the city"), and third he never mentions the possibility of execution. But the height of expansion on this Deuteronomic text occurs in rabbinic midrash. Here every detail of the biblical passage becomes a prerequisite before executing lethal parental judgment: the boy must be an early male adolescent drunkard who steals from his father, the parents cannot be lame, dumb, blind or deaf, the parents must both agree that stoning is required,

---

[341]E.g., CD XVI, 9-12; 11QTemple LIII, 16-21.
[342]Ps.-Phoc. 207; cf. Col 3:21; Eph 6:4.
[343]E.g., 11QTemple LXIV, 2-6.
[344]Josephus *Ant.* 4.260-265.
[345]Philo *Spec. Laws* 2.232.

and they must have previously brought their son to a court of three judges for scourging.[346] The increasing tendency throughout Second Temple literature to add to the Deuteronomic text indicates a certain unease with the harshness of executing a child. This results in attempts to render the biblical legislation difficult, if not impossible, to perform.

If discipline can be reactive to the moral ills of children, education in the Jewish religion can partly be conceived as a preventative.[347] In the heart of the *Shema,* which rabbinic law required to be recited daily, lies the command to teach the words of Moses to one's sons (Deut 6:7). The importance of this text for early Judaism, which can also be witnessed in its frequent employment in phylacteries from this period, serves as a reminder of the biblical stress on family-based religious instruction in Judaism. In a passage reminiscent of the *Shema,* Josephus indicates that parents have a duty to assure that their children are taught to read the Law and to imitate the deeds of their Jewish forefathers.[348] Both Josephus and Philo claim that Jews are instructed in the Law since youth.[349] Rabbinic texts indicate that compulsory religious ceremonies were part of the education of children, involving the reciting of the *Shemoneh Esreh* and of mealtime prayers, and including attendance at the temple for certain festivals.[350] Philo mentions that such education comes from parents as well as teachers and instructors.[351] This raises the question of the degree of community education in Jewish religion beyond parental teaching.

The revised edition of Schürer's *History of the Jewish People in the Age of Jesus Christ (175 B.C.-A.D. 135),* makes a strong case that at least by the second-century A.D. primary level education was available to some Jewish children.[352] Approximate ages for the different degrees of educa-

---

[346]See *m. Sanh.* 8:1-4; cf. *Sifre Deut.* 218-219. See O. Larry Yarbrough, "Parents and Children in the Jewish Family of Antiquity," in *The Jewish Family in Antiquity,* ed. Shaye J. D. Cohen, BJS 289 (Atlanta: Scholars Press, 1993), p. 51.

[347]On the home as a place of education, see ibid., pp. 42-45; John M. G. Barclay, "The Family as the Bearer of Religion in Judaism and Early Christianity," in *Constructing Early Christian Families: Family as Social Reality and Metaphor,* ed. Halvor Moxnes (London: Routledge, 1997), pp. 68-72.

[348]Josephus *Ag. Ap.* 2.204; cf. *Ant.* 4.211. Philo recasts the *Shema* as requiring not just instruction of sons but education of relatives and friends and all younger men (*Spec. Laws* 4.141).

[349]Josephus *Ag. Ap.* 1.60; 2.178; Philo, *Embassy* 210.

[350]See listing in Schürer, *History of the Jewish People,* 2:420-22. The temple attendance passages show that these rabbinic teachings could be Palestine centered and also impossible to perform after A.D. 70.

[351]Philo *Embassy* 115.

[352]Schürer, *History of the Jewish People,* 2:418-19.

tion in rabbinic circles are inscribed in the famous later rabbinic saying "At five years old [one is fit] for the Scripture, at ten years for the Mishnah, at thirteen for [the fulfilling of] the commandments, at fifteen for the Talmud."[353]

Even in the documents from Qumran there is reason to believe that at least some sectarians arranged for children's education in the religious precepts of the community. Children, along with women, are included in the sectarian gathering prescribed in 1Q28a (I, 4-5), where they will be taught "the precepts of the covenant." And the young man is likewise brought up in community instructions through a program that culminates in his ability to join the community at age twenty, to serve in the congregation at age twenty-five and to lead at the age of thirty.[354] An oath for sons enrolling in the community is required in the Damascus Document.[355]

One significant question concerns whether Jewish people sent their children to Hellenistic schooling in the gymnasium. An event that provides much insight concerns the introduction of a gymnasium in the region of Jerusalem by Jason the high priest; this was a source of great distaste in early Jewish literature.[356] The action itself indicates that some Palestinian Jewish families in the second century B.C. were longing for the gymnasium form of hellenizing education, whereas the strong opposition in the literature proves that others were quite opposed to it.[357] Yet elsewhere in the Diaspora by the third century A.D. one witnesses a Jewish synagogue meeting in a former civic basilica built alongside a gymnasium in Sardis. Clearly Hellenistic education was more acceptable to some than to others.

Adoption. Some Old Testament narrative texts provide possible examples of adoption, though these have been disputed.[358] J. M. Scott has argued that in Josephus, Philo and Pseudo-Philo several of these Old Testament texts are treated as instances of adoption (especially Pharaoh's daughter/Moses, Abra-

---

[353]See *m. 'Abot* 5:21. Translation from Danby, *Mishnah,* p. 458. Cf. *b. Qidd.* 29b-30a.

[354]1Q28a I, 6-16.

[355]CD XV, 6-7.

[356]E.g., 1 Macc 1:14; 2 Macc 4:12.

[357]On this incident and other aspects of education in Palestine, see Martin Hengel, *Judaism and Hellenism: Studies in Their Encounter in Palestine during the Early Hellenistic Period,* trans. John Bowden (Philadelphia: Fortress, 1974), 1:65-83.

[358]For a helpful list of texts, see Ben-Zion Schereschewsky, "Adoption," *EncJud* 2:298-301. Also Frederick W. Knobloch, "Adoption," *ABD,* 1:77-79. James M. Scott argues that at least Gen 48:5-6; Ex 2:10; Esther 2:7, 15 are valid references to adoption in the Old Testament; see James M. Scott, *Adoption as Sons of God: An Exegetical Investigation into the Background of ΥΙΟΘΕΣΙΑ in the Pauline Corpus,* WUNT 2.48 (Tübingen: Mohr [Siebeck], 1992), pp. 62-75.

ham/Lot and Jethro/Moses).[359] Scott also finds intertestamental Jewish meta-phorical use of adoption terminology, most notably in God's adopting as sons the proselyte, the Davidic line and Israel itself.[360] It is especially in these met-aphorical uses (most associated with 2 Sam 7:14) that Scott suggests possible Jewish influence in the Apostle Paul's use of adoption language.[361]

Certainly adoption was prevalent enough in Greco-Roman society that it could not be ignored by educated Jews. Thus Philo and Josephus recog-nized adoption in the Roman imperial family.[362] Nonetheless, the evidence for Jewish adoption in this period is sparse. An Elephantine text implies that a Jewish commander adopted a slave in the process of freeing him.[363] And the case that Diaspora Jewish people accepted the practice of adoption in Roman fashion can be made from a few third- to fourth-century A.D. funer-ary inscriptions from Rome.[364]

In any case, without Jewish legal teaching on adoption in the Old Testa-ment, it is perhaps less surprising that, even in the cultural context of a Greco-Roman society that had developed traditions of adoption, Second Temple and early rabbinic legal literature does not typically treat the subject.

Slaves. Slaves were properly part of the household in antiquity and thus often discussed in connection with family matters.[365] Documentary evidence of slavery in the fifth century B.C. may be found in the legal papers of an Elephantine Jewish lady who owns slaves that are inherited by her Jewish sons at her death.[366] In the rabbinic period, Safrai contends that "literature gives the impression that the average household included a manservant or a maidservant."[367] Opposition to slavery is occasionally apparent, as when Philo notes that the Essenes do not own slaves; however, this is also in the

---

[359]Scott, *Adoption as Sons of God*, pp. 75-77. This work (pp. 75-117) has significantly advanced the discussion of intertestamental views on adoption. My thanks to Robert Peterson for in-troducing me to Scott's work.

[360]Ibid., pp. 88-117. Scott also finds metaphorical use of adoption in Bosporan and Qumran adoption of proselytes (pp. 81-85); the evidence for adoption at Qumran appears to me scant and capable of alternative assessments (as Scott allows on p. 84 n.).

[361]Gal 4:5; 2 Cor 6:18; Rom 8:15, 23.

[362]Philo *Embassy* 23; Josephus *J.W.* 2.25, 248; *Ant.* 20.150.

[363]K 8. Kraeling, *Brooklyn Museum Aramaic Papyri*, pp. 223-31. Further discussion in Scott, *Adoption as Sons of God*, p. 85 (but see also p. 87 n. 123).

[364]See Noy, *Jewish Inscriptions of Western Europe*, vol. 2, nos. 25 (= *CIJ* 358); 246 (= *CIJ* 144); 531 (= *CIJ* 3). The Jewish origins of no. 531 is defended by Noy on p. 416. Scott (*Adoption as Sons of God*, pp. 79-80 n.), without complete argumentation, accepts only *CIJ* 3 and 144 as clear instances of Jewish adoption. See also Leon, *Jews of Ancient Rome*, pp. 232-33.

[365]E.g., Ps.-Phoc. 223-224.

[366]See C 28.

[367]Safrai, "Home and Family," p. 751 (note also his broader comments on pp. 750-52).

context of their overall avoidance of individual possessions in favor of community ownership.[368] And Philo's own contention that the Law allows for Jews to keep non-Jewish slaves[369] would seem to indicate that he did not hold the Essenes to be correct on this point. So, despite some sectarian opposition to slavery, it appears that slavery was an accepted part of early Jewish society.[370]

Much of the advice on dealing with slaves is focused on treating the slave well. Thus Pseudo-Phocylides encourages proper provision of food, advises against branding or slandering a slave; and mentions that one should accept advice from prudent slaves.[371] The motives for such good treatment include the well being both of the slave and of the master.[372] Ben Sira states that intelligent slaves are to be loved and eventually granted freedom; such a slave will even have freemen waiting on him.[373] Masters should treat slaves as equals since they are costly.[374] However, slaves ought not be left idle, and the bad servant should be tortured and enchained.[375] Regardless of the conditions in which slaves were maintained, they nevertheless were legally considered property that could be sold or inherited.

Property laws. Throughout history, family strife arises over possessions, and such is recognized in this period as well.[376] To prevent such strife optimally one arranged legal documents, though there were also a series of customs that Jewish people followed.

Generally the male head of the family was in charge of the family property. Nonetheless, we have numerous incidents from history in which it appears that women owned considerable property that had been granted to them apart from their husbands. Two documentary examples from the second-century A.D. Judean desert are Babatha and her stepdaughter Shelamzion.[377] Indeed, the Shelamzion example may indicate that a father (or mother) could give money to a daughter after marriage in order to avoid it

---

[368]Philo *Hypothetica* 11.4; in Eusebius *Praep. ev.* 8.11.4.

[369]Philo *Spec. Laws* 2.123.

[370]Further evidence in Dale B. Martin, "Slavery and the Ancient Jewish Family," in *The Jewish Family in Antiquity,* ed. Shaye J. D. Cohen, BJS 289 (Atlanta: Scholars Press, 1993), pp. 118-27.

[371]Ps.-Phoc. 223-27.

[372]Ps.-Phoc. 224-27.

[373]Sir 7:21; 10:25.

[374]Sir 33:30-31.

[375]Sir 33:25-28, contrast 33:25.

[376]E.g., Ps.-Phoc. 206.

[377]For Babatha, note comments in Lewis et al., *Documents,* p. 24. For Shelamzion, see P.Yadin 19 (in ibid., pp. 83-87).

being considered part of the dowry controlled by her husband.[378] Further, as was noted above (concerning "Widows"), wives whose spouses were deceased could inherit and control significant estates.[379]

Philo helpfully outlines the basic rules of inheritance: sons inherit the parents' property (daughters do so if there are no sons) with the eldest receiving a double portion, virgin daughters receive a portion for a future dowry, and if there are no children, the inheritance goes to a brother (or other family member if no brothers).[380] That daughters inherit property when there are no sons is also clearly stated in some of the Elephantine contracts mentioned earlier, and it appears to be the principle behind Tobit 8:21. Otherwise, rabbinic teaching distinguishes between sons, who receive an inheritance, and daughters, who receive maintenance until they are married.[381] However, as the documentary evidence from Elephantine and the Judean desert shows, parents could always deed property to a daughter (or a son) before death to guarantee that it would reach the right person.

CONCLUSION

As was remarked from the outset, Second Temple literature evidences widespread regard for the importance and centrality of the Jewish family. Although some sectarians practiced celibacy, the majority of Jewish authors convey the necessity of marriage and child rearing. Certainly some marriage and family practices could be left to custom, but other aspects of family life required legal discussion—especially when money was involved. Yet, marriage and family in antiquity cannot be encapsulated wholly in legislative terms. Undergirding these legal realities were relationships (some lifelong and others cut short by death or divorce). The study of Second Temple literary and material sources helps envision how ancient Jewish societies formed a complex collage of men, women and children relating to one another in marriage and family life.

---

[378] See P. Yadin 19; cf. the use of a trustee in *m. Ketub.* 6:7. Hannah M. Cotton and Jonas C. Greenfield, "Babatha's Property and the Law of Succession in the Babatha Archive," *ZPE* 104 (1994): 211-24, esp. 219-21.

[379] E.g., Jdt. 8:7. This was also true in rabbinic teaching: if a daughter is divorced or widowed in betrothal, the resulting property goes to the father's control; if she is widowed or divorced after marriage, the property stays with her (*m. Ketub.* 4:2). Note that a daughter is under the general control of her father until married (*m. Ketub.* 4:4-5).

[380] Philo *Spec. Laws* 2.124-139.

[381] See *m. Ketub.* 4:6.

6

Marriage and Family in the New Testament

ANDREAS KÖSTENBERGER

The following survey will take its point of departure from the biblical creation account. The first topic of discussion is that of homosexuality versus heterosexuality. This is followed by treatments of the New Testament teaching on marital roles: divorce, remarriage, singleness, and children and parenting. The importance of marriage and the family in church leadership and the issue of spiritual warfare as it relates to marriage and the family are briefly addressed as well. The conclusion sets forth the distinctiveness of the Christian understanding of the subject.

ROOTED IN CREATION

In his chapter on marriage and the family in ancient Israel, Daniel Block has demonstrated that the creation narrative presents the husband-and-wife relationship simultaneously in terms of ontological equality and functional complementarity.[1] By way of background to the present chapter, it will therefore suffice to briefly summarize his contribution. As pointing to ontological equality, Block lists the following observations: (1) the reference to man being created in the image and likeness of God as both male and female in Genesis 1:27 (cf. 1 Cor 11:7);[2] (2) the joint stewardship of creation expressed by plural pronouns and verbs in Genesis 1:28; (3) the expression

---

[1] See "Marriage and Family in Ancient Israel" above. One New Testament passage that holds these two aspects in tension is 1 Pet 3:7, where the woman is referred to both as the man's "fellow heir of the grace of life" and as the "weaker vessel" (NASB).

[2] The (roughly synonymous) Hebrew terms used in Gen 1:26-27 are *tselem* for "image" (in the sense of "replica"; cf. Num 33:42; 1 Sam 6:5, 11; 2 Kings 11:18; Ezek 7:27; 16:17; 23:14) and *demût* for "likeness" (in the sense of "resemblance"; cf. 2 Kings 16:10; 2 Chron 4:3-4; Ps 58:4; Ezek 23:15; see also Gen 5:3; 9:6; and Jas 3:9). Most likely, creation in God's image conveys the (functional) notion of representative rule by way of procreation, as seems to be borne out by the immediately following divine command for the man and the woman to be fruitful and

ʿēzer kᵉnegdô (suitable helper) in Genesis 2:18; (4) the woman's creation from the man's rib rather than his head or feet (Gen 2:22); (5) the man's recognition of the woman as his female counterpart in Genesis 2:23; and (6) the mutuality of the marital relationship conveyed in Genesis 2:24-25.

At the same time, Block observes indications of a "functional ordering" in the creation narrative's presentation of the male-female relationship. He names the following factors: (1) the man and the woman's consecutive (rather than simultaneous) creation (cf. 1 Tim 2:13); (2) the woman's creation to meet a deficiency in the man's experience (rather than vice versa; cf. 1 Cor 11:9); (3) the woman's creation from the man (rather than the man's from the woman; cf. 1 Cor 11:8, 12); (4) the woman's presentation by God to the man (rather than vice versa); (5) the record of the man's response to the creation of the woman but not the woman's to the creation of the man; and (6) the woman's being named by the man (rather than the man being named by the woman), and the woman's name being derivative of the man's.[3]

While it would be possible to add to the above list,[4] or to register certain differences of opinion,[5] these observations suffice to lay the groundwork

---

multiply, and to fill the earth and subdue it, and to rule (Gen 1:28). See the survey of the three major positions on what it means to be created in God's image in Millard J. Erickson, *Christian Theology*, 2nd ed. (Grand Rapids, Mich.: Baker, 1998), pp. 520-29, 532-34: (1) substantive (Luther, Calvin and more recently Wayne Grudem, *Systematic Theology* [Grand Rapids, Mich.: Zondervan, 1994], pp. 445-49); (2) relational (Barth, Brunner); and (3) functional (several Reformed scholars; Anthony Hoekema, *Created in God's Image* [Grand Rapids, Mich.: Eerdmans, 1986], esp. pp. 72-73, favors a combination of [2] and [3], with [3] being primary). For the ancient background, see esp. Hans Walter Wolff, *Anthropology of the Old Testament* (Philadelphia: Fortress, 1973), p. 160, followed by William Dyrness, *Themes in Old Testament Theology* (Downers Grove, Ill.: InterVarsity Press, 1979), p. 83 and passim. See also G. C. Berkouwer, *Man: The Image of God* (Grand Rapids, Mich.: Eerdmans, 1962), p. 70.

[3]As indicated, the apostle Paul explicitly makes the first three points in his writings. For a succinct summary of didactic passages in Paul regarding women based on the Old Testament teaching, see Andreas J. Köstenberger, "Women in the Pauline Mission," in *The Gospel to the Nations: Perspectives on Paul's Mission,* ed. Peter Bolt and Mark Thompson (Leicester: Inter-Varsity Press, 2000), pp. 236-37. On the authority implied by the woman's naming by the man, see James B. Hurley, *Man and Woman in Biblical Perspective* (Grand Rapids, Mich.: Zondervan, 1981), pp. 210-12.

[4]Cf. Raymond C. Ortlund Jr., "Male-Female Equality and Male Headship," in *Recovering Biblical Manhood & Womanhood: A Response to Biblical Feminism,* ed. John Piper and Wayne Grudem (Wheaton, Ill.: Crossway, 1991), pp. 95-112.

[5]Such as that the expression ʿēzer kᵉnegdô (suitable helper) in Gen 2:18 denotes not merely ontological equality but also functional complementarity, that is, the woman's subordination to the man in her role as "helper" (note that the man is never called the woman's "helper"). This, incidentally, is not mitigated by the fact that the term ʿēzer is repeatedly applied to God in the Old Testament (cf. Ex 18:4; Ps 20:3; 33:20; 70:6; 115:9-11; 121:1-2; 146:4). These passages refer to God's voluntary "submission" to meet human needs without necessary ontological implications. In the male-female relationship, likewise, it is not ontology but functional distinctions that are in view.

for the following discussion of the New Testament teaching on marriage and the family.[6]

HOMOSEXUALITY VERSUS HETEROSEXUALITY

Before turning to a discussion of marriage and the family, a few comments on the issue of homosexuality are in order.[7] The major source concerning the New Testament's view of homosexuality is the apostle Paul, who uses the term *arsenokoitēs* (not previously attested) in 1 Corinthians 6:9 and 1 Timothy 1:10 and refers to homosexuality in an important passage in Romans 1:27. The expression means literally "one who lies or sleeps with males," that is, those who engage in homosexual acts.[8] The term probably harks back to the proscription of homosexuality in the Levitical code (Lev 18:22; 20:13 LXX).[9] Wright calls it "that homoerotic vice which Jewish writers like Philo, Josephus, Paul and Pseudo-Phocylides regarded as a signal token of pagan Greek depravity."[10]

Some have sought to restrict the application of the term to male prostitution[11] or pederasty.[12] It has also been argued that the expression refers

---

[6]On the importance of the Old Testament teaching on marriage and the family for understanding the teaching of the New Testament, see Andreas J. Köstenberger, "Gender Passages in the New Testament: Hermeneutical Fallacies Critiqued," *WTJ* 56 (1994): 267-71. Note also the warning against efforts to interpret the Genesis creation narrative independently and apart from the apostolic interpretation of a given Old Testament passage in ibid., p. 271, n. 45.

[7]The following discussion of homosexuality is adapted from my forthcoming commentary on the Pastoral epistles in the New Expositor's Bible Commentary series (Grand Rapids: Zondervan). For a helpful treatment, see Thomas E. Schmidt, *Straight and Narrow? Compassion and Clarity in the Homosexuality Debate* (Leicester; Downers Grove, Ill.: InterVarsity Press, 1995).

[8]This is brought out by the NIV rendering "homosexual offenders" in 1 Cor 6:9 and perhaps even better in the TNIV's "practicing homosexuals"; the NIV translation "pervert" in 1 Tim 1:10 unduly dilutes the homosexual nature of the perversion addressed there (but note the commendable change to "those practicing homosexuality" in the TNIV).

[9]Cf. Jerome D. Quinn and William C. Wacker, *The First and Second Letters to Timothy,* Eerdmans Critical Commentary (Grand Rapids, Mich.: Eerdmans, 2000), pp. 88, 101.

[10]David F. Wright, "Homosexuals or Prostitutes?" *VC* 38 (1984): 145; see also idem, "Homosexuality: The Relevance of the Bible," *EvQ* 61 (1989): 291-300; and Richard B. Hays, "Relations Natural and Unnatural: A Response to John Boswell's Exegesis of Romans 1," *JRE* 14 (1986): 184-215.

[11]John Boswell, *Christianity, Social Tolerance, and Homosexuality* (Chicago: University of Chicago Press, 1980), esp. pp. 106-7, 335-53, decisively refuted by Wright, "Homosexuals or Prostitutes?"; see also idem, "Translating Ἀρσενοκοῖται (1 Cor. 6:9; 1 Tim. 1:10)," *VC* 41 (1987): 397.

[12]Robin Scroggs, *The New Testament and Homosexuality* (Philadelphia: Fortress, 1983); but see the critique in Hays, "Relations Natural and Unnatural," pp. 210-11; and Quinn and Wacker, *First and Second Letters to Timothy,* 88; see also the helpful summary and refutation of Boswell, Scroggs and Petersen by James B. De Young, "The Source and NT Meaning of Ἀρσενοκοῖται with Implications for Christian Ethics and Ministry," *MSJ* 3 (1992): 191-214 (apparently unaware of Wright, "Translating Ἀρσενοκοῖται").

merely to homosexual acts, not to "celibate" homosexual relationships (that is, relationships between persons with a homosexual orientation who are in a relationship but do not have sexual relations). Moreover, it has been alleged that the New Testament pertains merely to the negative dehumanizing pattern of homosexuality prevalent in first-century Hellenistic culture and that it therefore cannot be applied directly to contemporary mutually consenting, nonexploitative homosexual relationships.

In response, however, it must be pointed out, first, that *arsenokoitēs* is a broad term that cannot be confined to specific instances of homosexual activity such as male prostitution or pederasty. This is in keeping with the term's Old Testament background where lying with a "male" (a very general term) is proscribed, relating to "every kind of male-male intercourse."[13] In fact, the Old Testament "bans every type of homosexual intercourse," not just male prostitution or intercourse with youths. "Homosexual intercourse where both parties consent is also condemned."[14] Moreover, while it is true that homosexual *acts* are the specific focus in the Pauline prohibitions, this does not mean that he would have considered "celibate" homosexual relationships to be within the scope of the divine creative will; this would be to exchange a man's "natural" function for what is "unnatural":

> Because of this, God gave them over to shameful lusts. Even their women exchanged *natural* relations for *unnatural* ones. In the same way the men also abandoned *natural* relations with women and were inflamed with lust for one another. Men committed indecent acts with other men, and received in themselves the due penalty for their perversion.[15]

As the above passage shows, the apostle Paul considers homosexuality to be "unnatural," that is, contrary to the way God has ordained things to function according to the creation order.[16] This is borne out also by the Genesis narrative, which not only affirms repeatedly that God made every creature "after its kind" (Gen 1:21, 24 and so on) but also makes clear that God complemented the man, not by creating another man, but by creating a woman. It is intrinsic to creation that God made man "male and female," and it is together that they reflect the divine image (Gen 1:27). This is not mol-

---

[13]Gordon J. Wenham, "The Old Testament Attitude to Homosexuality," *ExpTim* 102 (1991): 362.
[14]Ibid.
[15]Rom 1:26-27 NIV, emphasis added; cf. 1 Cor 6:9-10.
[16]Cf. D. F. Wright, "Homosexuality," in *DPL*, pp. 413-14, notes that "unnatural" means not simply "contrary to accepted practice" but "the flouting of sexual distinctions basic to God's creative design" (p. 413).

lified by a mere denial that Paul in Romans speaks of homosexuality at large or by erecting a distinction between homosexual acts and homosexual orientation; that homosexuality is not in conflict with God's creation design can be maintained only by a decided rejection of the biblical creation account itself. Demonstrably, in the context of Genesis 1—2 there is no place for homosexuality in that it is not even potentially procreative and thus stands outside God's creative purposes of making humankind in two sexes in order to "be fruitful and multiply."[17]

MARITAL ROLES

Old Testament foundations. The divine institution of marriage is recorded in the foundational narrative of Genesis 2:24: "For this reason a man will leave his father and mother and be united to his wife, and they will become one flesh" (NIV). As Stott notes, this implies that the marriage union is (1) exclusive ("a man . . . his wife"); (2) publicly acknowledged ("leave his father and mother"); (3) permanent ("be united to his wife"); and (4) normally consummated by sexual intercourse ("become one flesh").[18] On the basis of Genesis 2:24, Stott provides the following biblical definition of marriage: "Marriage is an exclusive heterosexual covenant between one man and one woman, ordained and sealed by God, preceded by a public leaving of parents, consummated in sexual union, issuing in a permanent mutually supportive partnership, and normally crowned by the gift of children."[19] Despite occasional instances of polygamy, Israel's history generally presupposes the divinely ordained institution of monogamous marriage.[20]

Jesus. Jesus, when questioned about divorce, affirmed the permanent nature of marriage in no uncertain terms. Quoting both foundational Old

---

[17]Wenham, "Old Testament Attitude to Homosexuality," p. 363; Craig S. Keener, "Adultery, Divorce," *DNTB,* p. 15, comments that ancient Jews "usually viewed homosexual behavior as a pervasively and uniquely Gentile sin" and "regarded homosexual behavior as meriting death," noting also that "some Jewish people regarded homosexual intercourse as unnatural, . . . probably in part because it could not contribute to procreation."

[18]John R. W. Stott, "Marriage and Divorce," in *Involvement: Social and Sexual Relationships in the Modern World,* ed. John R. W. Stott (Old Tappan, N.J.: Revell, 1984), 2:163.

[19]Ibid. From a church-historical perspective, see also the interesting treatise entitled "On the Good of Marriage" written by Augustine around A.D. 400 (*NPNF,* 2:397-413). Attitudes toward sexuality, marriage and family in the patristic period are chronicled by Peter Brown, *The Body and Society: Men, Women and Sexual Renunciation in Early Christianity* (London: Faber & Faber, 1990).

[20]Craig S. Keener, "Marriage," *DNTB,* p. 683, notes that in early Judaism "the vast majority of Jewish men and all Jewish women were monogamous" and that some conservative sectarians forbade polygamy.

Testament texts, Genesis 1:27 and 2:24, he concluded, "So they are no longer two, but one. Therefore what God has joined together, let man not separate" (Mt 19:6 NIV). As Stott aptly notes, "The marriage bond is more than a human contract: it is a divine yoke. And the way in which God lays this yoke upon a married couple is not by creating a kind of mystical union but by declaring his purpose in his Word."[21]

While Jesus affirmed marriage and blessed children, however, he conceived of the community of believers in familial terms transcending those of people's natural relations. This is one of the most striking, distinctive and central aspects of Jesus' call to discipleship.[22] Leaving one's family behind, even literally, was regularly expected of Jesus' first followers. This is made clear by what is perhaps the earliest account of Jesus' calling of his disciples in Mark's Gospel:

> As Jesus walked beside the Sea of Galilee, he saw Simon and his brother Andrew casting a net into the lake, for they were fishermen. "Come, follow me," Jesus said, "and I will make you fishers of men." At once they left their nets and followed him. When he had gone a little farther, he saw James son of Zebedee and his brother John in a boat, preparing their nets. Without delay he called them, and they left their father Zebedee in the boat with the hired men and followed him.[23]

Conversely, those who resist Jesus' call to discipleship frequently are unwilling to forsake their natural ties in favor of total allegiance to Jesus. Luke records a series of three such memorable instances:

> As they were walking along the road, a man said to him, "I will follow you wherever you go." Jesus replied, "Foxes have holes and birds of the air have nests, but the Son of Man has no place to lay his head."
> He said to another man, "Follow me." But the man replied, "Lord, first let me go and bury my father." Jesus said to him, "Let the dead bury their own dead, but you go and proclaim the kingdom of God."

---

[21]Stott, "Marriage and Divorce," p. 167. On ancient Jewish marriage and weddings, see Keener, "Marriage," *DNTB,* pp. 684-86.

[22]Note the conclusion by Stephen C. Barton, *Discipleship and Family Ties in Mark and Matthew* (Cambridge: Cambridge University Press, 1994), p. 56, that there is "strong precedent for the apparent 'hostility' to family in the context of discipleship of Jesus found in the gospels," pointing to Judaism from the story of Abraham onwards, the renunciation of family life at Qumran (as idealized by Philo and Josephus), and the communities of Therapeutae (Philo). But see the perceptive review and critique by John Barclay, "Review of *Discipleship and Family Ties in Mark and Matthew* by Stephen C. Barton," *SCE* 9, no. 1 (1996): 47-50.

[23]Mk 1:16-20 NIV = Mt 4:18-22; cf. Lk 5:2-11.

Still another said, "I will follow you, Lord; but first let me go back and say good-by to my family." Jesus replied, "No one who puts his hand to the plow and looks back is fit for service in the kingdom of God."[24]

All three Gospels also record a rich young man's unwillingness to part with his wealth in order to follow Jesus, setting his refusal in contrast to the disciples' unconditional commitment to their Master.[25] Upon Peter's remark that he and his fellow disciples have left everything to follow him, Jesus responds with the promise that "no one who has left home or brothers or sisters or mother or father or children or fields for me and the gospel will fail to receive a hundred times as much in this present age (homes, brothers, sisters, mothers, children and fields—and with them, persecutions) and in the age to come, eternal life" (Mk 10:29-31 [NIV] par.).

Jesus himself set the example by repeatedly renouncing his own natural family ties where they potentially stood in conflict with higher spiritual loyalties. Thus the twelve-year-old Jesus retorted to his parents' anguished concern, "Why were you searching for me? Didn't you know I had to be in my Father's house?" (Lk 2:49 NIV). Later, Jesus rebuked first his mother and then his brothers for failing to understand the divine timing underlying his ministry (John 2:4; 7:6-8). Again, he refused to be drawn back into the confines of his natural relations when his concerned family went to take charge of him, fearing that the strains of his busy ministry had caused him to lose his mind. When told that his family was waiting for him outside, he queried in a dramatic gesture, "Who are my mother and my brothers?" And answering his own question, looking at those seated in a circle around him, he issued the weighty pronouncement, "Here are my mother and my brothers! Whoever does God's will is my brother and sister and mother" (Mk 3:20-21, 31-35 [NIV] par.). In due course, it appears that Jesus' mother and his brothers indeed acknowledged that they, too, must subordinate their familial claims to allegiance to Jesus as their Savior and Lord.[26]

Examples could be multiplied (such as Jesus' response to the woman

---

[24]Lk 9:57-60 NIV; cf. Mt 8:19-22.

[25]Mk 10:17-31 = Mt 19:16-30 = Lk 18:18-30.

[26]E.g., Acts 1:14; but see already Lk 1:46-47. James Francis's calling (in an otherwise excellent article) Acts 1:14 "a reaffirmation of family ties" strikes me as rather curious ("Children and Childhood in the New Testament," in *The Family in Theological Perspective,* ed. Stephen C. Barton [Edinburgh: T & T Clark, 1996], p. 81).

who called the mother blessed who gave him birth and nursed him in Lk 11:27-28), but the implications are clear. Rather than preaching a gospel urging believers to "focus on the family"[27]—though obviously family has a vital place in God's purposes for humanity—Jesus placed natural kinship ties into the larger context of the kingdom of God.[28] In keeping with Old Testament prediction, he came, not to bring peace, but a sword, "to turn 'a man against his father, a daughter against her mother, a daughter-in-law against her mother-in-law—a man's enemies will be the members of his own household'" (Mt 10:34-36 NIV). Thus, "If anyone . . . does not hate his father and mother, his wife and children, his brothers and sisters—yes, even his own life—he cannot be my disciple" (Lk 14:26 NIV).[29]

In sum, then, Jesus' teaching on natural family ties relativizes their significance and places them within the larger context of God's kingdom. Thus he lays the groundwork for Paul's teaching that "from now on those who have wives should live as if they had none . . . for this world in its present form is passing away" (1 Cor 7:29, 31 NIV). Marriage, while remaining the foundational divine institution for humanity, is therefore to be viewed not as an end in itself but as properly subordinated to God's larger salvific purposes. The culmination of this development will be reached in the eternal state where people will no longer marry but be like angels (Mt 22:30 par.). Many of the implications of Jesus' teachings on marriage and the family are further developed in the writings of Paul.

Paul. Of the New Testament writers it is Paul who elaborates on the nature of marriage in most detail. While he elsewhere extols the benefits of singleness, at least in certain circumstances (1 Cor 7; see further below), the same apostle has also provided us with the most extensive New Testament passage on marital roles (Eph 5:21-33; par. Col 3:18-19).[30] Rather than approaching this passage merely on a topical level, in order to appreciate its full import, one must understand it in the context of Paul's letter to the Ephesians as a

---

[27]Cf. Rodney Clapp, *Families at the Crossroads: Beyond Traditional and Modern Options* (Downers Grove, Ill.: InterVarsity Press, 1993), and the critique in Stephen C. Barton, "Biblical Hermeneutics and the Family," in *The Family in Theological Perspective,* ed. Stephen C. Barton (Edinburgh: T & T Clark, 1996), pp. 10-16; see also Nicholas Peter Harvey, "Christianity Against and for the Family," *SCE* 9, no. 1 (1996): 34-39, and the response by Linda Woodhead in *SCE* 9, no. 1 (1996): 40-46.

[28]Cf. Barton, *Discipleship and Family Ties.*

[29]Cf. Mt 10:37: "*loves* his father or mother/son or daughter *more* than me."

[30]For a discussion of 1 Thess 4:3-8 and 1 Cor 7, including bibliographic references to the New Testament teaching on marriage up to 1985, see O. Larry Yarbrough, *Not Like the Gentiles: Marriage Rules in the Letters of Paul,* SBLDS 80 (Atlanta: Scholars Press, 1985), esp. pp. 65-125.

whole.[31] The divine purpose is set squarely in an eschatological framework in the banner verse of the entire epistle: "to bring all things in heaven and on earth together under one head *[anakephalaiōsasthai]*, even Christ" (Eph 1:10). This establishes *Christ* as the focal point of God's end-time program, and more particularly, Christ *as head* (Eph 1:22), not only over the church (Eph 1:22) but over every authority, in the present as well as the coming age (Eph 1:21). Clearly, Christ's headship here conveys the notion of supreme authority, not merely that of provision or nurture, as is sometimes alleged.[32] As the exalted Lord, Christ is the head *(kephalē)*, and all things are subjected to him (*hypotassō;* cf. Phil 2:9-11).

Believers once were in the realm of Satan, but now they have been made alive in Christ, by grace (Eph 2:5). They have been raised and exalted *with him,* participating in his victory over Satan (Eph 2:6). God's end-time plan to bring together all things in and under Christ is nowhere more evident than in his inclusion of the Gentiles in the community of believers together with believing Jews (Eph 2:11-22; 3:6).[33] This is termed by Paul a salvation-historical *mystērion,*[34] hidden in the past in God's own purposes, but now brought into the open and unpacked by the apostle himself. As he comes to the close of his elaboration of believers' spiritual blessings in Christ in the first three chapters of Ephesians, Paul prays for all believers that Christ would live in their hearts by faith and that, rooted and established in love, they would know the love of Christ in their lives (Eph 3:17, 19).

The second half of the epistle is given to an exposition of the new life in

---

[31]See also the interesting recent discussion of Eph 5 by Francis Watson, *Agape, Eros, Gender: Towards a Pauline Sexual Ethic* (Cambridge: Cambridge University Press, 2000), pp. 183-259. Watson keenly observes that both viewing Eph 5 as "a legitimation of patriarchal marriage" and claiming that it "transforms patriarchal marriage by subjecting it to the criterion of love" simplifies the passage by ignoring its complexities (ibid., p. 229, n. 6), referring to Ben Witherington, *Women and the Genesis of Christianity* (Cambridge: Cambridge University Press, 1990), p. 156; Sarah J. Tanzer, "Ephesians," in *Searching the Scriptures,* vol. 2, *A Feminist Commentary,* ed. Elisabeth Schüssler Fiorenza (New York: Crossroad, 1994), pp. 325-48, 341.

[32]For Christ is not the source of demons, but their head. Contra Catherine Clark Kroeger, "Head," in *DPL,* pp. 375-77; see the critique by Wayne Grudem, "The Meaning of κεφαλή ('Head'): An Evaluation of New Evidence, Real and Alleged," *JETS* 44 (2001): 25-65.

[33]Note that Gentiles compose the majority of Paul's readership in Ephesians.

[34]The usual English translation of this expression by "mystery" is somewhat misleading in that *mystery* is at best a partial cognate of the Greek term *mystērion*. In fact, in a very important sense *mystērion* conveys the very opposite sense of *mystery,* for while the English term means "something secret or unrevealed" or even "something intrinsically unknowable," the Greek expression refers to a truth that was previously undisclosed but has now been made known (see Andreas J. Köstenberger, "The Mystery of Christ and the Church: Head and Body, 'One Flesh,'" *TJ* 12 n.s. [1991]: 80-83).

Christ that believers are to enjoy in the unity of the "body of Christ," the church. They are to walk in a manner worthy of their calling, give preference to one another in love and preserve spiritual unity in peace (Eph 4:1-3). In fact, the church has a sevenfold unity (Eph 4:4-6). God has given spiritual gifts and instituted various ministries in the church to equip believers for ministry of their own. In all this, his goal is the "perfect man" *(andra teleion,* Eph 4:13), who speaks the truth in love and in all things grows into him, who is the head, that is, Christ (Eph 4:13-16). Paul then contrasts the old with the new lifestyle: the old lifestyle was independent, unsubmitted, rebellious, defying authority, and in bondage to passions and lusts; the new lifestyle is submitted, respectful of authority and living in love. Becoming a Christian is like putting off old clothes and putting on new ones (Eph 4:22, 24; cf. Col 3:9-10): there must be a marked, noticeable change in spirit and behavior.

Moving to the more immediate context of the passage on marital roles, Paul exhorts believers to live lives of love, as Christ loved them. What kind of love did Christ show for believers? He gave himself as a sacrifice for them (Eph 5:1-2; cf. 5:25). Conversely, there must be no sexual immorality *(porneia;* cf. 1 Cor 6:15-16). As God's eschatological community, the church must be filled with the Spirit (which means that every believer must be likewise so filled; Eph 5:18). This corresponds to God's filling of the Old Testament sanctuary with his spiritual presence.[35] In the first instance, this Spirit filling refers to congregational worship (and is thus corporate, rather than merely individualistic, in import; Eph 5:19-20).[36] Still continuing the same sentence in the original Greek, Paul then relates Spirit filling also to the marriage relationship in Eph 5:21-24. Being properly submitted *(hypotassō;* Eph 5:21, 22) is thus a mark of Spirit filling, in contrast to believers' previous lifestyle, which was characterized by rebellion toward authority.

Several observations should be interjected at this point. First, the following instructions for wives and husbands (as well as those for parents and slaves/masters) are directed to Spirit-filled *believers,* that is, to committed Christians, rather than to those outside of Christ. It should therefore surprise no one that these instructions are foolishness to those who do not follow

---

[35]See my "What Does It Mean to Be Filled with the Spirit? A Biblical Investigation," *JETS* 40 (1997): 229-40, for a detailed discussion of Eph 5:18 and related passages.

[36]Cf. Timothy G. Gombis, "Being the Fullness of God in Christ by the Spirit: Ephesians 5:18 in Its Epistolary Setting," *TynBul* 53.2 (2002): 262-64, citing Thomas R. Schreiner, *Paul, Apostle of God's Glory in Christ: A Pauline Theology* (Downers Grove, Ill.: InterVarsity Press, 2001), p. 338; Köstenberger, "What Does It Mean?" p. 233; and Gordon D. Fee, *Paul, the Spirit, and the People of God* (Peabody, Mass.: Hendrickson, 1996), pp. 63-73.

the path of Christian discipleship. This does not mean that Ephesians 5:21-33 contains instructions on male-female relationships that are merely private in nature. Rather, these injunctions set forth the divine ideal for *all* (married) men and women because they reflect the Creator's abiding will and are part of his general revelation, instituted for all of humanity rather than merely for believers in Jesus Christ.

Second, what Paul has in mind here is not exactly "mutual submission" (in terms of identical roles), as may be supposed from reading Ephesians 5:21 in isolation from what follows.[37] Rather, "mutual submission coexists with a hierarchy of roles within the [Christian] household. . . . [T]here is a general sense in which husbands are to have a submissive attitude to wives, putting their wives' interests before their own. But this does not eliminate the more specific [role] in which wives are to submit to husbands."[38] Specifically, in Ephesians 5:22 wives are enjoined to submit to their husbands who in Ephesians 5:23-24 are called the "head" of their wives as Christ is the head of the church. The balancing command to husbands is for them to love their wives with the sacrificial love of Christ (Eph 5:25-28). To this the observation may be added that in the abbreviated parallel in Colossians 3:18-19, the statement "Wives, submit to your husbands, as is fitting in the Lord" (NIV), sums up the entirety of Paul's counsel to Christian wives with regard to their marital disposition (no word about "mutual submission" here). In that context, a husband's love is further defined as not being harsh with his wife (cf. 1 Pet 3:7).

Third, as can be seen from comparing the present passage with Ephesians 1:22 and 4:15 (see discussion above), "headship" entails not merely nurture (though it does that; see Eph 5:29) but also a position of authority. This position of the man is a function not of intrinsic merit or worth on his part but of God's sovereign creative will. Hence the husband's leadership, as well as the wife's submission, is to be exercised within the orbit of grace rather than legalism or coercion.

Fourth, the marriage relationship must be seen within the compass of God's larger salvation-historical, eschatological purposes, that is, the bring-

---

[37]See Wayne Grudem, "The Myth of 'Mutual Submission,'" *CBMW News* 1.4 (October 1996): 1, 3-4, who suggests that the force of the Greek term *allēlois* is "some to others." Rather than speaking of "mutual submission," it may be more appropriate to speak of "mutual humility" (note the shift from submission to humility in 1 Pet 5:5-6).

[38]Andrew T. Lincoln, *Ephesians,* WBC 42 (Dallas: Word, 1990), p. 366, quoted in Gerald F. Hawthorne, "Marriage and Divorce," in *DPL,* p. 596. See also the discussion in Watson, *Agape, Eros, Gender,* pp. 219-59.

ing of "all things in heaven and on earth together under one head, even Christ" (Eph 1:10 NIV). This includes spiritual powers, such as demons as well as Satan, who will be fully submitted to Christ (Eph 1:21); this includes the bringing together of Jews and Gentiles in one salvation-historical, eschatological entity, the church (Eph 2:11-22; 3:6-13); and it includes also the restoration of the male-female marriage relationship as realized by Spirit-filled, committed Christian believers, who overcome the cursed struggle of manipulation and dominance (cf. Gen 3:16)[39] in the power of Christ and relate to each other in proper submission and Christlike love. God's purposes are greater than marriage or male-female roles, though they significantly include this relationship (see 1 Pet 3).

Fifth, it is thus manifestly not true (as is regularly alleged by egalitarian scholars) that female submission is merely a result of the Fall.[40] For in the present passage, it is Christian women—in whom Christ's redemptive purposes are to be realized—who are nonetheless enjoined to submit to their husbands. And elsewhere in Paul, the apostle, with reference to Genesis 2:18, stresses that it is not the man who was made for woman, but the woman was made for man (1 Cor 11:9), so that "the head of every man is Christ, and the head of the woman is man" (1 Cor 11:3 NIV).

Moreover, sixth, it is likewise not true that the restored pattern for marriage in Christ transcends that of submission and authority. This understanding is not borne out by the New Testament, be it here or elsewhere. To the contrary, Paul's argument in 1 Timothy 2:9-15 "turns to the story of Adam and Eve in Genesis for scriptural support of an understanding of the authority structure, the order of creation, which exists between men and women. . . . Adam and Eve are called into service as normative examples of how men and women should interrelate and what can happen if the proper authority structure is adhered to [or not adhered to] by subsequent peoples."[41]

Notably, Paul refutes as heretical the understanding (as advocated by some in his day) that "the resurrection has already taken place" (2 Tim 2:18

---

[39]On Gen 3:16, see esp. Susan T. Foh, "What Is the Woman's Desire (Gen 3:16, 4:7)," *WTJ* 37 (1975): 376-83, who rightly interprets Gen 3:16 in light of Gen 4:7 where "desire" conveys a sense of attempted mastery or control. See also the scenario at the Fall (Gen 3), which is cited by Paul in 1 Tim 2:14-15 as one of two reasons for his prohibition of women teaching or exercising authority over a man in the church (cf. 1 Tim 2:12).

[40]See, for example, Stanley J. Grenz, *Sexual Ethics: A Biblical Perspective* (Dallas: Word, 1990), p. 28.

[41]Larry T. Kreitzer, "Adam and Christ," in *DPL*, p. 10.

NIV), that is, that the future has so invaded the present that believers' present lives no longer need to heed principles built into the fabric of creation by the Creator. Contrary to the false teachers, God's created order continues to provide the framework for human relationships (cf. 1 Tim 4:3). While subverted by the Fall, this order is not to be set aside by Christians. Rather, it is God's redemptive purpose in Christ to counteract the effects of sin in human relationships (and other spheres) by believers' new life in the Spirit. Only in heaven will people no longer be given in marriage, but they will be like angels (Mt 22:30 par.). Currently, they still marry, have children and are to fulfill the cultural mandate in keeping with the male-female roles established at creation.

Seventh, wives are to recognize and respect proper authority over them. In principle, this is true also of men; they, too, must submit to Christ, local church leadership and discipline, the civil authorities, or their employers; but clearly wives are called to submit to their husbands in a sense that is nonreciprocal (cf. 1 Pet 3:1-6 in the context of 1 Pet 2:13, 18). Husbands' exercise of authority, in turn, must not be arbitrary or abusive, but in love.[42] Again, Petrine teaching is found to cohere with that of Paul: "Husbands, in the same way be considerate as you live with your wives, and treat them with respect as the weaker partner and as heirs with you of the gracious gift of life" (1 Pet 3:7 NIV).

After these larger observations, we may look at Ephesians 5:21-33 in some further detail. For both wives and husbands Paul, using the format of the ancient household code, cites models to emulate: for wives, the church in her submission to Christ; for husbands, Christ's sacrificial love for the church, resulting in her cleansing, holiness and purity. The apostle adds a second, common-sense analogy from the nature of things, appealing to self-interest: everyone loves one's own body; in light of the one-flesh union between husbands and wives, if husbands love their wives, this is tantamount to husbands loving themselves.

Paul rounds out his discussion of marital roles with a quotation from Scripture: "and the two will become one flesh" (Eph 5:31 NIV; cf. Gen 2:24: "they"). Some believe that this allusion to the creation narrative draws a connection between the marriage union and Christ's relationship with the church by way of typology, that is, a "typical" correspondence along salvation-historical lines, with Adam prefiguring Christ, Eve foreshadowing the church, and Adam and Eve's relationship typifying the union of Christ

---

[42]Cf. Hawthorne, "Marriage and Divorce," p. 596.

and the church.[43] This is possible, though it is important to note that the apostle's focus here lies squarely on the union of Christ and the church (cf. Eph 5:30-32) and no longer on marriage (which dominated discussion in Eph 5:21-29).[44]

In any case, Paul's major point seems to be that marriage has the honor of embodying the "one flesh" principle that later in salvation history became true spiritually also for the union of the exalted Christ with the church, which is described by Paul in terms of "head," "members" and "body." This, too, like the inclusion of Gentiles in God's salvific plan, is a *mystērion:* it was hidden in the divine wisdom in ages past but now has been given to Paul to reveal. Marriage is thus shown to be part and parcel of God's overarching salvation-historical purposes of "bringing all things together under one head, even Christ" (Eph 1:10 NIV). The lesson to be drawn from this is that marriage in Christian teaching, rather than being an end in itself, is to be subsumed under Christ's rule. Just as Christ must rule over all heavenly powers (Eph 1:21-22) and over the church (Eph 4:15), he must also rule over the marital relationship (Eph 5:21-33), the home (Eph 6:1-4) and the workplace (Eph 6:5-9). A married couple is part of the church (understood as family of families), and it, too, is part of that spiritual warfare that resolutely resists evil (Eph 6:10-14) and seeks to promote God's purposes in this world (foremost the preaching of the gospel, Eph 6:15, 19-20).[45]

Thus the marriage relationship should also be viewed in the context of Christian witness in an unbelieving environment, both directly by the husband's and the wife's living out God's purposes for the Christian couple, as well as indirectly by being part of a biblical church that actively propagates the gospel message.

Peter. Peter's comments on the marriage relationship are penned in the context of believers suffering at the hands of unbelievers, in the present instance believing wives called to live with unbelieving husbands. Peter's general rule of conduct is submission "for the Lord's sake to every authority instituted among men" (1 Pet 2:13), including government and authorities at work and at home (1 Pet 2:13—3:1). In the case of work relationships, submission is urged not only to superiors "who are good

---

[43]Cf. Peter T. O'Brien, *The Letter to the Ephesians,* PNTC (Grand Rapids, Mich.: Eerdmans, 1999), pp. 429-35.

[44]See Köstenberger, "Mystery of Christ and the Church," pp. 79-94.

[45]On spiritual warfare in relation to marriage and the family, see further the discussion below.

and considerate, but also to those who are harsh" (1 Pet 2:18 NIV). Wives are to be submissive to unbelieving husbands "in the same way" (1 Pet 3:1 NIV).[46]

In all of this Christ has set the example (1 Pet 2:21), all the way to the cross (1 Pet 2:24; *epi* plus the accusative). Marriage, as well as other human relationships, is thus set in the larger framework of a believer's Christian testimony in the surrounding unbelieving world. While there is no guarantee (cf. 1 Cor 7:16), believing wives are to work and pray that their husbands "may be won over without words by the behavior of their wives, when they see the purity and reverence" of their lives (1 Pet 3:1-2 NIV; cf. 1 Cor 7:12-14). Such wives are to cultivate inner, spiritual beauty and not "give way to fear," being submissive to their husbands as Sarah was to Abraham, even when their directives are unreasonable or even unspiritual (1 Pet 3:3-6 NIV; cf., e.g., Gen 20).

The general principle issuing from Peter's counsel is that leading unbelievers to Christ is a greater cause than insisting on justice in human relationships. Believers are to defer their craving for justice until the eschaton, trusting God as Jesus did (1 Pet 2:23). While Paul enjoins believing wives in his letters to the Ephesians and Colossians to submit to their believing husbands, here Peter raises the bar further still. Wifely submission to an unbelieving husband—and any resulting suffering—is beautiful in the sight of God if borne reverently and with hope in God.

In the context of the third chapter of Peter's first epistle, there seems to be an almost imperceptible shift of focus from mixed marriages to those among believers. While 1 Peter 3:1-4 appears to apply primarily to the former, 1 Peter 3:5-6 evokes "the holy women of the past," including Sarah, whose husband Abraham, while occasionally sinning against Sarah, is hardly the prototype of the unbelieving husband. Thus Peter, like Paul, envisions that marital relationships between believers will be characterized by wifely submission and husbands' considerate treatment of their wives.

In the sole verse addressed to husbands, Peter admirably balances the recognition of distinctions between the marital partners and the notion of their equality in Christ. On the one hand, wives are called "the weaker partner" (whether the phrase is to be understood in physical or generic terms,

---

[46]This in no way amounts to a license for husbands to abuse their wives physically or in any other way, nor does it preclude the necessity for wives to separate from their abusive husbands in order to avoid serious harm. The delicate pastoral implications of such situations call for considerable wisdom in each individual case.

this is hardly a banner verse of egalitarianism). Yet on the other hand, wives are called "fellow heirs" together with their husbands of the gracious gift of life (1 Pet 3:7). The reference to removing any obstacles for joint marital prayer likewise presupposes that the initial focus on mixed marriages has now given way to those among believers.

Concluding thoughts. While marriage is, biblically speaking, not a "sacrament" in the Roman Catholic sense,[47] it—as well as parenting—is nonetheless a vehicle used by God to train the man and the woman (and their children) in the life of faith. For both the husband and the wife, living out their proper, God-willed roles becomes an important part of their discipleship. Moreover, it is an important part of their one-flesh union not merely that they produce physical offspring but that they pursue the nurture and facilitate the growth of spiritual offspring, that is, aid the Spirit's work in the lives of their children in conviction of sin, conversion, regeneration and sanctification. As Dietrich Bonhoeffer wrote,

> Through marriage men are brought into being for the glorification and service of Jesus Christ and for the increase of his kingdom. This means that marriage is not only a matter of producing children, but also of educating them to be obedient to Jesus Christ. . . . [I]n marriage it is for the service of Jesus Christ that new men are created.[48]

This is why a Christian marriage and family must be committed and subjected to Jesus Christ. And this is also why marriage and the family must be viewed not as an obstacle to true personal holiness, purity and sanctification, but as an important key to the development of these and other virtues. In godly homes husband and wife sharpen one another "as iron sharpens iron" (cf. Prov 27:17), and their children are drawn into the communal life of the family and into the path of discipleship pursued and modeled by their parents.

This, too, is part of obeying the risen Christ's commission for his followers to "go and make disciples" (Mt 28:18-20). What is more, in the case of one's own children, too, discipleship entails baptism in the name of the Father, Son and Holy Spirit and being taught to obey everything Jesus commanded his followers. Baptism and committed instruction, formal (such as by way of catechism) as well as informal (as opportunities arise), are not optional but an essential part of the life of the Christian family.

---

[47]Contra Germain Grisez, "The Christian Family as Fulfilment of Sacramental Marriage," *SCE* 9, no. 1 (1996): 23-33.

[48]Dietrich Bonhoeffer, *Ethics,* trans. N. H. Smith (London: SCM Press, 1955), p. 183, quoted in Banner, "Who Are My Mother and My Brothers?" *SCE* 9, no. 1 (1996): 8.

DIVORCE AND REMARRIAGE, SINGLENESS

Before moving on to a more extensive discussion of children and parenting, two important issues related to marriage must first be treated: (1) divorce and remarriage[49] and (2) singleness. In the case of the former, the marital union is ruptured, and the question arises whether or not remarriage is permissible. In the case of singleness, the unmarried person, whether widowed, divorced, not yet married or permanently single, faces a set of unique challenges and opportunities that likewise must be viewed in a scriptural framework.

Divorce and remarriage. *Jesus: The exception clause.* God hates divorce (Mal 2:16), and Jesus, reminding his listeners that God in the beginning had made man male and female (cf. Gen 1:27) and that the man, upon marriage, was to leave his father and mother and to be united to his wife (cf. Gen 2:24), taught that this one-flesh union was inseparable: "So they are no longer two, but one. Therefore what God has joined together, let man not separate" (Mt 19:4-6 [NIV] par.). Why, then, is divorce legislated in the Mosaic regulations (Deut 24:1, 3)? According to Jesus, this was done by concession to human hardness of heart rather than constituting the ideal. It was not the original vision and creative will of the founding Father (Mt 19:7-8 par.; cf. Mt. 5:31-32). Marriage was intended as a life-long, faithful union of a man and a woman. Recognizing the high standard set by Jesus, his original followers responded dejectedly, "If this is the situation, . . . it is better not to

---

[49]For a range of evangelical views, see H. Wayne House, ed., *Divorce and Remarriage: Four Christian Views* (Downers Grove, Ill.: InterVarsity Press, 1990). See also the excellent treatment of divorce and remarriage in David Clyde Jones, *Biblical Christian Ethics* (Grand Rapids, Mich.: Baker, 1994), pp. 177-204; the surveys by Raymond F. Collins, *Divorce in the New Testament* (Collegeville, Minn.: Liturgical Press, 1992); Pat E. Harrell, *Divorce and Remarriage in the Early Church: A History of Divorce and Remarriage in the Ante-Nicene Church* (Austin, Tex.: Sweet, 1967). Roman Catholic theology views marriage as a sacrament and hence indissoluble, although canon law makes provision for the annulment of marriages on certain grounds. Divorcees are barred from receiving Communion elements. However, while Scripture views marriage as permanent, it does not view it therefore as a sacrament (see Köstenberger, "Mystery of Christ and the Church," pp. 86-87). Moreover, as will be seen below, exceptions are made in New Testament teaching in the case of adultery and desertion by an unbelieving spouse, so a distinction ought to be made between legitimate and illegitimate divorces rather than discriminating against all divorcees, even those whose divorce is biblically legitimate. On the Roman Catholic debate about divorce, see also the works referred to in Joseph A. Fitzmyer, "The Matthean Divorce Texts and Some New Palestinian Evidence," *TS* 37 (1976): 225. A recent treatment is by David Instone-Brewer, *Divorce and Remarriage in the Bible: The Social and Literary Context* (Grand Rapids, Mich.: Eerdmans, 2002), who contends that (1) both Jesus and Paul condemned illegitimate divorce and discouraged divorce even on valid grounds; (2) both Jesus and Paul affirmed the Old Testament grounds for divorce, which were adultery and neglect or abuse; and (3) both Jesus and Paul condemned remarriage after an invalid, but not a valid, divorce (p. ix; see esp. pp. 133-212).

marry" (Mt 19:10).[50] To which Jesus replied, in essence, that to some it is given to remain celibate for the sake of the kingdom; otherwise people must subject themselves to God's original expectation for marriage.

There is one exception, however, mentioned in Matthew 5:32 and 19:9: "except for marital unfaithfulness" *[porneia]*."[51] This was infinitely stricter than the scenario mentioned in the opening statement of Jesus' interrogators, "for any and every reason" (Mt 19:3 NIV; cf. 5:31). While the challenge was aimed at eliciting from Jesus a response that would enable his questioners to assign him to one of the leading rabbinic schools of the day, be it the stricter Shammai or the more liberal Hillel, Jesus' answer confounded such hopes by refusing to endorse either position.[52]

According to the Mishnah,

> The School of Shammai say: A man may not divorce his wife unless he has found unchastity in her, for it is written, "Because he has found in her indecency in anything" (Deut 24:1). And the School of Hillel say: [He may divorce her] even if she spoiled a dish for him, for it is written, "Because he has found in her indecency in anything."[53]

---

[50]Some, such as Paul Ramsey, *Basic Christian Ethics* (Louisville: Westminster John Knox, 1993 [1950]), p. 71, argue that the disciples' response proves that Jesus' standard must have been extremely high—that is, no divorce or remarriage under any circumstances. If Jesus had merely aligned himself with the more conservative branch of Judaism of his day (the school of Shammai), why would Jesus' followers have been surprised? However, this assumes that the disciples' reaction was legitimate, which almost certainly it was not. More likely, they, like many of their Jewish contemporaries, assumed a somewhat more lenient standard and consequently were reacting against Jesus' pronouncement including the exception for adultery. See esp. Instone-Brewer, *Divorce and Remarriage,* p. 168, who argues that the disciples' answer most likely indicates that they held a type of Hillelite "any matter" view.

[51]The Synoptic parallels Mk 10:11-12 and Lk 16:18 mention no exception, though such a radical breach as adultery—a capital offense, albeit not enforced—was not in question as grounds for divorce (e.g., *m. Sota* 1:1, 5). See Stott, "Marriage and Divorce," pp. 169-70, who defends the authenticity of the exception clause, points out that adultery as grounds for divorce was not in dispute, and suggests that Matthew may have included this for his Jewish audience while Mark and Luke, both writing primarily to Gentile readers, did not have the same concern. Contra R. H. Stein, "Divorce," *DJG,* p. 197, who claims that "its authenticity [i.e., the exception clause in Matthew] is doubtful" and suggests that "Matthew has added an exception clause to Jesus' teaching." On adultery, see esp. Keener, "Adultery, Divorce," *DNTB,* pp. 7-10.

[52]See Instone-Brewer, *Divorce and Remarriage,* p. 173, who contends that "Matthew's version reflects a real rabbinic debate." For a similar dynamic, see Mk 12:13-17 par.

[53]From *m. Giṭ.* 9:10. The passage continues: "R. Akiba [ca. AD 135] says: Even if he found another fairer than she, for it is written, 'And it shall be if she find no favor in his eyes . . .'" See also Sir 25:26: "If she does not go as you direct, separate her from yourself" (lit., "cut her off from your flesh," that is, divorce her: Deut 24:1; up to this point they had been "one flesh": Gen 2:24).

In the present instance, then, Jesus aligned himself more closely with the more conservative branch of Judaism in his day. Yet he refused to get involved in legalistic squabbles, focusing instead on the original design of marriage in God's plan.[54] Not only must divorce be prevented by fostering commitment to marriage, but divorce is shown to be fundamentally at odds with God's creative purposes. Nevertheless, adultery is acknowledged as legitimate grounds for divorce, presumably since it violates the "one flesh" principle underlying marriage[55] and was at least in Old Testament times punishable by death.[56] After all, it would be difficult to continue a marriage if the partner guilty of adultery had been put to death by stoning!

Nevertheless, some would seek to delimit even further the exception stipulated by Jesus by taking him to refer here not to sexual infidelity in marriage, that is, adultery, but to some more narrow offense, be it incest (Lev 18:6-18; 20:17; Deut 27:22), the breaking of an engagement (Deut 22:20-21), or the like.[57] John Piper, for example, in two papers posted at his website,[58] doubts that adultery was assumed by Mark and Luke as a legitimate ground for divorce (and thus omitted in their parallel accounts) and so is led to explore the possibility that Matthew's exception clause conforms to the absolute statements in Mark 10:11-12 and Luke 16:18. He notes that *porneia* is used alongside *moicheia*—and thus distinguished from it—in Matthew 15:19. Does that not prove that it should also be distinguished in Matthew 19:9? Moreover, *porneia* in John 8:41 re-

---

[54]Cf. Keener, "Adultery, Divorce," *DNTB*, p. 6, who notes that Jesus "probably accepts but radicalizes the Shammaite position."

[55]So Stott, "Marriage and Divorce," p. 170, quoted in Jones, *Biblical Christian Ethics*, p. 202.

[56]Lev 20:10; Deut 22:22. Note that Jesus extends the scope of adultery even to a man's heart attitude (Mt 5:27-28). At the same time, if the tradition underlying Jn 7:53—8:11 is authentic, Jesus also recasts the issue of proper punishment for adultery: "If any one of you is without sin, let him be the first to throw a stone at her" (Jn 8:7 NIV). See also Joseph considering divorce when suspecting his fiancé Mary of sexual infidelity (Mt 1:19).

[57]See esp. Gordon J. Wenham and William E. Heth, *Jesus and Divorce,* updated ed. (Carlisle: Paternoster, 1997 [1984]); cf. Fitzmyer, "Matthean Divorce Texts," pp. 197-226, esp. 208-11, who thinks incest is in view. But note that Heth has changed his mind and now concurs with my position; see William A. Heth, "Jesus on Divorce: How My Mind Has Changed," *SBJT* 6, no. 1 (2002): 4-29. See also Mark Geldard, "Jesus' Teaching on Divorce," *Chm* 92 (1978): 134-43; and Abel Isaksson, *Marriage and Ministry in the New Temple: A Study with Special Reference to Mt. 19.13*[sic]*-12 and 1 Cor 11.3-16,* trans. Neil Tomkinson and Jean Gray, ASNU 24 (Lund: Gleerup, 1965).

[58]John Piper, "Divorce and Remarriage: A Position Paper" and "On Divorce and Remarriage in the Event of Adultery" (July 21, 1986) posted on Desiring God Ministries <www.desiringgod.org/library/topics/divorce_remarriage/div_rem_paper.html> and <www.desiringgod.org/library/topics/divorce_remarriage/dr_adultery.html>.

fers to (alleged) sex during the betrothal period. Is this the term's meaning also in Matthew? Piper thinks the answer is yes, and he construes the Matthean exception clause as written to show that Joseph's decision to divorce Mary (on account of her supposed premarital sexual infidelity) was just.[59]

Piper's view, though possible, is weakened by the following considerations. First, Piper inadequately recognizes the common rabbinic practice of abbreviating an account for the sake of making it more memorable.[60] Hence it is illegitimate to conform the longer Matthean version to the shorter Markan and Lukan accounts. Second, it is fallacious to argue from Jesus' "silence" in Mark and Luke regarding exceptions for divorce. Rather than indicating that Jesus did not teach any such exceptions, it is much more likely that he did not elaborate on points at which he agreed with the commonly held view in his day. As Instone-Brewer notes,

> If Jesus said nothing about a universally accepted belief, then it is assumed by most scholars that this indicated his agreement with it. He is never recorded as saying anything about the immorality of sexual acts before marriage (to the dismay of many youth leaders), but no one assumes that he approved of them. Similarly, everyone assumes that he believed in monotheism, but it would be difficult to demonstrate this from the Gospel accounts. Also, Jesus nowhere explicitly allowed or forbade remarriage after the death of a spouse, but we assume that he did allow this because all Jews, including Paul, clearly allowed it.[61]

Instone-Brewer proceeds to point out that on all these matters we find it easy to assume that Jesus agreed with these commonly held positions because we, too, agree with them. In the present case, however, some (inconsistently) construe Jesus' (alleged) silence on a subject as disagreement with

---

[59]Piper also believes that in Lk 16:18 Jesus excludes remarriage in the case of divorce and so interprets Mt 5:32 accordingly. Regarding Joseph's decision to divorce Mary, it should be acknowledged that the first-century Jewish understanding of an engagement was akin to marriage in the sense that breaking the engagement necessitated a formal divorce (be it private or public); see D. A. Carson, *Matthew*, EBC 8 (Grand Rapids, Mich.: Zondervan, 1984), p. 75, citing Num 5:11-31; *m. Soṭa* 1:1-5; David Hill, "A Note on Matthew i.19," *ExpTim* 76 (1964-1965): 133-34; A. Tosato, "Joseph, Being a Just Man (Matt 1:19)," *CBQ* 41 (1979): 547-51; Craig S. Keener, *A Commentary on the Gospel of Matthew* (Grand Rapids, Mich.: Eerdmans, 1999), p. 91, whose entire treatment of Mt 1:19 on pp. 87-95 repays careful study, cites *m. Giṭ.* 6:2; *m. Ketub.* 1:2; 4:2; *m. Yebam.* 2:6; *b. Giṭ.* 26b.

[60]Cf. Instone-Brewer, *Divorce and Remarriage*, pp. 161-67.

[61]Ibid., p. 185.

the prevailing practice in Jesus' day. This is illegitimate.

Third, while it is true that *porneia* may convey the notion of premarital sex in John 8:41, by Piper's own admission there are instances where the term, in context, refers to adultery (or a variety of other forms of sexual immorality). In the end, we are thrown back to the context at hand. Yet in Matthew 19:9, unlike in Matthew 15:19, *moicheia* is not used, so it is not necessarily legitimate to import the distinction made there into the present context. Unless it can be shown (which is exceedingly unlikely) that *porneia* functioned as a technical term for fornication apart from further contextual qualifiers, it is hard to see how the present reference can be limited to sex during the betrothal period.

In fact, the remaining New Testament instances of *porneia* are hardly limited to premarital sex during the betrothal period but extend to various forms of sexual immorality other than adultery.[62] While *porneia* and its cognates by themselves are very broad and nonspecific, the expression is regularly clarified by its context: if payment for sex is involved, the reference is to prostitution;[63] if close relatives are in view, the issue is incest;[64] in the case of same-sex relationships, it is homosexuality;[65] in the case of an unmarried couple, fornication; and if the context is marriage, sex outside its boundaries constitutes adultery.[66]

Since in the present case the subject is clearly marriage and its violation by one partner, *and the expression is otherwise not qualified,*[67] the sexual immorality referred to here is the breaking of the marriage vow by way of sexual relations with another woman (hence the NIV's "marital unfaithfulness") or perhaps by some other form of sexual immorality (hence the

---

[62]See now esp. the thorough discussion of the philological evidence for the meaning of *porneia* in Instone-Brewer, *Divorce and Remarriage,* pp. 156-59, who contends that the phrase is here used because it was judged to be the best translation of the phrase ערות דבר in Deut 24:1 and who sums up Jesus' teaching on divorce as follows: marriage should be monogamous and lifelong; divorce is never compulsory and should be avoided unless the erring partner stubbornly refuses to repent; marriage is optional; and Hillelite "any matter" divorces are invalid (p. 187).

[63]Mt 21:31-32; Lk 15:30; 1 Cor 6:13-18.

[64]1 Cor 5:1; Acts 15:20, 29; 21:25.

[65]Cf. Lev 18:22: *arsenos . . . koitēn*.

[66]Jer 3:9 LXX. Cf. *TDNT,* 6:579-95; BDAG, p. 854: "Of the sexual unfaithfulness of a married woman"; Joseph Jensen, "Does *porneia* Mean Fornication? A Critique of Bruce Malina," *NovT* 20 (1978): 161-84. As to Piper's argument from Lk 16:18, he fails to recognize that the second part of the phrase speaks of marrying an illegitimately divorced woman, not of marrying a woman whose divorce was legitimate (such as covered by the "exception clause"). His argument is circular, and he assumes what he sets out to prove at the outset.

[67]Cf. Stott, "Marriage and Divorce," p. 171, who notes the lack of further qualification.

TNIV's "sexual immorality").[68] Not that this betrayal of trust constitutes a *mandate* for divorce—God's desire always remains that forgiveness be granted and that the marriage be preserved (cf. 1 Cor 7:11). But while not required in such circumstances, divorce is nonetheless permissible.[69] Stott sums up Jesus' teaching well: "It seems, then, that he abrogated the death penalty for sexual infidelity, and made this the only legitimate ground for dissolving the marriage bond, by divorce not death, and then only as a permission."[70]

Paul: The "Pauline privilege." Paul addresses the same issue in a somewhat different context, that of a believer's desertion by an unbelieving spouse (1 Cor 7:12-16).[71] Since Jesus had not addressed the question, the apostle must adjudicate the situation himself ("I, not the Lord," 1 Cor 7:12), which in no way diminishes the authoritative nature of Paul's apostolic pronouncement. A mixed marriage in such circumstances is preferable (cf. 1 Pet 3:1-2), because it provides a Christian environment for the children of this marital union (1 Cor 7:14). Yet if the unbelieving spouse insists on leaving, the believer is not to hold him or her back, because God's desire is for peace, and there is no guarantee that the unbeliever will eventually be saved (1 Cor 7:15-16).[72]

Note the Corinthian context: apparently some were teaching the superiority of singleness over marriage on the basis of a Greek dualism that disparaged sexual relations as inferior to true spirituality expressed through an ascetic lifestyle.[73] To counter this entirely non-Christian notion, Paul wrote

---

[68]Cf. Stein, "Divorce," *DJG,* p. 194, who contends that "unchastity (i.e., *porneia*) has too broad a range of meaning to be interpreted so narrowly. It may indeed include these narrow meanings, but it cannot be restricted to them." Stein also points out that while Matthew elsewhere uses a more narrow term, *moicheia* (or the verb *moicheuō*), for adultery (Mt 5:27, 28, 32; 15:19; 19:18), and while elsewhere *moicheia* and *porneia* are distinguished (Mk 7:21-22 par. Mt 15:19; 1 Cor 6:9; Heb 13:4), *porneia* is a broader term that nonetheless includes *moicheia* (p. 195). See also the very thorough discussion in Carson, *Matthew,* pp. 412-19, who, before deciding in favor of the conclusion adopted in the present essay, discusses seven major interpretations of the Matthean "exception clause."

[69]Cf. Stott, "Marriage and Divorce," pp. 170-72.

[70]Ibid., p. 173.

[71]See the thorough treatment by Instone-Brewer, *Divorce and Remarriage,* pp. 189-212.

[72]On the entire pericope, see esp. the excellent treatment by Gordon D. Fee, *The First Epistle to the Corinthians,* NICNT (Grand Rapids, Mich.: Eerdmans, 1987), pp. 290-306. On the phrase "God has called us to peace," see Instone-Brewer, *Divorce and Remarriage,* p. 203, with reference to his earlier work, *Techniques and Assumptions in Jewish Exegesis Before 70 C.E.,* TSAJ 30 (Tübingen: Mohr-Siebeck, 1992), 21, 37, 82, 144-45, in which the author shows that "for the sake of peace" constitutes rabbinic legal terminology for what might be called "pragmatism" as opposed to a strict application of the law.

[73]Cf. 1 Cor 7:1, 5; cf. 1 Tim 4:3.

that a wife must not divorce *(chōrizō)* her husband; but if she does (disobeying the apostle's ruling), she must remain unmarried or be reconciled. The same applies if circumstances are reversed *(aphiēmi;* 1 Cor 7:10-11). In the case of the conversion of one spouse, the believer must not initiate divorce, but if the unbelieving spouse leaves, the remaining spouse is "not bound" *(dedoulōtai;* v. 15): divorce is legitimate, and (it may reasonably be inferred) the believer is free to remarry.[74]

In the Corinthian context, then, a married person must not divorce his or her spouse out of a desire to be more "spiritual." Neither is it legitimate for a married person to observe continence, that is, to refrain permanently from sexual intercourse with his or her partner in marriage (1 Cor 7:3-5). The only (minor) concession made by Paul is that believers who are deserted by their unbelieving spouse may divorce and remarry. It would appear that the same principle obtains today. The divorce of those deserted by their unbelieving spouses ought to be considered legitimate, with the implication that remarriage would also be legitimate in those circumstances.

Summary of New Testament teaching on divorce and pastoral implications. There are thus two legitimate reasons for divorce stipulated in New Testament teaching: sexual immorality or adultery (Mt 5:32; 19:9) and desertion by an unbelieving spouse (1 Cor 7:11-15).[75] Now it stands to reason that *if the divorce is legitimate, the person who has been legitimately divorced is*

---

[74]So rightly Instone-Brewer, *Divorce and Remarriage,* pp. 201-3. Needless to say, the dissimilarity between the Corinthian situation and the contemporary setting could not be greater since few today want to divorce their spouse in order to pursue a more perfect, sexless spirituality. In most cases, people have "fallen out of love" and simply want to get out of a present—now inconvenient—marriage to marry another, more desirable partner (cf. Fee, *First Epistle to the Corinthians,* p. 296). The injunction in 1 Cor 7:11, "but if she does separate, let her remain unmarried or else be reconciled to her husband," is at times taken as an absolute prohibition of remarriage under any circumstances. However, what is prohibited here is only remarriage after illegitimate, not legitimate, divorce (cf. 1 Cor 7:10: "the wife should not separate from her husband" with 1 Cor 7:11: "but if she does separate").

[75]Death of a spouse also allows the remaining spouse to remarry, "only in the Lord" (1 Cor 7:39 RSV; cf. Rom 7:3). To this may be added other extreme circumstances (such as persistent spousal abuse) when confronted through the process laid out in Mt 18:15-17. Cf. Hawthorne, "Marriage and Divorce," p. 599, who asks, "Is it possible to extrapolate from this that other such marital travesties, although not identical to these (e.g., cruelty, desertion, physical abuse, the systematic psychological destruction of one's marriage partner, and the like), might also have been included as exceptions to the ideal?" and urges that "any plan to divorce must not be made independently of the community of faith or apart from the advice and support of the authorized leaders of the church."

free to remarry.[76] This is borne out by the standard Jewish formula in the bill of divorce cited in the Mishnah, "See, you are free to marry any man" (*m. Giṭ.* 9:3).[77] It also seems to be the assumption underlying Jesus' statement that "anyone who divorces his wife . . . causes her to become an adulteress [assuming remarriage as a matter of course], and anyone who marries the divorced woman commits adultery" (Mt 5:32 NIV).[78]

The same would be true for those left widowed by the death of their spouse. Thus Paul encourages young widows to remarry (1 Tim 5:14) and elsewhere rules more globally that a widow "is *free* [to be] joined to another man" (Rom 7:3 NASB, emphasis added).[79] Still at another place, the apostle writes that "a woman is *bound* to her husband as long as he lives. But if her husband dies, she is *free to marry* anyone she wishes, *but he must belong to the Lord*" (1 Cor 7:39 NIV, emphasis added). Whether widowed or legitimately divorced, then, a person bereft of his or her spouse without fault is free, and frequently even encouraged, to remarry. The implications of these various exigencies on qualifications for church leadership will be discussed further below. At this point it will suffice to suggest three general pastoral implications for dealing with this issue.

First, everything should be done to preserve marriages (except in extreme cases, such as persistent spousal abuse). Second, one must determine if a

---

[76]Cf. Craig S. Keener, . . . *And Marries Another: Divorce and Remarriage in the Teaching of the New Testament* (Peabody, Mass.: Hendrickson, 1991), pp. 61-66; Stein, "Divorce," *DJG*, pp. 192-93: "'Divorce' therefore in our texts should be understood as assuming the right to remarry"; Jones, *Biblical Christian Ethics,* p. 199: "Where divorce is justified there is freedom to remarry"; Craig L. Blomberg, "Marriage, Divorce, Remarriage, and Celibacy," *TJ* 11 (1990): 196: "Divorce in biblical times virtually always carried with it the right to remarry; no NT text rescinds this permission." Contra Wenham and Heth, *Jesus and Divorce;* William E. Heth, "Divorce and Remarriage: The Search for an Evangelical Hermeneutic," *TJ* 16 (1995): 63-100: see the critique by Stott, "Marriage and Divorce," p. 171, who calls Wenham and Heth's view "extreme" and "not conclusive" (though "plausibly argued"; the reference is to a series of three articles by Wenham on "The Biblical View of Marriage and Divorce" published in *Third Way,* 1.20-22 [October and November 1977]). See also House, *Divorce and Remarriage: Four Christian Views.*

[77]Cf. Keener, "Adultery, Divorce," *DNTB,* p. 6: "the very term for legal divorce meant freedom to remarry."

[78]Cf. Stein, "Divorce," *DJG,* p. 195, who also notes that "divorce and remarry" are paired in Mk 10:11-12 (cf. v. 9) and that the link is also assumed in Deut 24:1-4.

[79]Cf. *m. Qid.* 1:1. Originally part of an illustration in a different context, the verse states that a woman may remarry if her husband has died. As Douglas J. Moo, *The Epistle to the Romans,* NICNT (Grand Rapids, Mich.: Eerdmans, 1996), p. 413 n. 24, rightly notes, "These verses are sometimes cited to prove that remarriage on any basis other than the death of one's spouse is adulterous. Whether this is the biblical teaching or not, these verses at any rate are probably not relevant to the issue. Paul is not teaching about remarriage but citing a simple example to prove a point."

given divorce is or has been legitimate. If so, a person may remarry, and a minister may perform the wedding ceremony. If not, the person may not remarry, and the minister should not officiate. Third, a clear distinction should be drawn between the guilty and the innocent party (rather than a "no-fault" approach to divorce): the innocent party should be treated as if single or unmarried, the guilty party as divorced.[80]

Singleness. Singleness, similar to adolescence, was probably not as clearly defined a concept in New Testament times as it is in the Western world today. If a person was "single," he or she more likely than not was in transition, whether that person was too young to be married, the death of a spouse had left the person widowed, or the like. Singleness as a settled state and a conscious life-style choice was comparatively uncommon, and marriage was the norm.[81] Having said this, however, both Jesus and Paul teach that there is such a thing as the "gift" of celibacy (1 Cor 7:7), or, as Jesus calls it, eunuchs "for the sake of the kingdom" (Mt 19:12 [RSV] par.), that allows unmarried persons to devote greater and more undistracted attention to religious service. As Paul comments in his major treatment on the subject,

> An unmarried man is concerned about the Lord's affairs—how he can please the Lord. But a married man is concerned about the affairs of this world—how he can please his wife—and his interests are divided. . . . I am saying this for your own good, not to restrict you, but that you may live in a right way in *undivided devotion to the Lord.*[82]

It is a remarkable fact that both Jesus and Paul, our Savior as well as the most significant proponent of early Christianity (Peter alone excepted), were single. Clearly, the reasons differed. It would have been unthinkable for the Christ, the Son of God, to enter into marriage with a human female during his brief earthly sojourn. In Paul's case, the divine gift of celibacy enabled this strategically called man to spearhead the Gentile mission in a way that a married man probably never could have. Paul's frequent travels and imprisonments also would have put great strains on a marriage. By contrast, the other apostles all had wives, as Paul himself makes clear: "Don't we have the right to take a believing wife along with us, as do the other apostles and the Lord's brothers and Cephas?" (1 Cor 9:5 NIV).

In keeping with contemporary Jewish custom, married men, with their

---

[80]So rightly Keener, . . . *And Marries Another,* p. 109.

[81]Thus Paul can stipulate that church leaders are to be "faithful husbands" (1 Tim 3:2, 12, my translation; cf. TNIV).

[82]1 Cor 7:32-35 NIV, emphasis added.

wives' permission, could leave home to study with a rabbi, as Jesus' disciples did (Mk 1:18-20; 10:28-29 par.). Paul also recognizes that spouses may temporarily refrain from sexual relations "by mutual consent and for a time" for the purpose of prayer (1 Cor 7:5 NIV). However, he urges marriage partners to resume such relations after this brief period of sexual abstinence so that Satan would not tempt them owing to their lack of self-control. Demonstrably, however, celibacy was not the norm for the apostles (1 Cor 9:5) or for those in charge of the first-century church (1 Tim 3:2, 12).[83]

For this reason evangelicals do not see celibacy as a ministerial requirement, contrary to Roman Catholic teaching, which requires celibacy of all priests, primarily because Jesus himself was unmarried. Since according to the evangelical understanding church leaders are not to embody or represent Christ himself, especially not in the sacramental sense of administering mass following the pattern of Old Testament priestly service, there is correspondingly no need for them to refrain from sexual relations in order to remain ritually pure. Thus singleness is considered to be a gift given by God to the select few rather than a requirement for all ministers. Despite efforts to demonstrate the contrary, the Roman Catholic understanding owes significantly more to later ecclesiastical tradition than it does to New Testament teaching.[84]

Applied to the contemporary context, singleness should be recognized as a gift for the select few that holds significant advantages for ministry but is neither intrinsically superior nor inferior to marriage. In fact, Paul assumes that church officers will be married (1 Tim 3:2, 12; Tit 1:6)—though this should not be construed as a requirement—and considers marriage and the family to be a training and proving ground for prospective church leaders.[85] In most churches married couples with children make up the fabric of the congregation, and they should be sensitive to include single people socially in order for them not to feel left out. Single individuals, for their part, ought to find their sufficiency in Christ and in serving him. Nevertheless, unless a single person feels satisfied in this state, it is likely that God will eventually lead that person to get married, which is the primary divinely instituted pat-

---

[83]On celibacy in ancient Judaism, including the Qumran community, see Keener, "Marriage," *DNTB*, pp. 682-83.

[84]See Köstenberger, "Review Article: The Apostolic Origins of Priestly Celibacy," *EuroJTh* 1 (1992): 173-79.

[85]1 Tim 3:4-5; cf. v. 15. See George W. Knight, *Commentary on the Pastoral Epistles*, NIGTC (Carlisle: Paternoster; Grand Rapids, Mich.: Eerdmans, 1992), p. 173: "the home is the proving ground of fidelity for all officers."

tern of human relationships in the Old Testament and reaffirmed in the New.

Finally, the last several decades have seen a marked rise in cohabitation without marriage as well as in the practice of premarital sex. It clearly follows from biblical teaching, however, that both are violations of God's design for male-female relationships. In biblical times, the Jews regarded (a woman's) premarital sexual activity as tantamount to prostitution, with the penalty for sex with a person to whom one was not married frequently being death.[86] In Scripture, marriage is presented as a sacred, inviolable and exclusive relationship between one man and one woman, properly entered into by the mutual pledge of lifelong marital faithfulness and consummated by sexual relations, which constitutes the marriage as a "one-flesh" union (Gen 2:23-24). As Jesus says, the marriage event issues in the man and the woman being no longer two, but one, having been joined together by none other than God (Mt 19:6 = Mk 10:8-9). Paul maintains that even sexual intercourse with a prostitute results in a one-flesh union, albeit an illegitimate one (1 Cor 6:16, referring to Gen 2:24); the same would be true for any form of sexual intercourse outside of a monogamous marriage relationship. For "the essential moral problem with nonmarital sexual intercourse is that it performs a life-uniting act without a life-uniting intent, thus violating its intrinsic meaning."[87]

Again, "Extramarital acts of sexual love are, no less than unloving begetting, attempts to put asunder what God joined together in ordaining that the one and selfsame act of human beings should have both a unitive and a procreative

---

[86]Cf. Deut 22:20-24; *Jub.* 20:4; 33:20; and others. See Keener, "Adultery, Divorce," *DNTB,* p. 10, who notes that this penalty was not enforced in New Testament times.

[87]Jones, *Biblical Christian Ethics,* p. 158; cf. Richard J. Foster, "Sexuality and Singleness," in *Readings in Christian Ethics,* vol. 2, *Issues and Applications,* ed. David K. Clark and Robert V. Rakestraw (Grand Rapids, Mich.: Baker, 1996), p. 157. Contra the unconvincing attempt by John F. Dedek, "Premarital Petting and Coitus," *Chicago Studies* 9 (1970): 227-42, to argue that there is no biblical condemnation of premarital sex. According to Dedek, *porneia* in Mt 5:32 and 19:9 means adultery; in 1 Cor 5:1 it means incest; in 1 Cor 6:12-20 (cf. 1 Thess 4:3-4) it means union with a prostitute; in Gal 5:19-20 and Eph 5:5 it might mean adultery; in 1 Cor 6:9 it probably means prostitution and promiscuous sexual relations; and in Acts 15:20, 29 it refers to irregular marriages listed in Lev 18, such as incestuous unions. Deut 22:1-29 condemns a woman's deceiving her husband prior to marriage into thinking she is a virgin when she is not, rape, and sleeping with a woman already engaged to be married to another man. However, Dedek's attempt to determine Scripture's stance toward premarital sex exclusively by a study of *porneia* is misguided, first and foremost because he unduly ignores the foundational Old Testament passage on marriage, Gen 2:23-24, and its covenant character. Moreover, even on Dedek's own terms, it clearly follows that if *porneia* means sexual immorality—which is everywhere forbidden in Scripture—and the only venue in which sexual relations are considered moral in Scripture is within the marriage covenant, sex relations without, outside, and before marriage are all equally beyond the pale of biblical morality.

end or good."[88] But what about engaged couples? In short, one may answer as follows: if the couple is ready to assume the full entailments of marriage in the here and now, why not get married immediately? "On the other hand, if an engaged couple is really contemplating *pre*-marital sexual relations in the authentic moral meaning of this phrase, then they *know* that they are seeking to justify something that is *not* fully responsible."[89] Premarital sex amounts to a futile attempt to act as if married while taking more and offering less than married love requires in terms of "the degree of responsibility and the kind of love and trust and fidelity" husband and wife are called to have for one another.[90]

While it is inevitable that those in the larger culture who are not committed to observing biblical teaching in this area persist in cohabitation or engage in premarital sex, there can be no doubt that this is not a legitimate option for believers. Sexual abstinence prior to marriage and sexual faithfulness in marriage are the biblical expectations, and it is evident that the practice of the former constitutes the best preparation for the observance of the latter.

CHILDREN, PARENTING AND THE HOME

Procreation and the metaphor of adoption. Procreation is an integral part of God's plan for marriage.[91] The Creator told the first human couple in the beginning, "Be fruitful and increase in number; fill the earth" (Gen 1:28 NIV; cf. Gen 9:1, 7; 35:11). Though originally two individual persons, husband and wife become "one flesh" (Gen 2:24) in their marital union, which is given visible expression by the children resulting from that union. Consequently, barrenness is regularly seen in the Old Testament as the result of divine disfavor (e.g., Gen 29:31), while children are regarded as a gift and blessing from God (Ps 127:4-5a).[92] Rachel's outcry to Jacob is symptomatic:

---

[88]Paul Ramsey, *One Flesh: A Christian View of Sex Within, Outside and Before Marriage,* GBE 8 (Bramcote, England: Grove Books, 1975), p. 13.

[89]Ibid., p. 18.

[90]Ibid.

[91]For a discussion of rabbinic attitudes toward procreation including references, see Keener, "Marriage," *DNTB,* p. 681, who notes that rabbis required husbands to divorce those wives who after a trial period proved unable to bear children (*m. Yebam.* 6:6). On the home, see the excursus on the ancient household below. On hospitality, see S. C. Barton, "Hospitality," in *DLNTD,* pp. 501-7.

[92]What is more, in the ancient world, prior to social security and health care systems, sons were also an economic necessity for women. On infertility and the Bible, see Judith Baskin, "Rabbinic Reflections on the Barren Wife," *HTR* 82 (1989): 101-14; Mary Callaway, *Sing O Barren One: A Study in Comparative Midrash,* SBLDS 91 (Atlanta: Scholars Press, 1986); David Daube, *The Duty of Procreation* (Edinburgh: Edinburgh University Press, 1977); and John Van Seters, "The Problem of Childlessness in Near Eastern Law and the Patriarchs of Israel," *JBL* 87 (1968): 401-8. Regarding contemporary implications, see the discussion below.

"Give me children, or I'll die!" (Gen 30:1 NIV). The removal of barrenness amounts to the lifting of divine reproach and is tantamount to being "remembered by the Lord" (Gen 30:22; 1 Sam 1:19-20). Without discriminating against childless couples, the general expectation for man and woman created by God is to be married and to have children.[93]

However, while in the Old Testament childbearing has not only an important biological function but also forms an integral part of God's covenant promise, leading to the birth of the messianic "seed" of the woman,[94] the New Testament significantly speaks of believers' "adoption" into God's family through Christ.[95] While in Old Testament times certain ethnic constraints applied, now we are "all sons of God through faith in Christ Jesus" (Gal 3:26 NIV). If anyone belongs to Christ, he is Abraham's descendant and included in the promise (Gal 3:28).

This is an eschatological, salvation-historical event of first import: through adoption, believers are introduced into the filial relationship between Jesus the Son and God his Father, sharing together in the new family of God.[96] While the distinction between Jesus as the unique Son of God and believers as sons and daughters of God in Christ is not obliterated (e.g., Jn 20:17), believers nonetheless become in a real, spiritual sense brothers and sisters of Jesus as well as of one another. "Both the one who makes men holy and those who are made holy are of the same family. So Jesus is not ashamed to call them brothers" (Heb 2:11 NIV). Even fruitfulness is to some extent transmogrified from physical childbearing to the harmonious, productive

---

[93]Contra Gerard Loughlin, "The Want of Family in Postmodernity," in *The Family in Theological Perspective,* ed. Stephen C. Barton (Edinburgh: T & T Clark, 1996), p. 323, who contends that "procreation, though natural, is an inessential part of marriage" (quoting Karl Barth *Church Dogmatics* 3/4 [Edinburgh: T & T Clark, 1961], p. 266). Opposing the comment that married couples need a good reason for not having children, Loughlin writes that, "[t]o the contrary, Christian couples need a good reason for having children, since faith in the resurrected Christ frees them from the necessity to reproduce" (p. 323 n. 48). However, there is no scriptural evidence that Christ "frees" believers from "the necessity to reproduce" (a potentially misleading phrase). No dichotomy must be erected between God's created order and life in Christ. Paul's teaching on marriage and parenting in Eph 5 and his qualifications for church leaders in 1 Tim 3 and Tit 1, for instance, clearly (re)affirm marriage and children as the general norm for believers (see also 1 Tim 2:15; 4:3; and so on).

[94]Gen 3:15; cf. Isa 7:14; 8:8; Gal 3:16, 19.

[95]Eph 1:5; Rom 8:23. See further the discussion below.

[96]Cf. Jn 1:12-13; Rom 8:14-17; Gal 3:23-36; 4:4-7; Eph 1:5; 1 John 3:1-2. See esp. Edmund P. Clowney, "Interpreting the Biblical Models of the Church: A Hermeneutical Deepening of Ecclesiology," in *Biblical Interpretation and the Church: Text and Context,* ed. Don A. Carson (Exeter: Paternoster, 1984), pp. 75-76, who also refers to Eph 3:14; 2 Cor 6:18; Mt 12:49-50; 23:28; and 1 Jn 4:21.

operation of the various members of the body of Christ according to the spiritual gifts supplied by God the Spirit.[97]

This does not mean that in Christ the family as such has ceased to exist or is of no or little importance. Surely Karl Barth's view is extreme that "the idea of the family is of no interest at all for Christian theology."[98] While the church as eschatological entity in some sense transcends natural ties—just as discipleship transcends family obligations in the teaching of Jesus—it embraces and undergirds rather than quenches or obliterates people's natural relationships. In his Spirit, Christ dignifies marriage and the family and enables husband and wife as well as children to be restored to God's original design prior to the Fall (cf., e.g., the reference to being filled with the Spirit in Eph 5:18 in relation to 5:21-33); in his church, he provides a larger framework for these Spirit-filled Christian entities to begin to flesh out the vision of a redeemed humanity under God in Christ that will be fully realized in the eternal state. Rather than being diminished in significance, families are elevated by being incorporated in God's grand program of "summing up of all things in Christ" (Eph 1:10 NASB).

Jesus. In Jesus' day, the extended family lived together (e.g., Mk 1:30), typically sharing a three- or four-room home. Like their mother, daughters were to take a domestic role (Mt 10:35; Lk 12:53), and boys were to emulate their father's example according to the maxim "like father, like son." Jesus himself learned his father's trade as a craftsman (Mt 13:55; Mk 6:3). The variety of terms used in the New Testament for "child"—such as *brephos, pais, paidion, paidarion, teknon, teknion,* or *nēpios*—indicates an awareness of children in their social settings and stages of development.[99] Jesus himself modeled obedience in relation to his earthly parents (Lk 2:51) and supremely toward his heavenly Father (e.g., Mk 14:36; cf. Heb 5:8).

Jesus' earthly ministry intersected with children at a number of occasions. Repeatedly, Jesus restored children to their parents by way of miraculous healing: Jairus's daughter in Mark 5:21-24, 35-43; the daughter of a Syrophoenician woman in Mark 7:24-30; and a demon-possessed boy in Mark 9:14-29.[100] In one instance, Jesus put a child in the disciples' midst in order to teach on the nature

---

[97]1 Cor 12—14; Rom 12; Eph 4. On the preceding two paragraphs, see Ray Anderson, "God Bless the Children—and the Childless," *Christianity Today* 31 (7 August 1987): 28.

[98]Barth *Church Dogmatics* 3/4, p. 241, cited in Loughlin, "The Want of Family in Postmodernity," p. 324.

[99]Cf. Francis, "Children and Childhood in the New Testament," p. 67, with reference to Hans R. Weber, *Jesus and the Children* (Geneva: World Council of Churches, 1979), pp. 52-53.

[100]See esp. Stephen C. Barton, "Child, Children," *DJG,* pp. 100-104; and Francis, "Children and Childhood in the New Testament," pp. 65-85 (note further bibliographic references to childhood in the ancient world on p. 66 n. 2 and to childhood and the teaching of Jesus on p. 72 n. 12).

of discipleship (Mk 9:36-37 par.). This must have been startling for Jesus' audience, since then as now it would have been uncommon for adults to think they could learn anything from a child. At another juncture, children were brought to Jesus to receive a blessing from him (Mk 10:13-16 par.).[101]

Clearly the climactic pronouncement, "I tell you the truth, anyone who will not receive the kingdom of God like a little child will never enter it" (Mk 10:15 NIV), ties together the earlier recorded instances of Jesus' receptivity toward children with an important characteristic of the kingdom, a humble lack of regard for one's own supposed status (cf. Lk 22:26 NIV: "Instead, the greatest among you should be like the youngest"). For Jesus, there is no better way to illustrate God's free, unmerited grace than pointing to a child.[102] For unlike many adults, children are generally entirely unpretentious about receiving a gift. Moreover, "little ones," that is, the least regardless of age, are a repeated focus in Jesus' teaching on discipleship (Mt 18:5; Lk 9:48).[103] Indeed, "the Kingdom . . . consists of the childlike,"[104] a lesson yet to be learned by Jesus' reluctant followers.

In sayings preserved by Matthew, Jesus focuses even more specifically on the dependency and trust that are characteristic of children and that are also traits essential for those who would enter his kingdom. In Matthew 11:25-26, Jesus praises the Father for concealing his truth from the self-proclaimed wise and understanding, and revealing it to little children. This statement turns out to be prophetic when in Matthew 21:15 the children are shouting in the temple, "Hosanna to the Son of David!" (NIV) while the chief priests and the teachers of the law are indignant at the sight of the children's praise of Jesus and of "the wonderful things he did." Jesus' words in Matthew 11:25-26 are further developed in his later pronouncement that people are not to call anyone "father" on earth, for there is only one Father, the one in heaven (Mt 23:9).

According to Jesus, the quality in children that is most emblematic of kingdom virtues is their humility. Unless an individual therefore turns and becomes like a child, he will never enter the kingdom of heaven (Mt 18:3). While children may not necessarily be humble—much less "innocent"—their lack of status and their dependence on others make them suitable illustrations of the

---

[101]See J. Duncan M. Derrett, "Why Jesus Blessed the Children (Mk 10.13-16 Par.)," *NovT* 25 (1983): 1-18; James I. H. McDonald, "Receiving and Entering the Kingdom: A Study of Mk 10.15," *SE VI* (1973): 328-32.

[102]Cf. Francis, "Children and Childhood in the New Testament," p. 75, who correlates this to the recollection of Israel's own experience with God in passages such as Deut 7:7-8; Hos 11:1-4; Ezek 16:3-8; Ps 74:21.

[103]For bibliography on children in Luke's Gospel, see ibid., p. 78 nn. 26 and 27.

[104]Ibid., p. 76.

need for would-be candidates for Jesus' kingdom to "become nothing" and be stripped of their earthly status (cf. Phil 2:6-7). Hence they embody Jesus' radical call for discipleship and his requirement for his followers to "take up [their] cross" in total self-abandonment (e.g., Mk 8:34-38 [NIV] par.).

Francis lists several other ways in which children came to typify desirable attitudes in believers in the early church: as an image representing the needy, the "little ones" who are members of the church;[105] as a "metaphor for learning in expressing the relationship of pupil to teacher as child to parent";[106] and as a symbol of hope and new beginning[107] in association with imagery of birthing as a new creation, be it in elaboration of the pupil-teacher relationship[108] or with reference to the birth pangs of the messianic age.[109] Also, as "little children," believers are to love one another (Jn 13:33).

In his personal experience, Jesus knew spiritual rejection even within his own family[110] and asserted that his own primary loyalty and that of his followers must be to God the Father.[111] Thus, while Jesus affirmed natural relations, such as the divine institution of marriage and the need to honor one's parents,[112] he acknowledged the higher calling of discipleship. One's commitment to truth may lead to division, not peace, in one's natural family,[113] and in this case following Jesus must take precedence.[114]

Paul. In light of the high value placed on procreation in the foundational creation narrative, Paul teaches that the woman is to devote herself primarily to "childbearing," that is, her domestic role related to the upbringing of children and managing of the home (1 Tim 2:15).[115] Thus motherhood is not only

---

[105]Mk 9:42; Mt 18:6-14; cf. Acts 20:35.

[106]Mk 10:24; 2 Cor 12:14; 1 Tim 1:2; 1 Jn 2:1.

[107]Is 9:6; cf. Lk 2:12-14.

[108]Gal 4:19.

[109]Jn 16:21; Rom 8:22; 1 Thess 5:3; Rev 12:2; cf. Is 26:16-19; 66:7-14. Francis, "Children and Childhood in the New Testament," p. 79. Francis also notes negative connotations conveyed by children in the New Testament—but remarkably not in Jesus' teaching—such as lack of maturity (p. 80).

[110]Mk 3:21; 6:1-6; Jn 7:1-9.

[111]Lk 2:49; Mk 3:31-35.

[112]Mk 10:8-9, 19 par.

[113]Mt 10:34.

[114]Lk 9:57-62. Cf. S. C. Barton, "Family," *DJG,* pp. 226-29.

[115]This pronouncement is almost unbearable for some contemporary scholars, such as Carolyn Osiek and David L. Balch, *Families in the New Testament World: Households and House Churches* (Louisville: Westminster John Knox, 1997), p. 122, who write, "It is theologically and morally outrageous when this 'Pauline' author argues that a woman 'will be saved through childbearing' (1 Tim. 2:15)." For a detailed treatment of the interpretation of 1 Tim 2:15, see my "Ascertaining Women's God-Ordained Roles: An Interpretation of 1 Timothy 2:15," *BBR* 7 (1997): 107-44.

not disparaged in biblical teaching (as it often is today); it is held up as the woman's highest calling and privilege. For this reason women's responsibility can be summed up by one biblical writer as follows: "to love their husbands and children, . . . to be busy at home, . . . and to be subject to their husbands" (Tit 2:4 NIV). Another important parental obligation is that of providing for their children's future, as Paul's aphorism in 2 Corinthians 12:14 makes clear: "After all, children should not have to save up for their parents, but parents for their children" (NIV). Conversely, if necessary, children ought to assume the responsibility of caring for their aging parents, for "if anyone does not provide for his relatives, and especially for his immediate family, he has denied the faith and is worse than an unbeliever" (1 Tim 5:8 NIV).

In a spiritual sense, Paul teaches that believers are adopted into God's family as his sons and daughters.[116] Rather than draw on the notion of divine adoption in Greco-Roman mythology or the Roman ceremony of *adoptio* (in which a minor was transferred from the authority of his natural father to that of his adoptive father), the apostle develops this concept by appropriating Old Testament exodus typology and the messianic adoption formula in 2 Samuel 7:14 ("I will be a father to him, and he will be a son to me," NASB) within the context of new covenant theology. Just as Israel was redeemed and received her covenant privileges at the exodus (cf. Ex 4:22; Hos 11:1), so New Testament believers were redeemed from their slavery to sin in and through Christ, receiving their adoption as God's children.[117] Significantly, this will be fully realized only in the future at the final resurrection (Rom 8:23).

As to children, their obedience was considered vital by both Jesus and Paul, in keeping with first-century notions. Yet such obedience could not be assumed to arise naturally; it must be inculcated from childhood. Ultimately, the standing and honor of the entire family were at stake. What is more, the hand of divine blessing could be withdrawn if one disregarded God's commandment to honor one's parents and his injunction for parents to raise their children in the nurture and admonition of the Lord. Thus the man of God must see to it "that his children obey him with proper respect" (1 Tim 3:4 NIV). Nevertheless, while trying to do their best, parents must recognize their own limitations and acknowledge that God alone is the perfect Father (Heb 12:5-11).

---

[116] Gal 4:5; Rom 8:15, 23; 9:4. See especially James M. Scott, *Adoption as Sons of God: An Exegetical Investigation into the Background of* ΥΙΟΦΕΣΙΑ *in the Corpus Paulinum*, WUNT 2.48 (Tübingen: Mohr-Siebeck, 1992).

[117] Cf. 2 Cor 6:18 citing 2 Sam 7:14. For a concise summary, see Scott, "Adoption," in *DPL*, pp. 15-18.

Above all, fathers must not be overly harsh or provoke their children (Eph 6:4; Col 3:21). This calls for wisdom. A balance must be struck between proper discipline and loving nurture and support. Neither the "encouraging parent" who neglects to discipline his child nor the strict disciplinarian fulfills the biblical ideal of parenting. Paul sought to strike just such a balance when he wrote to the Thessalonian believers that, on the one hand, he and his associates had sought to be "gentle among you, like a mother caring for her little children" (1 Thess 2:7 NIV) and that, on the other hand, they had "dealt with each of you as a father deals with his own children, encouraging, comforting and urging you to live lives worthy of God" (1 Thess 2:11-12 NIV). God's ideal is a godly father and a godly mother complementing one another in raising children in proper discipline and love.

Contemporary implications. There is perhaps no one who can better appreciate the value of children today than a woman who is unable to conceive and who desperately wants to have children of her own. Not that childless couples or single persons are not in the will of God or cannot make significant contributions to the kingdom; physical fruitfulness is but a part of God's overall desire for humans to be fruitful, which includes spiritual fruitfulness as well.[118] As Jesus told his followers, "This is to my Father's glory, that you bear much fruit, showing yourselves to be my disciples. . . . I chose you and appointed you to go and bear fruit—fruit that will last" (Jn 15:8, 16 NIV). This applies to single persons and childless couples as well as to married people.

Nevertheless, the bearing and rearing of children remains a vital part of the divine design for men and women today. God's overarching plan for humanity to "be fruitful and multiply" has numerous contemporary implications covering a wide range of issues, such as abortion, contraception, infertility, in-vitro fertilization, surrogate parenting, artificial insemination and adoption, to name but a few.[119] A few general remarks must suffice. At the outset, it should be noted that inability to have children does not necessarily indicate God's disfavor.[120] Barrenness is one of many effects of human-

---

[118]For contemporary implications with regard to marriage and the family, see esp. Part II in *The Family in Theological Perspective*, ed. Stephen C. Barton (Edinburgh: T & T Clark, 1996), a volume reflecting the editor's concerns as first articulated in Stephen C. Barton, "Marriage and Family Life as Christian Concerns," *ExpTim* 106.3 (1994): 69-74.

[119]On ancient Jewish attitudes toward abortion, see Keener, "Marriage," *DNTB*, p. 681. On contraception, see John T. Noonan Jr., *Contraception: A History of Its Treatment by the Catholic Theologians and Canonists* (Cambridge, Mass.: Harvard University Press, 1965); Angus S. McLaren, *A History of Contraception* (Oxford: Blackwell, 1992).

[120]Cf. Anderson, "God Bless the Children—and the Childless," p. 28.

ity's fall into sin. As Paul states in the book of Romans, "There is no difference, for all have sinned and fall short of the glory of God" (Rom 3:22-23 NIV). Unfortunately, however, redemption in Christ, while bestowing the divine gift of eternal life (Rom 6:23), does not yet reverse these general consequences. Believers may still desire to have children but not be able to do so without any fault of their own.

With the advances of modern medicine, childless couples have a much wider array of options than used to be the case (see the issues mentioned above). The vast field of medical ethics applied to issues facing contemporary Christians deals with these kinds of questions. Owing to space constraints I can only refer the interested reader to selected publications in this area.[121] The duties of parents and children are further taken up in the following excursus as part of the discussion of the adaptation of the household code by several New Testament writers.

EXCURSUS: THE ANCIENT HOUSEHOLD

Unlike the modern household, ancient households would include not only a married couple and children but other dependents, such as slaves, with the head of the household holding authority to which wife, children and slaves were to submit. The New Testament features several adaptations of the Greco-Roman "household code" (esp. Eph 5:21—6:9; Col 3:18—4:1), a device that addresses the various members of the household about their duties, usually progressing from the "lesser" (i.e., the one under authority) to the "greater" (i.e., the one in a position of authority).[122] The underlying assumption of this code is that order in the household will promote order on

---

[121]On birth control, see Helmut Thielicke, *The Ethics of Sex,* trans. John W. Doberstein (New York: Harper & Row, 1964), pp. 200-225, whose discussion is considerably more nuanced than that of Mary Pride, *The Way Home: Beyond Feminism, Back to Reality* (Westchester, Ill.: Crossway, 1985), who advocates letting God give a couple as many children as he desires by practicing no birth control. On infertility, see Martha Stout, *Without Child: A Compassionate Look at Infertility* (Grand Rapids, Mich.: Zondervan, 1985), and Kaye Halverson, *The Wedded Unmother* (Minneapolis: Augsburg, 1980).

[122]Cf. David L. Balch, "Household Codes," in *Graeco-Roman Literature and the New Testament: Selected Forms and Genres,* ed. David E. Aune, SLBSBS 21 (Atlanta: Scholars Press, 1988); idem, *Let Wives Be Submissive: The Domestic Code in 1 Peter,* SBLMS 26 (Chico, Calif.: Scholars Press, 1981); Craig S. Keener, "Family and Household," *DNTB,* pp. 353-68; idem, "Marriage," *DNTB,* p. 687; and Philip H. Towner, "Households and Household Codes," in *DPL,* pp. 417-19, who also notes the related passages 1 Tim 2:1-15; 5:1-2; 6:1-2, 17-19; Tit 2:1—3:8; 1 Pet 2:13—3:7; idem, "Household Codes," in *DLNTD,* pp. 513-20; James D. G. Dunn, "The Household Rules in the New Testament," in *The Family in Theological Perspective,* ed. Stephen C. Barton (Edinburgh: T & T Clark, 1996), pp. 43-63 (list on pp. 44-46; bibliography on p. 49 nn. 7-8).

a larger societal scale as well. Believers' conformance to the ethical standards of such a code would render Christianity respectable in the surrounding culture and aid in the church's evangelistic mission.[123]

The Christian duties of wives and husbands were already discussed under "Marital roles" above.[124] It remains to treat the responsibilities of children and parents in greater detail than was possible above. At the outset, it should be noted that children are often presented as metaphorical for those who are deficient in understanding (1 Cor 3:1-4; Heb 5:13). In 1 Corinthians 13:11-12, Paul contrasts adulthood with childhood as the stage of entering into maturity. Believers must "no longer be infants, tossed back and forth by the waves, and blown here and there by every wind of teaching" (Eph 4:14 NIV); together, they must grow up in Christ (Eph 4:15).

The major Pauline injunction on the role of parents and children is found in Ephesians 6:1-4, where the apostle writes,

> Children, obey your parents in the Lord, for this is right. "Honor your father and mother"—which is the first commandment with a promise—"that it may go well with you and that you may enjoy long life on the earth." Fathers [or parents], do not exasperate your children; instead, bring them up in the training and instruction of the Lord. (NIV)

The apostle's words in Colossians 3:20 are similar: "Children, obey your parents in everything, for this pleases the Lord. Fathers, do not embitter your children, or they will become discouraged" (NIV). Notably, in the more extensive passage in Ephesians, Paul roots children's obligation to obey their parents in the Old Testament Decalogue.[125] Disobedience to parents was considered to be a phenomenon characteristic of the end time (Mk 13:12; 2 Tim 3:1-2), which would draw divine judgment (Rom 1:30, 32). Children's responsibility to honor their parents also entailed caring for them in their old age (1 Tim 5:8). This was viewed as proper repayment for having been reared by them (1 Tim 5:4).

Fathers, in turn, were to provide for their children and to ensure proper nurture and discipline *(paideia),* which involved formal and informal education (2 Cor 12:14) and various forms of discipline, including physical discipline.[126] A father commanded great respect, but he was to use his position

---

[123]1 Tim 3:7; 6:1; Tit 2:5, 8, 10; 3:8; 1 Pet 2:12; 1 Thess 4:12.

[124]On gender roles in Palestinian and geographically related Jewish traditions, see Keener, "Marriage," *DNTB,* p. 690, who notes that wives' standard duties in first-century Palestine were largely domestic: grinding wheat, cooking, washing, nursing and sewing (*m. Ketub.* 5:5).

[125]Ex 20:12; Deut 5:16. Note also Jesus' reference to the fifth commandment in Mt 15:4 par. Mk 7:10 (as well as to negative consequences for disobedience in Ex 21:17 par. Lev 20:9).

[126]Prov 13:24; Heb 12:6; Rev 3:19; cf. Sir 3:23; 30:1-3, 12.

of authority not to exasperate his children but to display gentleness in his treatment of them.[127] As will be developed further below, the skills required to manage one's private household were considered to be the very ones also necessary for governing in a public setting (1 Tim 3:4-5).

It is an indication of the powerful dynamics of natural father-child relations that this kind of language was applied also to older and younger men who were not biologically related. Thus younger men could call older men "fathers," and older men could address younger men as "sons." Teachers likewise might refer to their disciples as children (Jn 13:33; 21:5; 3 Jn 4), while disciples might call their teachers "fathers" (2 Kings 2:12; Mt 23:9).

One of the primary roles of women was that of childbearing (1 Tim 2:15; 5:14). At times nurses were employed to care for infants.[128] In the same way, mothers, including widows, were to be honored by their children just as were fathers.[129] Their relationship with their sons was often particularly close, as in the case of Mary and Jesus[130] or the widow's son, "the only son of his mother" (Lk 7:12). As in the case of older men, older women were to be treated with respect (1 Tim 5:1-2). They also had the important obligation to mentor younger women with regard to their family responsibilities (Tit 2:3-5).[131]

MARRIAGE AND FAMILY AND CHURCH LEADERSHIP

The qualifications for church leadership stipulated in the Pastoral Epistles give prominent coverage to an applicant's marriage and family life. In 1 Timothy 3:1-13, the primary passage on the subject, it is required that both overseers and deacons be "faithful husbands" *(mias gynaikos andra);*[132] that

---

[127]1 Cor 4:15, 21; 1 Thess 2:11; Eph 6:4.

[128]See the imagery employed in 1 Cor 3:1-2; 1 Thess 2:7(?). Cf. Keener, "Family and Household," *DNTB,* p. 360.

[129]1 Tim 5:4, 8. Note that Lev 19:3 even mentions mothers before fathers, a fact that did not escape later Jewish rabbis (see references in Keener, "Family and Household," *DNTB,* p. 355).

[130]Lk 2:48-51; Jn 2:1-5; 19:25-27.

[131]On slaves as members of the ancient household, see esp. Keener, "Family and Household," *DNTB,* pp. 361-66.

[132]1 Tim 3:2, 12; cf. Tit 1:6. For a defense of this interpretation, see my forthcoming volume on the Pastoral Epistles in the New Expositor's Bible Commentary. Contra the NIV's "the husband of but one wife": there is no equivalent for "but" in the original (but note the commendable change in the TNIV: "faithful to his wife"). Cf. Stephen M. Baugh, "Titus," in *Zondervan Illustrated Bible Background Commentary,* ed. Clinton E. Arnold (Grand Rapids, Mich.: Zondervan, 2002), 3:501-2, who contends that, since polygamy was rather uncommon in the first century in the Greco-Roman world, Paul more likely prohibited church leaders from having concubines, a widespread practice at that time. According to Baugh, neither the Greeks nor the Romans regarded these practices as adulterous or polygamous. For Paul, however, concubinage was the same as polygamy, since he considered sexual union to be tantamount to marital union (cf. 1 Cor 6:16).

overseers keep their children under control with all dignity; and that they manage their own households well.[133] For, according to Pauline logic, "If anyone does not know how to manage his own family, how can he take care of God's church?" (1 Tim 3:5 NIV). Indeed, as the apostle makes clear later in the same chapter, the church is "*God's* household" (1 Tim 3:15).[134] There is thus a close relationship between church and family, and Christian maturity in the fulfillment of one's duties as husband and father becomes one of the most essential requirements for those aspiring to the office of pastor or elder.[135]

The implications of this are, first, that younger candidates who have yet to prove their ability to manage their own households well should ordinarily not be put in ultimate leadership positions in the church. They may possess proper formal training as well as be both eager and otherwise qualified in terms of character and disposition. However, maturity and life experience are such an integral part of a church leader's necessary equipment for his role that any diminishing of this requirement may come dangerously close to appointing a recent convert, which is discouraged in Scripture in the strongest terms (1 Tim 3:6; cf. 5:22).

Second, it is utter folly for someone to provide qualified, capable leadership for the church while neglecting his duties in his own family, be it owing to busyness in ministry or to improper priorities. Even while serving as pastor or elder, it is therefore imperative that men serving in this function regularly evaluate themselves to see whether they are able to oversee the church while continuing to be able adequately to fulfill their natural duties as husband and father. Otherwise, it may well be said with Paul that those men beware, lest possibly, after having preached to others, they may themselves be disqualified (1 Cor 9:27).

Third, theologically, by linking the family so closely to the church, the New Testament presents the latter as the eschatological extension of the former. That is, that which reaches all the way back to the divine creation of the first man and woman is seen to be further extended and explicated in the "household of God," the church (cf. Eph 5:31-32).

---

[133]1 Tim 3:4 (cf. Tit 1:6); 1 Tim 3:5.

[134]See Vern S. Poythress, "The Church as Family: Why Male Leadership in the Family Requires Male Leadership in the Church," in *Recovering Biblical Manhood & Womanhood: A Response to Biblical Feminism,* ed. John Piper and Wayne Grudem (Wheaton: Crossway, 1991), pp. 233-47.

[135]The terms "pastor," "overseer" and "elder" are used somewhat interchangeably in the New Testament (cf., e.g., Acts 20:17, 28; Tit 1:5-7).

One further issue (already touched upon above) must be taken up at this point: the question of whether divorced people may serve as elders or pastors. I believe that 1 Timothy 3 and related passages do not directly address this, focusing instead on the requirement of a candidate's faithfulness in a present marriage. In keeping with the general principles outlined above, if such a person's divorce was legitimate, there seems to be no immediate reason why he should be disqualified from consideration. If the divorce was illegitimate, service as elder or overseer is ruled out. However, even if the divorce was legitimate, the issue of a person's reputation with those outside the church should be considered, especially since there are many other avenues of service apart from the highest ecclesiastical office. Nonetheless, people should generally not be held to a stricter standard just to be "safe" and "conservative." If both Jesus and Paul were willing to make an exception, we should be willing to follow their lead without fearing that a high view of marriage will thereby be compromised.

Marriage, the Family and Spiritual Warfare

One final topic remains, that of marriage, the family and spiritual warfare. While there is a plethora of materials on marriage and the family, as well as a considerable body of literature on spiritual warfare,[136] rarely are these issues treated jointly. Thus I am aware of no current volume on marriage and the family that provides even the most cursory treatment of spiritual warfare.[137] Regularly, the focus is on fulfilling one's partner's needs in marriage,

---

[136]See esp. Clinton E. Arnold, *Three Crucial Questions about Spiritual Warfare* (Grand Rapids, Mich.: Baker, 1997); idem, *Powers of Darkness: Principalities and Powers in Paul's Letters* (Downers Grove, Ill.: InterVarsity Press, 1992); Sydney H. T. Page, *Powers of Evil: A Biblical Study of Satan and Demons* (Grand Rapids, Mich.: Baker, 1995); and the articles "Elements/ Elemental Spirits of the World," "Power," and "Principalities and Powers," in *DPL*, pp. 229-33, 723-25, 746-52.

[137]The only partial exception is Evelyn Christenson, *What Happens When We Pray for Our Families* (Colorado Springs: Chariot Family Publishers, 1992). There is no discussion of spiritual warfare in such popular books on marriage as Gary Chapman's *The Five Love Languages* (Chicago: Northfield, 1995), Larry Crabb's *Marriage Builder* (Grand Rapids, Mich.: Zondervan, 1992), Kay Arthur's *A Marriage Without Regrets* (Eugene, Ore.: Harvest House, 2000), Willard Harley's *His Needs, Her Needs* (Ada, Mich.: Revell, 1990), *The Language of Love* by Gary Smalley and John Trent (Pomona, Calif.: Focus on the Family, 1988), and Laura Walker's *Dated Jekyll, Married Hyde* (Minneapolis: Bethany House, 1997). There is nothing in bestselling books on parenting such as *Relational Parenting* by Ross Campbell (Chicago: Moody Publishing, 2000), *Raising Heaven-Bound Kids in a Hell-Bent World* by Eastman Curtis (Nashville: Thomas Nelson, 2000), *Children at Risk* by James Dobson and Gary Bauer (Dallas: Word, 1990), or *The Gift of Honor* by Gary Smalley and John Trent (Nashville: Thomas Nelson, 1987).

improving one's communication skills or resolving marital conflict. From reading any of these books, one would never know that spiritual warfare is a vital issue in marriage and the family.

Yet nothing could be further from the truth. Spiritual warfare has been a part of married life and child rearing almost from the beginning. The foundational biblical narrative in Genesis 3 recounts how the tempter, Satan, prevailed upon the first woman to violate God's commandment, and how her husband followed her into sin. Ever since, marriage has resembled more a struggle for control and conscious or unconscious efforts at mutual manipulation than an Edenic paradise. The first known instance of sibling rivalry resulted in Cain killing his brother Abel out of envy and jealousy. The rest of the Pentateuch chronicles a whole series of ways in which sin has affected marital and family relationships ever since the Fall.

A particularly egregious example in Israel's history is king David, whose sin with Bathsheba is recounted in 2 Samuel 11. David, being idle while others went to war, succumbed to sexual temptation, committed adultery and even murder, and his reign was never the same. The child born as a result of his adultery died. When rebuked by Nathan, he repented, but trouble never left his house again. His son Absalom rose up against his father, his son Solomon had multiple wives who led him into idolatry (1 Kings 11), and his kingdom was divided. From then on Israel's history took a sharp downturn, with the nation still languishing under foreign domination when Jesus appears on the scene.

The message of the New Testament is no different. Arguably the most important treatment of spiritual warfare, Ephesians 6:10-20 is preceded by an extended treatment of marriage (Eph 5:21-33) and child rearing (Eph 6:1-4). Unfortunately, these sections are regularly compartmentalized. In Paul's thinking, however, it is precisely in people's relationships with one another, be it at work or at home, among Christians or between believers and unbelievers, that spiritual warfare manifests itself and conscious dealing with it becomes a necessity. In fact, Ephesians 6:10-20 is "a crucial element to which the rest of the epistle has been pointing."[138] The main command governing Paul's treatment of marriage and the family in Ephesians 5:21—6:4 is "Be filled with the Spirit" (Eph 5:18).[139] The warfare passage in Ephesians 6:10-18 seamlessly picks up where Ephesians 5:18 left off, calling on believers to take up the sword of the Spirit (Eph 6:17), to pray in the Spirit (Eph 6:18), always remem-

---

[138]O'Brien, *Letter to the Ephesians,* p. 457.
[139]See my treatment of this passage in "What Does It Mean?" pp. 229-40.

bering that their "struggle is not against flesh and blood, but against the rulers, against the authorities, against the powers of this dark world and against the spiritual forces of evil in the heavenly realms" (Eph 6:12 NIV).[140]

There are several indications elsewhere in the New Testament in both Paul's writings and those of others that the devil's efforts to destroy marriages and to subvert family life did not stop at the Fall but continue to this very day. In 1 Corinthians 7:5, Paul counsels believers not to abstain from sexual relations, "except by mutual consent and for a time" (NIV) for the purpose of prayer, but then to come together again, so Satan may not tempt them because of their lack of self-control. This would seem to indicate that the sexual component of the marriage relationship is very much a regular target of Satan's attack and must be carefully guarded by the married couple.[141] Another Pauline passage is Ephesians 4:26-27: "Do not let the sun go down while you are still angry, and do not give the devil a foothold" (NIV). While not limited to marriage, this pronouncement certainly includes the marriage relationship, cautioning believers not to allow broken relationships to render them vulnerable to the devil.

Yet another relevant passage is found in Peter's writings. "Husbands, in the same way be considerate as you live with your wives, and treat them with respect as the weaker partner and as heirs with you of the gracious gift of life, so that nothing will hinder your prayers" (1 Pet 3:7 NIV). Here it is insensitivity on the part of the husband toward his wife that is mentioned as the potential cause for spiritual disruption in the family, and marital discord becomes a hindrance to united, answerable prayer.[142] Whether it is the couple's sex life, unresolved conflict or inconsiderateness, the New Testament makes clear that all are to be seen in the arena of spiritual warfare, with proper precautions needing to be taken.

Now what is the key element in spiritual warfare? According to Scripture,

---

[140]On Eph 6:10-20 in the context of the letter of Ephesians as a whole, see esp. the writings of Peter T. O'Brien: *Gospel and Mission in the Writings of Paul: An Exegetical and Theological Analysis* (Grand Rapids, Mich.: Baker, 1995), pp. 109-31; *Letter to the Ephesians,* pp. 456-90, esp. 457-60; and Andreas J. Köstenberger and Peter T. O'Brien, *Salvation to the Ends of the Earth: A Biblical Theology of Mission,* NSBT 11 (Downers Grove, Ill.: InterVarsity Press, 2001), pp. 196-98.

[141]On the Corinthian background to 1 Cor 7 and for an exposition of 1 Cor 7:5, see esp. Fee, *First Epistle to the Corinthians,* pp. 266-83.

[142]The question of whether it is only the husband's prayers (probably the immediate focus) or the couples' prayers (the necessary implication) that are hindered need not concern us here (see the relevant commentary literature; e.g., P. H. Davids, *The First Epistle of Peter,* NICNT [Grand Rapids, Mich.: Eerdmans, 1990], p. 123 n. 20). In the end, it is clearly the prayers of the entire couple that are negatively affected by the husband's insensitivity toward his wife.

it is human minds. "But I am afraid that just as Eve was deceived by the serpent's cunning, your *minds* may somehow be led astray from your sincere and pure devotion to Christ" (2 Cor 11:3 NIV, emphasis added). "For though we live in the world, we do not wage war as the world does. The weapons we fight with are not the weapons of the world. On the contrary, they have divine power to demolish strongholds. We demolish arguments and every pretension that sets itself up against the knowledge of God, and we take captive every *thought* to make it obedient to Christ" (2 Cor 10:3-5 NIV, emphasis added). Just as Satan reasoned with Eve about why she should disobey God in the Garden, it is people's thought life that is the arena in which our spiritual battles are won or lost. I conclude with three important principles pertaining to spiritual warfare and marriage.

First, an awareness of the fact that there is a battle is imperative for success. Anyone who, in the case of war, fails to realize that he is in it will no doubt be an early casualty owing to his failure to properly protect himself. It is the same in the realm of marriage and the family. Arguably, divorce rates are skyrocketing, not because of the lack of good intentions, the unavailability of resources and instruction on how to conduct a strong biblical marriage, or even the lack of love, but because many, unbelievers and believers alike, inadequately recognize that spiritual warfare is a certain reality that calls for a concerted, deliberately planned response.

Second, it is essential to know one's spiritual enemy. This enemy is not one's marriage partner. Nor is it one's children. It is Satan, the enemy of our souls, who employs a variety of strategies, methods and schemes. While he is highly intelligent, he nonetheless remains a creature. Thus he is neither omniscient nor omnipresent; God and Satan are not evenly matched. The devil can and in fact does miscalculate—the most striking instance being the cross, when what Satan thought would be his greatest triumph was turned into his final defeat three days later when Jesus rose from the dead. Satan specifically targets people's areas of weakness and greatest vulnerability, and every individual must be prepared for this in order not to be caught off guard. Yet like Paul, believers today will find that God's grace is more than sufficient for every challenge they face in the power of Christ, as long as they are diligent to "put on the full armor of God" (Eph 6:11).

Third and finally, spiritual battles must be fought by the use of proper weapons. As mentioned, some lose a spiritual conflict in which they are engaged because they fail to realize that they are in fact embroiled in such. Yet others may realize they are in a war but fail to use proper spiritual weapons. Once again, such persons will soon become casualties. In the context of

Christian marriages, as well as in parenting, it is imperative that believers, in order to overcome a spiritual enemy—be it their own sinfulness or evil supernatural opposition—employ spiritual weapons: truth, righteousness, peace, faith, salvation, the word of God and prayer (Eph 6:10-18). As Peter writes, "Be self-controlled and alert. Your enemy the devil prowls around like a roaring lion looking for someone to devour. Resist him, standing firm in the faith" (1 Pet 5:8-9 NIV).

As Christians are engaged in spiritual conflict, they must embrace the truth that there is in fact a spiritual battle raging; they must strive to know their enemy, the devil. And they must fight using proper, spiritual weapons. The apostle Paul wrote, "Our struggle is not against flesh and blood. . . . Therefore put on the full armor of God, so that when the day of evil comes, you may be able to stand your ground, and after you have done everything, to stand" (Eph 6:12-13 NIV). Spiritual warfare is the all-encompassing, ruling reality for all marital and family relationships. Those who ignore it do so at their own peril. Just as the devil attacks those with potential for church leadership, he seeks to subvert human marriages, because they have the greatest potential for showing the world the nature of the relationship between Christ and his church (Eph 5:31-32). If believers want to show the world by their marriages what a glorious and good God they have, they must, for God's sake as well as their own, engage in spiritual warfare, and they must do so using spiritual weapons. Then, and only then, will Christian marriages and families adequately reflect the image and design of the Creator.

CONCLUSION

In the above discussion, we have highlighted the following biblical teachings regarding marriage, the family and related subjects. Human sexuality and relationships were seen to be rooted in the eternal will of the Creator as expressed in the way in which God made men and women. Man and woman are made in God's image (Gen 1:27), called to representative rule (Gen 1:28) involving procreation, whereby the man, as first-created, has ultimate responsibility before God, with the woman placed alongside him as his "suitable helper" (Gen 2:18, 20). The Fall led to serious consequences affecting both the man and the woman individually in their areas of involvement as well as the marital relationship. Men's work and the relational sphere of women have both been significantly affected and turned into a struggle for control. Nevertheless, the image of God in man is not eradicated, and marriage and the family continue as the primary divinely instituted order for the human race.

From creation it also becomes clear that heterosexuality, rather than homosexuality, is God's pattern for men and women. The sexes are created in distinctness, which must not be blurred or obliterated, and humanity exists as male and female for the purpose of complementarity and procreation, neither of which can be properly (or at all) realized in same-sex (sexual) relationships. Moreover, the divine image was seen to be imprinted on man *as male and female,* so that homosexual unions fall short of reflecting God's own likeness as unity in diversity. It is for these reasons that Scripture universally views homosexuality in terms of rebellion against God and disregard for his creation order.

In keeping with the roles established by the Creator in the beginning, the New Testament defines marital roles in terms of both respect and love as well as submission and authority. While the husband and the wife are fellow heirs of God's grace (1 Pet 3:7) and while "there is neither male nor female" as far as salvation in Christ is concerned (Gal 3:28), there remains a pattern in which the wife is to emulate the church's submission to Christ and the husband is to imitate Christ's love for the church (Eph 5:21-33).[143] Thus a complementarian understanding of gender roles is borne out, not just by a few isolated problem passages but by biblical theology as a whole.[144] Apart from their joint stewardship, the married couple has an important witnessing function in the surrounding culture and ought to understand itself within the larger framework of God's eschatological purposes in Christ (cf. Eph 1:10).

Because marriage is a divinely ordained institution rather than merely a human contractual agreement, divorce likewise is permissible only in certain carefully delineated exceptional cases. These include sexual marital unfaithfulness (adultery) as well as desertion by an unbeliever. Even in those cases, however, reconciliation is to be the aim, and divorce, while permissible, remains the less preferable option. Where divorce is biblically legitimate, however, so is remarriage. The latter is apropos also in case of spousal death, "only in the Lord" (1 Cor 7:39 NASB). Another scenario different from marriage is that of singleness, which may present itself as premarried stage, widow or widowerhood or a permanent unmarried state. While premarrieds are to refrain from sexual relations prior to entering into marriage, and while widowed individuals are permitted, in certain cases

---

[143]On Gal 3:28, see esp. Richard Hove, *Equality in Christ? Galatians 3:28 and the Gender Dispute* (Wheaton, Ill.: Crossway, 1999); Köstenberger, "Gender Passages in the New Testament," pp. 273-79.

[144]See Köstenberger, "Gender Passages in the New Testament," pp. 259-83.

even encouraged, to remarry, permanent singleness (i.e., celibacy) is considered by both Jesus and Paul to be a special gift from God, though not a necessary requirement for church office (cf. 1 Tim 3:2, 12). By promoting undistracted devotion to the Lord, singleness can actually be a unique opportunity for kingdom service (1 Cor 7:32-35).

The bearing and rearing of children is part of God's plan for marriage. Children are a blessing from the Lord, while barrenness is generally viewed as a sign of divine disfavor. Parents are to bring up their children in the nurture and admonition of the Lord (Eph 6:4), and women are to place special priority on their God-given calling as mothers and homemakers (1 Tim 2:15; Tit 2:4-5).

Faithfulness in marriage, obedient children and proper household management are also considered paramount among the requirements for church leaders in the Pastoral Epistles (see esp. 1 Tim 3:2-5). For there is a close link between the family and the church, which is God's "household" (1 Tim 3:15), so that only those who are good husbands and fathers and who give adequate attention to managing their own homes are qualified to provide leadership also for the church.

The New Testament—indeed, the entire Bible—presents a coherent body of teachings pertaining to marriage and the family. Jesus, the early church and Paul all upheld a very high standard in this crucial area of life. Sexual purity was to be maintained in all human relationships, and marriage alone was considered to be the legitimate realm for sexual activity. In this as well as in other areas Christianity, in the first century as today, towers above pagan cultures and displays the character of a holy God in the lives and relationships of his people.

Contributors

S. M. Baugh (Ph.D., University of California, Irvine) is associate professor of New Testament, Westminster Theological Seminary in California. He is the author of *Pastoral Epistles and Philemon*, New Testament Background Commentary (Zondervan).

Daniel I. Block (D.Phil., University of Liverpool) is John R. Sampey Professor of Old Testament Interpretation, The Southern Baptist Theological Seminary. He is the author of *The Book of Ezekiel*, New International Commentary on the Old Testament (Eerdmans).

Ken M. Campbell (Ph.D., University of Manchester) was associate professor of biblical studies, Belhaven College. He has recently published *Our Awesome God* (Christian Focus Publications).

David W. Chapman (Ph.D., University of Cambridge) is assistant professor of New Testament and biblical archeology, Covenant Theological Seminary. He is the author of *Ancient Perceptions of Crucifixion Among Jews and Christians* (Mohr-Siebeck).

Andreas Köstenberger (Ph.D., Trinity Evangelical Divinity School) is professor of New Testament and Greek, Southeastern Baptist Theological Seminary. He is coauthor with P. T. O'Brien of *Salvation to the Ends of the Earth: A Biblical Theology of Missions* (InterVarsity Press).

Victor H. Matthews (Ph.D., Brandeis University) is professor of religious studies, Southwest Missouri State University. He has written *A Brief History of Ancient Israel* (Westminster John Knox).

Susan Treggiari (D.Litt., University of Oxford) is Anne T. & Robert M. Bass Professor Emerita in the School of Humanities and Sciences, Stanford University. She is the author of *Roman Social History*, Classical Foundations (Routledge).

Index of Topics